NORDIC LETTERS 1870-1910

Some other books from Norvik Press

P C Jersild: *A Living Soul* (translated by Rika Lesser)
Sara Lidman: *Naboth's Stone* (translated by Joan Tate)
Selma Lagerlöf: *The Löwensköld Ring* (translated by Linda Schenck)
Camilla Collett: *The District Governor's Daughters* (translated by Kirsten Seaver)
Jens Bjørneboe: *The Sharks* (translated by Esther Greenleaf Mürer)
Jørgen-Frantz Jacobsen: *Barbara* (translated by George Johnston)
Janet Garton & Henning Sehmsdorf (eds. and trans.): *New Norwegian Plays* (by Peder W.Cappelen, Edvard Hoem, Cecilie Løveid and Bjørg Vik)
Gunilla Anderman (ed.): *New Swedish Plays* (by Ingmar Bergman, Stig Larsson, Lars Norén and Agneta Pleijel)
Kjell Askildsen: *A Sudden Liberating Thought* (translated by Sverre Lyngstad)
Svend Åge Madsen: *Days with Diam* (translated by W. Glyn Jones)
Janet Garton (ed.): *Contemporary Norwegian Women's Writing*
Fredrika Bremer: *The Colonel's Family* (translated by Sarah Death)
Hans Christian Andersen (ed.): *New Danish Plays* (by Sven Holm, Kaj Nissen, Astrid Saalbach and Jess Ørnsbo)
Suzanne Brøgger: *A Fighting Pig's Too Tough to Eat* (translated by Marina Allemano)
Kerstin Ekman: *Witches' Rings* (translated by Linda Schenck)
Gunnar Ekelöf: *Modus Vivendi* (edited and translated by Erik Thygesen)
Robin Fulton (ed. and transl.): *Five Swedish Poets*.
Michael Robinson: *Strindberg and Autobiography*
James McFarlane: *Ibsen and Meaning*
Robin Young: *Time's Disinherited Children*
Knut Hamsun: *Selected Letters*, Vols. I and II (ed. and trans. by Harald Næss and James McFarlane)
Michael Robinson: *Strindberg and Genre*
A Century of Swedish Narrative (ed. Sarah Death and Helena Forsås Scott)
Aspects of Modern Swedish Literature (ed. Irene Scobbie)
Michael Robinson: *Studies in Strindberg*
Anglo-Scandinavian Cross-Currents (ed. by Inga-Stina Ewbank, Olav Lausund and Bjørn Tysdahl)
Victoria Benedictsson: *Money* (translated by Sarah Death)

The logo of Norvik Press is based on a drawing by Egil Bakka (University of Bergen) of a Viking ornament in gold, paper thin, with impressed figures (size 16x21mm). It was found in 1897 at Hauge, Klepp, Rogaland, and is now in the collection of the Historisk museum, University of Bergen (inv.no. 5392). It depicts a love scene, possibly (according to Magnus Olsen) between the fertility god Freyr and the maiden Gerðr; the large penannular brooch of the man's cloak dates the work as being most likely 10th century.

Cover design: V and A Vargo.

Nordic Letters 1870-1910

Edited by

Michael Robinson and Janet Garton

Norvik Press
1999

Selection © 1999 Michael Robinson and Janet Garton

Individual chapters and sections as indicated © 1999 :
Elias Bredsdorff, Lionel Carley, Kerstin Dahlbäck, Janet Garton, Katherine Hanson, Jorunn Hareide, Annegret Heitmann, Roger Holmström, Jørgen Knudsen, Barbara Lide, Henk van der Liet, Judith Messick, Harald Næss, Tor Obrestad, Michael Robinson, Alan Swanson, and Vigdis Ystad.

A catalogue record for this book is available from the British Library.

ISBN 1 870041 39 9
First published 1999

Norvik Press was established in 1984 with financial support from the University of East Anglia, the Danish Ministry for Cultural Affairs, the Norwegian Cultural Department and the Swedish Institute.

Managing Editors: James McFarlane, Janet Garton and Michael Robinson.

The Editors gratefully acknowledge the financial assistance given by Fritt Ord (Norway) towards the costs of publishing this book.

Printed in Great Britain by Page Bros. (Norwich) Ltd, Norwich, UK.

Contents

1. *Michael Robinson* — 11
   'The Great Epistolick Art' : An Introduction
2. *Vigdis Ystad* — 33
   Henrik Ibsen's Letters
3. *Jørgen Knudsen* — 65
   'I too believe in the good effect of hypnosis':
   George Brandes and his Correspondence
4. *Jorunn Hareide* — 87
   'Min anden Moder! Min kære og elskede Veninde!':
   Georg Brandes's Letters to Magdalene Thoresen
5. *Kerstin Dahlbäck* — 108
   'Six Worms and Nine Bees':
   The Vocabulary of Strindberg's Letters
   and Literary Works from the 1880s
6. *Barbara Lide* — 123
   Strindberg's Epistolary Wit
7. *Michael Robinson* — 146
   'Spela den så att Pontoppidan och Fru Nansen
   få blåskatarrh': Strindberg's Correspondence
   with Actors and Directors
8. *Tor Obrestad* — 172
   A Romantic Novel:
   The Correspondence between Alexander Kielland
   and the Drewsen Family
9. *Henk van der Liet* — 201
   'French Fungi': Some Snooping in Holger
   Drachmann's Letters
10. *Elias Bredsdorff* — 228
    Henrik Pontoppidan's Correspondence with
    Scandinavian Writers 1880-1910

11. *Harald Næss*   246
    Knut Hamsun and Denmark
12. *Janet Garton*   264
    'Why do Norwegians hate Denmark so much?':
    National Consciousness in Amalie and
    Erik Skram's Correspondence
13. *Judith Messick*   281
    Amalie Skram's Talking Cure Revisited
14. *Katherine Hanson*   306
    Amalie Skram and her Publishers
15. *Roger Holmström*   335
    The Modern Breakthrough's Author
    and his Publisher: Mikael Lybeck
    and Werner Söderström
16. *Annegret Heitmann*   352
    Letters from Munich: 'En Masse Kunst og
    storartet Bier.'
17. *Lionel Carley*   376
    An English Composer at the Heart of
    Nordic Culture: Frederick Delius and his Friends
18. *Alan Swanson*   398
    Style in the Letters of Carl Nielsen

Index   413

Notes on Contributors

Elias Bredsdorff was a lecturer and subsequently Reader in Scandinavian Studies and Head of the Department of Scandinavian Studies at the University of Cambridge from 1949 to 1979. Born at Roskilde he was active in the Resistance Movement during the war and edited *Frit Danmark* 1945-46. He is the author of many books on Scandinavian literature, including *Hans Christian Andersen. The Story of his Life and Works 1805-75*. He is a Fellow of the Royal Danish Society.

Lionel Carley has been a member of the Delius Society since its inception in 1962 and is currently its Vice President as well as its archivist. He took his Ph.D. at the University of Nottingham and for many years (1964-92) he pursued a career in the Government Information Service. He is the author of several books and has most recently edited a collection of essays, *Frederick Delius: Music, Art and Literature*. He is currently working on a book on Grieg and England and planning a new life of Delius.

Kerstin Dahlbäck is Professor in the Department of General and Comparative Literature at the University of Stockholm. She has written widely on both Hjalmar Bergman and Strindberg including a study of Strindberg's letters, *Ändå tycks allt vara osagt. August Strindberg som brevskrivare* (1994). She is also head of the data project devoted to Strindberg's letters.

Janet Garton is Reader in Scandinavian Studies at the University of East Anglia. She has published widely on contemporary Scandinavian literature, and has most recently been working on Norwegian women's writing (*Norwegian Women's Writing 1850-1990*, Athlone, 1993, and *Contemporary Norwegian Women's Writing*, Norvik Press, 1995). At present she is engaged in editing a complete Dano-Norwegian edition of the correspondence between Amalie and Erik Skram.

Katherine Hanson gained her Ph.D. in Scandinavian Languages and Literature at the University of Washington and is currently an Affiliate Faculty member of that department. Editor and translator of many of the selections in *An Everyday Story: Norwegian Women's Fiction* (Seattle, 1995). She collaborated with Judith Messick in translating three novels by Amalie Skram: *Constance Ring* (1988), *Professor Hieronimus* and *På St. Jørgen* (the last two published together as *Under Observation* in 1992).

Jorunn Hareide has been Professor of Nordic Literature at the University of Oslo since 1993. She has written on Norwegian literature, women's writing, children's literature, literature and psychoanalysis, and autobiography, including books on Aksel Sandemose and Dikken Zwilgmeyer. Most recently she has edited *Skrift, kjønn og selv. Nytt lys på Camilla Collett* (1998) and is co-editor of the three-volume *Norsk kvinnelitteraturhistorie* (1988-90) and *Norske tekster I-II* (1997).

Annegret Heitmann is Professor of Scandinavian Literature at the Ludwig-Maximilians-Universität in Munich, having previously taught at the universities of Norwich and Kiel. Her research in Scandinavian literature of the 19th and 20th centuries, women's studies and autobiography is exemplified in *Selbst Schreiben. Eine Untersuchung der dänischen Frauenautobiographik* (1994) and *Ästhetik der skandinavischen Moderne* (1998, ed. with K. Hoff).

Roger Holmström is Professor of Literature at Åbo Akademi. His extensive writings on twentieth-century Finland-Swedish literature include his 1988 thesis *Karakteristik och värdering. Studier i finlandssvensk litteraturkritik 1916-1929* and, most recently, a two-volume biography of Hagar Olsson and a study of Bo Carpelan's novel *Urwind*. He has also edited the volumes *Fem par finlandssvenska författare konfronteras* (1995) and *Från kulturväktare till nightdrivers* (1996).

Jørgen Knudsen taught at the University of Bonn and at Askov and Kolding High Schools, before becoming a free-lance writer. His many publications include *Tysk litteratur fra Thomas Mann til Bertolt Brecht* (1966) and the four volumes to date of his biography of Georg Brandes: *Georg Brandes, Frigørelsens vej 1842-77* (1985), *Georg Brandes, I modsigelsernes tegn 1877-83* (1988), *Georg Brandes, Symbolet og manden 1883-1895* (1994), and *Georg Brandes, Magt og afmagt 1896-1914* (1998).

Barbara Lide gained her Ph.D. in Comparative Literature at the University of Illinois, after writing her doctoral dissertation on *Strindberg's Comic Spirit*. Among her publications are numerous essays on

Strindberg, as well as on Friedrich Dürrenmatt and Lars Gyllensten. She is presently completing a book with the working title 'Strindberg and the Presence of Irony'. Professor Lide teaches at Michigan Technological University.

Henk van der Liet studied at the Universities of Groningen and Copenhagen. Lecturer in the Scandinavian Department at Groningen from 1985 to 1998 and, since then, Professor and Head of the Department of Nordic Languages at the University of Amsterdam. The author of numerous articles on contemporary Scandinavian (especially Danish) literature, his doctoral thesis, *Kontrapunkter. En studie i Poul Vads skønlitterære forfatterskab*, was published in 1997. He is the editor of *Tijdschrift voor Skandinavistiek*.

Judith Messick teaches writing at the Kellogg School of Management at Northwestern University. She gained her Ph.D. in English literature at the University of California, Santa Barbara, and together with Katherine Hanson she has translated three of Amalie Skram's novels: *Constance Ring, Professor Hieronimus* and *På St. Jørgen*, the last two published as *Under Observation* (1992). Her current research interests include Amalie Skram's correspondence with her professional colleagues – editors, publishers, and translators.

Harald Næss taught at King's College, University of Durham, from 1953 to 1959, when he was appointed Torger Thompson Professor of Scandinavian Studies at the University of Wisconsin–Madison, a post he held until his retirement in 1993. He is the author of many books and articles on Norwegian literature and Norwegian-American immigration history, including *Knut Hamsuns brev* (6 vols planned) and, with James McFarlane, *Knut Hamsun. Selected Letters* (2 vols).

Tor Obrestad was one of the prime movers of the "Profil" group in Oslo in the 1960s, moving from modernist texts to committed political poetry and documentary novels, e.g. *Sauda! Streik!* (1972). Since then he has been a prolific and wide-ranging author of novels, short stories, poetry and journalism. He has written a biography of Arne Garborg (1991) and one of Hulda Garborg (1992), and recently published an edition of the correspondence between Alexander L. Kielland and Louise and Viggo Drewsen, *To par* (1998).

Michael Robinson is Professor of Drama and Scandinavian Studies at the University of East Anglia. He has published books on both Beckett and Strindberg and written widely on modern drama and theatre practice. He has also edited and translated a two-volume selection of Strindberg's *Letters* (1992) and an anthology of Strindberg's *Essays*

(1996), for which he was awarded the Bernard Shaw Prize in 1997. A collection of Strindberg's plays in translation followed in 1998. He received the Strindberg Prize in 1999.

Alan Swanson is Professor of Scandinavian Studies at the University of Groningen. His chief interests are in theatre and music history, which are happily conjoined in a love of opera, however silly, and of song.

Vigdis Ystad is Professor of Scandinavian Literature in the Department of Scandinavian Studies and Comparative Literature at the University of Oslo. The editor of the series *Contemporary Approaches to Ibsen*, she has published numerous books and essays on Ibsen's work including *Henrik Ibsen: Dikt* (1981) and '– *livets endeløse gåde': Ibsens dikt og drama* (1996).

1

'The Great Epistolick Art': An Introduction

Michael Robinson
University of East Anglia

> We talked of letter-writing.
> JOHNSON. 'It is now so much the fashion to publish letters, that in order to avoid it, I put as little into mine as I can.'
> BOSWELL. 'Do what you will, Sir, you cannot avoid it.'

'Det är dumt att vara så öppenhjertig som jag är emot er,' the Swedish novelist Victoria Benedictsson writes to her critic and sometime lover, Georg Brandes, in 1887. 'Icke sant? Bref borde man aldrig sätta i verlden, ty det är med dem som med barn: man kan aldrig beräkna hvilka förargelser de komma att vålla en. Jag har också hållit mitt samvete rent, hvad brefsynder beträffar; man skulle kunna få trycka alltsamman tycker jag. Det skulle visst icke göra mig någon skada. Men brefven till er? Jag tror inte jag ville ha dem på trycket' (Being as frank as I am with you is stupid. Isn't that right? One ought never to give birth to letters because it's the same with them as with children: one can never anticipate the trouble they will bring one. But where letters are concerned, I've a clean conscience; it would be possible to publish all of them, I think. It wouldn't damage me at all. But my letters to you? I don't think I want to have them published).[1]

Benedictsson's words, which themselves form part of a personal letter, are, of course, symptomatic of the tensions which underlie the art of letter writing in general, and in particular of the wide-ranging correspondence to which many of the Nordic writers in the period under review here so readily committed themselves. Are these letters private or public? What may, or do, they reveal, and by association, what may they conceal? Should they have been preserved, or ought they to have been destroyed? And to whom, ultimately, do they belong? The writer? The recipient? Or the wider, largely anonymous public addressed in the letter writer's other works? On the one hand, letters had a particular significance for a generation of writers for whom the documentary aspect of literature was, in the light of literary naturalism, of great importance. They assumed the value of such documents, placed a premium on their preservation, and frequently assumed or intended that they should eventually be published. On the other hand, the compulsion to write openly and to reveal themselves with an immediacy that was again a consequence of naturalism but also part of the moral concern that their generation inherited from Kierkegaard, meant that they sometimes feared the exposure to the public gaze which the publication of their letters would bring. To publish, or not to publish; that is often the question. Thus, while Amalie Skram urges Viggo Hørup to burn her correspondence with him because of its self-revelatory nature, Strindberg declines to destroy the letters addressed to him by his third wife, Harriet Bosse: 'Att bränna dina bref vore att bränna Dig, och det kan jag icke' (to burn your letters would be to burn you, and I can't do that).[2]

In fact, many of the Nordic writers of the period 1870-1910 which, in deference to an 1883 collection of essays by Georg Brandes, is generally known as 'The Modern Breakthrough', have been treated to the publication of their letters, often in several volumes. In some cases, the process began while they were still alive. For example, the first collection of Ibsen's letters, edited by Halvdan Koht and Julius Elias, was published in simultaneous Danish and German editions in 1904 (Ibsen died in 1906), and was reviewed by Edvard Brandes in *Politiken* (19 November 1904), where he commented on the embarrassed sensation anyone who has received one of Ibsen's all too polite letters must feel on finding it published among so many similar letters here. Similarly, Georg Brandes wrote to Madame de Caillavet, also in 1904, about the recent publication of some of Nietzsche's letters: 'Ce sont seulement ses lettres à six correspondants, dont je suis. Il n'y a pas seulement les lettres, mais tous les réponses et une introduction par la sœur de Nietzsche très flatteuse pour moi. Mon dieu, je suis à présent si âgé qu'on édite mes lettres et les lettres qui m'ont été écrites' (These are only his letters to six correspondents, of whom I am one. Not only are there his letters, but all the replies and an introduction by Nietzsche's sister which is very flattering to me. Good Heavens, I am now so old that they are editing my letters and letters written to me).[3]

Meanwhile, Alexander Kielland took the initiative himself. Around the turn of the century much of his correspondence (with for example Bjørnstjerne Bjørnson, Edvard and Georg Brandes, and the publisher Jacob Hegel) is taken up with requests for the temporary return of his earlier letters, which he wishes to copy with a view to publication on his own terms. 'Ja, jeg samler mine Breve, idet jeg tænker, at hvis de skal udgives, vil jeg selv helst gjøre det,' he tells the Norwegian painter Frits Thaulow (Yes, I'm collecting my letters, because if they are to be published I'd rather do it myself).[4] Initially, he plans a volume in 10-12 printer's sheets in which the letters will be presented in strict chronological order without notes, index or commentary. Thus, to Edvard Brandes, he observes that he wants to avoid leaving his letters to the mercy of 'en Fremtidens Borchsenius, der da vil fremlægge et Monstrum paa 700 Sider med Noter' (a future Borchsenius, who will then produce a monster of 700 pages with notes).[5] But this scheme is soon supplanted by the possibility of a much longer 'Liv illustreret' (Illustrated Life)[6] with portraits and drawings of individuals, groups of people, and places mentioned in the correspondence. Nevertheless, as he tells Brandes, although 'jeg vil nok klæde mig noget af ved denne Leilighed…jeg vil beholde Buxerne' ([although] I really want to take this opportunity of undressing a little… I want to keep my trousers on).[7] What he wishes to preempt, in short, is what in Swedish is sometimes called 'kalsongsforskning' (literally, 'underpants research') at the hands of some future pedant like the ubiquitous nineteenth-century Danish editor and man-of-letters, Otto Borchsenius.

A striking feature of these subsequent collections is often the sheer volume of letters written by and to these authors. For example, a broad selection of Kielland's letters was eventually edited by Johs. Lunde in four substantial volumes while Bjørnson's letters to and from his Swedish correspondents fill three volumes, as does his correspondence with Danes. The correspondence of Georg and Edvard Brandes with other Nordic writers and scholars runs to eight large volumes and a selection of Georg Brandes' letters to other correspondents accounts for a further three; meanwhile Strindberg's extant letters run to twenty-two well-filled volumes and Knut Hamsun's to a mere six. Indeed, in the case of Georg Brandes who, with his brother Edvard, commonly acted as the nexus of an epistolary network that conveyed the ideas and emotions of the writers of the Modern Breakthrough back and forth across Europe, the statistics are frightening. It was quite normal for Georg Brandes to receive 20 letters a day and from the mid-1880s onwards, the number was frequently as many as 30 or 40. Jørgen Knudsen's modest estimation is that Brandes received at least a quarter of a million letters during the last forty years of his life, of which he preserved about 15,000 from some 2,500 correspondents. To these must be added the manuscripts, articles and books he was sent on a daily basis, often with dedications. The time he spent acknowledging and responding even to a small proportion of all these communications was prodigious as, too, might be the labour of his regular correspondents. Thus Kielland begins one of the many letters that Brandes could perhaps have done without by declaring: 'Jeg burde egentlig ikke skrive till Dem idag, thi jeg er træt efterat have skrevet otte Breve' (I really ought not to write to you today, because I am tired after having written eight letters).[8]

One obvious reason for the central role that letters played in these writers' lives is the fact that many of them lived outside Scandinavia, often for several years at a time. The theme of 'Home and Abroad' (Ude og Hjemme) is in fact a recurring motif in the writings of the Modern Breakthrough, and it was through their correspondence that (for example) Bjørnson, Georg Brandes, Hamsun, Verner von Heidenstam, Ibsen, Kielland, Jonas Lie and Strindberg first linked the one with the other. For them, Berlin, Munich, Paris, Rome or St Petersburg were frequently as important as Kristiania, Copenhagen or Stockholm and so, too, were many smaller places like Aulestad and Grez sur Loing or Skagen and Weggis which consequently emerge in these letters as important, if temporary, centres of European consciousness.

But what made a correspondence possible on this scale in the first place depended upon the revolution in the system of posts and communications, which was still in progress during the early years of the Modern Breakthrough. The kind of full and immediate exchange of opinion on which these writers relied was related to the practical exigencies of letter-writing, its cost, the ease with which letters could be posted and the frequency and dependability of the service that delivered them. There were, for example, four deliveries a day in Copenhagen in the 1880s and between four and eight in Stockholm, thus facilitating same day delivery within the city and the kind of everyday local contact which subsequently became the domain of the telephone as well as the distribution of more considered mail. Moreover, the extension of the railway system throughout Scandinavia and in Europe generally during the period under review contributed significantly to the ease with which the writers of the Modern Breakthrough corresponded as well as to the burgeoning modernity within which they worked. Formerly, distribution by horse-drawn mailcoach had governed both the rhythm of a regular correspondence (as Kerstin Dahlbäck points out, a frequent conclusion to many eighteenth-century letters alludes to the imminent arrival of the mailcoach)[9] and the speed with which a letter might reach its destination when previously bad weather and, especially in Northern and Eastern Europe, winter conditions generally, caused frequent delays. Similarly, the transition from sailing packets to steam-driven vessels had transformed the reliability of an overseas or coastal correspondence previously subject (among other things) to the caprice of contrary winds. The first regular service by steamer linking Sweden and Germany was established, between Ystad and Stralsund, in 1824, for example; Oslo was linked to Kristiansand by steamer in 1827, and to Hammerfest in 1841; and a regular postal service by steam packet between Europe and North America was initiated in 1840 (by 1845 the crossing from Liverpool to Boston took only nine days). All this is a far cry from the first years of the century when there was a single service a week linking Oslo with Kristiansand and Stavanger, and only two or three a year from Trondheim to the north. Even so, however, climate and geography continued to create particular problems in Norway where, for example, the question of a regular daily postal service between Bergen and Kristiania was not fully resolved before the turn of the century.[10] Likewise, anywhere north of Trondheim could also be problematic. When Trondheim to Hammerfest became a regular all-the-year-round route in 1859 a letter was expected to take 14 days in February and March, 8 days in April-August, 14 days in September and October and 3 weeks in November, December and January. But this was nevertheless a great improvement on the service around the beginning of the century when it would sometimes take a writer six months to receive a reasonably prompt reply to a letter sent from Hammerfest to Copenhagen.[11]

But to an impatient correspondent, even the most well-established routes could have their limitations. Thus, Erik Skram in Copenhagen is forced to write to an eager Amalie in Kristiania and explain: 'Du må ikke regne galt med Postgangen. Dit sidste Brev fik jeg ikke Onsdag Aften men Torsdag Morgen. Jeg kunde ikke have afsendt Brev før med den svensk-norske Post Fredag Morgen, den går kun en Gang om Dagen, og du vilde således under ingen Omstændigheder kunne have haft mit Svar før Mandag, da man i Kristiania – såvidt jeg ved – ikke omdeler Breve om Søndagen. Dette Brev kan først gå af imorgen Lørdag, og du vil efter min Beregning have det Mandag – er det rigtigt?' (You mustn't make the wrong calculations about postal deliveries. I got your last letter not on Wednesday evening but on Thursday morning. I could not have sent a letter before the Swedish-Norwegian post went on Friday morning, it goes only once a day, and therefore you could not under any circumstances have received my reply before Monday, since there is – as I understand it – no delivery of post on Sundays in Kristiania. This letter cannot catch the post until tomorrow, Saturday, and you will according to my calculations receive it on Monday – is that right?).[12] It was.

Price, too, and the availability of post offices or post boxes were also factors in the later nineteenth-century upsurge in letter writing to which the authors of the Modern Breakthrough contributed so prolifically. During the eighteenth century the frankage on a letter was various and could depend, for example, on the distance it had to travel as well as its size and weight. Where foreign post was concerned, there were also the different tariffs imposed upon letters or parcels by the various countries through which they passed on the way to their destination. (Thus, to take a non-Nordic example, during the 1850s, a letter of between 3/4 and 1 ounce cost 4s 4d to send from London to Belgrade via Paris while a similar letter from London to California via the Panama Canal cost a mere 2s 4d.)[13] It was only with the introduction of a standard postal rate and the stamps in which it was measured that the various national postal systems emerged in their modern form. Originally restricted to a ten mile radius of London, the penny post for a letter weighing half an ounce or less was introduced in England in 1840. France also acquired a standard rate during the 1840s and the Italian states in the 1850s. Norway followed suit in 1854 and Sweden in 1855 but a uniform rate irrespective of distance was adopted for north Germany only in 1867.

However, it still took some time before a comprehensive postal network developed. In Sweden, where post (or pillar) boxes were introduced in 1855, there were only 500 post-offices nationwide in 1870; in 1900 there were 2,600.[14] (In the same period the number of letters posted in Sweden rose from 10,700 in 1870 to 93,000 in 1900.) Meanwhile, in Norway, the number of postboxes multiplied from 638 in 1885 to 4,972 in 1910 and the number of post-offices increased during the same period from 617 to 3,206.[15] Thus, unless delivered personally, as in *A Doll's House*, the letters on which the plots of Ibsen and Strindberg's plays sometimes depend, were very much more easily sent and received at the end of these writers' careers than at the outset.[16] Moreover, the kind of foreign correspondence in which many of the Scandinavian writers of the period were necessarily engaged was likewise conducted with far greater ease after the first international postal convention had convened in Bern in 1874, and the creation of the General Union of Posts in 1875 (from 1878 the Universal Postal Union). With the establishment of a standard rate for all letters under half an ounce there was a significant reduction in the cost of sending a letter abroad and the introduction of standard rates for newspapers, parcels and books also facilitated the work of these writers and their editors and publishers, both at home and abroad.

The status of the letters which these writers addressed both to one another and to their other correspondents is, however, often problematic. For these are writers' letters and though a distinction may initially be made between the works that a writer produces for a multiple and anonymous public and the letters he addresses to an identified, private individual the fact remains that even with the most personal of these letters, 'on ne saura plus jamais où on en est, encore dans la vie ou déjà dans le texte'.[17]

For whom, indeed, were these letters intended and how should, or can, they be read now? The answer to both these questions seems at once immediately obvious: they were designed for the addressee named on the envelope or at the head of the letter and we read them now as documents of that relationship which he or she had with its writer and as source materials for the life of that writer in general. And yet both these responses are ultimately open to doubt not merely because they were written by practising authors given to transposing their experience into literature, but also because of the nature of the (private) letter as a genre, and our persistent desire to read letters as if they were always true and somehow free, because of their assumed spontaneity, naturalness and originality, of the artistry and stereotyping that characterizes all writing.

Setting aside such items as the contracts with theatres and publishers, the dedications in books and guest books and the inscriptions on his own paintings that Øyvind Anker includes in his edition of Ibsen's letters,[18] the great majority of these epistles are letters or postcards addressed to a named individual. Some of them were of course supposed to be read aloud to others like the triangular correspondence that Kielland conducted with Louise and Viggo Drewsen, discussed by Tor Obrestad in his contribution to this volume; a few might be 'kompanibref' (corporate letters) like the one that Strindberg addressed to Lie and Bjørnson in tandem on 12 February 1884;[19] and some were readily shared with others like the letter from Ibsen that Georg Brandes proudly enclosed with one of his own to the Danish philosopher Hans Brøchner in July 1869: 'À propos af Breve tillader jeg mig at vedlægge et fra Ibsen, som det har været mig kjært at modtage og som er blevet fulgt af flere' (A propos letters I take the liberty of enclosing one from Ibsen which I was very pleased to receive, and which has been followed by more).[20] Others contained information which the writer intended should be leaked either to those in the correspondents' intimate circle or to the press. Strindberg, for example, knew that his friend Georg Lundström would print any comments he sent him on women and his marriage to Siri von Essen in his (Lundström's) journal *Budkaflen* while Ibsen is even plainer when he concludes a letter to Sophus Schandorph, on *Gengangere* (Ghosts) with a P.S.: 'Skulde et eller andet af foranstående muligens kunne interessere nogen af Morgenbladets læsere, så har jeg intet imod at det meddeles' (If any part of the above letter is likely to be of interest to readers of *Morgenbladet*, I have no objection to its publication – 6 January 1882, Hundreårsutgave XVII, p. 451). Even so, misunderstandings could arise, and Hamsun is being transparently disingenuous when he writes to Arne Garborg to disclaim all responsibility for comments in an 'anerkendende Brev' (appreciative letter) from the latter about his (Hamsun's) novel *Sult* (Hunger) which had 'aldeles uden mit Vidende og naturligvis uden min Vilje' (entirely without my knowledge and naturally without my intending it), found their way into the papers.[21]

But the majority of these letters are nevertheless personal communications addressed to a specific correspondent and designed to be read by the recipient alone, one at a time, usually on or shortly after their arrival. This obvious point is worth bearing in mind since it provides one of the very few ways in which the texts of these letters may be distinguished from their author's other writings; it also particularizes our reading of them from their addressee's. For although a new letter may encourage its recipient to return to and read again any earlier letters in the correspondence that he or she has preserved, even this is a reading experience different in kind to that of the later reader or critic who encounters each letter in the uniformity of print, where the text of each collected item has been reduced to the similarity of a constant type face and any peculiarities of the handwritten text, even where noted by an editor, rarely, if ever, impact upon the eye of the reader. The printed letter is also not encountered in isolation but read in conjunction with the surrounding correspondence which may or may not be to the same addressee, depending upon whether the book is devoted to a single correspondence or forms part of the writer's collected letters, often in several volumes. Indeed, one of the advantages that a later reader of a writer's collected correspondence has over the original recipient of an individual letter is the possibility of juxtaposing communications sent to different addressees at the same time or comparing how the same information is formulated in letters to different correspondents. Thus, on the same day (26 May 1908) that Strindberg wrote a brief note to the Swedish chemist, The Svedberg, about 'Kisels övergång till Kol' (the transition of silicon into carbon),[22] he also addressed one of his most finely crafted suicide notes (a genre at which he excelled), to his brother Axel: 'Lägg krucifixet på mitt bröst i kistan. Min bruna kappa ofvanpå kistan. / Sätt endast ett svart träkors på min graf med: O crux, ave spes unica! Obemärkt enkel plats. Aldrig monument!' (Lay the crucifix on my breast in the coffin. My brown cape over the coffin. Place only a black wooden cross on my grave with: *O crux, ave spex unica!* An obscure, simple place. No monument).[23]

What is lost, however, in our contemporary reading is precisely the physical aspect of the letter in which meaning also resides.[24] For the physical appearance and texture of a letter, in the first instance its format, orthography, and layout, the colour of the paper and of the ink, the handwriting and whether or not it follows the writer's customary style together with any crossings out, dashes, marginalia, insertions, spacing, capitalization, underlinings or other ways of emphasizing a word or passage in the text plus, indeed, any of the sketches, doodles or blots with which the writer may embellish his or her text, and which, on paper, frequently give the impression at least of an immediate and personal communication, one written (in Samuel Richardson's fine phrase) to the moment and conveying the tone of voice and the physical aspect of the writer in such a way that s/he almost appears before the reader in person – all this, which is crucial to the original reading of a letter, is no longer readily apparent. And it is precisely this physical aspect that underlies what Richardson (again) terms 'the converse of the pen … that makes distance, presence; and brings back to sweet remembrance all the delights of presence',[25] and which supports the rhetorical strategies deployed by the writer as substitutes for gesture, vocal inflection, and physical context, as s/he appears, or performs, before the particular audience of the reader.

The idea that private letters are a substitute for conversation is commonplace. Stendhal, for example, maintains that 'pour avoir un bon style épistolaire, il faut dire exactement ce qu'on dirait à la personne si on la voyait, ayant soin de ne pas écrire des répétitions auxquelles l'accent de la voix ou le geste pourraient donner quelque prix en conversation.'[26] Strindberg, meanwhile, buttonholes his friend Eugène Fahlstedt at the start of a letter by exclaiming, 'Som Du förnärvarande är den enda människa jag kan tala vid och jag i detta ögonblick måste tala för Du vara goda läsa följande' (Since you are at present the only person I can talk to, and right now I've got to talk, kindly read what follows).[27] And even Henry James, who wonders 'what are letters but talk?',[28] considers the association a self-evident one. The letter, in short, claims to take the place of speech and hence abrogates to itself the values of immediacy, naturalness and veracity ascribed to speech by a logocentric tradition that privileges speech over writing because of the anteriority of the primary speaking voice over the supplementary writing hand in the individual's life and in history.[29]

But as writing all letters, from their inception, share in the artifices of literary composition, the processes of selection and reformulation, and the application of numerous, often extremely conventional rhetorical strategies for the production of a written text, some of them particular to letter writing, others common to writing in general. Get these wrong and the communication at which a writer aims may be seriously impaired, as is clear from Georg Brandes's response to Bjørnson's first contribution to what was always to be an uneasy correspondence. 'Høistærede!' (Sir), Brandes wrote:

De har under 15de April d. A. tilskrevet mig et Brev, der i flere Henseender har forundret mig. Det har været mig kjært at see at De ligesom jeg har den Mening, at smaaligt Fjendskab ei bør finde Sted i Litteraturen; men Brevets Form synes at mig beroe paa en Misforstaaelse eller paa et Ubekjendtskab med danske Sædvaner. Det er nemlig i Danmark Skik, at Enhver der i et privat Brev henvender sig til en Anden, taler i en høflig Tone, uden

Overlegenhed, næsten som til en Ligemand, hvad enten den Paagjælende er betydelig eller lille; vi ere blevne saa vante til denne høflige Form, at vi ere komne til at fordre den af Enhver, og aldeles ikke taale, at den udebliver; vi ere her komne saa vidt i vort demokratiske Væsen, at vi vide at tvinge Enhver, der søger personligt Samkvem med os, til den Høflighed, hvis Grad bestemt lader sig maale, og som vi derfor endogsaa foretrække for en Hjertelighed, der er tvivlsom. Jeg slutter af Deres Brev, at man i Norge stiller færre Fordringer og har mindre Stolthed.

(You have written me a letter, dated the 15th April of this year [1869], which has surprised me in various respects. It pleases me to see that you, like me, are of the opinion that petty enmities should not arise in literature; but the form of your letter appears to me to be due to a misunderstanding or ignorance of Danish customs. For in Denmark it is common practice for anyone addressing a private letter to someone else to write in a courteous tone, with no trace of hauteur, almost as to an equal, whether the person concerned is important or insignificant; we have become so accustomed to this polite form that we have come to demand it of everyone, and will not tolerate its absence; in this respect we have progressed so far in our democratic spirit that we are able to insist that anyone who seeks personal contact with us should observe this courtesy, the degree of which cannot be measured, and which we therefore prefer to a cordiality of dubious nature. From your letter I assume that correspondents in Norway make fewer demands and have less pride.)[30]

Even though Bjørnson frequently provoked an extreme response, Brandes's reply may appear unwarranted. Nevertheless, it serves to indicate that letters are accompanied by formal expectations and a writer needs to bear in mind what is appropriate to their various purposes. From begging letters to love letters and suicide notes to letters home there are proprieties to be observed, not least in the more or less conventional topping and tailing whereby a writer sets up his letter and rounds it off. Such proprieties, or their waiving, also impose on the writer a gesture of self-definition according to what is once again a generally standard epistolary gambit. The shift from one form of address to another marks a change in the writer's epistolary relationship with his correspondent, and where the Scandinavian languages are concerned, the all important shift from the impersonal to the personal form of address and the dropping of titles are crucial signifiers, though often lost in translation. Thus, even after she had declared her love for him, Amalie Skram found it impossibly embarrassing for quite some time to address her future husband, Erik, by his first name in the many letters she addressed to him; and the fact that Georg Brandes signed off so frequently with his full name (or as 'Georges Brandès' where his French correspondents were concerned) is as relevant to his epistolary relationships as is the multiplicity of soubriquets with which Strindberg liked to regale his addressees for whom he was variously (and in no particular order) 'Strind', 'Ågust', 'Gusten', 'Örnen', 'Strix', 'Augustus Imperator' and 'Rex' as well as 'Agustulus', 'August', 'Aug. Strindberg', 'August Sg.', or 'A.Sg.'. On one occasion, indeed, during Siri von Essen's flight to Copenhagen in order to precipitate the divorce from Carl Gustaf Wrangel that would enable her to marry him, he also became a suitably serious 'Ernest'.

As Elizabeth MacArthur observes, therefore, 'Letters are as much fictional constructions as they are transparent reflections. Letter writers do not merely reproduce the sentiment they feel and the events they observe; they transform them, whether consciously or unconsciously, into written texts whose organization, style, vocabulary, and point of view generate particular meanings.'[31] As in other forms of *belles lettres*, so in personal letters meaning is produced by figurative language, narrative or dramatic devices, stylistic choices and even the order in which the substance of a letter is relayed to its addressee. For example, the information that 'Fru Benedictsson har dræbt sig inat. Hun har paa fire Steder overskaaret sin Hals med en Barberkniv' (Mrs Benedictsson killed herself last night. She cut her throat in four places with a razor), is reported by Georg Brandes to Edvard only after a long paragraph in which he defends his recent book *Indtryck fra Polen* (Impressions of Poland) against his brother's criticisms.[32] Consequently, in reading them today, we need continually to look round the edge of these letters, and as much attention needs to be directed towards the verbal strategies that the writer employs in order to achieve his or her ends as to their documentary, or illustrative, value. Again, Richardson betrays the doubtful probity of the genre even as, like so many habitual letter writers, he extols it for its purity, when he tells Sophia Westcomb: 'This correspondence is, indeed, the cement of friendship ... more pure, yet more ardent, and less broken in upon, than personal conversation can be even amongst the most pure, because of the deliberation it allows, from the very preparation to, and action of writing.'[33]

Indeed, far from belonging to an uninhibited genre whose privacy and prompt despatch ensure the authenticity of the feelings they express and the accuracy of the information they contain, letters are in fact profoundly self conscious both in being so often preoccupied by the writer's self and in the frequency with which they reflect on themselves as letters. For even where they appear spontaneous letters are composed, not ready made. The process may even begin with a carefully meditated choice of format, for example between the possibilities offered by writing paper, manuscript paper, letter card, postcard (introduced in Austria in 1869 and quickly followed by Britain, north Germany and Switzerland in 1870), the picture postcard, telegram, or visiting card with inscription. The medium can be the message and a writer may (as Strindberg sometimes does) confine his communications with a specific correspondent to one or other of these formats.

Moreover, if the style is the man or woman, then letter writing also draws attention to the multifaceted nature of the individual who generally adopts a different persona in relation to his or her various correspondents, each of whom commands a different style and often a different vocabulary. In this respect, letters are theatrical. Where Samuel Johnson presumed (in a letter to Mrs Thrale, of course) that 'in a Man's Letters ... his soul lies naked, his letters are the mirrour of his breast,'[34] the reader of these late nineteenth-century letters is confronted by a very much less transparent subject. The writer assumes masks rather than strips him or herself naked before the reader (the latter being in any case merely a rhetorical strategy or figure of speech and thus a form of role play that is employed as readily to conceal as to reveal). As Bruce Redford suggests, in seeking to capture the artful spontaneity of conversation, the letter writer plays roles, dons masks, impersonates, much as an actor does, and 'the basic challenge is to find satisfactory equivalents to the resources of an actor: the ironic intonation, the raised eyebrow, the rueful smile, the sudden whisper, the emphatic change of posture, the meaningful glance across the room.' Redford quotes Janet Altman's assertion, in

Epistolarity: Approaches to a Form, that 'epistolary language, which is the language of absence, makes present by make-believe', and adds, with the subtlety of a theoretician of acting like Diderot: 'The letter-writer is an actor, but a *magician*-actor who works on his audience by sustaining the illusion of physical presence. Consequently the truest letter, we might say, is the most feigning.'[35]

Thus, although a letter is the act of 'a historically real person, occasioned and determined by a historically real universe,'[36] it is also a performance in which the writer creates as well as reports upon the given circumstances of his or her utterance, and employs language imaginatively and artistically in order to persuade, amuse, inform or otherwise engage its reader(s). And just as a story-teller adapts his narrative to capture and retain the attention of a specific audience so the letter writer always situates himself vis-à-vis another, and inflects his epistle in a manner that will appeal to the identity and interests of the recipient, who thus plays a generative role from the very inception of the letter.

Letters are therefore inherently dialogic, even though they do possess a monologic element. For while they are addressed to someone, and usually solicit a reply, they cannot normally be interrupted by the recipient in the course of composition. Only when despatched, delivered and read is a response possible, although one may be anticipated by the writer, in which case it is frequently written into the letter as it is being composed. Moreover, a further link between epistolary and dramatic discourse is to be found in its active intentionality. For letters are actions, designed to achieve something, from begging money, persuading a publisher, seducing a lover, entertaining the reader or simply enabling the writer to gain control over her own situation by formulating it in words. Consequently, just as all speech on stage is active, not passive, and an actor needs to understand his or her lines in terms of the circumstances each of them is intended to influence, so the reader of a letter might therefore reasonably consider its text to discover what the writer is seeking to accomplish with its writing. Not all intentions are as transparent as Ibsen's when he writes to Edvard Brandes about the young pianist, Hildur Andersen, 'Selvfølgelig er det ikke min mening at ville forsøge på at øve nogensomhelst indvirkning på den eventuelle musikkritik i Deres blad, men kun at bede om at hun må blive mødt med velvilje' (It is obviously not my intention to want to try and exert any kind of influence on any possible music critic in your paper, but only to request that she be treated benevolently),[37] yet most letters, when interrogated closely, yield their purpose, which is related to the persona assumed by the writer who (as Judith Messick points out, in her discussion of Amalie Skram's correspondence with Viggo Hørup below), frequently dons a mask in which to approach his or her various correspondents. 'Letter writers inevitably construct personae for themselves as they write, and if they are involved in a regular exchange they construct personae for the correspondent and plots for the story of the relationship as well.'[38] This is even the case where someone begins a correspondence anonymously, as in Amalie Skram's epistolary relationship with Bjørnson, where she signs her first letters 'ie' and he tries to guess who she is. He is correct in assuming she is a woman, but fails at first to get the right name. When he does (and he discovers that she is beautiful), the correspondence changes tone.

An extreme and obvious form of role play is to be found in Strindberg's exchange of letters with Nietzsche, where in response to a letter signed 'Nietzsche Caesar' Strindberg replies as 'Strindberg (Deus, optimus maximus)'.[39] But so blatant an example of epistolary performance is in fact only a self-conscious extension of a practice common to all letter writers, that is to say the role they employ to represent themselves both in a particular correspondence and the single letter. This may well be implicit in a letter's forms of address and salutation; it is always present in the writer's language and in the character necessarily projected upon the addressee by the writer and accepted or rejected by the former when he or she replies: 'Fortæl mig, naar De svarer mig, hvor gammel De er. Jeg tænker mig, at De er ung; jeg er 31 Aar' (When you reply, tell me how old you are. I imagine you to be young; I am 31), Georg Brandes writes, to Edmund Gosse, in 1873.[40]

Here, where 'writing ... becomes associated with the freedom to choose an identity by choosing a new relation to another,'[41] the association is again with drama, but because it is the product of writing this new identity, which is literally written into existence, comes in turn to be associated with fiction. Tor Obrestad raises the possibility of personal letters providing the novelist with the means of removing creative inhibitions, of acting as a Proustian mechanism for the release of hidden, or repressed, material. But as he points out, in his essay on Alexander Kielland's exchange of letters with Louise and Viggo Drewsen, some correspondences are already on the way to becoming fiction. This is also the case with Strindberg, whose letters to Pehr Staaff in 1887 prepare the way for his autobiographical fiction in French *Le Plaidoyer d'un fou*, and whose sequence of numbered letters on manuscript paper to Torsten Hedlund in 1896 is a preliminary attempt to organize the material ultimately published in 1897 as *Inferno*. More revealing even than any of these examples are the letters he exchanged with Siri von Essen during the 1870s, which he later described as 'en själs roman men icke diktad eller arrangerad, utan lefvad' (an intimate novel, not invented and arranged, however, but lived),[42] and sought in 1886 to publish as an epistolary novel. Although the collection, with the minimal editing that Strindberg had given it, did not appear until after his death, there is evidence here, if only in the fact that the reader can comprehend the unfolding drama of these letters and the references they contain with little or no editorial assistance, that in their original, ostensibly private form, they already belonged to the domain of literature.[43]

For the practising author, letters can therefore be trial runs, opportunities to explore material that may subsequently be developed in fictional form. Particularly for the young writer they provide an opportunity to experiment with different styles and to explore the expressive possibilities of various standpoints, ideas and emotions. A writer's letters are therefore frequently of a dual nature, both acts of immediate and personal communication and literary texts. But as part of his overall project, they offer a specifically autobiographical dimension in which the writer may often be observed writing his life into existence. 'To write a letter,' Janet Altman observes, 'is to map one's coordinates – temporal, spatial, emotional, intellectual – in order to tell someone else where one is located at a particular time and how far one has travelled since last writing.'[44] A correspondent is selected precisely for this purpose (in epistolary narrative, confidantes are chosen not given, and the same is frequently true of personal letters), in order to reflect the perception the writer has of his own self at the time or the narrative role he is seeking as he labours over the emplotment of his lived experience.[45] For although 'common opinion has it that the plot of a narrative imposes a meaning on the events that comprise its story level by revealing at the end a structure that was immanent in the events all along,'[46] it is nevertheless the case that in many of these correspondences, the writer is seeking to confer a meaning on his experience by projecting his life in progress in terms of existing forms of discourse, fictional or otherwise. Indeed, the great nineteenth-century letter writers, of whom Strindberg (like Keats and Flaubert) was undoubtedly one, deploy their correspondence to biographize themselves.

The essays collected here were originally presented as papers at a conference on Nordic letter writing at the University of East Anglia, in September 1997. They have been largely revised for publication and are presented in this guise as a contribution to our knowledge of The Modern Breakthrough in particular, and to an understanding of the epistolary genre in general. Unfortunately there are lacunae. Several major figures of the period – Bjørnstjerne Bjørnson, Herman Bang, J. P. Jacobsen, Victoria Benedictsson, Gustaf Fröding, Jonas Lie, Selma Lagerlöf and Verner von Heidenstam, of whom Kate Bang and Fredrik Böök observe that he was 'medveten artist på samma sätt som när han diktade ett poem eller formade ett tal' (the same conscious artist [in his many letters] as when he composed a poem or fashioned a speech),[47] figure only marginally, if at all, in this volume. For those who might have written about them other commitments intervened.

Finally, thanks are due to the following for their support in mounting the original conference from which these essays derive: Fritt Ord, The Royal Danish Embassy, The Royal Swedish Embassy, The Centre for Modern Nordic Studies and the School of Modern Languages and European Studies at the University of East Anglia.

Notes

1. Georg og Edvard Brandes, *Brevveksling med nordiske Forfattere og Videnskabsmænd* (henceforth GEB), 8 vols, edited by Morten Borup, with the cooperation of Francis Bull and John Landquist (Copenhagen, 1939-42), VI, pp. 222-3.
2. *August Strindbergs brev* (henceforth ASB), 22 vols, ed. Torsten Eklund and Björn Meidal (Stockholm, 1948-1999), XVI, p. 251. For Skram and Hørup, see Judith Messick's contribution to this volume.
3. *Correspondance de Georg Brandes. Lettres choisies et annotées par Paul Krüger*, 3 vols (Copenhagen, 1952), I, pp. 214-5; *Selected Letters*, edited and translated by W. Glyn Jones (Norwich, 1990), p. 189.
4. Alexander L. Kielland, *Brev 1869-1906*, 4 vols, edited by Johs. Lunde (Oslo, 1981), IV, p. 13.
5. Kielland, *Brev*, IV, p. 17.
6. Kielland, *Brev*, IV, p. 19.
7. Kielland, *Brev*, IV, p. 17.
8. GEB V, p. 333.
9. Kerstin Dahlbäck, *Ändå tycks allt vara osagt: August Strindberg som brevskrivare* (Stockholm, 1994), p. 24.
10. See August Schou, *Postens Historie i Norge* (Oslo, 1947), pp. 356-7.
11. See Schou, pp. 131, 225.
12. Letter dated 17 November 1882.
13. One of the most remarkable of all nineteenth-century correspondences in general (cost unknown) was the animated exchange of letters conducted during the 1850s by Alfred Wallace, moving between remote islands in the Malayan archipelago and towards a theory of evolution, and his fellow naturalist, Henry Walter Bates, some 2,000 miles up the Amazon – remarkable that is, until one remembers the correspondence maintained with Linnaeus by his informants worldwide in the previous century.
14. Prior to the establishment of an extensive network of post offices, the responsibility for receiving the mail and holding it until collected was assumed by one or other accredited citizen. In Grimstad, in Norway, the apothecary, Reimann, to whom Ibsen was apprenticed in 1844 aged 15 was also the town's postmaster. Thus Ibsen writes to a childhood friend, 'Reimann is also postmaster, so you can have my brother Johan put your letters in with the ones he writes, since in that way you won't have to pay the postage on them.' Henrik Ibsen, *Letters and Speeches*, edited by Evert Sprinchorn (London, 1965), p. 6.
15. Schou, *Postens Historie i Norge*, pp. 501, 504.

16. Front door letter boxes for the personal delivery of mail like the one that plays so central a role in *Et dukkehjem* (A Doll's House) were also introduced during this period.
17. Alain Buisine, 'Situations', *Revue des sciences humaines*, 195 (1984), p. 3.
18. Henrik Ibsen. *Brev 1845-1905*, ny samling (Oslo, 1979).
19. ASB, IV, p. 37.
20. GEB I, p. 69; *Selected Letters*, p. 21.
21. *Knut Hamsuns Brev 1879-1895*, utgitt av Harald S. Næss (Oslo, 1994), p. 169; Knut Hamsun, *Selected Letters*, translated and edited by Harald Næss and James McFarlane, 2 vols (Norwich, 1990-98), I, p. 119.
22. ASB, XVI, 319.
23. ASB, XVI, 320. There may also be editorial commentary and other explanatory material as in Harriet Bosse's collection of *Strindbergs brev till Harriet Bosse* or Lionel Carley's two-volume *Delius: A Life in Letters*, all of which situates the later reader in a different context to the original recipient, even where that material seeks to elucidate the latter's situation.
24. Or disclaimed: see Hamsun, to Arne Garborg, in the margin: 'Undskyld dette snobbede Papir. Jeg har ikke noget andet for Haanden i Aften. Det har Barter som Forklæderne i Hallingdal' (Please forgive the snobbish paper. I have nothing else at hand this evening. It has borders like the pinafores in Hallingdal). *Brev 1879-1895*, p.164, Hamsun, *Selected Letters*, I, p. 120.
25. See the letter to Sophia Westcomb in *The Correspondence of Samuel Richardson* (New York, 1966), III, pp. 244-9 passim for Richardson's own detailed exposition of his epistolary aesthetic.
26. *Correspondance*, 3 vols, edited by V. Del Litto and H. Martineau, I (Paris, 1962), p. 3.
27. ASB, I, p. 118.
28. Epigraph to the *Selected Letters of Henry James*, ed. Leon Edel (London, 1956).
29. See Jacques Derrida, *De la grammatologie* (Paris, 1967), for the now classic discussion of this opposition between writing and speech. In some cases (here it is Victoria Benedictsson writing to Georg Brandes), letter writing was a welcome substitute for what was experienced as the awkwardness of speech: 'Som jag sitter och pratar! Det värsta pennan orkar löpa. Men det är roligt. Jag önskar ibland att jag hörde till dem som kunna tala. Det måste vara behagligt. Men det är kanske bäst som det är; om jag icke tryckts af min skygghet, skulle jag kanske aldrig ha lärt mig att skrifva' (How I sit and talk! It's terrible how my pen can run on. But it's fun. I sometimes wish I was one of those people who can talk. But perhaps it's best the way things

are; if I hadn't been weighed down with shyness, I might never have learnt to write). GEB VI, p. 222.
30. GEB IVi, pp. 7-8; *Selected Letters*, pp. 18-19.
31. *Extravagant Narratives. Closure and Dynamics in the Epistolary Form* (Princeton, 1990), p. 118. For a rare study of the composition and style of some Nordic letters, see Kerstin Dalbäck, *Op. cit.*, Chapter Five, 'Några representativa Strindbergsbrev'. The analysis of a writer's shifts in style within a single letter and correspondence as well as across an entire corpus of letters is a much needed enterprise.
32. GEB, II, P.144; Georg Brandes, *Selected Letters*, p. 159.
33. Richardson, p. 245.
34. *The Letters of Samuel Johnson, with Mrs. Thrale's Genuine Letters to Him*, collected and edited by R. W. Chapman, 3 vols (Oxford, 1952), II, p. 228. Concerning what he calls 'the Great Epistolick Art', Johnson goes on: 'whatever passes within him is shown undisguised in its natural process. Nothing is inverted, nothing distorted, you see systems in their elements, you discover actions in their motives.'
35. Bruce Redford, *The Converse of the Pen. Acts of Intimacy in the Eighteenth-Century Familiar Letter* (Chicago, 1986), pp. 5-7. The Altman quotation is from p. 140 of her *Epistolarity: Approaches to a Form* (Columbus, Ohio, 1982).
36. Barbara Herrnstein Smith, *On the Margins of Discourse* (Chicago, 1978), p. 20.
37. GEB, V, p. 39.
38. MacArthur, *Extravagant Narratives*, p. 119.
39. ASB, VII, p. 216.
40. Georg Brandes, *Correspondance II*, p. 17; *Selected Letters*, p. 40.
41. Roy Roussel, 'Reflections on the Letter: The Reconciliation of Distance and Presence in *Pamela*', ELH 41 (1974), p. 346.
42. ASB, V, p. 357.
43. In fact both Strindberg and Siri von Essen wrote their letters influenced by numerous literary models. For detailed consideration of *Han och hon*, see Kerstin Dahlbäck, *Ändå tycks allt vara osagt*, pp. 321-330, and Michael Robinson, *Strindberg and Autobiography* (Norwich, 1986), pp. 94-104.
44. *Epistolarity*, p. 119.
45. As well as being the usual precondition for encouraging someone to write a letter, distance also permits reflection, introspection and self-analysis of a kind that approximates to the method which Freud was developing in Vienna during these same years. The blank page of writing paper serves as a screen on to which the writer may project his anxieties. Amalie Skram's correspondence with Hørup or Strindberg's many letters to Torsten Hedlund (a man he never even

met) are cures in which writing takes the place of talking, but which in other respects closely follow the dynamic of Freud's method, with its tension between objectivity and subjectivity and the perils of transference and counter transference. It is worth recalling that Freud accomplished much of his own self-analysis in which many of the ideas of psychoanalysis were first developed, by means of his correspondence with Wilhelm Fliess.
46. Hayden White, 'The Value of Narrativity in the Representation of Reality', in *On Narrative*, ed. W. J. T. Mitchell (Chicago, 1981), p. 19. Cf. also Janet Altman on how 'Epistolary narrative is by definition fragmented narrative. Discontinuity is built into the very blank space that makes of each letter a footprint rather than a path. Yet as any observer of perceptual behaviour knows, the illusion of a continuous line can be produced from a series of points.' *Epistolarity*, p. 169.
47. Verner von Heidenstam, *Brev*, utgivna av Kate Bang och Fredrik Böök (Stockholm, 1949), p. 5.

2

Henrik Ibsen's Letters

Vigdis Ystad
University of Oslo

In Ibsen's dramas, a *letter* can have fateful significance. The secret letter from Trond the priest, which contains the hidden truth about King Haakon's parentage, becomes a turning-point in the action of *Kongsemnerne* (The Pretenders). It is this letter which Bishop Nikolas receives and which he burns on his deathbed – without the contents being revealed either to him or to Skule, who from that moment becomes the victim of his own doubts. In *Vildanden* (The Wild Duck) Hjalmar interprets the letter Hedvig receives from old Mr Werle as a proof of his daughter's parentage – and thus the letter becomes a force which precipitates the drama's ultimate catastrophe. The 'strange letter' which the late Beate Rosmer once wrote to the journalist Mortensgaard in *Rosmersholm* tells of a secret love between Rosmer and Rebekka, and foreshadows the tragic outcome of their relationship in the present. And in *Lille Eyolf* (Little Eyolf) Aasta has preserved a collection of letters from her mother which show that she and Alfred Allmers are after all not half-sister and brother, as they had both believed. In this case too the letters are indirectly the catalyst for the play's denouement.

In other words, the fateful letters in Ibsen's plays are written evidence of concealed identities and secret motives, and have far greater repercussions than letters in an average play of intrigue. They contribute to precipitating the acknowledgement of identity and underlying motive which characterises Ibsen's tragic scenes of *anagnorisis*. But exactly what is *said* in these fictive letters – their precise wording and tone – we never discover. It is their *essence*, and not the actual words, which is important.

The same can be said of the letters Ibsen wrote in his own name. The author who was so acutely conscious of the explosive potential of a letter was careful about what he himself entrusted to paper, and therefore Ibsen's pen does not glide so easily over the writing paper as it does when it is used in the service of dramatic creation. Anyone who searches through his surviving letters looking for secrets about the writer's life or about his innermost thoughts, or who is interested in discovering more about Ibsen's opinions on contemporary literature, on the intellectual life of his time, or on his own writing, risks being disappointed. It is not without a certain justification that Ibsen is described as a boring – even bad – letter writer; a man who took great pains not to reveal anything intimate, and who in his letters as a rule presented the world with a formal facade. The reader of Ibsen's letters can therefore not be content with taking them at face value, but is enticed into looking for the meaning *between* the lines.

Amongst the most formal letters from Ibsen's hand one must reckon the so-called 'rimbrevene' (rhyming letters), philosophizing verses in which the poet is writing just as much for public consumption as he is for the recipient – whether the latter is called Johanne Louise Heiberg ('Rimbrev til fru Heiberg' (Rhyming Letter to fru Heiberg)), Fredrika Limnell ('Ballongbrev til en svensk dame' (Balloon Letter to a Swedish Lady)), or Georg Brandes ('Et rimbrev' (A Rhyming Letter)). Such 'letters' Ibsen immediately published. Here he writes about topical issues related to cultural, historical or social philosophy. One of his most famous formulations occurs precisely in the Rhyming Letter to Georg Brandes, written for publication in his journal *Det nittende Århundre* (The Nineteenth Century) in 1875. It is here that Ibsen writes: 'Jeg spørger helst; mit kald er ej at svare' (I prefer to ask; it is not my calling to answer) – words which could stand as a motto for all his correspondence, including that of a more private nature.

Even when the correspondence was of a more private nature, Ibsen as a rule preserved the facade. One of many such letters is addressed to his long-time business manager in Kristiania, the bookseller Nils Lund, and is dated Maximillianstrasse, Munich, 30 November 1879:

Ligeledes vil De bevise mig en stor tjeneste ved at lade bestille for mig en stor god gammelost og et par fine mysoste. Hvis afsenderen kunde ordne det så med sin kommisionær i Hamburg at sagerne blev mig hersteds leveret fortoldet og frit i huset, så vilde det for mig være en stor lettelse.

(You could in addition render me a great service by ordering for me a large mature sour-milk cheese and a couple of fine whey cheeses. If the sender could arrange with his agent in Hamburg for the cheeses to be delivered here to the house and with the import duties paid, it would be a great relief to me.)[1]

Ibsen went about these matters in a methodical and business-like manner – but the letter also reveals that the playwright was a great lover of traditional Norwegian cheeses.

Henrik Ibsen was quite conscious of the fact that much of his correspondence had a rather impersonal tone. He did not like letter-writing, and postponed putting pen to paper for as long as he could. Many of his friends lost patience with him because of his dilatoriness; one of them was Georg Brandes, who must have given strong expression to his irritation at not receiving a reply in a letter in the autumn of 1898. Ibsen replied as follows on 30 September 1898:

Og så kender De jo til overflod min indgroede aversion imod at sætte mig ned og skrive breve ... Jeg kan ... ikke finde, at min taushedsbrøde er så kvalificeret, at den berettiger Dem til at titulere en mangeårig ven for 'Deres Højvelbaarenhed' eller lignende. Og jeg synes aldeles ikke at det er en mand som Dem værdigt at tage sådan på vej for et par forsømte breves skyld, – og det oven i købet breve fra en mand [dvs. Ibsen selv], hvis hovedpassion det aldeles ikke er at udveksle epistler – selv med sine bedste og kæreste venner.)

(And then you are more than sufficiently aware of my deep-seated aversion to sitting down and writing letters.... I can ... not see that my offence of silence is so grave that it justifies you addressing a friend of many years' standing as 'Your High and Mightiness' etc. And it seems to me to be entirely beneath the dignity of a man such as you to get so worked up about a couple of missing letters – especially letters from a man [i.e. Ibsen himself] who does not regard exchanging letters as one of his favourite passions – not even with his best and closest friends.)[2]

No, letter writing was far from being Ibsen's 'favourite passion'.

It would be possible to make a comprehensive catalogue of the opening phrases in Ibsen's letters – they frequently begin with conventional excuses and explanations as to why he has not given any sign of life or replied to communications. Months could go by, even half a year, before Ibsen answered a letter. Øyvind Anker says that 'Det er som Ibsen kvier seg for å skrive og åpne seg, man kan ofte direkte merke at han skriver med uvilje, halvt ergerlig, tvungent' (It is as if Ibsen shrinks from writing and laying himself open, it is often clearly obvious that he is writing unwillingly, half crossly, under constraint).[3]

When the young literary historian Halvdan Koht was working on the first edition of a selection of Ibsen's letters in 1904, the writer himself is reported to have said that there were not all that many letters of any interest from his hand.[4] Fortunately Koht did not agree with this – and neither does posterity. A large proportion of the letters from Ibsen's pen which have been preserved may well seem to be trifling, dry, unimaginative and unremarkable – but there is nevertheless a great deal going on beneath the surface. Ibsen lived abroad for 27 years, and letters to and from Norway must have been of great significance for him, keeping him in touch with his native land in a similar way to his regular study of the newspapers. His letters in reply to those of friends and business contacts tell us not a little about his reactions to political and cultural developments back home. But also from the years before and after his residence abroad there are a large number of surviving letters to friends, fellow writers, translators and publishers – and in addition there are family letters and letters to two women who were particularly close to Ibsen. What all this material can tell us about Ibsen both as a private person and as an author is therefore of great interest – despite the rather dry and reserved tone of much of the writing.

In order to be able to evaluate the preserved correspondence, it would be helpful to have access to both sides of the dialogue. This opinion is shared by Ibsen himself, a playwright to his fingertips; he makes the following comment to Georg Brandes on 30 December 1898 about his letter-writing: 'det er aldrig heldigt for forståelsen af dialog at man kun kan høre den ene persons repliker og må gætte sig til den andens' (It is never a good idea, if you want to understand a conversation, that you can hear only one person's remarks and have to guess what the other one says – HU XVIII, p. 421). This is indubitably true. It is a very great pity that all the letters *to* Ibsen were destroyed by his family after his death. The same thing happened to a number of Ibsen's own letters to those closest to him, and to the woman with whom he had an especially intimate relationship in his later years. Much valuable material has been lost because of this. It will therefore never be possible to publish Ibsen's exchange of correspondence with anyone.

Editions of Ibsen's letters to date contain 2,674 letters from his hand. In addition to this there are a number of newly discovered but as yet unpublished letters, about a hundred in all. Compared to around 30,000 letters from Bjørnson, this may seem like a small number – yet it is nevertheless quite a considerable body of material.[5]

The first edition of letters from Ibsen was published whilst he was still alive – in 1904. It was edited by Halvdan Koht and Julius Elias, and contained, in addition to a judicious selection of 234 letters, a substantial commentary and lists of addressees, in which names like Bjørnstjerne Bjørnson and Georg Brandes figure most frequently – together with Ibsen's publisher, Frederik Hegel. The volume was extensively edited, which perhaps reflects the fact that it was a result of the editors' collaboration with the Ibsen family – particularly with the writer's son Sigurd. The emphasis was on providing documentation about 'the official Ibsen', whilst the private letters are few in number. Furthermore, it is particularly the author from the time of the Modern Breakthrough (the 1870s and 1880s) who is in focus in this early edition. Despite this fact, it is an excellent collection for anyone who is interested in Ibsen's relations with the literary scene. Most of the letters which are of interest from such a perspective are already included in this volume. The edition is also valuable because of its comprehensive commentary and factual information.

A couple of years later – a few months after Ibsen's death in 1906 – came Georg Brandes' notorious publication of Ibsen's twelve letters to the young Viennese girl Emilie Bardach. Needless to say, this happened *without* the collaboration of the family, and certainly without their approval.[6] In this edition, incidentally, Brandes had 'improved' some of the letters with misreadings which were repeated in the correspondence volumes of the later Centenary Edition of Ibsen's works, and only corrected in a supplementary volume to that edition. (HU XIX; cf. NS II, p. 107). In the letters to Bardach we meet quite a different Ibsen; here the private man appears, writing some of the few love letters which have been preserved from his hand.

It is not until the publication of the textually critical so-called 'Hundreårsutgave' (Centenary Edition) of Ibsen's works, edited by Francis Bull, Halvdan Koht and Didrik Arup Seip in 1928-57, that we have a more complete picture of Ibsen as a letter writer. Here it is Halvdan Koht who is responsible for editing the letters, which take up the whole of volumes XVI, XVII, XVIII and part of volume XIX. 1,414 letters are included in the Centenary Edition, drawn from a period of more than 60 years, from 1844 to 1905. The intention was that this edition should include all the known letters from Ibsen's hand, private as well as official ones.

However, the Centenary Edition is not complete. As soon as it began to appear, the editor explained that he was aware of the existence of letters which there had not been the opportunity to include. (Presumably the letters to Hildur Andersen were amongst these.) And since publication was completed in 1957, new letters have continued to come to light. Most of these are collected in Øyvind Anker's *Henrik Ibsen. Brev 1845-1905. Ny samling* (Henrik Ibsen. Letters 1845-1905. New Collection), published in *Ibsenårbok* (The Ibsen Yearbook) 1979. Here there is a register of letters which numbers 1,260 in all, and which includes both preserved letters and so-called 'minus letters', letters which Ibsen is known to have written, but which have disappeared. In his introduction to the collection of letters from 1979 Anker writes: 'Med år og stunder skulle det vel utgis et Tillegg til Brevregistranten' (In due course, it will no doubt be necessary to publish a supplement to the register of letters – NS I, p. 26). Time is now definitely ripe for such a project; for even after the publication of Anker's edition, many more unknown Ibsen letters have come to light. In the manuscript collections of the Oslo University Library there are now for example more than 80 still unpublished letters – some of them of great interest.

What kind of a letter-writer was Henrik Ibsen? Else Høst is one of the few people who asks the question explicitly, in an article in *Edda* in 1956.[7] She is not convinced that Ibsen's personality finds direct expression in his letters, and ponders why so great an author should be such a poor letter-writer. Her explanation is that there must be an unbridgeable gulf between Ibsen the poet and Ibsen the private person: Ibsen must have kept himself aloof from 'essensielt menneskelig samvær ved bevisst å sette diktningen foran livet' (essential human togetherness by consciously giving writing precedence over living), says Høst, who reads the letters as 'dokumenter om et ensomt sinn som ikke maktet å omsette sin rikdom til levet liv' (documents about a lonely mind, which could not manage to transmute its riches into actual living, *ibid.*, p. 40). She concludes also that it was 'som om de åndelige erfaringer dikteren gjorde under skaperprosessen aldri kom mennesket i ham til gode' (as if the poet's spiritual experiences during the creative process could never bear fruit for the human being in him, *ibid.*, p. 39). It is particularly Høst's evaluation of the family letters which prompts this observation. She finds that they give scant expression to feelings, being more taken up with trivialities about food, housekeeping and general comings and goings than with genuine concern and warm intimacy between father and son or husband and wife.

It is true that his letters to the family which have been preserved – the Centenary Edition prints 53 of them – do not take the form of open declarations of love or of really intimate confidences.[8] What might have been contained in the material which has been destroyed – amongst other things 50 'minus letters' to his son Sigurd, and no doubt a large number of letters to his wife – we do not know. But the letters which have been preserved are not without feelings; rather the opposite. They reveal a reserved warmth and a special kind of humour which presupposes a close and relaxed relationship between the sender and the addressee. Ibsen is economical in his use of language in letters too – he does not go in for a lot of big words.

A striking feature of the family letters is the fear that some accident will happen to his wife and son. But like the shy man he is, Ibsen conceals his anxiety behind irony and understatement. However, towards the end of his letters warm feelings and a kind of passion do find expression, but camouflaged behind a humorously worded exhortation. In a letter from Munich on 21 August 1877 to Suzannah, who is having a summer holiday in Norway together with their son Sigurd, Ibsen writes rather roguishly: 'Jeg håber at I froder jer godt deroppe; men vogt jer for alskens uforsigtighed, og pas godt på Sigurd og på dine penge og lad ikke Sogninger og Hardangere tage noget fra dig' (I hope you're enjoying yourselves up there; but be careful not to act incautiously, and take care of Sigurd and your money and don't let the folk of Sogn and Hardanger take anything from you – HU XIX, p. 323). From the same date is a letter addressed personally to the then eighteen-year-old Sigurd: 'Lad mig nu se du er forsigtig både tillands og tilvands; den mindste uforsigtighed kan drage de værste følger efter sig. ... vogt Dig for at komme formeget på vandet, og ikke ud i sejlbåd! Dette er alt, hvad jeg ved at skrive om idag' (let me see that you are careful both on land and on water; the least carelessness can have dire consequences. ...take care not to be on the water too long, and don't go out in a sailing boat! This is all I can think of to say today), says his father, before adding with a touch of self-irony: 'Mor Dig godt!' (Have a good time!). The letter is signed 'Din hengivne pappa Henrik Ibsen' (Your devoted pappa Henrik Ibsen – HU XIX, p. 324). When Ibsen calls himself *devoted*, it is safe to assume that *that* word is not ironically meant; it is heavy with meaning.

As late as 1884 – when Sigurd was 25! – Ibsen writes paternally from Gossensass to his son, on summer holiday in Trøndelag: 'vov dig ikke i bad deroppe; vandet er koldt og kan let fremkalde dødbringende krampetilfælder' (don't risk bathing up there; the water is cold and can easily bring on fatal cramps – 09.08.84. HU XIX, p. 341). The following week, this message is sent to Suzannah: 'Sigurd må du hilse mange gange, og sig ham at han endelig ikke må komme bag de trønderske heste, der er betrygtede for den vane at slå op' (Give Sigurd my warm regards, and tell him to make sure he does not walk close behind the Trønder horses; they are well known for kicking – 19.08.84. HU XIX, p. 343). And another week later, to Sigurd himself: 'Næsten i hver norsk avis læser jeg om ulykker, foranlediget ved forfjamset benyttelse af ladte geværer. Det vilde være mig overordentlig ukært om du ikke holdt dig langt borte fra folk, som håndterer slige våben. Skulde en ulykke passere, må der straks telegraferes til mig' (In practically every Norwegian newspaper I read about accidents caused by clumsy handling of loaded rifles. I would be most upset if you did not keep away from people who handle such weapons. If an accident does occur, a telegram must be sent to me at once – 27.08.84. HU XIX, p. 345). Is this the poet's imagination at work? Ibsen was at this time deeply absorbed in his work on *Vildanden*.

In the volume of the Centenary Edition in which Ibsen's letters to Sigurd and Suzannah are printed, Halvdan Koht writes in the preface that 'Så godt som hvert eneste brev er vitnemål om hvor omhyggelig, ja rent ut engstelig Ibsen var for hustruens og sønnens helse og velferd. Det er ingen ende på alle bekymringer han gjorde seg for deres skyld' (Practically every single letter bears witness to how considerate, not to say anxious Ibsen was about his wife's and son's health and wellbeing. There is no end to the worries that he suffered on their account – HU XIX, p. 313).

His fears for Sigurd can of course be a sign of a neurotic temperament. But they can also be seen as a symptom of an overdeveloped imagination, difficult to distinguish from the creative springs of Ibsen's artistic powers. To write was for him to 'see' – and in this way he was inventing also when he was addressing his nearest and dearest in the form of letters. That does not need to mean that the feelings which are expressed in his family letters are 'invented' or insincere – on the contrary, the congruence between letters and creative works may be due to the fact that both texts spring from the same deep level of imagination.

The letters to Suzannah Ibsen are not numerous – we can, as stated earlier, assume that the greater part of this material has been destroyed. But something has survived – including Ibsen's letter proposing marriage to the nineteen-year-old Suzannah Daae Thoresen. Here too he is to a certain extent 'a poet'. The letter, which is in verse form, is known today as the poem 'Til den Eneste' (To the only one). It is as if he is curbing his feelings in the confines of the stanza, where the strict form contributes towards a generalizing of his personal passion. The printed form is incomplete, as the four last lines of the final stanza have been omitted. This is the penultimate complete stanza (the fifth):

> Du unge, drømmende Gaade,
> Turde jeg grunde dig ud,
> Turde jeg kjækt dig kaare
> Til mine Tankers Brud,
> Turde jeg dukke mig ned i
> Dit rike aandige væld,
> Turde jeg skue tilbunds i
> Din blomstrende Barnesjæl

(You young, dreaming enigma, if only I dared to puzzle you out, if only I dared choose you boldly as the bride of my thoughts, dared dive down into your mind's rich fount, dared gaze into the depths of your blossoming childish soul)

And the last stanza, in its amputated version, is a repetition of which the concluding climax is missing:

> Du unge, drømmende Gaade
> Turde jeg grunde dig ut,
> Turde jeg kjækt dig kaare
> Til mine Tankers Brud...[9]

The text stops here. The last four lines of the verse have been suppressed – either by the family, or by Halvdan Koht, who published the poem in his edition of Ibsen's *Breve* (Letters) 1904, Vol. I. The manuscript is lost.

A number of the later letters to his wife Suzannah take the form of laconic, factual reports about his work on the plays, his meetings with people they both know, the routine of his meals and his daily rhythm. This material is primarily important as a source of information about Ibsen's working methods and discipline, and tells us less about the emotional relationship between husband and wife. Yet it does nevertheless tell us much about Suzannah's role as a stabilizing force in the poet's life.

Completely different in character are the love letters we know today from Ibsen's hand. They are not addressed to Suzannah, but to two other women, far younger than the poet himself. The letters Ibsen wrote to the Viennese girl Emilie Bardach after they had met in Gossensass in the summer of 1889 – 12 in all – are well known and have been used by many Ibsen researchers, perhaps first and foremost Else Høst in her monograph *Hedda Gabler* from 1958. Here Høst maintains – in contrast to what she believes to be the case with Ibsen's other letters – that there was in this case a connection between the life and the work: she regarded Emilie as the model for Hedda, and believed at the same time that the letters to Emilie expressed Ibsen's innermost feelings. This interpretation of the Bardach material was one she had also argued in her article about Ibsen as a letter writer two years earlier in *Edda*, in which she discussed Ibsen's relationship with the two young women Emilie Bardach and Hildur Andersen, and concluded that the relationship to Emilie was the most decisive.

However, after Høst published her studies, new information has been uncovered, mainly in the form of letters, which suggests that Hildur Andersen played a far greater role for Ibsen than had hitherto been believed. In Øyvind Anker's *Henrik Ibsen. Brev. Ny Samling* from 1979 there are registered in all 15 numbered letters from Ibsen to Hildur Andersen. In some of these letters, as well as in Anker's detailed commentaries, new material has come to light.

Ibsen had met the young Hildur for the first time during his visit to Norway in 1874, when she was a child of ten. They met again after his definitive homecoming in 1891, when Ibsen himself was 63 and Hildur a young and celebrated pianist of 27. Hildur Andersen was the daughter of Oluf Martin Andersen, a city engineer, and his wife, Anne Fredrikke, née Sontum, from Bergen. The latter Ibsen had known in his youth, when he rented a room with the Sontum family during his stay in Bergen in the 1850s. After returning to Kristiania as an old man, he reestablished contact with the family. Hildur's uncle, Dr. Chr. F. Sontum, was Ibsen's doctor right up until his death in 1902, and the young pianist became the poet's close friend and confidante, his companion to concerts and theatres – and perhaps something more. The relationship between them lasted throughout the 1890s, until Ibsen around the turn of the century was confined to his flat because of illness. The last preserved letter from him to her is a visiting card, where he writes quite openly: '9 røde roser for dig, 9 rosenrøde år for mig. Tag roserne med tak for årene' (9 red roses for you, 9 rose-red years for me. Take the roses with thanks for the years.)[10]

The card must be from the year 1899, and Anker suggests that the likely date is 19 September, because it is known that this date played a special role in the relationship between the two of them. This date is also incorporated into the play *Bygmester Solness* (The Master Builder), in which Hilde arrives at the master builder's house on precisely 19 September – ten years to the day after his memorable ascent of the tower at Lysanger. Later Ibsen presented Hildur Andersen with the final version of the manuscript of this play with an inscribed dedication.

Almost all letters from Ibsen to Hildur Andersen were destroyed by her, presumably on the advice of other people. Øyvind Anker refers to an interview Hildur Andersen gave in 1910, in which she explains that Ibsen had asked her to look after his letters to her. 'Hennes brev til ham skulle hun få [og fikk] etter hans død, og så skulle hun en gang offentliggjøre dem' (Her letters to him she was to be given [and was given] after his death, and one day she was to publish them).[11] That was however not to happen. It is probable that Hildur Andersen had intended to carry out Ibsen's wishes, but also had considerable reservations, which clearly derived from the Ibsen family's reactions to Brandes' edition of the Bardach letters. She sought advice from others regarding what she should do with the material. We do not know in detail what advice she received, but the result at any rate was that in her advanced old age – around 1954 – she instituted an autodafé which more or less destroyed all the material.[12] Only very few letters escaped destruction, and those are included in Øyvind Anker's *Ny samling*, where, as earlier stated, he registers 15 definite numbered letters, including the so-called 'minus letters'. The list includes in part brief notes or directions on envelopes, but there are also preserved a few deeply personal letters, which have an unusually direct form for Ibsen. To Hildur, who is on a tour of performances abroad, he writes on 7 January 1893:

Min vilde skogfugl!
Hvor flyver du nu? Jeg véd det ikke ... Å, hvor jeg længter efter prinsessen! Længter ned fra drømmenes højder. Længter efter at gå ned på jorden igen og gøre det, som jeg sa' – så mange mange gange!
Tusind inderlige hilsener sålænge!
Din, din bygmester. (NS I, p. 393f.)

(My wild forest bird!
Where are you flying now? I do not know ... Oh, how I long for my princess! Long to come down from the heights of my dreams. Long to walk on the earth again and do what I said to you – so many, many times!
A thousand heartfelt greetings in the meantime!
Your, your master builder.)

During the autumn of that same year Hildur is away travelling again, and Ibsen writes:

Min egen kjæreste, dejligste prinsesse! Hvor usigelig længe jeg synes det er siden jeg sidst hørte fra dig. Det vil da sige direkte og i vort eget sprog....Jeg vil ha' dig igen således som du var. Hører du det, Hildur? Lover du mig det? Tusend hilsener flyver til dig
    fra din trofaste H.I. (22.10.93. NS I, p. 401f.)

(My own dearest, loveliest princess! How unspeakably long it is since I last heard from you. I mean directly and in our own language....I want to have you again just as you were. Do you hear that, Hildur? Do you promise me that? A thousand greetings are flying to you
    from your faithful H.I.)

What Ibsen calls 'our own language' was clearly reserved for direct communication, and did not occur in the letters – even though they are among the most intimate things Ibsen has written to another person. But he is consciously holding something back:

Jeg tør ikke skrive, som jeg helst vilde. Postgangen er jo så usikker. Tusind inderlige hilsener fra prinsessens unwande[l]bar treu-ergebener
    H.I. (05.10.93. NS I, p. 401)

(I dare not write as I would most like to. The mail is not dependable. A thousand heartfelt greetings from the princess's unwande[l]bar treu-ergebener
    H.I.)

Thus the few letters which are preserved show that Ibsen refrained from putting into words the most important matters – even when writing his warmest and most personal letters. The letters to Hildur are moreover strikingly similar in their language to the play about Hilde and the master builder which Ibsen wrote in 1892, and which it has long been accepted was inspired by the relationship to Hildur

Andersen. Despite the reservation and the paucity of the surviving material, the tone in these love letters is so intimate that it is difficult to take them as anything other than deeply sincere expressions – despite their literary flavour. In other words, the correspondence with Hildur Andersen contradicts Else Høst's assertion about the lack of connection between Ibsen the poet and Ibsen the man.

If one examines Ibsen's letters to his friends, it can be seen that here too Ibsen is always holding something back. There are a great number of such letters which have survived. They are addressed in particular to friends from his early years – men like Ole Schulerud, Paul Botten Hansen and Lorentz Dietrichson. One of these contacts originating in the 1850s and 60s is also Bjørnstjerne Bjørnson, who is the recipient of a long series of very important letters from Ibsen, mainly written from Rome in the 1860s, when the relationship between the two of them was still good. During this period Ibsen was undergoing a process of major development as a writer and as a person, for which Bjørnson can take a great deal of the credit, since he had been centrally involved when it came to providing the means for Ibsen's journey, partly by recommending him for a state travel stipend and partly by collecting in private subscriptions to finance Ibsen's stay in Rome. Ibsen writes to Bjørnson about his overwhelming experiences of the Italian landscape and of the cultural treasures of antiquity – in letters in which he gives unusually frank expression to his emotions. He writes of his reactions after visiting Villa Borghese and the Vatican's collections of sculpture, of his meeting with Michelangelo and Bernini, of the political situation in Poland, of conditions in the theatre in Kristiania – and of his own creative idleness: 'Jeg ligger mangengang halve Dage ude mellem Gravene paa Via latina eller på den gamle Via appia og tror det er en Lediggang, som ikke kan kaldes Tidsspille' (I often spend half the day lying between the graves on Via latina or on the old Via appia, and I believe that it is an idleness which cannot be called a waste of time – 28.01.65. HU XVI, p. 107).

To Bjørnson he can open his heart and complain about his fear and nervousness when anticipating the reaction to *Brand*:

i disse Dage udkommer formodentlig min Bog [Brand] ..... og hvorledes jeg altsaa nu er situeret, ventende, fortæret af Spænding og Uro, imødeseende Bogen og dermed maaske Kamp og Anfald af alle Slags, ude af Stand til midt i alt dette at tage fat paa noget nyt, som dog allerede ligger fuldbaaret i mig ... – Kære Bjørnson, jeg synes, at jeg ligesom ved et stort uendeligt Øde er skilt baade fra Gud og Mennesker... (04.03.66. HU XIV, p. 125f.)

(I expect my book [Brand] to be published any day now ... and how I am feeling right now, waiting, consumed by tension and nervousness, anticipating the book and with it perhaps battles and attacks of all kinds, incapable in the midst of all this of getting going on something new which lies already fully formed within me ... – Dear Bjørnson, I feel that I am cut off by a great endless wasteland from both God and my fellow men...)

Ibsen, of course, recovered his ability to write after the success with *Brand*. *Peer Gynt* was published the following year, but did not meet the same warm reception as its predecessor. The Danish critic Clemens Petersen's uncomprehending review, with his well-known rejection of this masterpiece because it did not meet Petersen's aesthetic standard, caused Ibsen to explode in violent rage. Clemens Petersen's friend Bjørnstjerne Bjørnson received the following flood of abuse in the post:

Kære Bjørnson!
Hvad er det igrunden for Helvedesskab, som paa hvert eneste Punkt kommer og stiller sig imellem os? Det er som om den personlige Djævel kom og skyggede ... Hvis *jeg* var i Kjøbenhavn og der havde nogen, der stod mig saa nær, som Clemens Petersen staar dig, saa havde jeg slaaet ham helseløs, før jeg havde tilladt ham at begaa en slig tendentiøs Forbrydelse mod Sandhed og ret. (09.12.67. HU XVI, p. 197f.)

(Dear Bjørnson,
What kind of infernal design is it which sets us at odds with each other all the time? It is as if the devil incarnate were casting a shadow... If *I* were in Copenhagen and had someone there who was as close to me as Clemens Petersen is to you, I would have beaten his brains out before I had allowed him to commit such a tendentious crime against truth and justice.)

The letter continues with the pronouncement that *Peer Gynt* is poetry and that future notions of the beautiful will conform to this book, not vice versa.

Thus speaks a self-confident author – but also a person with strong passions. He appears here like a raging Jupiter who allows his flaming temperament to flow unhindered through his pen. Ibsen was right when he once in his old age complained that his plays had not been fully understood – for, he said, I am a *passionate* writer. The same is clearly true of him as a private person, and at times even as a letter writer.

Hildur Andersen was fully aware of his temperament as well. In 1907 she had heard Professor Gerhard Gran deliver a lecture about Alexander Kielland's letters, and this reinforced her worries at the thought that all the letters from Ibsen's hand which had been preserved might be published. In a letter to one of her advisors she wrote: 'Hvor Kielland spotter og haaner og er vittig paa andres bekostning, der hugger og flænger og saarer Ibsen. Jeg har været saa bange for at glemme *det* og hva det vil si for dem det gaar ud over' (Where Kielland mocks and derides and is witty at the expense of other people, Ibsen stabs and tears and wounds. I have been so fearful of forgetting *that*, and what it would mean for the people affected).[13] Hildur's description fits quite a number of Ibsen's letters to friends in which he discusses a third person. It also applies to a number of cases where the person attacked is the addressee in person.

Ibsen's temperament could run away with him when it came to dealing with his author's rights as well. In the nineteenth century, of course, the laws of copyright when it came to intellectual works were practically non-existent. Norway was the first Scandinavian country to ratify the Bern convention of 1866, which it did as early as 1896, whereas Denmark, where both Ibsen and other Norwegian authors published their books, did not become a signatory to the convention until 1903.[14] Therefore it was up to Ibsen himself to keep an eye on what he regarded as his lawful property, and this he did with a vengeance. There have been preserved around 1,000 business letters from his hand, addressed to printers, publishers and translators, theatres and directors. As his own business manager Ibsen most often adopted an exceedingly correct and formal manner, but here too there are examples of a fury which could become white-hot. One such reaction was precipitated by the illegal pirated publication of *Hærmændene på Helgeland* (The Vikings at Helgeland). In the autumn of 1871 the printer Hans Jacob Jensen in

Kristiania published a so-called second edition of this play, which had however been completely re-set after the first printing of the play in 1858. Ibsen had been told of the plan in a letter from Jensen himself, and answered forthrightly in a letter from Dresden dated 17 September 1871:

Med den største forbauselse modtog jeg idag Deres frække og uforskammede brev, hvoraf jeg erfarer, at De agter at udgive et nyt oplag af mine dramatiske arbejder....De har ikke det fjærneste skin af ejendomsret til de nævnte arbejder....Deres påtænkte svindleri [vil ikke] indbringe Dem andet end skam og skade. ...vover De at fremture i Deres forsæt, så skal jeg såvel gennem pressen som for domstolene vise Dem, hvad deslige kæltringstreger fører efter sig. (HU XVI, p. 373)

(It was with the greatest astonishment that I today received your impudent and impertinent letter, from which I discover that you intend to publish a new edition of my dramatic works....You have not the smallest jot of right to ownership of any of the above-mentioned works....Your intended swindle [will not] bring you anything other than shame and hurt.... if you dare to proceed with your intentions, I shall demonstrate to you both in the press and in the courts where such villainy will lead.)

Ibsen was as good as his word. He protested publicly in the Danish paper *Dagbladet*, and the case was actually brought to court, where it went all the way to the High Court. Jensen was fined and forced to pay compensation, and the whole edition was confiscated and pulped.[15]

The letters to Ibsen's own publishers, Gyldendal, and to the publisher Frederik Hegel, have a quite different tone. Here we have epistolary material which is without strongly personal statements or messages, but clearly influenced by Ibsen's respect, indeed by his deferential gratitude. His relationship to Hegel was in fact extremely polite and correct: Ibsen knew well how dependent he was on his publisher. Nevertheless, these letters are of great interest for Ibsen research. Here we can watch from outside the author's work on his plays. He provides constantly updated information on how far he has got with the writing process, and shows an interest in discussing when would be the right strategic moment to put a new book on the market. The letters also contain information about how Ibsen regarded the publishers' production process, his attitude to proofs, his views on the choice of fonts, paper quality and other technical aspects of book production. If one examines the letters to Hegel closely, it becomes clear that Ibsen had a lot of specialized knowledge about production techniques and typography – a matter which is not without interest for the work on a new, complete historical and critical edition of Ibsen's works which is at present under way.

In his letters to Hegel Ibsen also comments on his economic circumstances; he mentions royalties from the publisher and the placing of the money in shares and securities. In addition he sends thanks for the receipt of annual parcels with Gyldendal's fiction (?) list. He also from time to time mentions explicitly an author or a work which he has found of particular interest. In other words, the correspondence with Hegel suggests that Ibsen kept up with – and perhaps himself read – the majority of what was published of Danish and Norwegian literature in the latter part of the nineteenth century. However, anyone interested in Ibsen's literary judgements, his views on literature and his opinions on contemporary writing, will not find very much in the letters to Hegel. From this point of view, Ibsen's letters to and about Georg Brandes are more informative – both as direct commentary and because of what they do *not* say.

Ibsen mentions Georg Brandes' name as early as 21 October 1867, in a letter to Jonas Collin, son of the great Danish collector of manuscripts Edward Collin. In this letter he promises moreover to present Collin's father with the manuscript to *Peer Gynt*. (This is, incidentally, the reason why the manuscript of *Peer Gynt* is today in the Royal Library in Copenhagen, where Collin's great collection was deposited.) In the letter to Collin, sent from Sorrento, Ibsen writes about the notorious positivism debate, in which the opponents were Georg Brandes and Rasmus Nielsen (HU XVI, p. 191f.). In 1866 Brandes had attacked Rasmus Nielsen's attempts to reconcile religion and science, and began a discussion with Nielsen which in later articles, in the newspaper *Dagbladet* and elsewhere, led to sharp criticism where he opposed modern positivism to the religious philosophy and the reactionary cultural life of Denmark. The feud extended also to the newspaper *Fædrelandet*, in which Bjørnstjerne Bjørnson had published anonymous attacks on Georg

Brandes. Thus there were clearly opposing sides in the literary debate. Ibsen, who was an avid newspaper reader, must have followed developments closely in the publications which reached the Scandinavian Club in Rome.

Despite the fact that Ibsen at that time had a close relationship to Bjørnson, he did not in his letters to Collin take Bjørnson's side in the conflict. Neither did he declare himself unreservedly for Georg Brandes. Perhaps Ibsen was so unsure of Collin's views that he chose a diplomatic course: he characterizes the cultural battle as 'en pennekrig mellem filosofer og teologer' (a pen-and-ink battle between philosophers and theologians), and continues: 'Jeg er ikke tilstrekkelig inde i sagen til at kunde danne mig nogen mening' (I am not sufficiently au fait with the matter to be able to form any opinion). But when he observes as it were in passing that Georg Brandes' contributions to the debate demonstrate 'overbevisningens kraft og styrke' (the power and strength of conviction), this perhaps conveys a hint of his own evaluation. It is not until two years later, when he mentions this cultural feud in a letter to Georg Brandes himself on 26 June 1869, that he dares to speak slightingly of Rasmus Nielsen's 'akkordfilosofi' (philosophy of compromise – HU XVI, p. 249)

The relationship between Ibsen and Brandes can hardly be called a warm friendship; it had more the character of a strategic alliance in the name of progressive ideology. Nevertheless, it must be said that the relationship between them was a close one, especially in the 1870s and 80s. The critic and the playwright were each in his own field among the leading figures in contemporary European intellectual life, and they could clearly see the mutual benefit of their links. Towards Brandes Ibsen played the role of the radical and anarchist for as long as it seemed appropriate, and it is in the letters to Brandes that we find some of the most revolutionary statements he has ever penned. But it is quite obvious that he is editing his pronouncements; most of the major letters to Brandes have a less straightforward and more calculating tone than the ones Ibsen had written to Bjørnson the decade before. Furthermore, the number of anarchistic 'letter-bombs' decreases at the same rate as Ibsen's dramas change their character.

There is one of the letters to Brandes which is particularly well known and often quoted, and that is Ibsen's thanks for the first volume of *Hovedstrømninger* (Main Currents in Nineteenth-Century Literature), dated 4 April 1872. It is here he writes the famous words:

Farligere bog kunde aldrig falde i en frugtsommelig digters hænder. Den er en af de bøger som sætter et svælgende dyb mellem igår og idag ... Om tyve år vil man ikke kunne begribe, hvorledes det åndelig taget var leveligt hjem [sic!] før disse forelæsninger. (HU XVII, p. 31)

(A more dangerous book could never fall into the hands of a pregnant writer. It is one of those books which creates a yawning gulf between yesterday and today....In twenty years people will not be able to understand how any intellectual life was possible back home before these lectures.)

Here it seems as if Ibsen's allegiance to the standard-bearer of the Modern Breakthrough is total. But as Brandes published the later books in the series, Ibsen's reactions were expressed with more reservation and more delay. It is not until 16 October 1873, in a letter which Georg Brandes had to remind him to write, that he sends thanks for receipt of the second volume of *Hovedstrømninger, Den romantiske skole i Tyskland* (The Romantic School in Germany – HU XVII, p. 105f.) It was in this volume that Brandes had included an analysis of Søren Kierkegaard's pseudonymous writings, which he interpreted as an example of modern, subjective and 'sick' literature. Ibsen's relationship to Kierkegaard was very different and much more sympathetic than Georg Brandes'.[16] Yet he does not enter into any polemics; the only thing he says about the book is that: 'De véd godt, at jeg betragter Deres værk som epokegørende i vor livsbetragtning, og at dette vil blive almindelig erkendt hjemme, om end nogle år først må hengå' (You know well that I regard your work as a watershed in our philosophy of life, and that this will be generally acknowledged at home, even though it will not be for some years). When we come to 1874, however, Ibsen is expressing clear and explicit reservations about the whole project: in a letter of 20 April 1874, in which he also makes some critical remarks about the Brandes brothers' journal *Det nittende Aarhundre* (The Nineteenth Century), he writes:

... mine tanker er oftere hos Dem, end De af min forsømmelighed i brevskrivning skulde formode ... Hele første bind af Deres litteraturhistorie er mere en polemik imod den københavnske end imod den nordiske bornerthed; det er specifikt københavnske retninger i literatur, kultur og kunstbetragtning der bekæmpes, og det er denne begrænsning af slagfeltet, som jeg mener at en forfatter hos os som andetsteds må komme ud over, hvis han skal kunde slå igennem. (HU XVII, p. 130f.)

(... my thoughts are more often with you than you might imagine considering my deficiencies as a letter-writer ... The whole of the first volume of your literary history is more a polemic against Copenhagen than against Nordic bigotry; it is specifically Copenhagen attitudes in literature, culture and the study of art which are the object of attack, and it is this narrow perspective of the field of battle which I believe that an author – at home as elsewhere – must overcome, if he is going to make a name for himself.)

Here Ibsen is actually suggesting that the great Georg's views of art or aesthetics are too narrow! The explanation may be that there was a real difference of opinion. It may also be of a more personal nature. More probably both interpretations are partly correct. Between the first letter about *Hovedstrømninger* and this one from 1874, Brandes had written negatively about Kierkegaard and Ibsen had published *Kejser og Galilæer* (Emperor and Galilean), which did not elicit superlatives of praise from Brandes. Ibsen is rather tart about this in a letter on 30 January 1875, in which he says to Brandes that he 'finder nogen indre modsigelse i Deres dom om den i min bog indeholdte nødvendighedslære' (find an inner contradiction in your evaluation of the philosophy of necessity contained in my book – HU XVII, p. 160).

From the material which has been preserved, it seems that the correspondence between the critic and the dramatist dried up after 1875. It is not until 1882 onwards that we again find several letters to Brandes, clearly precipitated by the latter's positive review of *Gengangere* (Ghosts). Yet even if the revived correspondence continues right until the end of the 1890s, it is from now on markedly more sporadic than in the earlier period. This may mean that the relationship between the two was no longer so straightforward and relaxed, which no doubt is connected with the fact that they in actual fact did not understand each other as well as they had professed in the first blaze of enthusiasm. When Georg

Brandes had published the second edition of his book on Ibsen in 1882, the latter did write to him from Gossensass on 21 September and thanked him for a literary portrait which he placed 'højest af alle dem, der hidtil er blevne mig til del...' (highest of all those which have been written about me so far – HU XVII, p. 483). But it is not certain that he was being entirely truthful; for Brandes was not the only one who had written a book about Ibsen and received praise for it from the object himself. There was also a Finnish professor named Valfrid Vasenius, who had published firstly a doctoral thesis called *Henrik Ibsens dramatiska digtning i dess första skede* (Henrik Ibsen's dramatic writing in its first phase, 1879), later followed by the book *Henrik Ibsen. Ett skaldeportrett* (Henrik Ibsen. Portrait of a Poet, 1882).

Ibsen thanks Vasenius for his first book as early as 30 March 1880, when he writes: 'aldrig kunde jeg ønske ... en bedre advokat, end jeg har fundet i Dem' (never could I wish for ... a better advocate than I have found in you – HU XVII, p. 396). He continues by praising Vasenius for having brought out precisely what he himself intended with regard to characterization and conflict in his dramas. Ibsen and Vasenius met several times, and in a later letter to his German translator Ludwig Passarge, on 22 December 1881, Ibsen writes that 'Ingen kender mit liv og min literære virksomhed så nøje som han' (Noone knows my life and my literary work as intimately as he – HU XVII, p. 444). It is worth noting here that Vasenius includes a long passage in his 1882 study of Ibsen which is extremely critical of Georg Brandes' interpretation of Ibsen's writings. Which of these two critics had the finer perception is not a matter for discussion here – but we may safely say that one cannot simply take Ibsen's own words about the validity of the various interpretations as gospel.

What Ibsen really thought about Brandes' writings does not emerge with any clarity from the letters. It is striking how vaguely he expressed himself as time went on, even though the formulations on the surface seem complimentary enough. He can speak of Brandes' books as something new, and find that they contain 'et fremtidselement, som meget ofte beskæftiger mig; ...en dyb og stor digtning' (a forward-looking element which very often engages me; ...a deep and rich poetry). But *Den romantiske skole i Tyskland* he does not wish to write about – it must wait until they meet, he says in a letter of 12 June 1883. (HU XVII, p. 514). He expresses himself just as vaguely the following year, when he writes to Brandes that the two of them 'er kommet hinanden imøde under vor udviklingsgang. Herom og om beslægtede emner kunde jeg nok have lyst til mundtlig at tale med Dem. I et brev går det ikke' (have drawn close in the course of our development. I would like to meet you to talk about this and other related matters. In a letter it is not possible – HU XVIII, p. 27). So most of it remains unsaid.

Ibsen's letters to Brandes can in many ways be seen as an extension or offshoot of his own plays of social criticism, and they decrease in frequency accordingly as his own writing changes direction. When writing to Brandes he tries out shocking and radical opinions, which are incorporated into the dramas he was simultaneously working on. Ibsen himself indirectly confirms that his correspondence with the Danish critic can have had this kind of function. In a letter to Brandes of 21 September 1882, after the publication of *En Folkefiende* (An Enemy of the People), in which Ibsen allows Stockmann's many provocative statements free rein, he writes to Brandes:

Når mit nye skuespil kommer Dem ihænde, vil De kunne forstå hvorledes det har interesseret, og jeg kan sige, moret mig at bringes [sic!] i erindring de mange spredte og henkastede ytringer i mine breve til Dem. (HU XVII, p. 483f.)

(When my new play comes into your hands, you will be able to see how it has interested, and, I may say, amused me to recall the many scattered and casual expressions in my letters to you.)

One can trace formulations from his letters directly in this play – as indeed one can find similar echoes of formulations and opinions from his correspondence with Brandes in other of Ibsen's plays too.

But we must ask how sincere Ibsen was when he served up his anarchistically formulated radicalism in the form of letters to Brandes. Was it a mask he adopted? In the earliest phase of the correspondence, even before they had met in person, it was clearly of importance to Ibsen to appear as a genuine radical and man of the Modern Breakthrough. On 17 February 1871 he writes:

Jeg går aldrig ind på at gøre friheden ensbetydende med politisk frihed. Hvad De kalder frihed, kalder jeg friheder, og hvad jeg kalder kampen for friheden er jo ikke andet end den stadige, levende tilegnelse af frihedens idé ... Staten er individets forbandelse ... Staten må væk! Den revolution skal jeg være med på ... Ombytning af regeringsformer er ikke andet end pusleri med grader, lidt mere eller lidt mindre, – dårlighed altsammen ... al religion vil falde. Hverken moralbegreberne eller kunstformerne har nogen evighed for sig. Hvor meget er vi i grunden forpligtet til at holde fast ved? Hvem borger mig for at ikke 2 og 2 er fem oppe på Jupiter? (HU XVI, p. 349f.)

(I shall never agree that freedom is synonymous with political freedom. What you call freedom, I call freedoms, and what I call the fight for freedom is no other than the constant living appropriation of the idea of freedom ... The state is the curse of the individual ... The state must go! That revolution I shall join ... Changing the forms of government is simply tinkering about with degrees, a little more or a little less, – folly the lot of it ... all religion will fall. Neither concepts of morality nor art forms will last eternally. How much are we actually obliged to retain? Who can guarantee that 2 and 2 doesn't make five on Jupiter?)

So speaks an anarchist and revolutionary. But it is a completely different Ibsen who only one week later writes a crawling letter in bureaucratic language to the Department of Church and Education in Copenhagen, in response to the announcement that he has been made a knight of Dannebrog:

I det jeg pligtskyldigst erkender modtagelsen af det kgl: ministeriums 2de skrivelser, henholdsvis af 30te Januar og 20de Februar ... tillader jeg mig at frembære min ærbødigste tak for den af ministeriet nedlagde allerunderdanigste forestilling, der har bevirket den mig til del blevne allerhøjeste anerkendelse. (26.02.71. NS I, p. 137, no. 175)

(In response to the communications from His Majesty's Ministry of 30th January and 20th February respectively... I beg to assure the Ministry of my most respectful gratitude for their generous consideration, which has occasioned the award to me of this most prestigious honour.)

No trace of the anarchist can be found in these phrases! And the accompanying letter which Ibsen wrote when he sent his first real socially critical play, *Samfundets støtter* (The Pillars of Society) as a gift to King Oscar II, has a ring of pure opportunism. Here there are barely concealed references to Bjørnstjerne Bjørnson's iconoclastic social plays *Kongen* (The King) and *Redaktøren* (The Editor) – and reassuring explanations to the king that Ibsen's own play from 1877 is much less dangerous:

> At skrive og udgive dette arbejde just nu, forekom mig at være en tidsmessig gerning. Det har nylig fra andet hold gennem digtning været rettet angreb på institutioner, som er sammenvoksede med vor hele nationale fortid, og af hvis bevarelse vor hele folkelige velfærd og fremgang afhænger. Jeg har derfor troet, at det kunde være gavnligt at lede almenhedens syn og tanke hen i en anden retning og vise at usandheden ikke ligger i institutioner, men i samfundsindividerne selv....Min højeste løn vilde være opnået, hvis Deres Majestæt måtte bifalde dette arbejdes grundtanke og form. (20.09.77. NS I, p. 218, no. 360)

> (To write and publish this work at this moment seemed to me to be a timely act. Recently attacks have been made from other quarters through literature on institutions which are an integral part of our history as a nation, and on the preservation of which our entire national welfare and progress depends. It is therefore my belief that it would be beneficial to direct the attention and thoughts of the common people in a different direction, and to show that untruth derives not from institutions but from the social individuals themselves....It would be my greatest reward if Your Majesty were able to approve the ideas and form of this work.)

Thus it is apparent that Ibsen's anarchism is a highly debatable affair. And despite numerous coincidences of expression between formulations in his letters and in his plays, Ibsen is hardly a reliable guide when it comes to discovering the intentions and forming interpretations of his dramatic work. His letters are those of a consummate tactician, and he emphasizes different ideas and literary qualities of his writings depending on the addressee.

If one searches in Ibsen's letters for information about his reading and his literary preferences, or for what he might there say about his own approach to writing, one is yet again confronted by considerable problems. The greatest candour is perhaps to be found in his early letters, from the period before he became world famous. But not even these letters are entirely reliable. The most interesting observations are perhaps those where he indirectly reveals something of his wide reading.

He himself was fond of denying that he had received any literary impulses, and he was most reluctant to admit what he had actually read. But now and then the mask slips. He writes several times to the Danish critic Peter Hansen. It is in a letter to him that Ibsen maintains that he has read little and understood even less of Søren Kierkegaard, a claim which is it very difficult to take seriously given both the evidence of other sources and what one can read out of his own plays (28.10.70. HU XVI, pp. 315-19). But in the same letter he nevertheless reveals a familiarity with Shakespeare which is taken for granted; for *Brand*, he explains, was written under the influence of the mood which filled him during his first years in Italy – it was just like in Shakespeare's *As You Like It*! When Ibsen claimed that he had lived completely in a Shakespearean mood, this must indicate that he felt his relationship to Shakespeare to be just as self-evident and intimate as was his love of the Holbergian comic universe. It is well known that Ibsen in his younger years was given the nickname Gert Westphaler (after a character in the Holberg comedy *Gert Westphaler eller Den meget talende Barber* (Gert Westphaler or The Garrulous Barber)), and even in his later years he constantly alluded to Holberg's comedies both in letters and in speech.

Almost twenty years after *Brand* and the Shakespearean intoxication, in 1888, Ibsen congratulates Peter Hansen for his translation of *Faust*, which is in his opinion much better than the corresponding Swedish translation by Viktor Rydberg (12.03.88. HU XVIII, p. 157). And the Norwegian translator Fredrik Gjertsen received as early as March 1872 an unusually warm letter where Ibsen thanks him for having sent his Norwegian version of Horace's *Ars Poetica*, a translation which Ibsen knowledgeably describes as 'et påtakelig vitnesbyrd om, hvor vel skikket vort sprog er, når det benyttes på rette måde, til at gengive de antike tankers indhold og form ...' (tangible proof of how well adapted our language is, when it is used in the right way, to reproduce the content and the form of the thought of the ancients... – 21.03.72. HU XVII, p. 25). In the same letter Ibsen expresses some interesting reflections on the theory of translation, and makes some critical remarks about Chr.K.F.Molbech's famous Danish translation of Dante's *Divina Commedia*. He also discusses critically the translations of Meisling and Wilster – and it is presumably S.S. Meisling's Danish translations of Vergil's *Aeneid* and Christian Wilster's translations of *The Iliad* and *The Odyssey* to which he is referring when he maintains that the hexameter is unusable in the Nordic languages. Meisling had also at the same time published a translation of Ovid's *Metamorphoses*, which it is probable that Ibsen was familiar with. Furthermore, when Goethe uses such a verse form in *Hermann und Dorothea*, it is unsatisfactory according to Ibsen. Ibsen recommends in addition that Giertsen should set about Byron – but at the same time he expresses reservations when it comes to the possibility of having himself been influenced from that quarter:

Jeg kender ikke synderlig til Byron; men jeg har en følelse af, at hans værker, overførte i vort sprog, mægtig vilde bidrage til at feje en hel del moralistiske fordomme ud af vor æsthetiske betragtning, og derved var meget vundet.

(I am not very familiar with Byron; but I have a feeling that his works, translated into our language, would contribute immensely to banishing a large amount of moral prejudice from our aesthetic judgements, and we would profit greatly from this.)

The letter to Gjertsen, composed at the height of the Modern Breakthrough, thus indirectly reveals that Ibsen was more than familiar with a number of major works from the classics, which he had studied in various Scandinavian translations, and most likely also in the original. In addition he has detailed knowledge of authors like Shakespeare, Goethe and Byron. But we have to read between the lines in order to find these revelations.

To sum up, it can be said that Ibsen's own letters rarely or never assume the fateful character of some of the letters in his plays; Ibsen the letter writer is a man in full control, who guards himself and adapts the message to the receiver. This becomes more and more pronounced as he becomes more famous. It seems he becomes increasingly watchful in order to protect both his private and his public life.

Despite the buttoned-up, reserved, tactical and formal style which characterizes Henrik Ibsen the letter-writer, there do nevertheless exist letters in which he with his own hand exposes his most intimate circumstances. The archivist at Riksarkivet (the State Archive), Per Heggelund Dahl, published on 24 March 1996 in the Norwegian newspaper *Aftenposten* a hitherto unknown letter from Ibsen which is actually of the same kind as the most fateful letters in his own plays. It dates from 1846, and I here quote it in full:

Hr. Byfoged Preus.
Opfordret af Deres Velbaarenhed til at erklære om jeg vedgaaer eller nægter at være Fader til et af Pigen Else Sophie Jensdatter Birkedalen født Drengebarn, som i Daaben den 25de October sidstleden er kaldet Hans Jacob, maa jeg herved ærbødigst meddele, at jeg ikke, uagtet Pigens Samqvem ogsaa med andre Mandspersoner paa den vedkommende Tid, bestemt tør fralægge mig bemeldte Paternitet, da jeg desværre med hende har pleiet legemlig Omgang, hvortil hendes fristende Adfærd og samtidige Tjeneste med mig hos Apotheker Reimann i lige Grad gav Anledning.
   Jeg er nu i 20de Aar gl:, eier aldeles Intet, uden nogle tarvelige Klæder, Skoetøi og Linned og skal om kort Tid forlade Grimstad Apothek, ved hvilket jeg som Lærling og altsaa uden nogen anden Løn, end Kosthold og de ovennævnte Fornødenheder, har opholdt mig siden Sommeren 1843. Min endnu levende Fader, til hvem jeg nødsages for det første at begive mig, er en af de mindre Handelsmænd i Skien og befinder sig i høist maadelige Kaar.
   Grimstad den 7de Decbr: 1846
   Ærbødigst
   Henr. Ibsen

(To His Honour Mr Preus
Justice of the Peace.
In reply to the letter from Your Honour enquiring as to whether I admit or deny the charge of being the father of the male child born to the maid Else Sophie Jensdatter Birkedalen and christened Hans Jacob on 25th October just past, I must respectfully state that, despite the fact that the girl also had relations with other male persons during the period in question, I am unable to rule myself out categorically from the said paternity, as I have unfortunately had intercourse with her, to which both her provocative behaviour and her concurrent service with me in the house of Mr Reimann the pharmacist gave occasion.
   I am now in my twentieth year; I own precisely nothing, with the exception of some shabby clothes, shoes and linen, and in a short while I shall leave Grimstad Pharmacy, at which I have resided as an apprentice – i.e. without any other pay than my keep and the above-mentioned necessities – since Summer 1843. My still surviving father, to whom I am obliged to turn in the immediate future, is one of the small traders in Skien, and his

circumstances are extremely modest.
Grimstad 7 December 1846
Your humble servant
Henr. Ibsen)

The information that the young Ibsen was the father of a child born out of wedlock is of course not new. Nevertheless this is a most interesting letter, because of what it tells us about the eighteen-year-old who wrote it. The letter falls within the stylistic conventions of a legally binding paternity declaration, and like the texts it is modelled on, is couched in formal bureaucratic style. Yet it also contains expressions and information of a less objective character, which show how even the *young* Ibsen edited his own self-presentation. For one thing, Ibsen, who was born in March 1828, makes himself a year older than he actually is. It is not possible that he was in his twentieth year; he was eighteen and a half in December 1846. This inaccurate information can of course be understood both as an expression of responsibility and as a manifestation of pride. Less impressive are the excuses, where Ibsen points out that the child's mother had 'relations with other male persons during the period in question', and where he cites her 'provocative behaviour' as a contributory cause of the affair. It is also difficult to avoid the impression that when addressing the justice of the peace who had the responsibility for collecting paternity payments, he presented his material circumstances in as poor a light as possible - although the information he gives about his property and his working conditions is in all probablility correct. At any rate, this is a letter which it must have pained the impoverished and proud young boy to write. Perhaps the form and the style served as a shield against the oppressive content of the text.

One of the last letters Ibsen sent to Georg Brandes, on 3 June 1897, has a very different character. Here it is the famous poet and world citizen who is speaking. Yet this too gives direct expression to human pain:

Kan De gætte hvad jeg går og drømmer om og planlægger og udmaler mig som så dejligt? Det er: at slå mig ned ved Øresund, mellem København og Helsingør, på et frit åbent sted, hvor jeg kan se alle havsejlerne komme langvejs fra og gå langvejs. Det kan jeg ikke *her*. Her er alle sunde lukkede i enhver ordets betydning, – og alle forståelsens kanaler tilstoppede. Å, kære Brandes, man lever ikke virkningsløst 27 år ude i de store fri og frigørende kulturforhold. Her inde eller, rettere sagt, her oppe ved fjordene har jeg jo mit *fød*eland. Men – men – men: hvor finder jeg mit *hjem*land? Havet er *det*, som drager mig mest. (HU XVIII, p. 397)

(Can you guess what I am dreaming about and planning and imagining to myself as so lovely? It is: to find a place to settle by Øresund, between Copenhagen and Elsinore, a free open place, where I can see all the ocean-going sailing ships coming from afar and going afar. I cannot do that *here*. Here all the sounds are closed in every sense of the word, – and all the channels of understanding are blocked. Oh, my dear Brandes, one cannot escape the effects of living for 27 years out in free and liberating cultural circles. In here, or rather, up here, by the fjords, is the land of my *birth*. But where will I find my *home*land? It is the sea which draws me most.)

Ibsen is no doubt sincere in what he writes here. But even in this letter there are echoes of other texts: Ibsen is quoting Ballested (and himself as an author!) in *Fruen fra havet* (The Lady from the Sea), a quotation which he in his turn had borrowed from his Danish fellow-poet Adam Oehlenschläger, who in the final act of the tragedy *Haakon Jarl* (Earl Haakon) had placed these words in the mouth of the slave Kark, just before he kills his master: 'Snart er alle sunde lukket' (Soon all the sounds will be closed). The dramatist Oehlenschläger and the slave Kark, the quasi-artist Ballested and the poet Ibsen – all share these words, which are used here to convey the private Ibsen's heart-felt complaint, and can stand as our final example of how consummately edited Ibsen's letters are – even when they express his innermost feelings. In other words, Ibsen's correspondence, despite its occasionally dry, impersonal and controlled tone, is written by a man of letters to his fingertips. But *behind* the literary flavour of the letters is concealed a personality which is vulnerable and at the same time strong, almost volcanic. As a rule, however, Ibsen kept his passions on a tight rein. His letters tell of a man who wished to build a wall around his private existence. That wish we should respect – to the extent that a poet who belongs to world literature can demand such a thing.

Notes

1. Øyvind Anker: *Henrik Ibsen. Brev 1845-1905. Ny Samling, I-II, Ibsenårbok 1979.* Letter no. 416, Vol. I, p. 245. Further references to this collection will be abbreviated as NS.
2. Henrik Ibsen: *Samlede verker.* Hundreårsutgave, ed. Francis Bull, Halvdan Koht og Didrik Arup Seip, I-XXII. Oslo, 1928-57. Vol. XVIII, p. 417f. Letter to Georg Brandes, Kristiania 30.9.98. Further references to this edition will be abbreviated as HU.
3. Øyvind Anker: 'Bjørnstjerne Bjørnson fra en annen side' in *Samtiden* 63 (1954), p. 114.
4. Halvdan Koht and Julius Elias (eds.): *Breve fra Henrik Ibsen* I-II, Kristiania 1904, Vol. I, p. 7.
5. Øyvind Anker, *Samtiden* 1954.
6. Brandes first published the Bardach letters (which were written in German) in a Danish translation in the Danish newspaper *Politiken*, and later he published them in their original form in his little illustrated book on Ibsen in the series *Die Literatur*, 1906.
7. Else Høst: 'Brev fra Henrik Ibsen', in *Edda* 56:1 (1956), pp. 1-40.
8. The letters to the family which are published in HU were printed in a supplementary volume (XIX) in 1952. Four years earlier Ibsen's daughter-in-law Bergljot Ibsen had published excerpts and fragments from this material in her memoir *De tre*, 1948. Sigurd Høst had also published a couple of Ibsen's letters. They appeared as a supplement to the book *Ibsens diktning og Ibsen selv*, 1927. In both cases the material was later included in HU. Individual letters from Ibsen have in addition been published from time to time in newspapers and journals. These too were later published in HU or NS.
9. Koht and Elias, 1904, I, p. 67ff. The last four lines of the verse were suppressed as early as this. The title is 'Til Susanna [sic!] Thoresen', and it is dated [Bergen] January 1856.
10. NS I, p. 467, letter no. 1100. To Hildur Andersen. Anker's suggested dating: 19.09.1899.
11. NS I, p. 25. Cf. Vol. II p. 123, notes to letter no. 762.
12. NS II, pp. 120-27 refers to the relevant data in connection with Ibsen's relationship to Hildur Andersen. The editor, Øyvind Anker, gives further information about Andersen's correspondence with Halvdan Koht, the editor of the *Efterladte Skrifter* I-II, 1909 and HU 1928-57, and refers to Francis Bull's explanation of the whole affair in *Edda* 1957. It is here that it is stated that Andersen's reservations about publishing are presumably due to the Ibsen family's reactions.
13. NS II, p. 124. Note to letter 762, which reproduces a letter from Hildur Andersen to V.Hammer 27.10.1907.

14. Cf. Koht and Elias 1904, Vol. II, p. 234, note to letter 151. The note explains that the MP Hagbard Berner proposed on 1 February 1882 that an extra sum should be added to the authors' stipends of both Ibsen and Bjørnson, on the grounds that they had 'lidt store økonomiske tab ... uden traktatmæssige overenskomster til beskyttelse af deres litterære ejendomsræt' (suffered considerable economic loss...because of the lack of contractual agreements for the protection of their literary copyright). The proposal was not accepted by the Storting.
15. Koht and Elias 1904, Vol. I, p.329.
16. Much has been written about Ibsen's views of Kierkegaard. For a presentation of his actual knowledge of Kierkegaard's writings, see Vigdis Ystad: ' – *livets endeløse gåde*'. *Ibsens dikt og drama* (' – life's endless mystery'. Ibsen's Poetry and Drama), Oslo, 1996, p. 215, where it is argued that he must have read at least *Enten-Eller, Kjærlighedens Gjerninger, Afsluttende uvidenskabelig Efterskift* and *Stadier på Livets Vej* (Either-Or, The Works of Love, Final Unscientific Postscript and Stages on Life's Way). The types of conflict in Ibsen's plays reveal a striking similarity to the basic premises of Kierkegaard's thinking. See the discussion of this point in Ystad 1996.

3

'I too believe in the good effect of hypnosis': Georg Brandes and his Correspondence

Jørgen Knudsen
Copenhagen

Let me begin by establishing what I am not going to do. I shall not attempt to describe Brandes the brilliant letter-writer – always eager to learn, always asking good questions, sometimes very blunt ones, often caring, often stating clear opinions, often very open-minded. Consequently, I am not going to discuss the letters to his parents, edited in six volumes, nor his correspondence with Scandinavian authors in eight volumes, nor his correspondence with other European authors in three, equally bulky, volumes.[1] My concern here is not with literary relations and influences, therefore. But even when speaking about the man himself as seen through his correspondence I shall not be focusing on any one aspect of his personal development over time, nor what might be called the multiplicity – or unpredictability – of his character, his incontinence and capriciousness. My intention is rather to proceed from a discussion of the central role which his correspondence played in his life to a consideration of what I take to be an important pattern in his personality, and then to suggest one of the reasons for his enormous influence upon this pre-Freudian era.

The extent of his correspondence is remarkable. One of the main themes in his own letters is a recurring complaint about the prodigious number of letters that he receives. Just how prodigious is indicated by his remark that every day the postman – and in late nineteenth-century Copenhagen the postman called four times a day – brought with him requests to Brandes to write or do things that would in fact take him three months to write or to do. More specifically: of his own letters, those to a little over 500 addressees have been preserved, and these are evidently not a representative selection. Meanwhile, he himself has kept letters from about 2,500 correspondents, in all some 15,000 items.[2] From the mid 1880s on, he claims repeatedly that he receives twenty, and sometimes thirty or forty letters a day, to which must be added the manuscripts, books and articles sent to him by their various authors and editors. Consequently, taking the conservative estimate of twenty letters a day and multiplying that by the last forty years of his life, it would appear that during this period he received at least a quarter of a million letters. Thus, according to an estimate that has, inevitably, to be very rough, he preserved only one in twenty of them. And it would seem that the letters he kept are those which he bothered to answer.

A very broad idea of the nature of this correspondence may be achieved by considering the first one hundred of his correspondents whose surnames begin with the letter 'T', and whose letters have been preserved in the Brandes Archive in Copenhagen. This letter suggests itself because it is both neutral as regards nationality and would seem to offer a fair cross-section of those with whom Brandes corresponded. The number of extant letters from these one hundred persons varies between 1 and 80, although in by far the majority of cases it is a question of only one or two. The great majority of these letters date from after 1900 (in fact 90 of the correspondences begin after this date), and this again hardly gives a fair picture of what would have been Brandes' correspondence as a whole. Rather it suggests that he was more careful to keep the letters he received towards the end of his life. Also, and for obvious reasons, there is a distinct falling off in the flow of letters from abroad during the First World War.

The accompanying table distinguishes these correspondents by nationality and profession.

Georg Brandes

From Tao di Bruno, Gloria, to Thorgils, Maria Magdalena

Nationality		Profession	
Denmark	39	Wives, widows	14
Germany	11	Authors, poets	12
USA (incl. Danish emigrants)	9	Editors of newspapers and journals	10
Norway	8	Professors of Lit.	5
France	4	Students	5
Finland	4	Artists	3
Sweden	4	Publishers	3
Hungary	3	Teachers	3
Armenia	3	Various professions	17
Iceland	2	Unknown	28
Austria	2		
Japan	2		
England	1		
Poland	1		
Italy	1		
Tunisia	1		
Persia	1		

What is designated here as 'Various professions' brings few surprises, although it does include a barber, two nurses, a theosophist, and a perfume-vendor from Tunisia. 'Wives, widows', meanwhile, are the wives or widows of authors and artists often well-known to Brandes, such as Hippolyte Taine or the Norwegian painter, Fritz Thaulow. Finally, of these 100 correspondents, 74 are men and 26 women.

What do they want from him? A little more than half of these letters contain requests and invitations ranging from those who wish to come and see him or who want a picture or his autograph to others requesting advice as to what they should read. There are those who ask him to write something to help a critic in distress or an artist pursued by a malignant press and others who seek to enlist his help for a periodical by writing an article, while yet others want him to review their book or privately to give his opinion of the enclosed poem, or to make a speech at some occasion or other, or to help them find an editor for (say) this Norwegian author in (say) Germany. Still others contain requests to be allowed to translate him (Brandes) or want him to serve on a committee for this or that noble purpose or else to write something to secure world peace according to the infallible method invented by the undersigned. A female translator asks for advice as to how to handle her shy fiancé, and also tries to get Brandes to support his case at the theatre. A waiter who is out of work asks him to read a manuscript, and wants to know what he should do now that his wife has left him.

Again, an English woman asks for a contribution to her Christian work among sailors from the Navy while from a Dane who has emigrated to the States he receives the following letter:

Dr Brandes
De er klog Mand. De maa kunne sige mig hvordan jeg skal faa et Maal at arbejde mod. (Jeg ønsker at tjene Penge); fremfor alt at blive en dygtig Mand min Vilje er god. Ærbødigst Eli Thomsen

(Dr. Brandes, you are a clever man. You must be able to tell me how I shall get an aim to work for (I want to make money), first of all become a skilful man, my will is good. Yours etc.)

The worst of Brandes' tormentors among these hundred correspondents chosen at random is a nurse who in the course of two years writes to him eighteen times, evidently with the sole purpose of obtaining an answer. 'Thank you for your last lovely little note which for many days kept me above water', she gushes. Her attempts to be humorous and coquettish are, moreover, evidently in vain, but he must have answered her letters, patiently and perhaps out of some pity, though in principle he is much against pity. After sixteen letters he ceased to respond but a few years later she tried once more, though evidently with scant reward. Nevertheless, there are some more deserving petitioners like the Armenian student, Thadewassian, who invites him to speak on the Armenian question in Berlin (Brandes did so in 1903) or the sculptor Rudolph Tegner, whose wife, in describing how the reactionary newspaper *Nationaltidende* is pursuing her husband, demonstrates that she knows very well how to activate Brandes.

So much for those who write to him asking favours. The remainder of this correspondence comprises business letters from translators and editors or approaches from those who are arranging festivities for him or who wish to congratulate him on his birthday or his last, wonderful article or recent lecture, or who do not agree with his interpretation of *Macbeth*. Or it may be the Norwegian Cecilie Thoresen, who is so totally confused with love that she doesn't know what to write although she uses many words, or a Japanese who sends him the gospel of a new prophet. Finally, there are letters from various personal friends informing him about their books, families, and friends or arranging to meet him, etc.

To read the letters that Brandes received from this almost random selection of correspondents is to confirm an impression that his correspondence is one of the most pathetic aspects of his literary life and comprehensible only when it becomes clear that this celebrator of the will, this adamant no-sayer in principle, had one defect, one weakness: he was almost incapable of refusing a request. Even if he left most of the letters he received unanswered, and even if he wrote very quickly, he must have devoted several hours of every day to his correspondence – to read, to sort out, to answer.

Why did he do this? Or why didn't he at least get a secretary? Eventually he did, of course, but not before 1910, and for the simple reason that he did not trust anybody to poke into his private affairs, apart from his good friend Bertha Knudtzon whose help for many years was indispensable. But even so, why did he take this enormous burden upon himself, knowing, as he must have done, that the rumour would spread, and the more letters he answered, the more he would get.

A first answer is that he loved to be used, to be useful if not indispensable, and what is more, to be asked for more than he could possibly achieve. That goes for his correspondence but also for requests to deliver speeches or to write articles. But there is, in the relationship between this type of work produced at the request of others and his own major creative writing, a vicious circle. After finishing his study of Shakespeare in 1895 the important project that has recently governed his life, the endeavour that makes him put everything else to one side, is missing. Apart from his autobiography, which he writes mainly at Carlsbad where he is sheltered from the postman, he produces no major works after the

Shakespeare book until the – postally speaking – peaceful years of the First World War. Then, suddenly, the large-scale biographies of Goethe, Voltaire, Michelangelo and Caesar appear. And note how they are written: he writes the first chapter, delivers the manuscript – and has four compositors working on it at the printing-house, so that he is forced to write at an insane speed merely to keep up with them. Meanwhile, there is clearly no time for letters or other interruptions. The evident necessity, the incontestable excuse is at hand. But if he did not write his book on Goethe immediately after the study of Shakespeare, then his susceptibility to these distractions is part of the explanation. Maybe the writing of his book on Goethe was an excuse for not answering letters in 1915. But until then, the letters had been an excuse for not writing about Goethe.

Evidently, this weakness of Brandes became well known, and more and more people who wanted to immortalize themselves by means of his written word thronged around him. In a humorous article, 'Magnet for Gale' (Magnet for Madmen)[3] he describes the kind of strange characters who force themselves upon him. Everybody, it seems, abused his weakness, even those who should know better. For example, during a lunch in London in 1896 he promised – after 'outrageous persuasion', as he calls it – his British publisher William Heinemann that he would write a history of Danish-Norwegian literature, a task to which he was evidently far from inclined, and this promise worried him for seven years, until at last he paid Heinemann to release him from the agreement.[4] By 1904, in a letter to Madame de Caillavet,[5] he calls himself 'la bonne à tout faire' (or in German, 'Mädchen für alles'); everybody seems to have a right to call upon his help from morning till night.

This fatal weakness of Brandes' was interpreted as a kind of naïveté. A journalist, Andreas Vinding, writes:

Naiv var Georg Brandes, og misbrugt blev han. Ofte maatte han sælge sine kostbareste Bøger for at hjælpe litterære Plattenslagere, der paakaldte hans Medlidenhed. Han skrev artige og anerkendende Breve til Folk, som sendte ham de ligegyldigste Publikationer ... I sin Godhed nænnede han ikke at afslaa Opfordringer til at tage Ordet ogsaa ved mindre Begivenheder ... og efterhånden blen han fast Gratulant ved alle litterære Fødselsdage.

(Georg Brandes was naive, and misused, too. He had frequently to sell his most valuable books in order to come to the assistance of literary cheats who made demands upon his pity. He wrote polite and appreciative letters to people who sent him the most indifferent publications ... In his goodness he did not have the heart to refuse to speak at minor occasions ... and he ended up the permanent congratulator at every [man of letters'] birthday.)[6]

In a letter of 1908, he writes:

Die Art wie mich die Leute ausnutzen ist eine solche, dass es ein Wunder ist, mir selbst kaum verständlich, dass ich nicht längst wahnsinnig geworden bin. Von Morgen bis Abend, Tag aus, Tag ein, von 5-6000 Menschen bestürmt zu werden, die Aufmerksamkeit fordern, alle beleidigt werden wenn das nicht geschieht, oder nicht genügend ... In diesem Herbst ist es einfach furchtbar. Keine Fest wo ich nicht die Hauptrede halten muss, und eine solche Rede nimmt mir einen ganzen Tag, oft zwei.

(The way people use me makes it a wonder, hardly understandable to myself, that I have not gone mad a long time ago. From morning till night, day after day, to be pestered by between five and six thousand people who want attention, are offended when they do not get it, or not enough of it ... This autumn it is simply horrible. No party where I must not make the main speech, and it often takes me a whole day to prepare, often two days.)[7]

This outburst is to be found in a letter to a certain Sophia della Valle di Casanova, who was married to an Italian poet writing in German. Brandes visited the couple several years running at their estate on Lake Garda, so it is no wonder that Mr Casnova hopes for something in return. Brandes describes the situation in yet another letter, this time to an acquaintance of the poetical landowner; they are the words of a man on the verge of a nervous breakdown:

Ich soll Herrn Casanova betrübt haben. Ich mache den redligsten Versuch etwas von ihm in den Buchhaufen zu finden, denn alle Bücherregale sind doppel voll, die Bücher liegen in Kisten, auf Tischen, Stühlen usw. Es ist mir, obwohl ich fast einen ganzen Tag verschwendete, unmöglich seine Gedichte zu finden ... Ich sehe ich soll ihm gesagt haben, er soll italienisch schreiben. Ich nehme unendlich gern das unselige Wort zurück. Wie kann ich wissen, dass ich es gesagt habe. 5000 Menschen fragen mich im Laufe des Jahres, was ich von ihrer Produktion meine.

(I am supposed to have saddened Mr Casanova. I do try honestly to find something by him in these heaps of books, for all bookshelves are stacked double, [and I] also have books lying in boxes, on tables and chairs, etc. Even if I wasted a whole day it isn't possible for me to find his poems ... I understand that I must have told him to write in Italian. With infinite willingness I take back that disastrous word. How can I be sure I said it? 5,000 people ask me in the course of any year what I think of their production.)[8]

By now it is clear that this is a man who is terribly weak, and that he suffers from his weakness and its miserable consequences for himself and for his work. The question is how this fits in with the way both he and those about him regarded him as a strong and determined personality, the 'field marshal' as he was called by Alexander Kielland, the commander who from the height of his rostrum seizes the attention of his audience and authoritatively directs his troops into battle.

When in 1897 he was seriously ill with phlebitis, was in terrible pain and looked death in the face every day for several weeks, he wrote a letter to the painter Agnes Slott-Møller, which deserves to be quoted at length:

De Ord Malgré tout, der stod som Motto for min Bog om Polen bad jeg i 1867 for lige 30 Aar siden en øm Veninde at brodere paa min Tegnebog og de Ord er jeg blevet tro, tiere end jeg til daglig Brug taler om. Man skal være født *uovervindelig*, man skal være den Hest der sejrer i Væddeløbet - det er simpel Pligt for de tre første Rangklasser (alt det som er over Etatsraad) og det er baade Deres fyrstelige Højhed og Undertegnede.

Jeg respekterer til Nød Pengenød - skønt ikke meget - saa sælger man noget ... Misfornøjelse med Omgivelserne respekterer jeg ikke. Omgivelser *eksisterer* ikke, eller dog kun som Voks i de tre første Rangklassers Haand. De er kun at tage humoristisk. Dem lærer man efterhaanden hvad de skal mene. Det er den store Puddel, der skal dresseres til at gaa oprejst paa to Ben og som bestandig falder ned igen paa fire, men hvad saa? Man arbejder ej for Puddelens Skyld - den har at bjæffe sit Bifald til sidst - men for sin egen for at lade sine Kræfter spille, tumle et eller andet Stof, sætte sit Stempel paa det og leve det udødelige Liv alt her paa Jorden, som gamle Spinoza levede sit i ærlig og beskeden Overlegenhed. Man maa heller ikke være for hidsig for at Medgangen skal indfinde sig. Medgang er Luksus, Firkløver, Gevinst i Lotteriet - skidt med Medgang!

(In 1867 I asked a tender girlfriend to embroider the words 'malgré tout', which I have as a motto in my book on Poland, in my wallet, and to these words I have been faithful, more often than I would usually like to mention. You must be born *invincible*, you must be the winning horse in the race – that is simple duty for the three first ranks (everything above councillor of state), and that is the case, both with your princely highness and the undersigned.

If needs must be I can respect lack of money – though not much – then you sell something ... Dissatisfaction with your surroundings is not to be respected. Surroundings do not *exist*, or only as wax in the hands of the three first ranks. They can only be taken humorously. You teach them by and by what to think. They are the big poodle to be trained to walk upright on two legs and which constantly falls down on four, but so what? You do not work for the sake of the poodle – it has to bark its applause at the end, but for your own sake, to use your full power, to handle some stuff, put your stamp upon it and live the immortal life already on this earth, as old Spinoza did in honest and humble superiority. You must not be too eager to be successful. Success is luxury, four-leaved clover, prize in the lottery, never mind success!)[9]

Here is Brandes as he wished to be seen. But it is clear from what has already been said that the 'surroundings' he dismisses so lightly here really *did* exist – four times a day, when the post arrived. So why this weakness?

There are two lines of explanation. One is this: the female side in him, which was the very basis of his critical ability, his ability to understand and identify himself with the object of his attention, was in this very concrete way also a threat to his existence, when so many people misused his sympathy and consideration. In order not to be overwhelmed by it, he mobilized whatever he had in himself of the field marshal, of fighting-will and of scorn for this race of apes euphemistically calling itself humans: a will and a scorn which vanished with the next delivery from the postman.

The other line of explanation, which goes some way towards explaining the eighteen replies he addressed to the silly and coquettish nurse or to so many of the other 2,500 hopeful letter-writers, looks for clarification in the fact that throughout his life Brandes was afflicted by a fear of being pushed out into the dark, expelled from good company, and emerging superfluous, betrayed by friends, forgotten by everybody. The experience, indeed the shock, that he went through in 1871-72 when the promising young scholar found himself suddenly a scandal in person, unworthy of the professorship that had been his hope and firm ambition, excluded from all the newspapers and then, five years later, his – as he saw it – forced exile to Germany, the continued experience of being set aside, mistrusted, regarded with contempt and ignored – not becoming a member of the Academy of Sciences, not getting the Nobel Prize, not getting the mansion of honour which the philosopher Høffding got etc., etc. – all this marked him. Whereas abroad he was called the greatest critic in Europe, even in the world. Of course he had his ardent followers in Denmark too, but hardly had he been partially and half-heartedly acknowledged by the conservative press, before those nearest his heart, respectless youth, began to treat him as an antiquity.

No wonder therefore if he – as Pontoppidan asserts in his portrait of Dr Nathan in *Lykke-Per* (1898-1904) – worries about what even the youngest student thinks about him. As he wrote to Pontoppidan:

Intet kan være mere polært fjernt fra mit Væsen. Det er ikke min Fortjeneste men mit Liv har ført det med sig at jeg er kold som Is over for hvad man mener om mig. *For ikke at gaa til Grunde* nødtes jeg til ved mit 30te Aar formelig at extirpere hos mig den Nerve, i Kraft af hvilken man sørger over at udskældes og nedsættes. Jeg gjorde mig meget haard ... selv naar jeg har skullet tale under vanskelige Forhold som første Gang i Petersborg eller første Gang i Paris paa et fremmed Sprog over for en fremmed Forsamling, har jeg til mine Omgivelsers Forundring ikke følt den allerringeste Uro, fordi Publikums Dom om mig var blevet mig ligegyldig.

(Nothing can be further from my nature. It is not my personal merit, but my life which has led me to be cold as ice towards what others think about me. *In order not to perish* I had at thirty to extirpate the nerve by which it hurts you to be scolded or cut down. I made myself very hard ... even when I had to talk under very difficult circumstances like the first time in Petersburg or the first time in Paris in a foreign language to an alien audience I did not, to the astonishment of my surroundings, feel the slightest anxiety, because the verdict of the audience had become indifferent to me.)[10]

Note Brandes' words: 'to the astonishment of my surroundings'. Of course that nerve has not been extirpated. And nor does

Pontoppidan believe it, as his response demonstrates:

en saadan Kastration af Æresfølelsen vilde efter min Antagelse umuliggøre en saa overvældende Frugtbarhed som Deres. En anden Ting er det jo, at selve det attraaede kan være én ligegyldigt.

(... in my supposition such a castration of the sense of honour would make a fertility as overwhelming as yours impossible. There is another story that once you have what you desired it becomes unimportant to you.)[11]

He went on to say that the desire to conquer which Dr Nathan shows even towards a young student seemed to him so remarkable and so charming, all the more so since the student's applause in itself was and must be absolutely worthless to him, the world-famous man.[11]

The desire to conquer. When Brandes again and again took on new tasks, now urging his fellow-countrymen to fight for free thought and against the clergy, now supporting the Danes in German Schleswig, now spurning Europe to protest against the Turkish slaughter of the Armenians, he did so because the cause was good, and because he loved to have a good cause, and these two aspects cannot be separated. Every day he had once more to fight the dragon of world-wide stupidity and to maintain his own position threatened by the same stupidity, and answering letters from people with an interest in him and his writing was evidently one way of doing this. In spite of every assurance from his friends and admirers, in spite of all the speeches and poems and torchlight processions in his honour: in a dark corner of his soul the worm of doubt was gnawing away and through all the years grew ever worse, and in a sense all too justly. He saw only too clearly that the liberation of thought and feeling for which he had hoped and fought, had no earthly chance against the immense power of sheer stupidity, kept alive by instinctive humility towards clerical authorities and by antediluvian superstition, fertilized by a cynical press and steering towards the disastrous world war and the destruction of civilization. Indeed he did talk to deaf ears, indeed his misanthropy was all too justified.

In a way it was easy: his world fell into two parts, those who needed (and normally hailed) him – and those who hated and haunted him. In the latter group were also those who had formerly admired him, and they had, of course, to be seen as traitors. Despite everything, and in spite of all doubts as to their future behaviour: he could not let down those who wrote and told him that they needed him. They had to have a letter. And that is the marvellous thing about him: however snobbish he was, however attracted to the idea of aristocracy, and to all kinds of spiritual nobility – if somebody was in distress, and turned to him for help, then this person was his first priority. Here he combined his compassion with his position as a field marshal.

To give an example. There are, for instance, the three pathetic letters from one Anna Land. She presents herself as an elderly teacher, at the end of her tether, and at the mercy of money-lenders, to whom she has pawned all her belongings. She only wants to die, that is, to kill herself, but she is so afraid of eternal life and of the punishment to come, that she dares not do so unless Brandes can guarantee that there is no life after death. To her mind he is *the* expert in this matter. Will he therefore please give her a definite promise that death is the end? – What he replied we shall never know, but it is evident from her second and third letter that not only has he answered, but he has also, or so it would appear, had a talk with her in person. Indeed, how could he have turned down such misery?

A chapter in Brandes's life that has aroused much interest concerns his relations with women. As far as the correspondence is concerned we are in the – happy or unhappy – situation of there being practically no extant letters from him apart from the pathetic and terrible ones written to Gerda, his fiancée, and from 1875 his wife. I shall omit them here, since I have written about them in the second volume of my biography.[12] It is my theory that he gave his other female friends an absolute ultimatum: if they want letters from him, they must burn them after reading them. They would seem to have obeyed, and that is why most of his love-life is mercifully spared the curiosity of posterity.

It is nevertheless the case that he could not live without some kind of connection with the opposite sex. Since, however, he was a very busy man indeed, and women took up much time and were not only loveable, but also rather troublesome, he was drawn to correspond with what he took to be non-erotic women. With these women he enjoyed a holiday, so to speak, and they were allowed to keep his letters. Take, for example, the very beautiful young Swiss girl, Margrethe Klinckerfuss, who was endowed with the most wonderful eyes (her photo is among her letters in the Brandes archive). He is happy to tell her: 'Ich kenne kein so ernstes, echtes und doch (meiner Meinung nach) unerotisches Mädchen. Sie sind so ladylike, dass Sie eine Distanz um sich haben. Und gleichzeitig dieses rein geistiges Wohlwollen; Sie scheinen mir einmalig' (I know no such serious, genuine and yet (in my opinion) unerotic girl. You are so ladylike, and you have a distance around you. And at the same time this purely spiritual sympathy; that seems unique to me). Here he felt safe, therefore, and there are many letters to her, especially those in which he took her into his confidence over his affair with a certain Talitha Schütte, his mistress in the years from 1907 to 1912, when she deceived him with Anatole France, before returning to him a few months later. He has had an immense need to confide in someone about these very upsetting events, and an understanding woman like Margrethe, who lived in far-off Switzerland and had a distance around her, was well qualified to receive his confidences.

He had a similar relationship with other women, including for example the Swedish writer Ellen Key, although in her case he could not stop teasing her with hints of his own sexual conflicts precisely because of her very unsexy nature. But he evidently liked her because of her female delicacy and intuition, and because she was a free zone, erotically speaking. A third instance is the crippled Marie Hjort, a sister of his lawyer, who lived in an institution near Nyborg, from where she sent him platonically infatuated letters for many years. His replies are both simple and beautiful.[13]

However, perhaps the most remarkable of these platonic letter-relations to a distant woman emerges from his correspondence with Vera Spasskaja. The 146 extant letters that he addressed to her are in St Petersburg, but there are copies in Copenhagen, where her letters are also to be found. I have not counted them, but there are between three and four hundred.[14]

When Brandes was in Moscow in 1887 a young woman came

to him and asked him to visit her sister, who was ill and in bed and therefore could not attend his lectures, much to her vexation, since she had read his books and greatly admired him. Brandes immediately agreed, they took a cab, and he was at her bedside for twenty minutes. Her illness, it appeared, was of a nervous nature; when scared she lost the ability to speak. In her later letters she speaks very frankly about her 'ubønhørlige Hysterie' (inexorable hysteria), as she calls it herself.

There are several reasons why this correspondence developed as richly as it did. One is her humble and fervent admiration and her sympathy with his great and noble cause to educate mankind. Another is her very distant position, a third her terrible weakness plus the stubborn will to overcome it. This we recognize from other situations, most strikingly from Brandes' efforts for persecuted minorities. Indeed, wherever somebody is persecuted – by fate, by a bloody suppressor, by any superior force – there he is immediately at hand, spontaneously and irresistibly identifying himself under one condition: that the persecuted in question is already fighting back. 'Det er ydmygende at være svag ...,' he says in a speech to compatriots from the minority in Schleswig, 'men det er opløftende at være Den, som trods Lidenhed og Svaghed ikke giver tabt og aldrig falder i aandelig Søvn eller Døs' (It is humiliating to be weak ... but it is elevating to be the one who in spite of being small and weak does not give in and never falls asleep spiritually or descends into lethargy).[15] Or whimpers, one may add. Whimpering disgusts him most of all.

Vera could not control her voice. Sometimes she was mute, at others she was forced to cry out again and again the name of a sister, to whom she was violently attached in hate and love. She tells Brandes about her dark insistent ideas and her fits of fear. She also suffers from hysterical lameness in her legs and now and then in her hand – it is visible in her handwriting – and sometimes she cannot open her eyes, so that she is virtually blind. She also suffers from agoraphobia and cannot walk on her own in the street. She is often so weak that she has to stay in bed, now in her own little flat, or just a hired room, now in some institution or a hospital. She is treated by various doctors, sometimes with electric shock treatment, or 'franklinization', and sometimes with injections of arsenic, which makes her very dizzy. She talks about writing the story of her disease under the title 'Injured by medicine'. To this may be added her financial worries, since she is an orphan and her younger sister is also very poor, even though she helps her now and then. Apart from that, her only income is what she can get for her translations from German, and later from Danish.

The decisive thing is that she is brave. In one of her first letters she writes: 'Ich habe mich so schwach gefühlt, so mutlos, so ausser Stande meinen Kampf gegen diese Schmerzen fortzusetzen, und war von schmerzvollen Gedanken verfolgt. Wenn jedoch man von warmen treuen Herzen umgeben ist und fest darauf besteht, wie bescheiden auch immer, an der grossen menschlichen Aufgabe teilzunehmen, dann steht man schliesslich auf und ist nicht länger ein Opfer der Apathie und der Verzweiflung' (I felt so weak, so discouraged, so unable to prolong my fight against these pains, and was pursued by painful thoughts. When, however, you are surrounded by warm faithful hearts and firmly insist on participating, however humbly, in the great human project, then you rise in the end and are no more a victim to apathy and despair). – This was precisely what Brandes liked to hear!

In the first period of their correspondence she translated some minor pieces by him from German, but after a few years she did what, astoundingly, so many young girls of his acquaintance did: she learned Danish. She begins to write her letters in Danish, not faultlessly, but fairly well. Brandes, of course, gladly replies in the same language, and the tone of the correspondence gets warmer. She translates and publishes parts of his study of Shakespeare. She admires him immensely and writes about her feelings again and again. 'Deres Billede, som De gav mig for tre Aar siden, ser saa velvilligt ned paa mig naar jeg sidder ved mit Skrivebord, og synes at styrke mig i mit Forsøg paa saa meget jeg formaar at udbrede i mit Fædreland de geniale Værker af en af de største moderne Aander' (Your picture, which you gave me three years ago, looks so benevolently down upon me when I sit at my writing desk, and seems to inspire me in my attempt to spread in my fatherland the works of genius of one of the greatest modern spirits as much as I can). – And again: 'For mig er De ogsaa den største Personlighed i den moderne Verden, an Aandens Helt, troende paa sin Sag (hvad saa sjældent ses for Tiden) og stadig gaaende og førende andre mennesker fremad. Lykkeligt det Land, hvilket ejer en saadan Bærer af Lys!' (You are the greatest personality in the modern world, a hero of the spirit, believing in your cause (which is so rarely seen these days) and still leading others along. Happy the land that has such a bearer of light!).

'Kære Frøken!' he replies, 'Kære Barn, er jeg fristet til at sige. Jeg er ganske rørt over Dem. Blandt de hundreder af Mennesker jeg lærte at kende i Rusland, er De den eneste, der er blevet mig tro ... Jeg kan ikke undvære Deres Hengivenhed' (Dear miss, dear child I am tempted to say. I am quite touched by you. Among the hundreds of people I was acquainted with in Russia you are the only one who has remained faithful.... I cannot do without your devotion). He takes confidence from her enthusiasm and starts to confide in her. After some six months he tells her:

Der Aufsatz über Bjørnson ist lange nicht so gut wie der über Ibsen, ist überhaupt nicht gut, besonders weil er, wie fast alle meine für den Export geschriebene Sachen allzu lobend ist und in seiner Auffassung so idealistisch dass er unwahr wird. Eigentlich ist dieser Bjørnson wie recht viele Genies, ein eitler und recht schlechter Mensch. Indessen wenn schon gelogen oder übertrieben werden soll, ist es besser dass es in diese Richtung geschieht als in die herabsetzende.

(The article about Bjørnson is not nearly as good as the one about Ibsen, especially since it – like almost all the things I have written for export – is far too full of praise and in its interpretation so idealistic that it becomes untrue. In fact this Bjørnson is, like quite a lot of geniuses, a vain and very bad person. However, when you have to lie and exaggerate anyway, it is better that it goes in this direction rather than in a disparaging one.)

It transpires that she has translated the fifth volume of his *Hovedstrømninger i det 19de Aarhundredes Litteratur* (Main Currents in Nineteenth-Century Literature). It then turns out that another translator has done the same and, furthermore, sold his translation. All her work has been in vain, which also means an economic catastrophe for her. But she tries to console – not herself, but him: 'De kan ikke forestille Dem hvor velgørende Oversættelsen af Deres Skrifter virker altid paa mig; De er sandelig den bedste Læge og Deres Værker det bedste Lægemiddel for alt det som nedslaar mig. ... Jeg lader mig ikke knække af Skæbnens Slag, De har ikke forgæves opfordret mig ikke at tabe Modet' (You cannot imagine how beneficial the translating of your works always is to me; you are certainly the best of doctors, your works the best cure for everything that depresses me. I will not let myself be broken by the strokes of destiny, it is not in vain that you have told me not to lose courage). He replies: 'Ja gid jeg kunde lægge min Haand i Deres. Men jeg gør det nu, føler De det ikke?' (Yes, I wish I could lay my hand in yours. But I do it now, don't you feel it?). And she:

Ja, jeg *har* følt, hvor De lagde Deres Haand i min, og de ømme Ord De rettede til mig, gjorde et rigtigt Underværk. Hver Gang det Tvangsraab jeg skrev om til Dem vilde senere begynde paany, gentog jeg disse Ord i Mindet og blev atter rolig. Det var som en 'Suggestion' og den virkede paa en saa velgørende Maade. Og det var mig en saadan Glæde at tænke, at netop De var blevet min Læge i dette Fald. Der er ingen Overdrivelse i hvad jeg siger: fra den Dag jeg læste Deres Brev blev disse Anfald overvundne.

(Yes, I *have* felt how you put your hand in mine, and your tender words to me caused a regular miracle. Whenever the involuntary cries which I wrote to you about, were about to begin again, I repeated these words in my memory and they calmed me. It was like a 'suggestion' and it worked so beneficially. And I was so glad to think that you of all men had become my doctor in this case. I do not exaggerate when I say: from the day I read your letter these fits were overcome.)

Evidently, he enjoys this unexpected power and tries it once more: 'Hvor herligt at jeg har kunnet fordrive hint Tvangsraab. Men nu befaler jeg Dem af min inderste Vilje og mit hele Hjerte at blive rask. Tag din Seng og gaa! som der staar skrevet. Sig Dem selv, at det er mit hede Ønske og min bestemte Vilje' (How glorious that I have been able to expel this involuntary cry. But now I order you with my innermost will and all my heart to be in good health. Take up thy bed and walk, as it is written. Tell yourself that this is my hottest wish and my firm will).

But as this unfortunately does not work, she turns to a Russian doctor and treatment by hypnosis. She is hopeful: 'Hypnosen *skal* lykkes; jeg vil bære i Mindet Deres opmuntrande Ord og vil adlyde Dem og blive rask ... Jeg vil forestille mig, at naar jeg skal blive hypnotiseret, vil *De* lægge Deres Haand paa mit Hoved - ak, der er et Sted, som smerter saa meget og deraf kommer al den Uro' (The hypnosis must succeed; I will bear in mind your encouraging words and obey you and be well ... I will imagine that you will lay your hand on my head – alas upon that very painful spot from where all the unrest comes). Brandes promptly reassures her: 'Ja kunde jeg i Virkeligheden være den, der lagde Haanden paa Deres Hoved og kunde god Vilje gøre det - saa vilde det visselig hjælpe. Ogsaa jeg tror paa Hypnosens gode Virkninger' (Yes, could I be the one to put my hand on your head, and could good will work, then it certainly would help. I too believe in the good effect of hypnosis). But unfortunately, it did not help in this case. It may even have been counterproductive. This Russian doctor was so un-Brandeslike! He did his best, but: 'Det er mig som vaktes noget modstræbende i mit Indre naar denne fremmede Haand saa haardt trykker sin Vilje paa min Pande og mine Øjne' (It is as if some reluctant force is awakened in my interior when this strange hand of his is pressing its will so roughly on my forehead).

Take up thy bed and walk: the method does not work by letter. But it is evident that she associates Brandes with Christ himself. About his helpful friend and secretary, Bertha Knudtzon, who sometimes was a stand-in for Brandes in the correspondence with Vera, she wrote: 'Hun har et saa elskeligt Væsen, og hun vækker i Mindet Billedet af den Maria, som sad ved Jesu Fødder og lyttede til hans Ord' (She has such a loving nature and she calls to mind the picture of the Maria who sat at Christ's feet listening to his words). But so unreservedly does Vera lay her life in his hands that he has to do something in return. He does so by telling her his most painful secrets. '"Min Prinsesse" har forelsket sig i en anden' ('My princess' has fallen in love with somebody else), he tells her in June 1895. And so it was. His young love, Anna Tutein, had lost patience with him, since he evidently would not or could not get a divorce, and had chosen a Norwegian doctor in his place. Vera Spasskaja's first reaction about the master's loss is simply hysterical, but in her following letter she is more composed: 'Hun var for tom til at kunne følge en Ørn i sin Flugt; det var langt mageligere at gifte sig med et Hverdagsmenneske' (this so-called princess was too empty to follow an eagle in its flight. It was far more comfortable for her to marry an everyday person). – And in the same vein she writes about 'de Danskes sorte Utaknemlighed mod deres store Fører og aandelige Høvedsmand. Det er saa smerteligt at tænke, at Menneskene hader Geniet, kun fordi det bringer dem Lys og lærer dem at elske Frihed, Kunst og Deres ved det samme Geni omformede Sprog' (the black ingratitude of the Danes towards their great leader and spiritual chief. It is so painful to think that men hate the genius only because it brings them light and teaches them to love freedom, art and a language formed and changed by the same genius).

In return he tells her what until now has been a secret between him and the former princess, that when placed together the first letters in each chapter of the second volume of his study of Shakespeare form the words: 'Anna Tutein min elskede din er jeg' (Anna Tutein my love yours I am), as indeed, they do.

Indeed, Brandes recalls King Midas' barber, who could not keep his frightful secret, but had to whisper it into a hole in the riverside. By 1901 he had written an article about Vera, in which he called her Nadjesjda and blurred the story by letting it be an English novelist who corresponds with her. I quote: 'Hun har ingen Hemmeligheder for mig; vort Forhold er jo som et Forhold mellem Aander, og hun udsætter sig ikke for nogen Fare ved at betro sig fuldstændigt til mig' (She has no secrets to me; our relation is like a relation between spirits, and she exposes herself to no danger by confiding herself totally to me).[16] Neither did he by confiding to her. To his biographer, however, his letters yield quite a lot of confidential information, for instance about his daughter Edith whose development under the influence of her mother he did not approve of. He is afraid she will some day marry 'en Frisørsvend' (some barber's boy) – which to his mind she eventually does. He also brags about his different triumphs, as when, in London in 1913, he is greeted 'næsten som en Konge, allevegne kaldt den største Kritiker i Europa eller Verden' (almost as a king, and everywhere called the greatest critic in Europe or in the world). Interestingly enough, however, he says nothing about his terrible disappointment in love of 1912, perhaps because here he prefers other confidants, perhaps because he does not wish to confuse her about the role of Bertha Knudtzon sitting at his feet.

Let me end by quoting his last letter to Vera, from 31 December 1925, a year before his death. He never returned to Russia, so they never met again.

Min kære Veninde Tak for Deres aldrig svigtende Interesse efter 38 Aar, hvor vi mødtes i maaske et Kvarter ... De er meget utaalmodig med mig som en forsømmelig Brevskriver. Men naar den første Morgenpost - og der er fire Ombæringer om Dagen - bringer 59 Bøger, for hvilke en Tak forventes, og 25 Breve, som for nylig; og naar man arbejder uafbrudt fra Morgen til halv tre Nat, ikke har nogen Hjælp og er 84 Aar gammel, saa bliver det umuligt at overkomme den forventede Brevskrivning, selv om den Forventende udmærker sig særligt ved aldrig svigtende Hengivenhed og god Vilje.

De maa ogsaa huske at mindst et Dusin Mennesker ønsker at tale med mig hver Dag, og at aandelig Virksomhed er den Form for Arbejde, som kræver mest Samling. Saa længe Frk. Bertha Knudtzon levede, havde jeg i det mindste nogen Hjælp, nu ikke længere ... Og naar jeg ikke skriver, husk saa Mængden af mine Korrespondenter, som kan beløbe sig til 5000. Sidst men ikke mindst, mine Kræfter slår ikke til, jeg er ofte syg. For ikke at tale om at jeg er fattig. Verdensberømmelse er ikke indbringende, når man er Dansker.

(My dear friend thank you for your unfailing interest after 38 years, when we met for maybe a quarter of an hour.... You are very impatient with me as a negligent writer of letters. But when the first morning post – and there are four posts a day – brings 59 books, for which thanks are expected, and 25 letters, as recently; and when you are fully occupied with work from morning until half past two at night, have no help, and are 84 years old, then it becomes impossible to manage the expected letter-writing, even if the expecting person is especially distinguished by unfailing devotion and good will.

You must also bear in mind that at least a dozen people want to speak to me every day, and that spiritual creation is the kind of work demanding the utmost concentration. As long as Miss Bertha Knudtzon was alive, I had at least some help, but I have none now.... And when I do not write, then remember the number of my correspondents, which can be as many as 5,000. Last but not least my strength is insufficient, I am often ill. Not to mention that I am poor. World fame brings you nothing, when you are a Dane.)

He ends with news of Edith, whose bad luck has made her surly and cutting. 'I Danmark har Krigen skabt megen Elendighed. Det vil jeg dog ikke tale om, kun takke Dem min kære Vera for de mange Aars aldrig svigtende Venskab. Jeg er Deres meget hengivne ...' (In Denmark the war has caused much misery. However, I will not talk about that, but only thank you, my dear Vera, for your unfailing friendship over many years. I am your quite devoted ...).

Here, Brandes might be said to whimper. But after 84 years, should he not be allowed to? And what is more important: whether this correspondence appears parodic or verging on the ridiculous, or touches the latterday reader with its beauty or even its serenity, it serves to demonstrate one way in which Brandes influenced his contemporaries – as, indeed, it illustrates their susceptibility to him. 'I wish I could lay my hand in yours. But I do it now, don't you feel it?' – 'Yes, I *have* felt how you put your hand in mine...'

Notes

1. *Breve til Forældrene* I – III, ved Morten Borup (Copenhagen, 1978), *Breve til Forældrene* 2. række, I – III, ved Torben Nielsen (Copenhagen, 1994). Georg og Edv. Brandes, *Brevveksling med nordiske Forfattere og Videnskabsmænd*, ved Morten Borup (Copenhagen, 1939-42). *Correspondence de Georg Brandes* I – III, ved Paul Krüger (Copenhagen, 1952-66).
2. By far the majority of these letters are in the Brandes Archive in The Royal Library in Copenhagen. Some of them are in the Ny Kgl. Samling in the same library, and a few in Rigsarkivet.
3. 'Magnet for Gale', *Politiken* , 13 May 1901; *Samlede Skrifter* XVII.
4. 7 January 1903, to Vilh. Andersen (Brandes Archive).
5. *Correspondence de Georg Brandes*, Notes I, 70.
6. *Sorgløse Tider*, 1942.
7. To Sophia Casanova, 22 October 1908 (Brandes Archive).
8. To Margrethe Klinckerfuss, 27 September 1904 (Brandes Archive).
9. Ny Kgl. Samling.
10. 17 July 1902, in Elias Bredsdorff, *Henrik Pontoppidan og Georg Brandes. En dokumentarisk redegørelse for brevvekslingen og den personlige kontakt* (Copenhagen, 1964), I.
11. 19 July 1902, *ibid.*
12. *Georg Brandes. I modsigelsernes tegn, 1877–83* (Copenhagen, 1988).

13. Among letters from Niels Hjorth in Rigsarkivet.
14. Both collections are in the Brandes Archive.
15. 'Tale til Sønderjyderne i Kjøbenhavn', 1902, in *Taler* (Copenhagen, 1920).
16. 'Nadjesjda', *Samlede Skrifter*, vol. XVII.

4

'Min anden Moder! min kære og elskede Veninde!' Georg Brandes's letters to Magdalene Thoresen

Jorunn Hareide
University of Oslo

On the occasion of Magdalene Thoresen's eightieth birthday in 1899, the then fifty-seven year old Georg Brandes wrote to her:

Kjære fru Thoresen.
Tillad mig som en af Deres gamle Venner, der aldrig har glemt hvad Godhed De for mange Aar siden viste mig, at indfinde mig med min Tak i Anledning af den 3. Juni. Da jeg kan tænke mig, der bliver Trængsel imorgen, prøver jeg at komme Aftenen forud.

De gjorde i min Ungdom et smukt og dybt Indtryk paa mig, og Præget staar bevaret uforvansket i mit Hjerte. Hav Tak derfor og for Deres hele varme, rige Kvindelighed.

Hvis jeg ikke, som bunden til et Sygeleje, skrev i min Seng, vilde jeg sige mere.

Deres Georg Brandes.

(Dear Mrs. Thoresen.
Allow me as one of your old friends who has never forgotten the kindness you showed me many years ago, to turn up with my thanks on the occasion of the 3rd. of June. As I anticipate a great crowd tomorrow, I will try to arrive the evening before.

In my youth you made a deep and beautiful impression upon me, and this impression is preserved uncorrupted in my heart. Receive my thanks for this and for all your warm, rich womanliness.

If I were not ill and writing from my bed, I should say more.

Your Georg Brandes.)[1]

This brief letter, the last of all those that have been preserved from Georg Brandes to Magdalene Thoresen, reveals some of the features that were also evident in the letters of his youth to her: the politeness, the gratitude, and not least, the coquetry: what is it that he would have liked to tell her, but which he cannot express because he writes from his bed? What is more: he praises the woman Magdalene Thoresen, but says nothing at all about her writing.

The purpose of this essay is to take a closer look at the letters which Georg Brandes wrote to Magdalene Thoresen as a young man. Her letters to him will be discussed only in passing, as it is my aim primarily to study Brandes' comments on her literary works and about the literary debate in general, as well as the account of her character that emerges from these letters. It is my contention that the impression Brandes received of her when he was in his mid-twenties, was decisive for the way in which she is presented in his memoirs *Levned* (Life, 1905). This is half admitted in his birthday letter: 'Præget [the impression she made upon him in his youth] staar bevaret uforvansket i mit Hjerte.' Because of the literary position Brandes enjoyed both in his own time and in posterity, this youthful impression to a great extent determined her posthumous reputation both as a writer and as a human being.

Today we know how Georg Brandes looked upon Magdalene Thoresen in his youth mainly from two sources: one private, which consists of his letters to her and of remarks about her in letters to others, and one public: an essay that he published in *Illustreret Tidende*, 22 April 1866, at the very start of their friendship. The letters were not accessible to the public until after his death in 1927.

Brandes did not write much about her in his later career. He did not review any of her books, and it seems that he did not have first-hand knowledge of the many works she published after their friendship had come to a close in 1868. He mentions her very briefly in *Det moderne Gennembruds Mænd* (The Men of the

Modern Breakthrough, 1883) for her poignant characterizations of the clergy, probably thinking of one of the central characters in the novel *Signes Historie* (Signe's Story, 1864), and of several other clergymen in some of her early short stories. He also wrote an obituary about her, as he did about quite a few other women authors whose works he also did not review.[2] His third and last public mention of her is in *Levned*, in which he included some of the main points from his obituary. He chose not to reprint the essay of 1866 in his collected essays since he believed that Magdalene Thoresen had idealized her life story for him to the extent that the portrait of her in the essay was untrue.[3] Therefore his presentation of her in *Levned* must be looked upon as his final assessment of her.

The remarkable thing about *Levned*, considered as the presentation of an author, is that Brandes is far more interested in Magdalene Thoresen's personality than in her works. He mentions only three titles, all of them from the 1860s, and he does so only briefly, *en passant*. This limitation may perhaps be explained by the fact that these were the only books Magdalene Thoresen published during the period of their friendship, and that the context in his memoirs is the years of his early manhood. Nevertheless, this elision is curious.

But how can the presentation in *Levned* have consequences for the evaluation of Magdalene Thoresen as an author, when her works are not presented?

Firstly, there is a negative signal in the mere fact that nothing is said about them: the implication is that these books are not even worth mentioning.

Secondly, Brandes still gives the impression that he is characterizing Magdalene Thoresen as an author and a human being simultaneously. The presentation in *Levned* has until recently been considered the authoritative assessment of her. Later literary historians have used this source somewhat uncritically, without reflecting that Brandes may have wanted to present a certain picture of *himself* to the world, by treating Magdalene Thoresen (and others) in a certain way. Literary historians seem especially to have loved – and repeated and enlarged upon– his final verdict on Magdalene Thoresen as an author: 'Iøvrigt var hun langt mere

Kvinde end Forfatterinde' (Moreover, she was far more of a woman than of an authoress).

The very wording here can be found in later works by literary historians such as Kristian Elster Jr. and Vilhelm Andersen. Francis Bull states bluntly that Magdalene Thoresen's works are no longer read, and that she is interesting only because of her relationships with the great literary (male) names of her time, and as a model for female characters in the works of Ibsen and Bjørnson.[4]

The scope and character of the correspondence

Apart from the birthday greeting from 1899 the twenty-two letters from Georg Brandes to Magdalene Thoresen cover the period from July 1865 to January 1868.[5] For most of this time she lived in Christiania [Oslo] after having spent some few years in Copenhagen, in the hope of a literary breakthrough there. A letter from Georg Brandes, dated 15 May 1866, reveals that they met for the first time in July 1864 at Klampenborg on the outskirts of Copenhagen, when he was 22 and she was 45,[6] but it seems that the correspondence between them did not start until a year later. Her earliest letter is also dated July 1865. But one may safely deduce from his letter that they had seen each other at least once since their first meeting.

His first letter is reverential, as befits a young man addressing a middle-aged woman who is also a well-known author. He writes: 'Høit ærede Fru Thoresen' (Honorable Mrs Th.). But the tone quickly changes. From his sixth letter on, of July the following year, he often writes to his 'kjære Veninde' (dear friend), with variations like 'Min godt oprigtige alvorlige Veninde' (my very sincere and earnest friend, Sept. 1866), 'Min kjæreste Veninde' (my dearest friend, 30 Oct. 1866), 'Min hjertenskjære Veninde' (my beloved friend, Febr. 1867) and 'Min inderligt kjære Veninde' (my very dear friend, 1 Aug. 1867). Once he writes: 'Min anden Moder! min kjære og elskede Veninde' (My second mother! my dear and beloved friend, 30 Aug. 1867), and one day, when he is angry with her for not having written for some time, he again becomes more formal: 'Kjære Fru Thoresen' (Dear Mrs Th., 16 Jan. 1867). He most often signs his letters 'Deres Georg Brandes'

(Your G.B.; they used the polite, formal form of address, except in some notes from the summer of 1868), sometimes 'Deres Ven'(your friend) before his name or just his initials, once also more cryptically: 'Deres Ven. (De veed nok Navnet, De kjender Røsten)' (Your friend. You guess the name, you know the voice, June 1866).

They soon exchange photographs, something fairly common in those days. And the tone quickly becomes more intimate, the contents likewise – but clearly within certain limits, especially on Brandes' side. He writes about newspaper feuds and literary debates he took part in, about the political situation and the possibility of his being drafted for the Dano-Prussian war, about travels he would like to undertake and people he has met, about his accomplishments and ambitions, and his imperfections. His own life is, naturally, in focus. But he also discusses Magdalene Thoresen's work and her style of writing with her; he is interested in her health and her daughters, and he offers characterizations of her personality; among other things he accuses her of lacking a sense of humour. He approaches her as his motherly friend and comforter, as one who understands him and sees through his false poses, and who elucidates matters for him with her clear opinions (which he sometimes rejects). He scolds her, pretends to be offended by her once in a while, but reassures her that he will always be her devoted friend.

At the same time there are many things he keeps from her, things of a private nature that he cannot or will not tell her: 'Det er mig umuligt, uden at gøre Brud på en Delicatesse, der er mig en Lov, at meddele Dem det ringeste angaaende Naturen af det, der sysselsetter mine Tanker' (It is impossible, without transgressing a sense of delicacy which for me is a law, for me to impart the smallest thing to you of the nature of that which is occupying my thoughts), he writes to her in a letter of 12 April 1867 after his return from Paris, where he had apparently fallen seriously in love and even asked for the hand of the young lady. (At the same time he gives fairly detailed accounts of these events in his letters to his friend Emil Pettersen, so the Law of Delicacy does not seem to have been absolute.) On the ninth of November that year, in the penultimate letter of their correspondence, he writes:

De forundrer Dem med Rette over min lange Taushed. Ak ja vist er der Noget i Veien – ikke for mit gode Forhold til Dem, men for min Ro og min Lykke. Jeg kan ligesaa gjerne sige det, da De dog gjætter det; jeg lever i den desperateste Kjærlighetshistorie hvori Nogen kan leve. Men De vil ei fordre eller vente at jeg skal betroe Papiret mere eller Dem mere paa denne Maade. Min Aands Blufærdighed vilde vaande sig derunder.

(You wonder – rightly – about my long silence. Alas, yes, there is something the matter – not with my good relationship to you, but with my peace and happiness. I may as well tell you, as you will certainly guess it: I am living in the most desperate love affair that anyone could live in. But you will not ask or expect that I confess more to this paper or more to you in this way. The modesty of my spirit would lament at such a thing.)

The letters are friendly, then, without being really intimate, and they are by no means love letters. But although many commentators have drawn attention to Brandes' filial attitude to Magdalene Thoresen, there is no doubt also a certain titillating, flirtatious tone in some of his letters, as when in a letter from Paris in November 1867 he writes about his young female French language teacher, and adds (as if he wants to suggest the opposite) that there is no reason for Magdalene Thoresen to be jealous. Likewise, he describes his successful private lecture evenings for 'en snes unge Damer (for en del av Noblessen)' (a score of young ladies (partly of the nobility)), confiding that he is constantly being inspired by 'de mange smukke Øine' (the many beautiful eyes), or he informs her excitedly about his acquaintance with other beautiful, attractive and amusing ladies.

The letters are fairly long, mostly a couple of pages in print, but some fill twice that space. The longest letters describe a walk on Zealand during a fine summer's day and night, and his experiences and impressions from his stay in Paris between November 1866 and January 1867. Some are written over several days, and may start by describing feelings of *tristesse*, happiness or inner turmoil.

If, for the sake of comparison, we look briefly at Magdalene Thoresen's letters to Brandes, the relationship seems at first sight to have been uneven: against his twenty-two letters, there are seventy-five letters from her to him during approximately the same period. On closer inspection, however, this impression changes, since many of her letters are no more than short notes and invitations, often undated. From what I would term the central period, the years 1866-1868, they wrote almost the same number of letters: there are ten letters by her in 1866 (as against his eleven), six in 1867 (as against his eight) and nine in May to August 1868 (as against his one letter). There is a lacuna in her letters from the summer of 1868 until December, and the tone of the December letter is totally changed. She feels that he is dissatisfied with her and that therefore she should not write; all the same, she ventures to ask him for some practical help. The letter gives the impression that she is trying to sound him out. Judging from some hastily written notes in her hand, probably from the summer of 1868, something happened that led to a rupture in their relationship. From later years there remain only five short letters from Magdalene Thoresen to Brandes; three from 1869, one from New Year 1870 and the last one from February 1872, in which she informs him of a change of address in case he should make good his promise to come and see her. His reply, if there was one, has not been preserved.

What happened?

The relationship between Georg Brandes and Magdalene Thoresen has preoccupied quite a few Brandes scholars, many of whom declare without hesitation that Mrs Thoresen was first and foremost baby snatching. In support of this view they point to a letter that Brandes wrote to his mother in February 1871, in which he complains that Magdalene Thoresen had tried to seduce him while she was staying at Klampenborg – it may have been the summer of 1868 – and that he found this abominable.[7] Henning Fenger, who discusses this topic in *Den unge Brandes* (The Young Brandes), apparently feels sorry for the young man: 'Den store Lucifer [Brandes] var fra første færd en sølle Forfører, et offer for en Megære og ingen Don Juan. Nu havde han Held til at gennemskue fru Th.' (The great Lucifer [Brandes] was from the very start a poor seducer, a prey to the furies and no Don Juan. Now he had the good fortune to unmask Mrs Thoresen.)[8] Francis Bull in his article 'Magdalene Thoresen' (1970) does not agree. He takes it for granted that a sexual relationship had existed between

Brandes and Mrs Thoresen for some months, and finds Brandes' description of her in the letter to his mother less than courteous, in his effort to 'unnskylde seg med å si at han så å si var blitt voldtatt,– noe som vel neppe er den fulle sannhet' (excuse himself by saying that he had more or less been raped – something which was hardly the whole truth).[9]

More interesting than Francis Bull's coming to Magdalene Thoresen's rescue, is the causality he sees between this story (whatever may have happened) and the fact that Brandes hardly ever published anything about her later in his life. I shall return to this point shortly.

As already suggested, Henning Fenger is not the only one to depict Magdalene Thoresen as 'the bird of prey' in this relationship, as a woman who did her utmost to enmesh the young man in her erotic net.[10] Even if there may be a grain of truth in this (a letter from Magdalene Thoresen to Johanne Louise Heiberg of 26 October 1867 has been interpreted in this direction),[11] it seems fair to point out that the young critic may have had his own intentions concerning this relationship, intentions just as honorable or disreputable as hers (if this is the place to pass moral judgment). One of his letters suggests that he had felt a sting of truth in a remark from her about his egoism, for in connection with his request that she reveal to him her personal impression of her son-in-law Henrik Ibsen, for an article he is working on, he writes (2 September 1867):

Har De Ulyst, skal De ikke gjøre det. Og tro dog endelig ikke, hvad De til min Forundring i Deres Brev gav en Antydning af, at jeg er en saadan Egoist, at jeg skulde ville søge Næring og Nytte for mig alene af ethvert Forhold; dertil er jeg om ikke for god saa dog visselig altfor stolt.

(If you don't want to, you shall not do it. And do not believe what you to my surprise suggested in your letter, that I am such an egoist that I should seek nourishment and advantage for myself alone from all relationships: I may not be too good for this, but I am certainly too proud.)

Nevertheless, in a letter to Emil Pettersen written two years earlier, he had said flippantly that he was in need of a Muse, and it did not matter if she was old: 'de gamle have en vis Moderomsorg, som er

Ungdommen meget tjenlig. Var der En, som var saa smuk som Fru Thoresen og som havde saa meget tilovers for mig som hun, skulde det være mig meget kjært' (the old show a certain motherly care, which is very useful for youth. I should be immensely pleased were there one as beautiful as Mrs. Thoresen and one that cared for me as much, 16 December 1865).

It is advisable not to attach too much importance to such youthful foolishness, but for a young eagle (it is very difficult to see Brandes as a mouse or some other easy game for a bird of prey), Magdalene Thoresen may have been useful in the attempt to build a desirable image of himself and to find his literary identity. It seems that he was aware of this, at least retrospectively, judging from phrases in the friendly birthday letter for her eightieth anniversary, and more ambiguously – in the presentation in *Levned*.

The fact that Brandes did not keep up the contact between them that Magdalene Thoresen seems to have desired may have been due not only to his pronounced distaste (viz. the letter to his mother), but also to the fact that his life took a new direction from the end of the 1860s. He became involved in love affairs with other women, and he developed acquaintances of greater intellectual value to him. In the autumn of 1871 he delivered his lectures on 'Hovedstrømninger i det nittende Aarhundredes Literatur' (Main Currents in Nineteenth-Century Literature) at the University of Copenhagen, and all at once found himself a well-known, famous and infamous figure of the Nordic Parnassus. The correspondence with a middle-aged woman, whom he came to consider as not very knowledgeable, vaguely romantic, religious and annoyingly emotional, could hardly be important to him any longer.

Literary criticism

Relatively early in their correspondence Georg Brandes and Magdalene Thoresen start to discuss literary matters. At the beginning of September 1866 he thanks her for a short story she has sent him. It was 'Pilt-Ola', which was to be published just before Christmas in the anthology *Vintergrønt* (Wintergreen) edited by Brandes's friend Christian Richardt. In 1873 Magdalene

Thoresen had this story reprinted in her collection *Nyere Fortællinger* (New Stories). Brandes starts by praising it:

Fortællingen gjør Dem helt igjennem Ære: de opstillede Forhold have Sandhed og Dybde, ere sete med et sjælekyndigt Øie og skildrede med levende og stærke Farver. Der er rystende Alvor i Fremstillingen af Kampen mellem Ola og Thore og i Dødsscenens simple Poesie. Den lille Vise er holdt i den rette Stil og Dictionen er paa mange Steder charakteristisk og ny.

(The story really does you credit; the relationships portrayed have truth and depth, are seen with a soul-searching eye and depicted with living and strong colours. There is moving earnestness in the description of the fight between Ola and Thore and in the simple poetry of the death scene. The little song is cast in the right style and the diction is in many ways characteristic and new.)

But Brandes also has some objections. In his opinion the story would benefit from being reworked especially with a view to style. He and Christian Richardt would be happy to suggest amendments. Then he goes on to what he calls 'en uforskammet Udtalelse om Deres Talent, betragtet i sin Almindelighed' (an impudent utterance about your talent, generally speaking). First he emphasizes that she possesses the most important prerequisite, 'en vingestærk Phantasie' (a strong-winged imagination). On the other hand she lacks 'en vis bon-sens' (a certain sensibility):

Deres store Omrids ere altid skarpe og klare; men i Enkeltheder, i Metaphorer og Billeder viser De ikke bestandig den mandlige Sky for det Ubegrænsede og Dunkle, De holder ikke meget af at lade et lille Naturtræk staa, ufortolket, i dets hele Simpelhed, De giver tidt en symboliserende Omskrivning, der er mere eller mindre vilkaarlig.

(Your broad outlines are always sharp and clear, but in details, in metaphors and images you do not always shrink from what is undefined and vague, as would a man; you do not like to leave a small feature of nature uninterpreted, in its total simplicity, you often turn to paraphrasing, employing symbols that seem to be more or less haphazard.)

The expression 'den mandlige Sky for det Ubegrænsede og Dunkle' is strikingly similar to the vocabulary of post-structuralist discussions on gender and language; in Julia Kristeva's terminology one might say that Magdalene Thoresen had not completely emerged from the semiotic, pre-Oedipal 'female' chaos, that she had not quite submitted to the Law of the Father. It may be seminal to study her works from this angle. However, in our connection the most important point is that Brandes establishes the dichotomy male – female in his discussion of literature, and that he even at this early stage, although with different phraseology, suggests that Magdalene Thoresen is 'langt mere Kvinde end Forfatterinde'.

His other letters reveal further that he has quite fixed ideas about the two genders. In the Paris letter of February 1867 he writes, after having spoken generally of his appreciation of French theatre, philosophy and literature:

... jeg vil heller fortælle Dem lidt om de Mennesker, jeg omgikkes, da jeg veed, at De som Kvinde nødvendigvis foretrækker saadant Noget som Personligheder, Ansigter, Typer af det virkelige Liv for det Andet man kalder Videnskab, Kunst og upersonlige aandelige Indtryk.

(... instead I will tell you a little about the people I met, as I know that you, being a woman, necessarily prefer things like personalities, faces, characters from real life to what is usually called science, art and impersonal spiritual impressions.)

We shall return to Brandes's comments on her literary works, however. In his letter of September 1866 he goes on to say that she uses too many Norwegian words and idioms, something which has a tiresome effect on Danish readers. When asked to give examples, he does so in a letter of 6 October, at the same time pinpointing his main objection, that there is 'noe Urent' (something impure) in her style, and that she ought to be more careful and fastidious in choosing 'mellem de utallige Billeder og Lignelser, der bestandigt strømme ind over Deres Phantasie' (between the innumerable images and similes that are forever flooding your imagination). But he ends by saying: 'De er i det Hele god som De er, for god for Mange' (On the whole you are good as you are, too good for many). The overall impression is encouraging, even if it becomes clear that his stylistic ideal is very different from hers – because she is so 'kvindelig', and he is a man?

Later he informs her of the reception of 'Pilt-Ola' in Denmark:

Jeg kan fornøie Dem med at fortælle, at Deres lille Fortælling Pilt-Ola har gjort en ganske overordentlig Lykke. De forskjelligste Mskr [Mennesker], og Folk, der ikke anede at jeg kjendte Noget til Dem, have prist den for mig, som det bedste Prosa-Stykke, den forresten kummerlig vintergrønne Bog indeholdt.

(I may delight you by telling you that your little story 'Pilt-Ola' has had an overwhelming success. The most diverse people, people that had no idea of my acquaintance with you, have praised it to me as the best piece of prose this incidentally miserable wintergreen book contains, 12 April 1867.)

And he adds:

Skal jeg, Deres gamle Kritiker og Beundrer sige Noget om Deres Fortælling, da er det, at medens andre slige skjænker den største Nydelse, mens man læser dem (som f. Ex. Goldschmidts) ved det soignerede og smagfulde Foredrag, men ikke erindres uden naar man har Bogen i Haanden, virker Deres allerstærkest naar mange smaa Enkeltheder ere glemte og Figurerne staae levende og virkelige for Phantasien.

(Should I, your old critic and admirer say something about your story, it is that while others offer the greatest pleasure while being read (e.g. Goldschmidt's) through their polished and tasteful discourse, but are not remembered unless one has the book in one's hand, yours is most effective when many small details are forgotten and the characters stand living and real before one's imagination.)

This is the same type of criticism that Brandes has previously offered, and again it seems that he attaches more importance to her fine powers of characterization than to her, in his opinion, somewhat uneven style. However, Magdalene Thoresen paid attention to his detailed critique concerning some descriptions of scenery in 'Pilt-Ola', so that her style seems more stringent in the 1873 edition of *Nyere Fortællinger*.

The only other literary work of hers that Brandes mentions in these letters is 'Min Bedstemoders Fortælling' (My Grandmother's Story), which was originally published in the anthology *Ved Løvfaldstid* (When the Leaves Fall) in the autumn of 1867 and ten years later reprinted in Magdalene Thoresen's collection *Livsbilleder* (Images of Life), but in a greatly altered version. The story had moved him deeply, Brandes writes on 9 November 1867, adding: 'Hvori ligger det, at enhver god Bog synes saa mærkelig at spille ind i Læserens eget Liv. Her endog indtil Enkeltheder. Denne Fortælling er jo desværre det Eneste, som duer i Bogen' (Why is it that any good book seems in such a wondrous way to play a part in the reader's own life. In this case even down to details. This story is, unfortunately, the only one of value in this book).[12]

'Min Bedstemoders Fortælling' had not been published when Brandes wrote his essay in *Illustreret Tidende* one and a half years earlier. This essay is primarily biographical in its approach, a fact which he underlines. But he finds space for a brief characterization of her literary works, which he regards as belonging to the national genre of 'folkelivsskildring' (stories of folk life). He finds that Magdalene Thoresen possesses all the prerequisites necessary to succeed in this field:

Som Kvinde har hun besiddet den Modtagelighed, der maatte til for at hun, en Datter af et andet Folk, skulde kunne leve sig ind i den norske Natur og fornemme det sproglige Udtryks ganske særegne Form og Farve *saa* klart og reent, at hun kunde gjengive det uforvansket. Som Barn af Almuen har hun havt det sjeldne Indblik i Bondens Sjæl og den dybe Sympathi med hans Stræben, som ene muliggjør en Fremstilling af hans Liv, der vil være Andet og Mere end ethnografisk. Og som digterisk Aand har hun eiet en Phantasi, der netop udmærker sig ved den Evne til at løse store og faste Skikkelser ud fra Stemningens Baggrund og lade dem vandre deres Gang paa egen Haand, som svarer til det Materiale, hun behandler.

(As a woman she possesses the impressionability necessary for her, a daughter of another people, to become attuned to the natural surroundings of Norway and sense the very special form and colour of the linguistic expression *so* purely and clearly that she could imitate it without flaw. As a child of the common people she owned a rare insight into the peasant's soul and the deep sympathy with his toil which is indispensable for a portrayal of his life that pretends to be other and more than merely ethnographic. And as a poetic spirit she possesses an imagination that is outstanding in its ability to lift great and vividly realized figures from out of the evocative background and let them wander their way on their own, in a manner compatible with the material she treats.)

His presentation is full of praise, more so here than in later comments in his letters to Magdalene Thoresen herself – we might remember his critique of her use of Norwegian idioms in 'Pilt-Ola'

– and perhaps also more laudatory than he felt he could maintain in later years, as a man of The Modern Breakthrough. In his obituary he places her admirers among the conservatives.

Posthumous assessment

Consequently Brandes does not repeat this literary evaluation from *Illustreret Tidende* in *Levned*, which will now be the object of this discussion. On the other hand, several of the personal characterizations from the letters of his youth reappear in his memoirs. He had reported some of his opinions to her directly, for example those concerning her ardour and passion, both features that indirectly suggest a lack of control and moderation. An eternal topic of discussion between them turned on the question of which to prefer, French or German philosophy and literature. Even as a young man Brandes loathed 'Tydskeriet' (letter dated 26 November 1866), which he associated with sentimentality, romanticism and vagueness, while she admired the German fervency. Therefore his 'kolde Forstandighed' (cold common sense) must be to her a 'Torn i Øiet' (thorn in the eye), he suggests (2 September 1866):

Ak jeg frygter for, at en uklar Begeistring, der har et Ord at hviske baade til Følelsen og Phantasien, men lader det Allerhelligste: Fornuften i Stikken, vilde være Dem langt kjærere, hvis De kjente den i personlig Skikkelse, end min haardnakkede og upoetiske Rationalisme.

(Alas, I fear that a vague enthusiasm, that has a word to whisper both to sentiment and imagination, but leaves out the most sacrosanct, common sense, would be far dearer to you had you known it in the shape of a person, than my stubborn and unpoetic rationalism.)

In *Levned* he transforms this fear into an evaluation: 'Uklare Følelser frastødte hende ikke, men al skarp og spids Forstand ... Franskhed var hende imod ... I alle Spørgsmaal om rene Tanketing var hun umaadelig uklar' (She did not detest muddled sentiments, but all kinds of sharp and pointed reason ... Everything French repelled her... In all questions concerning purely intellectual processes she was immensely vague).[13]

However, he continues to admire her ability to understand and assess people. In his letters to her he says repeatedly that she has seen him and seen through him as no other person. She has discovered his faults and imperfections, but also his aspirations and unclear dreams. She tells him that he is self-indulgent, which he must admit to, and she takes him aback by stating that 'det mere er Poesien end Videnskaben, der kan begeistre mig [Brandes] eller løfte mit Sind' (it is poetry rather than science that makes me enthusiastic or lifts my spirit, 30 August 1867); however, he argues against her at this point by contending that he is 'en stor Skepticus ligeoverfor Idealismen i Videnskaben' (a great sceptic concerning idealism in science). If he can tolerate her corrections and admonitions, it is because he knows that 'De – selv sandhedskjærlig – ogsaa troer paa Andres Sandhedskjærlighed, og fordi De, naar De dadler mig, tidt rammer mig saa sikkert, at jeg gjerne hører Dem og lydigt bøier mit Hoved for Deres rene og strenge Tale' (you yourself loving truth, believe in other people's love of truth and because you, when you call me to account, often strike home so precisely that I desire to hear you and obediently bow my head to your pure and critical discourse, 3 October 1866).

In *Levned* he also praises her for being 'en fin, næsten genial Sjælekender, der stundom overraskede ved de træffende Ting, hun sagde, og forbavsede ved sit rigtige Skøn i vanskelige, psykologiske Tilfælde' (a fine, almost brilliant connoisseur of souls, who sometimes surprised by her precise remarks and astonished by her exquisite discernment in difficult psychological cases).[14] But he does not state here that she unfolded this psychological insight in her literary works, as he had done in a letter to her and also in the presentation in *Illustreret Tidende*.[15] This ability of hers has, however, been fruitful for him personally, Brandes says retrospectively, as he came to see himself with her eyes and therefore in a new light. To Mrs Thoresen he was above all a rational being, to others, passionate or determined by his will. 'I alt dette laa en Opfordring til selv at naa fuld Klarhed over mit virkelige Væsen' (All this encouraged me to try and reach full insight into my real self), he says, and concludes that he must find the answer in the fruits of his work.[16]

The image of the ideal woman

Brandes may have had many reasons for not presenting Magdalene Thoresen's literary works in *Levned*, and concentrating instead on her character, her attitudes and her faculties. As already suggested, he may not have wanted to confirm his evaluation of her from *Illustreret Tidende*, but submitting a totally different assessment at this later stage would amount to admitting that his original literary judgment had not been sound. Therefore it would seem better to be silent.

Another reason may be that he did not know the many and varied works she published in the 1870s and 1880s well enough to be able to say anything interesting about them. Nothing seems to indicate that he had read the four dramas, the eight collections of short stories, an extended historical novel and the three widely praised volumes of travel sketches from the west coast of Norway and from The Land of the Midnight Sun (an epithet Magdalene Thoresen seems to have coined).

A third reason may be the one that Francis Bull suggests in his article: the disappointment and disgust resulting from her erotic initiative may have made Brandes decide not to have anything more to do with her. If Bull is right, his strong reaction may perhaps be explained by the suggestion that Magdalene Thoresen at this point destroyed the ideal image Brandes had created of her.

When Brandes praises Magdalene Thoresen in his letters to her, and this he does quite often, he especially emphasizes her 'rene og strenge Kvindelighed' (her pure and strict womanliness). In a letter from Stockholm, in July 1866, he writes: 'jeg længtes fra Alt det Stygge, Haarde, Tillukkede og Aabenmundede, hvoraf Verden er saa fuld, efter Renhed og Kvindelighed, efter en Følelse paa eengang dyb, ædru og sanddru. Derfor vendte min Sjæl sig uvilkaarligt til Dem' (I long to escape from everything ugly, hard, buttoned-up and gossipy of which the world seems so full, I long for purity and womanliness, for a sentiment at once deep, sober and truthful. Therefore my soul naturally turned to you).

It is remarkable how in his letters Brandes glorifies Magdalene Thoresen as a mother figure, pure, truthful and demanding, who may be his spiritual star. Expressions like 'ædel og udviklet Kvinde' (noble and fully-developed woman, 9 August 1866), 'en Valkyrres Aand og en Moders Hjerte' (the spirit of a Valkyrie and the heart of a mother, *ibid.*), 'De har med deres Ord grebet mig saaledes i Hjertet, som De ellers kun har grebet mig med Deres Blik' (with your words you have gripped my heart in such a way as you have previously only gripped me with your glance, 3 October 1866), 'det er mig et Savn, at undvære Deres kjærlige Breve' (I miss your loving letters, 29 July 1867), 'Veed De hvad jeg foruden Deres Kvindehjertes varme Følelse finder i Deres Brev? ... Jeg finder Visdom' (Do you know what I find in your letters, besides the warm sentiments of a woman's heart? ... I find wisdom, 30 August 1867) all underscore this attitude. It seems safe to assume that Magdalene Thoresen incarnates for Brandes the idea of the virginal woman characterized by chastity, purity and honesty. Some comments about one of her daughters in a letter of 18 May 1867 emphasize this point: 'Elskeligheden straaler hende ud af Øinene og der er kommen en Alvor og dyb sædelig Kvindelighed over hele hendes Væsen, som ganske har vundet mit Hjerte' (Amiability glows in her eyes and earnestness and a deep chaste womanliness have suffused her being: this has completely won my heart).

May the psychological cause of the rupture in the summer of 1868 be that this ideal image was pulverized as the vestal priestess he himself had created (for her own letters seem to contradict this image somewhat, in that they seem rather sensuous) in a very direct way revealed that she was a woman of flesh and blood? He calls her his 'anden Moder', and often underlines the filial character of his relationship to her, for example jokingly in the already discussed letter to his friend Emil Pettersen of December 1865. Her fall from Madonna to Harlot may have been too much of a shock to him. The very fact that the letter to his mother in which he describes Magdalene Thoresen's attack on his virtue is written with great emotion even several years after the incident, seems to substantiate such a suggestion. There may also have been something frighteningly incestuous in the situation.[17]

Even so, perhaps the worst aspect of it all lay somewhere else. Brandes starts the letter to his mother by complaining that Magdalene Thoresen had not been truthful to him. She had not told him that she had been travelling abroad as the wife of another man (Dr Danielsen) while still married to Thoresen; she had always spoken very warmly of her husband. But she had told him, Brandes goes on to say, that she had wanted to be Bjørnstjerne Bjørnson's mistress and that she had not been able to understand why he had rejected this offer even though he was married. Magdalene Thoresen has thus revealed herself to be neither chaste nor honest, but immoral and full of lies. So what is left of the high ideal Brandes had erected of her?

Brandes' reaction may seem dramatic and exaggerated in view of the fact that by the time he wrote this letter to his mother, in 1871, he had already had certain experiences with married women. But they had probably not been mother figures for him. His abusive language seems to indicate that exceedingly strong and perhaps unconscious emotions had been involved. If he can no longer trust her, the woman he had called his second mother, who can be trusted? One is reminded of the Norwegian medieval ballad 'Olav og Kari', in which Olav's mother asks him how grass can grow if a son can't believe the words of his mother; nothing less than life itself is at stake.

If this is so, why should Brandes' understanding of Magdalene Thoresen as a person influence his perception of her literary works? One of his early letters to Emil Pettersen may perhaps throw some light on this question. Brandes writes (2 October 1865) that he has been to see Magdalene Thoresen, and that she had talked 'i eet væk om Kjærlighed og det i sine Døtres og en gammel Jomfrus Nærværelse' (incessantly of love, even in the presence of her daughters and an old maid). The tone is one of disapproval. Then he goes on to make a more general observation:

I den Anledn. tænkte jeg paa, at saa vist som det er, at det, vi kalde Kvindelighed, tidt er *dyrekøbt* af Kvinden og derfor i sand Forstand ogsaa af Manden, saavist duer det ei for en Kvinde at være Forfatterinde. Denne Digterinteresse for Lidenskaberne er fordømt ukvindelig. Men jeg er dog ei vis paa om den ikke i det Hele er umenneskelig, saa det ei er saa meget ukvindeligt at være Forfatterinde som umenneskeligt at være Digter.

(In that connection I was thinking that, since what we call womanliness often is acquired at a cost by the woman and therefore in actual fact also by the man, it does not do for a woman to be an author. This authorial interest in the passions is damned unfeminine. However, I am not certain that it is not altogether inhuman, and so it would seem to be less unfeminine to be an authoress than inhuman to be an author.)

Brandes's ambivalence towards Magdalene Thoresen was present from the start, but the attraction was originally stronger than the disgust. In youthful enthusiasm he gave her a promise which we, knowing the development of their relationship, may perhaps find somewhat comic today:

Der var Meget hos Dem, der tiltrak mig, Noget, der snarere frastødte, men hele Deres Væsen bandt sig fast i min Erindring, og dette Væsen har jeg nu gjennem ikke mange Timers Samliv lært saaledes at kjende, at De sandelig aldrig, mens jeg lever, skal staae ene som Kvinde, hvis De nogensinde maatte ønske at stille en Ridder i Marken.

(There was much about you that attracted me, something that I found rather repellant, but your whole being made an imprint on my memory, and this being I have now learnt to know through our few hours of togetherness in such a way that as long as I live you shall never stand alone as a woman, should you at any time require a knight to fight for you, 15 May 1866.)

In a way – in his own way – Brandes kept this promise, in so far as what he finally did in *Levned* was to carve a rune to her 'Kvindelighed'. The older Brandes was apparently able to regard a woman's sexual life and possible double moral standards with greater tolerance than the twenty-nine year old could muster. As a mature man he could be generous enough to praise Magdalene Thoresen for being 'kvindelig', and to thank her 'for Deres hele varme, rige Kvindelighed', as he did in his birthday letter in 1899. But it was hardly meant as praise when he pronounced as his final, public opinion that she was 'langt mere Kvinde end Forfatterinde.'

Notes

1. The letter dated 2 June 1899 is kept in the Brandes Archive, The Royal Library, Copenhagen, reg.nr. NKS 2065, 2. Several letters from Magdalene Thoresen to Brandes can also be found here.
2. Pil Dahlerup has commented on Brandes' presentation of Magdalene Thoresen in *Det moderne gennembruds kvinder* (Copenhagen, 1983), p. 72. She also writes about Brandes' obituaries in her essay 'Sol', siger De – hvor skulle jeg få den fra? Det moderne gennembruds kvinder', in Hans Hertel, ed., *Kønsroller i litteraturen* (Copenhagen, 1975), p. 36. His obituary of Magdalene Thoresen was published in *Politiken*, 29 March 1903, and signed 'G. B.'. Here he characterizes her as 'en mærkelig Personlighed med stærke Følelser og ualmindelig digterisk Evne' (a striking personality with strong feelings and uncommon poetic faculties), at the same time suggesting that she would never have become a writer were it not for Bjørnson and his peasant tales.
3. Georg Brandes, *op. cit.*, p. 149.
4. Georg Brandes, *Levned*, vol. I (Copenhagen and Kra, 1905), p. 151. See also Kristian Elster Jr., *Fra tid til anden. Bøker og digtere*, (Kra, 1920), p. 68, Vilhelm Andersen, *Illustreret dansk litteraturhistorie*, vol. IV. (Copenhagen, 1925), p. 119 and Francis Bull, 'Magdalene Thoresen. En dansk-norsk kvinneskjebne' in his *Land og lynne* (Oslo 1970).
5. The letters can be found in the Manuscript Collection, University Library, Oslo (Bs. 154).
6. In *Levned* (p. 148) Brandes makes her one year older at their first meeting.
7. The letter is quoted in Henning Fenger: *Den unge Brandes. Miljø, venner, rejser, kriser* (Copenhagen, 1957), p. 57. Brandes's relationship with Magdalene Thoresen is discussed pp. 53-57 and p. 162.
8. *Den unge Brandes* (Copenhagen, 1957), p. 57.
9. Francis Bull, *op. cit.*, p. 106. In a short preface Bull states that he partly utilizes oral sources that may not be reliable in each and every detail, but that he includes them all the same as they can add to the picture of Magdalene Thoresen's fate and personality.
10. Jørgen Knudsen offers the same view in *Georg Brandes. Frigørelsens vej. 1842-77* (Copenhagen, 1985), where he writes: 'Hun [M.Th.] har sværmet for sin yndige unge ven på hunedderkoppens fasong' (she has wooed her sweet young friend in the fashion of the female spider, p. 84). Furthermore, he suggests that a young man who 'så pinligt og så enfoldigt lader sig misbruge, må endnu mangle meget i selvstendighed og modenhed' (in such a compromising and naive manner lets himself be misused, must still lack a lot in the way of

independence and maturity, p. 85).
11. The letter to Johanne Louise Heiberg is reprinted in *Breve fra Magdalene Thoresen 1855-1901* (Copenhagen, 1919), p. 79-84. Before commenting on her relationship with Brandes she discusses her erotic nature, her nature of 'a bird of prey' ['Rovfuglenatur']. Concerning Brandes she focuses upon his 'Væsen', his being, of which she wants to have her part. Maybe this has given rise to a contamination, in some people's minds?
12. *Ved Løvfaldstid* was edited by Bjørnstjerne Bjørnson and also contained contributions by himself and Andreas Munch, Theodor Kierulf, Christopher Janson and Lorentz Dietrichson. For a closer analysis of 'Min Bedstemoders Fortælling', see my essay 'En kvinneprotest mot Magdalene Thoresen' in *16 skribenter søker en leser. En kollegial hilsen til Willy Dahl på 60-årsdagen 26. mars 1987*, Eigenproduksjon nr. 30, Nordisk institutt, University of Bergen.
13. *Levned*, p. 150.
14. *Levned*, p. 151.
15. Harald Næss has drawn my attention to the fact that Knut Hamsun was interested in the works of Magdalene Thoresen, and that it was above all her insight into people's psychology that he admired. In an interview in *Stavanger Avis*, 13 March 1891, Jens Tvedt reported that Hamsun had told him: 'Magdalena Thoresen dikta for diktinga si eiga skuld. Ho fortalde ikkje merkverdige hendingar, men om dei fine rørslene i menneskesjela der "sprog og form og tone smelter sammen til et stemningsrikt dikt"' (M.Th. was writing for the sake of writing. She did not recount marvellous events, but depicted the fine movements in the human soul 'in which language and form and tone blend together into a poem full of sentiment').
16. *Levned*, p. 152.
17. This idea was suggested to me by Jørgen Knudsen at the Norwich conference on Nordic Letters, and it seems rather obvious once pointed out.

5

'Six Worms and Nine Bees':
The Vocabulary of Strindberg's Letters and Literary Works from the 1880s

Kerstin Dahlbäck
University of Stockholm

The title of this essay – '"Six Worms and Nine Bees": The Vocabulary of Strindberg's Letters and Literary Works from the 1880s' – could well be supplemented with the more seemingly prosaic 'two text corpora compared in computer runs'. In what follows I shall report on just such a computer run; but I need first to outline the background to this project.

During the 1980s I worked alone on a project that was partly financed by the Swedish National Research Foundation for the Humanities and Social Sciences. There were two principal tasks involved. One was to encode all the printed and unprinted letters of Strindberg (about 10,000 are extant) and to produce concordances of the wordstock. This material is now in a data bank at the Institution for the Swedish Language, formerly known as Språkdata, in Gothenburg from where it is accessible on the internet. The second task was to write a monograph on August Strindberg's letters.

In my book *Ändå tycks allt vara osagt. August Strindberg som brevskrivare* (Everything still seems to be unsaid. August Strindberg as Correspondent),[1] I place Strindberg in an epistolary context, give a general account of the development of correspondence and of the postal revolution of the nineteenth century. I discuss categories of letters and explain these categories while also producing the relevant statistics of, for example, the number of letters per decade, year and addressee, the number of addressees per decade and year, distribution by sex, nationality, etc. The most important chapters of the monograph are devoted to analyses of individual letters and exchanges of letters with the aim of characterizing Strindberg's epistolary style; this is in fact a matter of several styles which change between different periods and addressees. In particular I focus on the genre characteristics of an author's letters in general and Strindberg's in particular, their 'dual character' of communicative and literary text. Throughout I pay attention to the literary character of the letters and to the relationship between the letters and Strindberg's literary works. This aspect is refined in the concluding chapter in which I look at Strindberg's various 'epistolary' projects, i.e. the more or less autobiographical works of fiction that are wholly or partly based on his letters and which are close to them. In this chapter I also discuss genre problems and elucidate Strindberg's letters in the light of the increasingly intensive theoretical treatment of the narrative self, wherever it appears, in the letters, journals, autobiographies and first-person novels. At this point I should like to deal briefly with these two aspects that are treated at greater length in my book before presenting the computer run and its results.

The Strindberg letter project is a result of the high value that he placed upon his letters. He was aware not only of their importance to biography and literary history but counted them as part of his literary *oeuvre*. In the various 'wills' pertaining to his literary remains drawn up at various moments of crisis in his life the letters are included as an essential component. Strindberg was aware from an early age of the close relationship between letters and literature and as early as the 1860s and 70s he used his correspondence as a means of developing his literary style.

In 1875 he gave his first wife, Siri von Essen, who was then still married to the aristocratic guards' officer Carl Gustaf Wrangel, a correspondence course in how one becomes an author by writing letters. Strindberg acted with the tacit agreement of Siri's husband and his intention was that she should abstain from her acting ambitions which were unsuited to her position in society, and concentrate instead on becoming an author. There is good reason to consider the love letters which August and Siri exchanged after her divorce – perhaps the most beautiful love letters ever written in Swedish – as an element in Siri's education as an authoress. The 'letter trick' – i.e., pretending to write letters and then erasing the dedications and the dates to reveal a short story – was afterwards recommended by Strindberg to other presumptive authors.

During the 1880s Strindberg made use of letter writing as a way of 'producing literature without fiction' which he then put a premium on and in the 1890s he used it – I am thinking primarily of the letters he addressed to Leopold Littmansson and Torsten Hedlund – to practice a new style and new subjects in order to try out a modernistic style, one rich in associations.

In itself this is not necessarily remarkable. Many young authors have developed their powers of observation and their narrative abilities by writing letters – Fyodor Dostoievsky was one such, as was his Swedish disciple Hjalmar Bergman. Nor is the transfer of phrases between literary works and letters unique or surprising – Charles Dickens is an example as is Pushkin's Arzama circle in St. Petersburg. And in epistolary novels, fictitious letters have traded as authentic and authentic letters as fiction.

When in the middle of the 1880s Strindberg suggested to his publisher, Bonniers, that he should publish his correspondence from the 1870s with Siri von Essen under the title *Han och hon* (He and She), this was in accord with the ambitions of the Modern Breakthrough, with its concern for documentary authenticity. He could refer to several authors who had brazenly transposed documentary into literary material. One source of inspiration was probably the Danish actress Johanne Louise Heiberg who had, in 1883, published *Peter Andreas Heiberg og Thomasine Gyllembourg. En beretning, støttet paa efterladte breve* (Peter Andreas Heiberg and Thomasine Gyllembourg. A Tale based on their Letters), of which there was a copy among the book collection that Strindberg sold in 1892.

Strindberg was, I make bold to claim, exceptional in his conscious and intensive re-use of the letters. This was facilitated both by his lack of respect for genre (for example, he offered to let

Bonniers publish *Han och hon* either as a novel or as part of his autobiography) and of the extraordinary literary quality of his letters – even given the fact that they are the work of a practising author.

Other examples of what I have called 'letter projects' are the novel *En dåres försvarstal* (A Madman's Defence) in which the same letters were used, *Kvarstadsresan* (The Sequestration Journey) in which a fictive August Strindberg writes letters that are not identical with but similar to the letters that Strindberg himself actually wrote to Carl Larsson, Jonas Lie and others during the period when he was on trial for blasphemy over the collection of short stories in *Giftas* (Getting Married, 1884), the short story 'Hjärnornas kamp' (The Battle of the Brains) which made use of the correspondence with the young sociologist Gustaf Steffen from 1886, and *Klostret* (The Cloister) which was commenced in 1898 and in which Strindberg renders and quotes letters exchanged with his second wife, Frida Uhl. It is probable that while he was writing the letters to Frida, Strindberg was expecting to publish them in due course in a new *Han och hon*.

Of interest in this connection are, of course, the letters that Strindberg wrote to the theosophist Torsten Hedlund during the 1890s, in particular the sequence of eight letters on manuscript paper which are numbered consecutively pages one to fifty-nine that he wrote during July 1896. Strindberg informed Hedlund that these letters were a substitute for a book that he did not have the time and peace to write and he gave the addressee the right to publish them. Scholars have considered them a sketch for the autobiographical novel *Inferno* (1897).

Yet another striking example of Strindberg's use of letters is the play *Kristina* (Christina) from the autumn of 1901. His third wife, the Norwegian actress Harriet Bosse, had left him and in a sequence of letters written parallel with the play he flattered her and offered her the title role as a way of persuading her to return. At the same time he painted a very much gloomier picture of Harriet in his so-called *Occult Diary*. But it was only when he was protected by fiction that Strindberg could fully disclose his ambivalent attitude to Harriet and in the relations between the male characters and the queen, behind whom Harriet can be glimpsed, he gives expression to his longing, admiration, disappointment and contempt. The letters are quoted in the dialogue of the play while dialogue from the play reappears in the letters; thus, words and phrases move between the two – indeed, three – texts and consequently appear in new contexts and reference systems. As with his correspondence with Siri von Essen in 1876 and Frida Uhl in 1893, the extant exchange of letters with Harriet Bosse from 1901 exists in an 'edited' state and Strindberg presumably intended to publish it in some form.

The question of the letters' literary status and the genre to which they belong is discussed in my book in connection with the letter-writer, the letter ego, the recipient and the text. Here I can only emphasize some of the matters that I considered there.

Strindberg is, as Michael Robinson has noted in his study *Strindberg and Autobiography*, continually occupied with 'writing his ego'.[2] This he does both in his literary works and in his letters. At the same time as his plays, novels and poems are unusually autobiographical in nature (both critics of the older school and postmodernist commentators are agreed on this), the letters – as Strindberg himself pointed out – are unreliable as sources. His letters fictionalize his ego and are endowed with aesthetic and mythical dimensions. This is achieved by exposing the self alongside figures such as Jesus, Hamlet and Werther who are given a figurative and emphasizing function, or by placing it in situations which are portrayed with symbolic overtones and references to his own writing and to other authors. Like the German poet and letter writer Heinrich von Kleist Strindberg created a succession of 'blödigkeitstopoi' in order to portray the letter writer's loneliness, rejection and suffering.

While the letter writer is extratextual the 'I' of the letter is an integral part of the text. I consider the signatory of the letters a hybrid of these. Analogously, there are two addressees that exist within and outside the text of the letter respectively. The intratextual addressee lives in a hard-to-define symbiosis with the 'I' of the letters. The extratextual addressee also raises problems. The form of address may have a representative function. This is very evident when Strindberg is writing to his daughter Kerstin but actually addressing his mother-in-law; more subtly when we latter day readers are faced with Strindberg's letters. Letters from authors are, perhaps, never wholly private but, consciously or unconsciously, aimed at a wider public – over time. This means that letters from authors aim beyond the stated addressee and beyond the time in which they are composed, that they exceed their 'psychosocial terms of production' and have 'the ability to escape the intentional horizon that limits the author', to borrow Ricoeur's terminology. The letter can be 'decontextualized' and then 'recontextualized' when, a century later, we provide it with a new context and thereby liberate an aesthetic dimension out of the rhetoric whose primary task was to persuade, to inform, etc.

The genre to which the letters belong has been discussed with reference to the letter writer, the addressee and – most suitably in my opinion – the text of the letters. Their literary status, it has been claimed, depends on their complexity. Strindberg's letters fulfil stringent requirements as to complexity. Strindberg exploited the full expressive resources of the language, varying denotative and informative passages with connotative and suggestive ones. There are a great number of images since reactions, reflections and statements are translated into images and it is not least these images that make the Strindberg letter hard hitting and entertaining. The powerful emotional tension, echoes from other texts – innumerable Biblical references act as a sounding board, for example – and the composition which is both associative and rhetorically exact make Strindberg's letters something more than a mere report from reality.

It thus came naturally to me, after the linguistically oriented monograph, to continue studying the relationship between the literary works and the letters and to look more closely at the stylistic differences between the language of Strindberg's letters and that of his literary works. I shall here present a few advance glimpses from this later project which I am conducting with the help of the large amount of data available on Strindberg – besides the computerized letters, the material generated by some forty volumes of the new national edition which have already appeared.

With the help of the computerized material I shall be able to investigate extensive masses of text in order to answer such questions as: does the style of Strindberg's letters differ in certain respects – vocabulary, syntax, etc. – from the style or styles of his literary works? Can one pinpoint Strindberg's literary style with the help of this sort of comparison?

My new project is at an embryonic stage and here I can only reflect upon and present preliminary results from a limited case study of the letters and the literary works of the 1880s. The material that I have studied comprises the letters from the decade 1881-90 (text corpus 1) and nine prose works from the period: *Det nya riket* (The New Kingdom), *Svenska öden och äventyr* (Swedish Destinies and Adventures) I-II, *Giftas* (Getting Married) I-II, *Tjänstekvinnans son* (The Son of a Servant) I-II, *Utopier i verkligheten* (Utopias in Reality), *Bland franska bönder* (Among French Peasants), *Vivisektioner* (Vivisections), *Skärkarlsliv* (Life in the Skerries), *Blomstermålningar och djurstycken* (Flower Paintings and Animal Pieces) and *I havsbandet* (By the Open Sea) (text corpus 2).

For the time being I have chosen in text corpus 2 to mix literary works in prose with non-literary works – novels and short stories with reportage, essays and autobiography. The selection should give a reasonably accurate picture of Strindberg's writing in the 1880s when, at times, he sought to avoid the so-called 'fabricated' novel (konstruktionsroman) in order not to 'hallucinate', or invent. A different selection would have offered different premises for my comparative studies of the language of the letters and literary works. If I had only chosen fiction, for example, it is probable that certain tendencies in the material would have been emphasized.

To begin with, however, it is necessary to say something about the techniques and material of my study since this entails the analysis of a complicated and often intransigent material with a computer. Thus, after conducting some preliminary manual analyses on the letters and literary texts from the 1880s respectively, the two text corpora were run against each other. The letters from this decade amount to 397,159 words and the chosen literary works to 633,443; in total a matter of more than a million words which is a large, though not a huge, number in the field of computer linguistics.[3]

Strindberg's Vocabulary

355.7610	VÄNLIGA	62	13	582.4420	DÄRFÖR	6	948			
358.4808	PORTFARANDE	70	16	607.7680	AFFÄR	68	10			
359.7031	SKRIFTER	75	18	613.7774	NOUVELLE	47	5			
364.5792	BERLIN	31	9	613.9718	KOMMER	661	416			
365.8283	SVENSKT	37	5	614.5464	LES	72	11			
366.0045	SEPTEMBER	60	12	625.2055	OM	4382	4801			
368.7067	VORO	82	829	637.9809	LA	202	65			
370.5361	RIKET	71	16	640.5062	PENGAR	313	132			
377.5861	TROR	530	372	642.8004	LE	165	46			
384.2241	EMELLERTID	367	219	645.4030	HOPPAS	124	28			
384.3451	JOHAN	6	632	649.4413	SOM	4790	11018			
385.6959	FÖRSKOTT	49	8	663.6875	NU	2738	2682			
386.7225	TIDNINGAR	116	36	671.9326	ALBERT	141	34			
387.7523	SÖK	38	5	688.7249	BOK	257	92			
391.2790	MAN	1093	3144	712.1533	LÄNA	110	21			
396.5048	C	65	13	712.2262	FRANSKA	324	131			
403.4332	SÄNDE	50	8	715.1713	HONOM	517	2520			
404.6459	SITT	156	1086	729.1585	JUL	102	18			
424.3037	GÖR	464	294	741.9405	TRYCKT	129	27			
429.1359	BROR	173	65	776.2330	DE	2240	6384			
430.0322	ÖNSKAR	73	15	779.0243	LÄS	95	15			
430.3944	FÖRETAGET	44	6	782.2416	TEATER	88	13			
430.3944	FÖRFATTERI	44	6	787.3729	DEL	302	110			
431.1061	VÄN	307	159	809.6540	LÖRDAG	64	7			
435.9086	HENNE	141	1099	811.0903	ÄMNAR	59	6			
440.2543	PROGRAM	62	11	816.2019	AFFÄREN	69	8			
449.7733	RESA	255	117	818.5357	BED	86	12			
455.4945	STYCKET	128	38	821.5349	EN	5101	12121			
455.6242	SINA	185	1247	858.0709	JANUARI	55	5			
457.5056	FRANSK	75	15	895.4516	FRU	350	129			
459.4432	GICK	100	1027	902.2101	BÖR	160	34			
464.5605	DITT	265	122	925.4041	ROMAN	95	13			
474.5809	VORE	395	221	925.5240	GÖTEBORG	57	5			
495.0214	KONTANT	51	7	929.7323	PÅ	1527	1137			
495.3198	SÅG	76	1018	930.3575	ANRUD	87	11			
496.1596	BOKEN	176	61	931.8131	OCH	13020	27114			
503.6618	UPP	271	1547	959.5124	RESER	156	31			
516.8771	TIDNING	143	42	965.4782	HANS	313	2436			
517.5932	SADE	58	1002	996.1391	SIN	313	2487			
523.0723	RESAN	118	30	999.2555	VAD	7	1616			
526.6036	TEATERN	189	66	1010.9703	TACKAR	71	7			
555.6518	DANSKA	105	25	1016.3267	SVAR	280	82			
559.6863	MONSIEUR	58	8	1044.9786	ERT	153	28			
560.7935	SVEA	54	7	1053.2997	BLIR	800	428			
566.4130	LÄST	248	98	1090.9975	SKALL	1480	1025			
574.6942	SVENSK	118	28	1099.4331	FÅR	903	502			

Fig.1

Essential comments:

1. The material has not been lemmatized, that is, different paradigms of the words have not been put together. I work, in other words, with so-called graphemes.
2. The words have not been separated into homographemes - i.e., different words with the same spelling have not been separated.
3. The spelling in the two corpora differs - the new national edition uses modern orthography; in the letters, the original spellings have been preserved. This naturally leads to misleading results but appropriate adjustments have been made at all strategic points.
4. Words with a frequency lower than five have been excluded. Obviously this group of words, containing radical neologisms is of interest. I shall devote a special study to it in due course.

Nordic Letters 1870-1910

1143.1947	O	63	5					
1166.0189	ÖDEN	126	18	3907.2398	APRIL	125	6	
1183.6494	BETRÄFFAR	119	16	4218.5711	BJ	2415	1114	
1190.4350	FÖRHOPPNING	111	14	4223.5653	GIFTAS	169	10	
1237.0924	F	104	12	4441.3483	FARVÄL	354	39	
1255.0341	MITT	899	467	4450.9230	TACK	378	44	
1352.3759	REVUE	93	9	4484.8066	FÖRLÄGGARE	155	8	
1424.3067	UTMÄRKT	220	42	4692.7777	MIN	1920	728	
1434.1795	PARIS	354	96	4717.4337	MINA	969	230	
1446.3374	HON	462	3631	4837.2193	BER	353	36	
1464.5750	JUNI	144	19	4845.5884	MARS	171	9	
1487.8967	DIG	1029	525	5006.5808	OKTOBER	141	6	
1496.1144	SVENSKA	454	142	5237.2962	SÄNDER	156	7	
1568.9274	HERR	942	446	5304.6265	M	291	23	
1578.0589	Å	198	32	5456.7869	V	244	16	
1609.5311	LÅT	400	109	5693.0494	BRANDES	174	8	
1657.5197	HADE	364	3714	6202.7243	HÄRMED	233	13	
1682.5003	VILL	1292	695	6331.8193	HAN	1562	14658	
1698.0286	ÄR	5556	5133	7185.1309	OUCHY	207	9	
1709.1976	KORREKTUR	91	7	8506.6626	A	404	28	
1766.9073	STOCKHOLM	365	87	8565.3663	KÄRE	167	5	
1785.7881	ET	139	15	8670.2270	UPPLAGAN	168	5	
1811.6961	BR	759	292	8974.1933	EDER	348	20	
1822.1588	DANMARK	119	11	9082.2091	BRODER	489	38	
1826.5821	O	461	127	10046.0120	B	348	18	
1850.8102	TRYCKA	186	25	10915.0549	SÄNDA	239	8	
1856.0041	DIN	766	292	12455.1863	MIG	4005	1302	
1878.2137	KÄRA	331	70	14837.7824	MANUSKRIPT	295	9	
1948.6666	NI	1698	971	24003.3774	B	352	8	
2002.2273	VAR	1336	6786	31614.4328	JAG	12155	4434	
2006.0648	FR	193	25	41524.9838	P	399	6	
2177.1243	SIG	820	5811	52933.5635	S	665	13	
2302.6916	HAR	3296	2331	55981.0079	DER	735	15	
2304.5718	KAN	1942	1093	83015.5671	D	608	7	
2440.7295	JULI	123	9	329433.6812	HVAD	1117	6	
2483.5949	MAJ	194	21	1860577.8958	AF	3749	12	
2516.1617	VÄNNEN	391	75					
2524.6282	BJÖRNSON	125	9					
2552.9006	KRONOR	408	80					
2724.4559	HÄFTET	105	6					
2879.5419	SNÄLL	247	29					
2918.1654	POLITIKEN	126	8					
3052.8414	ETC	152	11					
3430.4633	DU	3605	2245					
3741.0509	KÖPENHAMN	142	8					
3875.0803	AV	31	6279					

Fig.1 (cont.)

Three separate arrangements of the material were produced:

- an alphabetic word listen giving frequencies of words in the respective corpora;
- a list of words, with frequencies greater than five, that appear only in one of the corpora, i.e. only in the letters or in the literary works;
- a table, constructed using the well known chi-square test, showing the so-called 'p' value of words. The last two pages of this table are reproduced in figure 1.

The p value shows the difference in frequency between the two corpora but does not indicate which corpus shows the highest frequency. This is a measurable variable that is calculated with the help of the following formula:

$$p = \frac{\left(E_{Sk\mathring{a}ne} - N \cdot P_{Sk\mathring{a}ne}\right)^2}{N \cdot P_{Sk\mathring{a}ne}}$$

where Skåne is a randomly selected word
E = frequency in the letters (16)
N = total of words in the letters (397,159)
P = relative frequency in the literary works, i.e. 25: 633,443
N.P = expected frequency in the literary works (i.e. starting from the = 0 - hypothesis, that there is the same frequency in both directions

$$\frac{25}{633443.39715} = 15.6746$$

i.e. (formula in words): p = (frequency in the letters - expected frequency in the literary works)^2; the result divided by the expected frequency in the literary works
i.e. (16 - 15.6746)^2 divided by 15.6746 = 0.68

A low p value for a word means that the word appears with just about the same frequency in both corpora and a high p value indicates a difference between the corpora; frequencies can, of course, be low in both corpora and still generate a high p value.

The values that are generated must, of course, be analyzed and appraised. This can be done with the help of existing concordances of the letters and the literary works; the concordances, in which words are listed alphabetically with their contexts indicated, make it possible for me to take note of the individual contexts of words and to define the words and identify the homographemes.

The statistical pitfalls are legion. I shall indicate a couple of examples: the letter 'O' is used not only in abbreviations such as 't.o.m.' (till och med), 'o. fl.' (och flera) and 'O.H.' (Ola Hansson) but also as the interjection 'O' which appears particularly in the letters that are powerfully rhetorical. With the rhetorical 'O'-style Strindberg had, for example, tried to achieve parity with the Norwegian author Bjørnstjerne Bjørnson.

The relatively high frequency of the colour words 'red' and 'yellow' in the letters depends largely on the fact that Strindberg discusses his novel *Röda rummet* (The Red Room, 1879) and that on several occasions he orders 'Lessebo gul bikupa', his customary yellow manuscript paper.

Analysis of the data in many cases merely confirms more or less self-evident matters. It is entirely natural that many of the values calculated lack interest. But this does not prevent values in other cases confirming suppositions about more intricate matters and, indeed, in their foregrounding central aspects of Strindberg's vocabulary and language that are otherwise difficult to discern. Statistics can sharpen our vision.

It is a matter of detecting patterns and trends in the material with the help of the p values. Certain words and categories appear more frequently in the literary works and others in the letters. I shall comment first on some that predominate in the literary works.

In the 1880s, Strindberg was preoccupied with outer reality which is reflected in the numerous, differentiated names for concrete phenomena in the descriptive literary texts; in the letters, on the other hand, he seldom devotes space to descriptions.

Thus in the literary works there is a considerable preponderance of species names of flora and fauna; perhaps it is a discovery that insects appear sparingly in Strindberg's animal world: in the literary works there are six 'worms', nine 'bees' and an equal number of 'flies' - in the letters only two 'flies' and one 'firefly'. Nouns such as 'water', 'snow', 'earth', 'fire', 'sun', 'air', etc. appear in vastly superior number in the literary works - 'the dew', 'the fog', 'star', 'the star' and 'the stars' appear only there. More 'dreams' appear in the literary works than in the letters - though things may be different in the 1890s - and, leaving physical reality, there 'conscience' appears more regularly. Strindberg was not interested in his own conscience but that of others!

The adjectives he employs are interesting in this context. They are far more abundant in the descriptive works and thus emphasize the specific characters of the two types of text. The most noticeable discrepancy between the letters and the literary texts is the matter of colour words: yellow, gold, blue, red, green, grey, black, etc. occur very much more frequently in the literary works. In this sense the letters are colourless.

That the adverbs 'quite', 'certain' and 'almost' appear more frequently in the literary works may indicate that Strindberg used more nuances there. Though drawing any conclusions at this stage is hazardous; it may just indicate a different choice of words to cover instances that the high frequency of 'partly' and 'probably' in the letters may otherwise be employed to indicate.

On the other hand I dare claim that the greater number of co-ordinating and subordinating conjunctions in the literary works: 'and', 'as', 'regardless of', 'while', 'like', 'for', 'by means of which', etc. indicate a syntax different from that of the letters. While the letters are constructed using short, independent sentences and contractions, the literary works depend on parataxis and hypotaxis.

With words and word categories that are more frequent in the letters one finds that of the ca. 140 words with a p value greater than 500 - a singularly high value indicating an extremely uneven distribution (I have shown the 500 limit in figure 1) - more than 120 are found in the letters and barely 20 in the literary works. The fact that there are so many imbalances where the dominance lies in the letters is probably due to the fact that these contain standardized elements of vocabulary.

Among the formulae characteristic of the letter are, above all, those that pertain to the date, preamble and conclusion - 'Dear', 'Mr', 'Brother' (being a common mode of address among Swedish men), 'thanks', 'thank you' and 'farewell' - but even words such as 'hereby', 'expectation', 'hope', 'answer', 'request' and, if we go beyond figure 1, naturally 'post' and 'letter'.

But words like 'excellent', 'distinguished' and 'kind' are also typical of the letters; from the concordances it is evident that 'distiguished' frequently appears in a standard Swedish formula for concluding a letter (some 300 times in Strindberg's 10,000 letters). And 'kind' is a polite word that Strindberg often uses to soften the demands that he is making of his addressee.

Several of the words in figure 1 - and a very large number of letter words in the study - belong to Strindberg's correspondence with his publisher. Examples include 'manuscript', 'edition', 'publisher', 'proof' while even 'offer', 'transaction' and 'crown' (krona) belong to the same sphere. From Strindberg's perspective, authorship included business transactions. Strindberg's correspondence with his publishers was particularly lively in the 1880s and it is hardly surprising that such vocabulary makes itself so strongly felt in this material.

The letter's character of communication or address in a 'now' situation is demonstrated by the present-tense forms of verbs like 'is', 'have', 'request' which have a much higher frequency in the letters while imperfect forms like 'said', 'had', 'was' and 'were' have a higher frequency in the literary works. The letter is a 'present' text - this is particularly true of Strindberg's letters which are seldom retrospective - while the novel and the autobiography usually take place in past time. The dominance in the letters of imperative forms such as 'read', 'pray' and 'let' is also typical. Strindberg often commanded his addressees to perform services of various sorts.

In almost all the texts we encounter personal pronouns; words that are widely distributed and very frequent. Legal texts are an extreme exception: in the 500,000 words of legal text that have been encoded for computer reading at Språkbanken in Gothenburg, the pronoun 'I' appears only four times. That personal pronouns appear in large number in my material is no surprise, nor is the fact that the letters and the literary texts favour different pronouns: 'I' and 'you' in the letters, 'he' and 'she' in the literary texts. The tendency is reinforced by the fact that *Tjänstekvinnans son* (The Son of a Servant) is written in the third person.

The egocentricity of the letters shows itself in a further way. Adjectives such as 'ill' and 'tired' dominate in the letters - I am departing from the published table - while 'overexerted' only appears in the letters. These words are often directly coupled with the letter writer. Strindberg's constant complaints about his being tired and ill during the 1880s should be viewed against the background of his extreme productivity. Frequency tables for the 1890s and the 1900s will show whether the Strindberg of the letters became increasingly tired; and whether his literary heroes did too!

Strindberg makes frequent use of abbreviations in his attempts to compress and improve the efficiency of his epistolary style. In the table we find abbreviations for 'The' or 'The same', 'Postscript', 'Best' and 'Brother' as terms of address, 'Friend', 'August'. The abbreviation 'Etc.' is used to indicate that a series or argument really continues but is discontinued, a practice that works best when the recipient, as in extended correspondence, is acquainted with the context.

The vocabulary of invective, swear words and words with sexual connotations which Strindberg made use of in his letters is absent from the literary works; not surprisingly there is a difference between the private text, i.e the letters, and the public or literary works. These types of words appear only in certain sequences addressed to men. 'Hellish', 'hell', 'devil', 'devilish', 'idiot' and 'whore' belong to the letters as does 'coition' - this last word is unthinkable in the literary works. But these differences are only valid for the letters (to male addressees) of the 1880s. A study of the frequency of appearance of words of this type for the entire corpus of letters reveals the Inferno crisis as a watershed. The vocabulary of the letters changes after 1895: 'hellish' appears 40 times prior to 1895 but only once subsequently; 'devil' and 'devilish' 83 times before and only twice after 1895.[4] Invective, swear words and words with sexual connotations represent an oral element in the letters and one can naturally ask oneself whether the letters are not more speech oriented than the literary works in terms of vocabulary. The distribution, between the two corpora, of spoken forms and standard written forms of various common words supports this.

It is time to summarize our findings. My study of the letters and the literary texts respectively suggests that Strindberg used two different languages, or rather one language with different ingredients in the letters and the literary works. The differences - which I have only been able briefly to exemplify here - tell us something about the divergences between the language of the letters and that of the literary texts.

In the literary works, which are addressed to an anonymous readership, Strindberg needed both to articulate more clearly and to employ a language suited to the general public. The language is dictated by the work's subject, theme and literary characters; the perspective is expanded in various directions, the vocabulary is broader than in the letters; reality is reflected in descriptions that are rendered concrete by using nouns and coloured using adjectives.

In the letters, which are often aimed at an addressee who is familiar with the subject matter, Strindberg could imply ideas and shorten arguments. He made use of both accepted epistolary formulae and private language which was adjusted to the present and to direct communication and in which spoken language makes itself felt in the choice of words. Strindberg's private perspective rules and the mirroring of the outer, concrete reality is narrow.

These and other divergences indicate that there are constitutive differences between the language of the letters and that of the literary works. But this does not contradict what I have reported in my book about the close relationship between the letters and the fiction.

But most important to the language of the letters and that of the literary works is not, of course, the actual words Strindberg used - and he was probably the most successful user of words in the Swedish language - but how he fitted them together, charged them and gave them metaphorical functions.

I shall therefore conclude by quoting Strindberg when he combines some of the most frequent and trivial words of the Swedish language into a dialectical formulation which reveals the dual references of the language, to the world and to itself, thus demonstrating his fundamental scepticism in a simple line from a letter that suddenly broadens in its perspective and undermines our existence: 'Allt är och allt är inte. Det är så och det är inte så! Hvad är då är?' (Everything is and everything isn't. It is thus and it is not thus! What, then, is is?)[5]

Notes:

1. Kerstin Dahlbäck, *Ändå tycks allt vara osagt. August Strindberg som brevskrivare* (Stockholm, 1994)
2. See Michael Robinson, *Strindberg and Autobiography* (Norwich: Norvik Press, 1986).
3. The computer run was conducted by Christian Sjögreen of the Swedish Language Institution at the University of Gothenburg.
4. *Ändå tycks allt vara osagt*, p. 150f.
5. *August Strindbergs brev* IX, edited by Torsten Eklund (Stockholm, 1965), p. 264.

6

Strindberg's Epistolary Wit

Barbara Lide
Michigan Technological University

Rarely, if ever, do people think of Strindberg as a writer of sparkling – or even appreciable – wit. Some might even question the possibility of discussing at any length the topic of Strindberg's wit. As is well known, his reputation rests primarily on his naturalistic tragedies *Fadren* (The Father) and *Fröken Julie* (Miss Julie); on his expressionistic 'station dramas' *Till Damaskus* (To Damascus) and *Ett drömspel* (A Dream Play); and on his chamber plays, the most prominent of which is *Spöksonaten* (The Ghost Sonata). Thus Strindberg is best known as a creator of works generally regarded as dour and pessimistic. This holds true not only for countries outside his native Sweden, countries where his satirical writings or his letters either are not available or not widely read; it also applies, to a considerable extent, in Sweden, where many do indeed regard him almost exclusively as a neurotic, misogynistic, irascibly contentious writer of plays full of doom and gloom, and where a number of scholars, critics, and writers – happily, not all of them – seem to share that opinion.

In support of the prevailing image of Strindberg, scholars and critics like to cite the following words from his preface to *Fröken Julie*: 'Jag finner livsglädjen in livets starka, grymma strider' (I find the joy of life in life's fierce and ruthless battles).[1] Admittedly, these lines are appropriate for discussions of the conflicts that Strindberg depicts in a number of his tragic plays. But one must acknowledge a hint of tragicomic incongruity in these lines about finding the joy of life in its fierce and ruthless battles – in its wars, so to speak. Also, it should be pointed out that these lines are taken out of a highly satirical context – a context in which Strindberg attacks Ernst Lundqvist, literary advisor to the Royal Dramatic Theatre in Stockholm at the time Strindberg wrote *Fadren* and *Fröken Julie*.

Two of Strindberg's letters, written in December of 1887, several months after he had completed *Fadren*, reveal the background of this attack on Lundqvist. In the first, written to his friend Claes Looström and dated 4 December, he stated, 'Ernst Lundqvist har nu gifvit svar om Fadren. Nix! Den är för dyster och pinsam! (Jemf. *Macbeth* och *Hamlet* och *Gengångare*!)' (Ernst Lundqvist has just given his answer on The Father. Nix! It is too gloomy and too painful! (Compare *Macbeth* and *Hamlet* and *Ghosts*!)).[2] Shortly thereafter, on 19 December, Strindberg wrote essentially the same message to his brother Axel, to which he added, 'Har han sett några muntra sorgespel, han?' (VI, p. 334 – Has the fellow seen any jolly tragedies?).

The lines in the preface to *Fröken Julie* about finding the joy of life in its grim struggles ought to be read in their proper context: they appear as part of Strindberg's attempts to explain the necessity of Julie's tragic fate. Following Darwin, Strindberg explains that, as a weak member of the human species, Julie must necessarily die, while those more fit for life will survive. In his plea for the necessity or validity of tragedy, Strindberg refers to Lundqvist's criticism of *Fadren*:

Man förebrådde nyligen mitt sorgespel *Fadren*, att det var så sorgligt, liksom om man fordrade muntra sorgespel; och man ropar med pretention på livsglädjen och teaterdirektörerna skriva rekvisitioner på farser liksom om livsglädjen låge i att vara fånig och att rita av mänskor som om de voro alla behäftade med danssjuka eller idiotism.

(My tragedy *The Father* was criticized recently for being too sorrowful, as if people wanted jolly tragedies; and now people are demanding the joy of life, and theatre directors are writing requisitions for farces, as if the joy of life lay in being ridiculous and portraying people as if they were all seized by St. Vitus Dance or idiocy – SV 27, p. 103.)

It is at this point that the lines appear about finding the joy of life in life's grim battles, and these lines, in turn, are followed by the words, '...och min njutning är att få veta något, att få lära något' (SV 27, p. 103 – and my enjoyment is in being able to know something, in being able to learn something). In other words, Strindberg is not at all describing himself as any kind of tragic protagonist or gloomy figure, but as a man with a healthy intellectual curiosity who is rising up against the philistines and what he considered to be their idiotic farces.

Also, he is tweaking Ibsen a bit here. There was a time when Strindberg was a great Ibsen enthusiast. In his autobiographical work *Tjänstekvinnans son* (The Son of the Servant), he describes his profound admiration for *Brand* and *Peer Gynt* (SS 18, p. 335f.).[3] But when Ibsen wrote *Et Dukkehjem* (A Doll's House), Strindberg's enthusiasm turned to scorn, for in his eyes Ibsen had become a spokesman for women's emancipation and, consequently, a turncoat and an enemy. Strindberg took to calling him 'blåstrumpan Ibsen' (VII, p. 81 – that bluestocking Ibsen), who had become one of the 'f.d. män' (VI, p. 155 – former men) by joining a number of women writers in order to perpetrate 'Ibsen och systrars skändliga angrepp på mannen' (VI, p. 148 – Ibsen and the sisters' infamous attack on men). Although Strindberg did genuinely admire Ibsen's play *Gengangere*, in the criticism of the Swedish theatre that he vented in the preface to *Fröken Julie*, he played satirically upon the word 'livsglädjen', a key concept and a verbal leitmotif in that play.

Rarely mentioned in discussions of Strindberg is that he was able to find the joy of life not only in life's fierce struggles, but also in its simple pleasures – something clearly evidenced in his letters. As he expressed in a letter to his colleague Axel Lundegård on 31 October 1887, in which he described his 'rolig och ... grofkornig kostlig bok' (comic and ... crudely funny book) *Hemsöborna* (The People of Hemsö), 'Jag har äfven haft mycket roligt i mitt lif' (VI, p. 293 – I also have had many good times in my life). Even at times when he was being heavily bombarded by negative criticism, Strindberg was able to take pleasure in recalling happier days, as is illustrated by a letter he wrote to the artist Carl Larsson in May 1887. In this letter, he mentions the good times they once had at

Kymmendö, the island in the Stockholm archipelago where he had spent some of the happiest days of his life. He wrote,

Mins (sic) du så ung jag var den rosenröda tiden på Kymmendö, då vi och Stux ännu voro roade av att kasta smörgås! Andra stenkastningar nu!
   Skit i lifvet! Det var djefligt roligt emellanåt! Och jar har haft det godt, herrligt emellanåt. Sådana studentår 70-73 och nygiftasår! Åh Gud! – Ja!'

(Do you remember how young I was in the rosy-red days at Kymmendö, when we and Stux still got a kick out of playing ducks and drakes! Well, there's a different kind of stone-casting going on now!
   Shit on life! It was a hell of a lot of fun sometimes, though. And I have had it good, wonderful at times. My student years from 70 to 73, and my years as a newlywed! Oh, God! – Yes! – VI, p.207.)[4]

There appears, however, to be little or no interest in such lines – lines that help to balance somewhat the critical image of Strindberg. This is understandable, for they lack the dramatic incisiveness that we have come to expect of Strindberg. And it is true that only a portion of Strindberg's wit – perhaps a third of it at most – actually derives from his happier moods. Most often, it derives from his anger and his frustration, and it is inherent in his criticism of literature, theatre, people, politics, his native Sweden, and the world as he perceived it.

One who recently has shown an appreciation of Strindberg's incisive wit is the Swedish journalist Annette Kullenberg, in her book *Strindberg – murveln* (Strindberg – Hack Journalist). Kullenberg concludes her book with an excerpt from Strindberg's 1907 novel *Svarta fanor* (Black Banners), in which Strindberg includes some very sharp satirical observations of devotees of Wagnerian opera and of cultural snobs in general, who follow 'fashionable' opinions. Kullenberg's final comments on this excerpt, which also are the concluding words of her book, are: 'Strindberg var dräpande. Och rolig' (Strindberg was crushing. And funny).[5]

Returning to the question, posed above, of whether one could discuss at length the topic of Strindberg's wit, a perusal of his letters confirms that such a discussion is not only feasible, but that examples of his wit are in such abundance that unless it were to fill a book, any discussion must necessarily be strictly limited. I have, therefore, resorted to the traditional division of Strindberg's works into the pre-Inferno and post-Inferno periods, limiting the sources of my examples to the letters that Strindberg wrote up through 1895. The examples, however, are representative of the kind of wit that Strindberg displayed throughout his entire life. While he might have changed the style of his plays after his Inferno period, the style of his wit, as displayed in the letters, remains constant, although its volume diminishes.

My discussion will centre on Strindberg's quick-wittedness, his talent for clever and witty expression, based on both his knowledge and intelligence. Quick wit is not to be confused with humour, for wit and a sense of the comic are not at all synonymous with humour. To cite some dictionary definitions of 'wit' in order to clarify my own use of the word, it is 'more purely intellectual than humour,' implying 'swift perception of the incongruous.' It 'consists typically in a neat turn of speech by which disconnected ideas are unexpectedly associated.' 'It may take the form, as in poetical or whimsical composition, of association of the trivial and sublime, the literal and figurative, the corporeal and abstract, or of things between which there is apparent contrariety, or of various senses of the same word. It may consist of deft and spontaneous play with unperceived or artificial analogies, often with a severely critical or satirical or maliciously personal application, always expressed in a way to give mental stimulation and entertainment.'[6] Strindberg's letters do indeed display such wit.

I have attempted to arrange my examples of Strindberg's wit rather loosely into four categories, all of which are characterized by the playful use of language, and which also, in many of the letters, overlap, blurring the distinctions between the categories.

The first is the wit arising out of Strindberg's youthful exuberance and his snobbishness. He was, after all, a student in Uppsala, he was successful as a young writer, and he hobnobbed with some of the more prominent and talented figures among Stockholm's young writers and artists. With the wit of an intellectual, as well as of a student of language, he plays not only with his own language, but with Latin, German, French, English, and a little Greek. He also displays a zesty exuberance in some of the letters from his younger days, especially those to Carl Larsson, in which he jokes about sex and fornication and uses a good many obscenities, demonstrating that, like his character Jean in *Fröken Julie* he 'hade samma fula tankar som alla pojkar' (SV 27, p. 155 – had the same dirty thoughts that all boys had).

The second category is perhaps best characterized by the words 'charming wit,' a kind of wit that Strindberg sometimes employed in his criticism, couching that criticism playfully in polite and charming language, using few, if any, obscenities, and writing with varying styles – sometimes tongue-in-cheek, sometimes flatteringly, sometimes feigning flattery.

A third category is exemplified by sharp, biting wit, born out of frustration and anger and directed mostly at his publishers, at theatre directors, at Sweden and his fellow Swedes, at Parisian life, or at his fellow writers. To paraphrase Annette Kullenberg's lines, quoted above, Strindberg could be very funny while being very nasty.

The fourth and last category is the wit arising from puns and playful allusions to the Bible, to works of literature, or to philosophical works, sometimes with variations, sometimes with ironic juxtaposition, and almost always resulting in a comic or parodic twist.

Beginning with the playful letters that Strindberg wrote to his friends, one can easily observe that, whether he was writing to his contemporaries in the happy, youthful days of the early 1880s or writing to younger colleagues for whom he served as a mentor when he was in his mid-forties, the tone of his letters is essentially the same.

In the 1880s, he wrote a series of letters to his friend Willehad Lindström, a Stockholm businessman who was helping research some points for his study *Gamla Stockholm* (II, p. 121 – Old Stockholm). Strindberg's ludic spirit abounds in these letters, in which he addresses Lindström by a number of names, proving perhaps the Swedish saying, 'Kärt barn har många namn' (We have many names for what we love (literally, A beloved child has many names)). Among those names are: 'Lind af Hageby,' 'Lindy,' 'Hagel,' 'Hagelby,' and 'Hagelstam,'[7] as well as 'Lind af Hagelstam, Esq.' (II, p. 178), and 'Välborne Herr Robert Lind af Hageby, född Lindström.' (II, p. 161 – Honourable Sir Robert Lind of Hageby, born Lindström). In one letter, in which he tries to tempt Lindström to celebrate Midsommar at Kymmendö, he writes playfully in German, 'Wir zieh'n den Linden h'naus!'[8] This he follows with, 'Öfversättning! Nu ska vi (ta mig djefvuln) dra ut Lind af Hageby till Midsommar!' (III, p. 37 – Translation! Now we'll (devil take me) drag Lind af Hageby out here for Midsommar!).

In another invitation to Lindström, Strindberg writes, in a joyful and witty style characteristic of a young man planning a party with his friends,

Helsa Stuxberg och gif honom en brinnande
FÖRBANNELSE!
och säg honom att umgänget med menniskor icke blott skall bestå uti att man lånar pengar af hvarann utan äfven, och mest kanske, uti att man håller landskap!
Som jag icke utöfvat fyllerilasten på nära fjorton dagar, törstar min själ efter dåligt sällskap; jag har inte fått säga ett svinaktigt ord sedan jag var i staden sist och derför ber jag Dig: tag en droska först vackra dag och hemta Stuxberg, full eller nykter, fatig eller rik! och släp honom ner till en Dalaröbåt! (Har han viggat af Dig ännu?). Släpp honom sedan ej förr än Du har honom i Gästbådshamn. Ligg efter honom som en rem! . . .
P.P.S. Skulle Du vilja fullständigt krossa mig med din godhet så köp två burkar Star-Lobster (Hummer) och två Champignoner (à 1 Krona.) Disconto claro contanto à Kymmendö.

(Give Stuxberg my regards and a hearty
CURSE!
and tell him social intercourse doesn't only consist in borrowing money from one another, but also, and probably even more importantly, in getting drunk together!
As I haven't gone boozing for almost a fortnight, my soul is thirsting after bad company; I've not uttered a single dirty word since I was last in town; therefore, I beg you, the first fine day, to take a cab and fetch Stuxberg, drunk or sober, poor or rich, and drag him down to a Dalarö boat! (Has he sponged off you yet?) Don't let go of him until you get to the jetty at Gästbåd. Keep a tight hold on him! . . .
P.P.S. If you'd like to entirely smother me with kindness, buy two tins of Star Lobster and two of Mushrooms (at 1 Krona). Disconto claro contanto on Kymmendö. – II, pp. 157-8.)[9]

The phrase 'Disconto claro contanto' illustrates Strindberg's penchant for flavouring his speech, in the facetious manner of a student, with expressions from Latin and other languages common to learning in his day. In preparation for one of his parties at Kymmendö, for example, he asked Lindström to 'Medför *Contantibus i manibus* en låda af dina fina cigarrer samt ett paket *Kymendötobak* – (svart du vet)' (II, p. 262 – Bring with you *contantibus i manibus* (with cash in hand) a box of your *fine* cigars, along with a package of *Kymmendö tobacco* – (black, you know the kind)).

In the summer of 1881, Carl Larsson lived with Strindberg at Kymmendö, when he was working on the illustrations for Strindberg's *Svenska folket*, his history of the Swedish people. Strindberg was married to Siri von Essen at the time, but Larsson was still single, and Strindberg enjoyed joking with him about his sex life – or lack thereof. He sent Larsson a note on 19 June 1881 that read: 'Artisten Carl Larsson inbjudes att med en (eller två) brun Kognackstoddy reperara sin genom Onani och Samlag förstörda mage. Nu genast' (II, p. 264 – The artist Carl Larsson is invited to repair his stomach, destroyed by masturbation and fornication, with one (or two) brown cognac toddies. Now, immediately). The letter is signed 'August', followed by the words, 'Litteratör – Hamnbuse' (*litterateur* – harbour bum), and next to the names 'Carl' and 'August,' Strindberg drew pictures of Larsson and himself.

It was not unusual for Strindberg to include illustrations in his letters, especially in his earlier letters to friends. He concluded a series of two lengthy letters to Carl Larsson, regarding *Svenska folket*, with one of his better-known illustrations – a drawing of himself as an Egyptian Sphinx. The letters express Strindberg's reaction to criticism of both his text and Larsson's illustrations. On 16 November 1881, Strindberg wrote to Larsson,

Wie steht's mit Ihnen! Här må du tro det har pipit om öronen, men jag har bara lyftat på ena bakbenet och pissat på kopplet!
    Nu skall du inte vara ledsen för det, ty det går galant ändå, fast bröderna Fritze äro ledsna, men de hafva också haft ett helfvete, att behöfva stå och höra åsneskrien! Emellertid! Vi öfvergå nu till 1500-talet och du har ju fått manuskript! till Staden och Landet. Go on Sir! ... Men ålägges du för hela

vårt väl: att icke mer rita någon af följande artiklar: Hor- och Skithus, horeri ... fylleri – (med kräkning!), halshuggningar – (med nakna qvinnor), veneriska sjukdomar – emedan efterfrågan på sådana varor lär vara ringa. ... Deremot efterfrågar Hofbokhandeln starkt följande: Kungar med kronor på hufvet. Englar med palmer i hand, Unga väl klädda qvinnor. Officerare. Högre embetsmän, helst kommendörer, Sidenklädningar, Hofbokhandlare, Guds ord, Juveler, Kröningsprocessioner, Intåg, och sådant som du vet.

Nå gamle Kymendit, du knullar väl ordentligt dina mål om dygnet! Du skall icke trissa middag, ty det för man slag efter!

(Wie steht's mit Ihnen! [How are things with you!] You can believe that the arrows are whistling around our ears here, but I have simply lifted one of my hind legs and pissed on the leash!

Now you shouldn't be unhappy about that, for things are going along splendidly anyway, although the brothers Fritze are unhappy, but they also have had a hellish time, to have to stand and listen to the asses braying! However! We'll now proceed to the 1500s, and you have received the manuscript! to The City and The Country. Go on Sir! But for the good of all of us, you are hereby instructed: to no longer draw any of the following articles: Whore- and shithouses, whoring ... drunkenness – (with vomiting!), beheadings – (with naked women), venereal diseases – because the demand for such wares is said to be limited. ... On the other hand, the court bookseller [the publisher Fritze] strongly requests the following: kings with crowns on their heads. Angels with palms in their hands, young, well-dressed women.[10] Officers. Higher officials, preferably commanders, silk dresses, court booksellers, the word of God, jewels, coronations, parades, and such, as you know.

Now, old Kymennö friend, you're probably fucking your quota properly around the clock. You should not miss dinner for it, though, because you'll get a stroke afterwards! – II, p. 305.)

In his follow-up letter, written a few days later in response to criticism by Oscar Montelius in the *Nordisk tidskrift*, Strindberg changes from writing in a relatively unruffled and facetious manner to displaying a bit of anger and employing some pretty strong language – mostly with the intention of consoling Larsson, whose illustrations Montelius described as 'alltför fantasibetonade' (much too coloured by fantasy) and 'delvis smaklösa' (in part, tasteless). Strindberg wrote, 'Hvad Montelius beträffar så träcka på honom, jag skall knulla honom i peruken så att han skall bli flintskallig. Gå på du bara med dina gubbar! Nu ha vi strömmen med oss! Det har varit satan så hett om örlapparne men är nu mest öfverståndt' (II,

p. 320 – As far as Montelius is concerned, shit on him! I'll fuck him in his wig until he gets bald. Just go ahead with the figures that you're drawing! We're swimming with the current now! It's been hellishly difficult, but we've survived most of it.) It is at the end of this letter that Strindberg drew a picture of himself in the form of a sphinx, which he titled 'Egyptisk sphinx pissande på Bronsåldersfolk Ritarakademiens Prisämne' (Egyptian sphinx pissing on the Bronze-Age folk of the Academy of Art and their prize).

Not only does Strindberg use crude language from the sexual sphere in some of his coarse wit. As Michael Robinson points out, he also carried on 'a lively and often scatological correspondence with a succession of male friends' (MR, I, p. xi). One example of the scatological aspects of Strindberg's letters can be seen in a letter to his friend Pehr Staaff, which he wrote while traveling on a train between Bremen and Osnabrück on his way to Paris, and which he did indeed embellish with some unusual flourishes:

Jag har i egenskap of smutsförfattare särskildt studerat klosetterna på hotellen. Den mest glänsande uppfinningen träffade jag i Hamburg. Der träckade man i något som liknade en soppskål och när man tittade sig om så var det ingenting att se, oaktadt man kunnat svära på att man nedlagt ett par meter; skålen var så fin efter förrättningen att man kunnat äta äkta skåldpaddsoppa ur den; dock det hördes intet vattensqvalp såsom i Stralsund der fjölen gaf efter när man satt sig och ett strömmande vatten började gå. Det var ett fullständigt trolleri. Nog om Klosetter!

(In my capacity as a purveyor of filth, I have made a close study of the hotel toilets. The most brilliant invention was the one I came across in Hamburg. There you shat into something resembling a soup tureen and when you looked round there was nothing to be seen, even though you could have sworn you'd put down a couple of meters; the bowl was so fine after the proceedings that you could have eaten genuine turtle soup from it; however, there was no sound of any splashing water as in Stralsund, where the seat activated a stream of water as soon as you sat down. It was just like magic! But that's enough about Toilets! – III, p. 302-3; MR I, p. 114.)

Strindberg could also be witty without resorting to biting attacks, the use of obscenities, or scatological references. He could tone down his criticism considerably and take the edge off of it – which did not, however, lessen its effect. In the following example, the wit derives from the incongruity between the subject matter and the flowery formal tone. It is from a letter to the publisher Joseph Seligmann, for whom Strindberg, in collaboration with Claes Lundin, was writing *Gamla Stockholm*. On 18 July 1880 Strindberg wrote to Seligmann,

Efter den angenäma sammandrabbningen med Farbror Claes på J.S. et C:is byrå förliden försommar har Undertecknad förlorat all lust att uppträda som Censor öfver merbemälde Farbror, hvilken ju då tog sig den sällsynta friheten att så godt som klandra författaren Sg:s plan med arbetet sådan just denna plan yttrar sig i Sg:s skenbart ytliga behandling af ämnena, hvilken ytlighet just är arbetets hufvudplan (annorlunda uttryckt – att icke skrämma bort läsare och för egen lärdomshögfärds tillfredsställande ruinera förläggarne.) Skulle Herrarne deremot vilja ta itu med gubben C.L. vore det ganska kärt. Hans nyssläsrta ms är högst förtjenstfullt – men för grundligt. Hvem t. ex. bryr sig om Bagar Kammeckers vidlyftiga lefnadsomständigheter?! Denne bagares uppträdande i en lång not förefaller den misstänksamme Sg. som en löjlig polemik mot författaren till Inledningen, hvilken i förbigående omrör den berömde ökände enkhusgrundaren. Och att två förf. uppträda och ge hvarandra på nosen inom samma omslag – det är visserligen mycket *nytt* och roligt, men fasligt opraktiskt.

(After the pleasant encounter with Uncle Claes at J.S. & Company's office this past spring, the Undersigned has lost all desire to appear as Censor over the frequently aforementioned fellow, who did indeed take the unusual liberty to so much as find fault with the author Strindberg's plan for the work, precisely as this plan is evident in Strindberg's apparently superficial treatment of the subjects, which superficiality is precisely the major plan for the work (expressed differently – to not scare readers away and ruin the publishers for the sake of satisfying the pride we take in our own erudition.) Should the gentlemen, on the other hand, wish to take up the matter with the fellow (C.L.), that would be very nice. His recent ms. is most worthy of merit – but too thorough. Who, for example, cares about the wordy descriptions of the shady life of Kammecker the baker? This baker's appearance in a long note strikes the suspicious Strindberg as a ridiculous polemic against the author of the introduction, who in passing touches upon the notorious founder of a 'home for widows.' And for two writers to step forward and poke each other on the snoot between the same covers – surely that is very new and delightful, but frightfully impractical – II, p. 153.)

Here we have Strindberg expressing his dissatisfaction in a diplomatic and witty way, exhibiting a somewhat charming restraint, a soft-pedaling of his criticism, through which, however, his displeasure can clearly be seen. This style is one that Strindberg uses primarily in his younger years, rarely in his later years. It also is evident, however, in some letters that he wrote to friends in the mid-to-late 1890s, in combination with what might be called the exuberant, persistent spirit of the Kymmendö letters.

In the mid-1890s, Strindberg formed some friendships – some of them rather short-lived – with men younger than himself, for whom he served as a mentor of sorts, and with whom he engaged in lively correspondence. Among them was Bengt Lidforss, a botanist and writer whom Strindberg had met in Lund in 1890,[11] and with whom he became closer acquainted during his time in Berlin, when Lidforss was there as a correspondent for the Stockholm newspaper *Dagens nyheter*. Lidforss was one of a group of artists and writers who gathered at Strindberg's 'Stammlokal' (regular haunt) 'zum schwarzen Ferkel' (The Black Piglet), a group including the Scandinavians Edvard Munch, Adolf Paul, Dagny Juel, Christian Krohg, and Ola Hansson; the Germans Laura Marholm, Ludwig Schleich and Richard Dehmel; and the Pole Stanislaus Przybyszewski.

A letter to Lidforss dated 2 February 1894 exemplifies the playful wit that Strindberg frequently displayed in letters to his male friends – in this case combined with an admonition to Lidforss to be more productive as a writer. Then follows some of the caustic wit that often flavours his criticism, especially of Swedish writers:

Men gubbe! lite flit, då och då! (Mycket supa emellanåt skadar inte.) Du var i dåligt sällskap i våras – med mig nemligen! Jag söp djefligt och immer, men Du glömde att jag flitat en meter böcker. Il faut faire quelque chose, ser Du! Och man förvexlar så lätt hvad man på krogen velat göra med hvad man gjort. Äran och guldet ligga framför Dig! Tag det! Men Du måsta sträcka ut armen! Bara det!

(But my dear fellow! A little diligence, now and then! (Boozing a lot doesn't hurt, however.) You were in bad company last spring – that is to say, with me! I boozed a hell of a lot, and constantly, but you forgot that I produced a meter of books. Il faut faire quelque chose, you see![12] And one so easily confuses what wanted to do at the pub with what one actually has done. Honour and money are lying at your feet! Grab them! But you have to stretch out your arm for them! That's all! – X, p. 5.)

Now follows the critique of the Swedish writers, which Strindberg begins with the lamentation, quoted from the Book of Jeremiah, '"O Land! Land!" (Jeremias!),' and in which he distorts the name of at least one writer, that of Oscar Levertin, whom he refers to as 'Levertran' (cod-liver oil):

Nu kifvas det om hvem som är den förste i Sverge. Rydberg vill vara det men Snoilsky vill också, och Heidenstam tror bestämdt han är det, men Wennerberg är det säkert, om inte Levertran sjelf trodde sig var näst Wirsén. O Land! Land! ... Fiskar G af G, den lilla skiten, efter mig! – Med vilken propos slog han opp språklådan? Det är en komisk djefvel. Han var född pensionerad. Pensionerades vid fyllda 28 år af R. Wall med 1,800 Kronor för att han skulle låta bli att skrifva i D.N.
Nu har v Steijern pensionerat honom igen! Född barhufvud med glasögon och ögon som en pissträngd kanin.

(Now they're squabbling over who is number one in Sweden. Rydberg claims to be the one, but so does Snoilsky, and Heidenstam believes that it definitely is he, but surely it's Wennerberg, if Levertran himself did not consider himself next to Wirsén. O Land! Land! ... Is G af G, that little shit, fishing after me! – Apropos of what did he reopen lines of communication? He's a comical devil. He was born pensioned. He was pensioned at the age of 28 by R. Wall, with 1,800 Crowns, so that he would stop writing for D[agens] n[yheter].
Now v. Steijern has pensioned him again! He was born bald with glasses, paunch, pension and the eyes of a rabbit in need of a piss. – X, p. 5.)[13]

Here, in the midst of his biting wit, Strindberg has created a very playful analogy, as well as what appears to be an anthromorphic rabbit.

Besides forming new friendships and gaining new partners with whom to exchange letters, Strindberg also renewed old acquaintances from time to time. One of these was Leopold Littmansson, an old friend from the Stockholm and Kymmendö days of the early 1870s, with whom Strindberg reopened correspondence in 1894, around the same time that his friendship with Lidforss was coming to an end. Strindberg was living in Austria at the time, and Littmansson, who had married into a wealthy French family, was living in Versailles. There ensued what Michael Robinson describes as 'one of the central sequences of letters in his [Strindberg's] entire correspondence,' with Strindberg writing, 'between 19 June and 15 August 1894, when he moved to Paris ... an extraordinary series of thirty-five, often extremely long, letters, sometimes writing more than one a day, and adopting in many of them a burlesque jargon, full of puns, private allusions and verbal jokes which generally resist translation' (MR I, p. 343).

Strindberg's particular use of jargon, believed to have developed among his friends at Kymmendö in the 1870s, included, among other characteristics, distorting personal names and using the letter y in place of i.[14] The following lines from the first letter in the series, dated 19 June 1884, are exemplary:

Broder Lyktmanntson,
Vÿ äro nu bortät femtio är och ha dansat bort mjolktänderna sambt skol tänka på ändalykten, men jag kan ändå icke låtta blÿ att le när jag tänker på detta gÿckel som likfullt är rätt allvorsamt gÿckel emellanåt.
    Att det är derför som jag ännu en gång skrÿffwer och frågar om Du lefwer, och om Du wÿlle ha mig öfver sommaren i en Kymmendöpension likasom. För att lära mig tala franskt, så godt en Svensk kan.
    Jag är nu visserligen djäfligt stor; har byst i finska (!) Nationalmuseum, sÿtter i 2 ponoptikonar med stort luderhår och fläckiga kläder (som Hjalmer Hyrsch förr); har blifwit uthwÿslad i Neapel och spelad en (I!) gång I Rom (och Den Fredlöse) samt nerskällad af Sarcey y Parys, etc. ...
    Jag är gyfft två gånger och är ändock monogamit, samt har afslöjat hela Universum, och Gud och Jesus samt Englarne.

(Dear Lykmanntson,
We're now getting on for fyfty, have danced away our mylk teeth and should be thynking of our tail end, yet I can't help laughing when I thynk of this joke called lyfe, which is nevertheless pretty serious between tymes.
    That's why I'm wryting to you again to fynd out if you're alyve and would lyke to put me up over the summer – pension à la Kymmendö as it were. So I can learn to speak French a well as a Swede can.
    I really am damned big now; my byst is in the Finnish (!) National Museum, and in 2 waxworks with a whorelike mane of hair and dirty clothes (like Hjalmar Hyrsch once had); have been hyssed in Naples and played once (1!) 'In Rome' (and *The Outlaw*), as well as crytycyzed by Sarcey yn Parys, etc. ...
    I've been married twyce but remain a monogamist; have also unmasked

the whole Unyverse along with God, Jesus and the Angels. – X p. 94; MR II, p. 47.)

As Kerstin Dahlbäck points out in her study of Strindberg as a correspondent, the paradoxical words 'allvorsamt gÿckel' (serious joke) establish not only the tone of this particular letter, but also that of the entire correspondence.[15] Because Strindberg is seeking here to reestablish his relationship with Littmansson, he brings him up to date, as it were, on events in his life. His style, which combines baby talk with grandiose statements regarding unmasking 'the whole universe along with God, Jesus and the Angels,' and his juxtaposition of the grand and the low – defining, for example, being 'djäfligt stor' as having rather grotesque figures of himself in two wax museums – gives rise to the ironic tone characteristic of the 'serious joke' that pervades the correspondence.

The salutation in this letter, 'Broder Lyktnanntson,' is typical of the variations on Littmansson's name with which Strindberg addressed him. Some of the others are 'Broder Luitpold' (IV p. 85; VIII, p. 179), referring to Luitpold, regent of Bavaria from 1886 to 1912; 'Broder Leopold (af Belgien)!' (IV, p. 234); 'Broder Lyknant' (X, p. 96), 'Broder Thomas' (X, p. 175), when Littmansson was exhibiting doubt; and 'Hej! Lyktnam! Hej!' X (p. 375).

While a few of the letters are somewhat esoteric, most are accessible, and many are quite witty. The following, somewhat lengthy, excerpt from a letter written in early August, 1894, in which Strindberg attempts to persuade Littmansson to join him in Austria and then take a trip to Hungary, is rife with comments and witticisms on Prince Esterhazy, Hungarian violinists, the German industrialist Krupp, and Littmansson's mother-in-law:

Du som har fiolen kan ju gå eller bicyklera verlden rundt med en fiolpåse på ryggen. Hör!
I Ungern vid Totis under Pressburg bor Fursten Esterhazy. Han är så djäfligt rik att han håller eget kapell, egen teater, bibliotek, stall med 1 000 hästar, och vyn har han i en underjordisk kyrka fullt. Denna Furste åsåg *Créanciers* i Berlin, och blef exalterad (jag såg aldrig mannen – inte rifvit honom ens! Mycket mindre ...); för honom var *Cavalleria Rusticana* och *Gläubiger* det högsta af modern konst etc. Nå...låtom oss som fin-de-siecle Buddhor med lån från Troubadourerna tåga dit, anonymt, och låta upptäcka

oss. Du spelar, och jag reciterar Nordiska (pseudo-) fin-de-sieclestumpar som jag skrifver först på Tyska.

Så demaskera vi oss; du blir hofkapellmästare och komponist med Ungerska Jernkronan på fracken, och jag furstlig bibliotekarie och Alchemist!

Det är inte filisterleben det! Men Du vet väl hur ungrarne spela fiol: utan taktstreck, utan D-moll immer tempo rubato som när menskor qvida.

Jag åt middag på Hotel Bristol i Berlin (betalade inte naturligtvis sjelf) Champanen var high och jag hade strålande materia – Då hör jag ljud från salen bredvid sådana att jag trodde mig ha fått norrsken i örona. Det lät som gråtande, jemrande menskor, som emellanåt snyftade och skrattade – etc. Det var ett Ungerskt fiolkapell som spelade för Krupp hvilken åt middag för 50,000 Rixdaler med sina vänner.

Det är ett godt valg! utan askes! Det är aristos från den gamla goda tiden, då lekare och fiddlare kröpo för furstar och ej för pack som nu.

Du kunde direkt gå in och be om plats i kapellet, profspela och bli Gud!

Men du måste bära en suggestiv skalp, helst en nordisk som står emot luften med dina blonda mustascher, ty tyskar äro hatade i Ungarn. Eller en frankisk med Spanska skägget. ...

Skrif en enaktare på Franska på åtta dagar och säg svärmor att du blir författare, men måste göra en studieresa för att träffa mig. Och att Du börjar med att öfversätta mig för att öfva franskan, lära stil och komma in med förläggare och teaterdirektörer. Da blir gumman glad och stolt! Tag så straxt ett franskt författarnamn och var Fransk.

(With your fiddle you can walk or cycle round the world with a violin case on your back. Listen!

Prince Esterhazy lives in Hungary, at Totis near Pressburg. He's so damned rich that he has his own orchestra, theatre, library and stables with 1,000 horses, and a subterranean church full of wyne. This Prince saw *Creditors* in Berlin and was carried away (I never met the man – didn't even touch him! Far less...!); he thought *Cavalleria rusticana* and *Creditors* the summits of modern art. So...let us emulate the Troubadours, make our way there anonymously, as fin-de-siecle Buddhas, and have them discover us. You can play and I'll recite some Scandinavian (pseudo) fin-de-siecle pieces, which I'll write beforehand in German.

Then we'll unmask: you'll become court conductor and composer with the Iron Crown of Hungary on your tail-coat, and I the royal librarian and Alchemist!

No philistine life, that! But you're aware of how the Hungarians play the violin: without bar lines, not in D minor, and *immer tempo rubato* [always flexible tempo], like people whining.

I had dinner one day at the Hotel Bristol in Berlin (didn't pay myself, of course). The champagne was flowing and I felt radiant. – All of a sudden I heard a sound from the adjoining room which made me think I had the Northern Lights in my ears. It sounded like people weeping and wailing, and now and then sobbing and laughing, etc. It was a band of Hungarian violinists playing for Krupp, who was dining out with his friends for 50,000 Riksdaler.

This is a fine choice! Not ascetic! Aristocratic as in the good old days when players and fiddlers bowed down to princes, and not as now to the mob.

You could walk right in and ask for a place in the orchestra, audition, and become God!

But you must have a fetching hair cut, preferably a Scandinavian one to counter the effect of your blond moustache, for the Hungarians hate the Germans. Or a French one, with a Spanish goatee. ...

Spend a week writing a one-acter in French and tell your mother-in-law you're going to become a writer but need to make a study trip in order to meet me. And that you're starting off by translating me so as to practise your French, learn style, and get to know some publishers and theatre directors. That'll make the old woman proud and happy! Then adopt a French pseudonym and become French. – X, pp. 190-1; MR II, 498-9.)

In a letter written shortly thereafter to Littmansson, Strindberg closes with the following strophe:

Då jublar min anda
Då pissar jag blod
Och menskor beblandas med djuren!
    (Runeberg)
(Then my spirit is jubilant
Then I piss blood
And mankind and animals are united!
    (Runeberg) X, p. 226)

As Torsten Eklund's note points out, this stanza, apparently a travesty of a religious revival song, appears in a number of letters that Strindberg wrote at the beginning of the 1880s, and it is attributed to various poets – Tegnér, Snoilsky, and Runeberg. Strindberg especially used the first lines to signify that he was suffering from cystitis (X, p. 226).

Strindberg seemed to be particularly fond of misquoting, or falsely attributing what he quoted. In another letter to Littmansson, he wrote, for example, 'Wo die Geldfrage fängt an, hört der Buddaismus auf' (X, p. 177 – Where the question of money arises, Buddhism ends), followed by 'Goethe' in parentheses. Michael Robinson notes that this quotation is, indeed, not from Goethe, but 'a play on the phrase "Bei Geldfragen hört die Gemütlichkeit auf"' (In matters of money, geniality ceases), uttered by David Hausemann in the first German Parliament of 1847' (MR II, p. 841).

Strindberg's correspondence is, however, rife with parodies of quotations from Goethe. In one instance, for example, he parodies both Schiller and Goethe in a letter in which he thanks Verner von Heidenstam for a tin of anchovies: 'Hvilken herrlig anjovis! O Land wo bist Du? Kennst Du das Land wo die Anjoven glüh'n?' (VI, p. 84 – What wonderful anchovies! O land, where are you? Do you know the land where the anchovies glisten?) The first question, 'O Land, wo bist Du?' is a play on the line 'Schöne Welt, wo bist du?' (Beautiful world, where are you?) from Schiller's poem 'Die Götter Griechenlands' (The Gods of Greece), and the second question parodies the frequently quoted lines, spoken by Mignon in *Wilhelm Meister*, 'Kennst du das Land, wo die Zitronen blüh'n? (Do you know the land where the lemons bloom?).[16]

Besides citing or parodying Goethe to create witty formulations, Strindberg often achieved wit by quoting, or twisting quotations from – among many others – Martin Luther, Heinrich Heine, the German humanist Ulrich von Hutten, the Bible, and Schopenhauer. Thus on 19 June 1893 he writes to Frida Uhl, from a hotel in Hamburg where he is stranded, 'Hier sitze ich! und kann nicht Anders, vorläufig' (IX, p. 210 – Here I sit! And cannot do otherwise, for the time being), parodying Luther's famous words, 'Hier stehe ich. Ich kann nicht anders!' (Here I stand. I cannot do otherwise!).

With regard to his references to Heine, it is perhaps noteworthy that, in his younger days, Strindberg appeared to cite Heine's verses naively – in letters, for example, that he wrote to Siri von Essen in the early days of their courtship.[17] Later, in the early days of his marriage to Frida Uhl, he took to citing Heine with a certain irony. He repeatedly wrote the words, 'ich grolle nicht' (I'm not angry) to Frida, words from Heine's *Buch der Lieder* (and also from one of the better-known Lieder set to music by Robert Schumann). This he did when he wanted to express that, though in an undesirable situation, he would not complain. And yet complaining, albeit mildly, was precisely what he was doing. The following instances are exemplary: In July of 1893, he wrote to Frida, 'Wie kannst Du mir so zuschreiben! So! Aber ich grolle nicht! Sei ruhig!' (IX, p. 231 – How can you write such things to me! But I'm not angry! Don't worry!). Then, about a week later, he wrote to her in French, translating 'Ich grolle nicht': 'Deux jours sans de lettres! Et je ne gronde pas' (IX, p. 240 – Two days without any letters! And I'm not angry).

What appears to be one of Strindberg's favourite lines, one that he alludes to exuberantly in favourable situations, and sometimes with a hint of melancholy in adverse situations, apparently comes from a letter written by the German humanist Ulrich von Hutten to his colleague Willibald Pirkheimer: 'es ist eine Lust, zu leben' (It's a joy to be alive).[18] Shortly after his arrival in Berlin in October 1892, he met with some good fortune, and was in the happy position of being able to invite a few of his new friends to celebrate. He wrote enthusiastically to a colleague, the Finnish writer Adolf Paul,

Wenn Strindberg Geld kriegt, kriegt auch Paul och Przybyszewski, und Priapus will im Müggelschloss den todten Russen bei drei (3) klavieren tanzen.
Die Sonne scheint, Der Blumenthal schreibt in Börsencourier und der Stier will Geld machen! Es ist eine Lust zu leben!

(When Strindberg gets money, Paul and Przybyszewski get some too, and Priapus wants to dance the dead Russian with three (3) pianos in the Müggelschloss.
The sun is shining, Blumenthal is writing in the *Börsencourier*, and the bull wants to make money! Es ist eine Lust zu leben! – IX, p. 71.)[19]

In contrast to the celebratory mood of this letter is the spirit of a letter written from Djursholm outside Stockholm roughly a year before the trip to Berlin in 1892. Here Strindberg writes of 'produktionsglädjens smärta och fröjd' (the pains and the joy that come with the delights of being productive). His position is that of a recently divorced man, burdened with debts that he cannot pay. He nevertheless has been productive and is able to write, '- och likafullt - es ist eine Lust zu leben i inbillningens rosenröda verld der man styr allt sjelf till det bästa' (VIII, p. 367 - and nevertheless - es ist eine Lust zu leben in the rosy-red world of the imagination, where you manage everything by yourself, all for the best).

This letter ends with Strindberg parodying the first chapter of the Book of Genesis: 'Jag har nu skrifvit mitt nya Sorgespels 1a Akt på 4 dagar och se: allt är mycket godt!' (VIII, p. 368 - I have now written the first act of my new tragedy and behold: it is good!).

Strindberg's correspondence is rife with Biblical allusions and puns. One finds many travesties that would perhaps strike some as unduly profane, and others as cleverly witty. They range from falsely solemn words, such as those that he wrote in a letter to Verner von Heidenstam upon returning from a research trip to France in 1886: 'Det är fullkomnadt. Utan att jag uppgivit anden!' (VI, p. 67 - It is finished. Without my giving up the ghost),[20] to his exclamation, after waking up with a hangover on 28 December 1892, 'Kater noster qui es in coelo!' - in which he substitutes the word 'Kater' (German for 'hangover') for 'Pater' (IX, p. 110).

From literary to religious to philosophical texts, Strindberg delights in parody. At least one example of a parodic reference to a philosophical tractate should be added to the parodic allusions presented here: in a letter to Ola Hansson of 22 March 1889, Strindberg wrote,

> Jag har länge tänkt skrifva en bok:
> Die Welt als Lügen und Verstellung
> oder
> Das Wesen der Simulation.

(VII, p. 288 - I have been thinking for a long time about writing a book: The World as Lies and Distortion - or - The Essence of Simulation), clearly parodying Schopenhauer's title, *Die Welt als Wille und Vorstellung* (The World as Will and Representation)).

A number of examples of the wit that permeates Strindberg's correspondence have been presented here, and yet they offer but a small sampling. After reading so many quotations, however, one might question the purpose of so much anecdotal evidence. One of my aims is to bring to light some aspects of Strindberg that for many years generally have been ignored in Strindberg scholarship and criticism – to uncover Strindberg's sometimes wonderfully incisive, sometimes cynical, wit, and to illuminate his comic side, which has been stifled for so many years. While one cannot deny the gloomy aspects of Strindberg's image, surely they ought to be complemented by the more delightful aspects of Strindberg, aspects which, while prevalent throughout Strindberg's literary œuvre, are found in perhaps greater concentration in his correspondence.

Notes

1. *August Strindbergs Samlade Verk*, Vol. 27, edited by Gunnar Ollén (Stockholm, 1984), p. 103. Subsequent references to this edition will appear in parentheses after a quotation as SV, with volume and page number in Arabic. References to Strindberg's *Samlade Skrifter*, 55 vols (Stockholm, 1912-20), are distinguished in parentheses as SS, followed by the volume and page number, also in Arabic.
2. *August Strindbergs brev*, edited by Torsten Eklund and Björn Meidal (Stockholm, 1948-97), VI, p. 315. Subsequent references to this edition will appear in parentheses after a quotation, with the volume number in Roman numerals and the page number in Arabic numerals.
3. See also Martin Lamm's chapter on *Mäster Olof*, in which he discusses the influence of Brand on Strindberg's original concept of Olaus Petri. Martin Lamm, *Strindbergs dramer*, Vol. 1 (Stockholm, 1924), pp. 90-96.
4. 'Stux' refers to Anton Julius Stuxberg (1849-1902), zoologist, explorer, and a friend of Strindberg from his student days in Uppsala.
5. Annette Kullenberg, *Strindberg – murveln. En bok om journalisten August Strindberg* (Stockholm, 1997), p. 357.
6. The source of these definitions is Webster's *New International Dictionary*, 2nd ed.
7. See note, *Brev* II, p. 158. Hagelstam possibly refers to a member of the Swedish parliament, O. J. Hagelstam, who specialized in alcohol legislation; Hagel to a well-known innkeeper from the 1700s, made famous by the poems, songs, and illustrations of Carl Michael Bellman and Elias Martin.

8. 'We're going to pull out the linden tree!' While Strindberg's meaning is clear, his reference is not. One can assume that he was writing his own abbreviation, 'den Linden', of 'den Lindenbaum' (the linden tree).
9. This translation is from Volume I, pp. 74-5 of Michael Robinson, *Strindberg's Letters*, Vols I & II (Chicago: The University of Chicago Press, 1992). In his notes on p. 384, Robinson explains that 'Gästbådshamn' (Gästbåd) is 'the main harbour on Kymmendö' and translates 'payment in ready cash' from the Latin. Subsequent references to Robinson's translations will appear in the parentheses after quotations as MR, followed by volume number in Roman and page number in Arabic. All other translations into English are my own.
10. Michael Meyer quotes the same letter up to this point, following with the comment, 'But such cheerfulness was infrequent'. Michael Meyer, *Strindberg: A Biography* (New York, 1985), pp. 93-4). A perusal of Strindberg's letters, especially of the letters he wrote in his pre-Inferno period, provides considerable evidence to the contrary.
11. For an account of the relationship between Strindberg and Lidforss, see MR I, p. 348f.
12. 'It's necessary to do something, you see!'
13. The last sentence, describing Gustaf af Geijerstam, appears in English translation as a caption under Geijerstam's picture in MR II, between pp. 696 and 697.
14. See Torsten Eklund's note, X, p. 95.
15. Kerstin Dahlbäck, *Ändå tycks allt vara osagt. August Strindberg som brevskrivare* (Stockholm, 1994), p. 180f. For a more thorough analysis of the Strindberg-Littmansson correspondence, see pp. 341-66.
16. See also Torsten Eklund's note, VI, p. 84.
17. See, for example, the verses cited from Heine's *Buch der Lieder* in a letter to Siri, dated 8 August 1875 (I, p. 216).
18. The lines in the letter to Pirkheimer read, 'O große Zeit der Wissenschaft, noch ist nicht der Augenblick, sich zur Ruhe zu setzen, mein Willibald, die Geister erwachen, die Studien blühen, es ist eine Lust zu leben' (O great time of learning, the moment has not yet come to settle into idleness, my Willibald, the spirits are awakening, knowledge is blooming, it is a joy to be alive). Cited in Fritz Martini, *Deutsche Literaturgeschichte*, 12th ed. (Stuttgart, 1963), p. 116.
19. Torsten Eklund has included a number of explanatory notes after this letter. Przybyszewski is a Polish writer who was a prominent member of the 'zum schwarzen Ferkel' circle, as was Adolf Paul; 'Priapus', according to Adolf Paul's *Min Strindbergsbok*, was a Polish lawyer;

the 'Müggelschloβ' was a restaurant on the shores of the Müggelsee east of Berlin; the 'dead Russian', a Russian funeral march that was one of Strindberg's favorite compositions; and Oscar Blumenthal, the director of the Lessing Theater in Berlin, who wanted to stage *Fadren* (The Father).
20. See the Book of John, Chapter 19, Verse 30.

7

'Spela den så att Pontoppidan och Fru Nansen få blåskatarrh': Strindberg's Correspondence with Actors and Directors

Michael Robinson
University of East Anglia

In October 1902 Max Reinhardt staged Strindberg's *Brott och brott* (Crimes and Crimes) at the Kleines Theater in Berlin, with Emanuel Reicher as Maurice and Gertrud Eysoldt as Henriette. It was Reinhardt's third major Strindberg production in twelve months and both these performers were also experienced at acting in Strindberg's plays (Reicher had created the title role in the German première of *Fadren* (The Father) in 1890, for example). Anticipating a success, his German translator, Emil Schering, therefore encouraged him to travel down and see the production for himself. However, Strindberg's response was characteristically discouraging: 'Tacksam för de goda förhoppningarne Ni dagligen insänder,' he told Schering,

och önskar se de efter hand förverkligas. Att jag går till Berlin är för studier och för att få nya tankar, ty här råder vintersömn hela året, och jag har nu lefvat upp hela förrådet som jag medförde hem från utlandet förra gången. Men Ni har väl aldrig trott att jag fore till Berlin för att låta fira mig eller 'uppträda' (som Björnson!) Jag anser mig visserligen skyldig skådespelarne att se en föreställning, från en osynlig plats, en qväll då ingen af publiken vet att jag fins der, och fastän det redan är tortyr att se mina skuggor och höra mina ord, skall jag göra min pligt....Allt offentligt är mig emot, rent patologiskt!¹

([I'm] grateful for the high hopes you send me every day, and look to see them realized in due course. My going to Berlin would be to study and to get some new ideas, for here we're sunk in a winter sleep all year round, and I have now lived up the entire supply I brought home from abroad last time. But you surely never believed I would go to Berlin to be lionized or 'perform' (like Bjørnson!). I certainly believe I owe it to the actors to see a performance, from a concealed seat, one evening when no one in the public is aware I am there, and even though it is a torture to see my shadows and hear my words, I shall do my duty....I am opposed to everything of a public nature, quite pathologically so!)

To anyone familiar with Strindberg's correspondence this response will come as no surprise. For while he was always pleased to travel the world in pursuit of the capital of experience that he exploited in his writings, he was unwilling to expose himself to the paying public in person. Shy and frequently tongue-tied in public gatherings, he left his writing to speak for him, and a director or impressario (Schering at this time enjoyed playing the latter role alongside that of translator) had to be prepared for Strindberg to cry off an opening night. At best he might attend a dress rehearsal and follow up his visit with a formal note of thanks to those involved in mounting the production.

Such notes form only a small proportion of the some 9,000 items in Strindberg's extant correspondence. The sheer volume of his letter writing, which in this respect represents his principal genre, is to be accounted for only in part by the many years he lived abroad during the 1880s and 1890s. In fact, the volume of his correspondence in no way diminished when he returned to Sweden, either in 1889 or again in 1898, and it is clear that from an early stage in his career letter writing fulfilled a vital need for self-expression, one which could only be adequately satisfied in this immediate fashion. Moreover, for Strindberg, the private letter was not only the most honest and individual form of communication, which implied spontaneity, naturalness, and originality; it was also the basis for other kinds of writing, whose affinity with the personal letter seemingly masked for him the element of artifice and stereotype present in all written compositions.

At first sight Strindberg's epistolary aesthetic may recall Stendhal's approach to autobiographical prose, which he sometimes regards as a form of letter: 'Je me suis imposé d'écrire ces souvenirs à vingt pages par séance, comme une lettre', he writes, in *Les Souvenirs d'égotisme*, and again, 'J'écris ceci, sans mentir j'éspère, avec plaisir comme une lettre à un ami', in Chapter One of *La Vie de Henry Brulard*.[2] But Strindberg's practice is very much more far-reaching. Just how far-reaching is most clearly articulated in the lengthy epistle on writing with which he initiates his correspondence with his first wife, Siri von Essen, in 1875. 'Att skrifva för Er är endast att erinra' (I, p. 193 – For you, writing is simply a matter of remembering), he tells her, and goes on to demonstrate how she may arrive at a work of literature by taking and dating a sheet of stationary, and addressing on it all she cannot say aloud to a dear friend. Then, by removing the date, the superscription and the signature the text of this and other such 'letters' to which she has confided herself may be published as a book. Again, in 1882, he tells his younger sister Elisabeth, 'Är ditt hjerta fullt och du icke kan tala, så skrif! Hvarje menniska med uppfostran kan skrifva, det vill säga sätta sina tankar på papperet. Du kan skrifva bref; en god och sann bok är ett bref. Att författa är icke att dikta, hitta på hvad som aldrig varit, utan författa är att berätta hvad man lefvat' (III, p. 41 – If your heart is full and you cannot speak, then write! Every educated person can write, that is, commit their thoughts to paper. You can write letters; a good and true book is a letter. Writing is not inventing, making up something that has never happened; to write is to relate what one has lived). And in 1907 letter writing remains the touchstone for that immediate and truthful form of writing to which he aspires when he seeks to console Schering for the break up of his (Schering's) marriage by advising him to 'Skrif sjelf, skrif ur Er smärtan! Ni skrifver ju mästerliga bref! och är således skriftställare' (XVI, p. 30 – Write yourself, write out your pain! You write such masterly letters! and are thus a writer). Or as he writes in *En blå bok* (A Blue Book) of his own published work and with the outrage it so frequently occasions uppermost in his mind: 'Jag anförtrodde det åt det tysta tryckta ordet på det vita papperet. Det var ett konfidentiellt meddelande; och den som förrådde det var en förrädare. Våra böcker äro gjorda att läsas tyst, att viskas i örat' (SS 48, pp. 941-2 – I confided it to the silent, printed word on the white paper. It was a confidential communication; and he who betrayed it was a traitor. Our books are produced in order to be read silently, to be whispered in [the reader's] ear).[3]

Nevertheless, Strindberg's response in this otherwise practical letter to Schering about Reinhardt's production of *Brott och brott* touches upon a notion that lies behind much of his writing in general, and his letter writing in particular, namely that where he is concerned social intercourse is 'en väv av hyckleri och lögn' (SS 17, p. 68 – a web of hypocrisy and lies) which people deploy 'endast i avsikt att bedraga varandra' (SS 48, p. 1061 – only with the object of deceiving each other), and that in spoken discourse one therefore runs the risk of losing one's identity. Through shyness or social convention one is unable to represent oneself accurately when speaking; this can only be done in writing. Moreover, 'tungan och det talade ordet äro så orenade av dagligt vardagsbruk att de icke kunna säga högt det vackra som pennan säger tyst' (SS 47, p. 731 – our tongues and the words they speak are so sullied by everyday use that they cannot say aloud what the pen says silently).[4] Strindberg is in fact deeply suspicious of the notion of a full and present speech, embodied in the person of the speaker, and likewise of a presence that is immediately recoverable from language as spoken, a language that is denied transparency and truth by the need always to accommodate oneself to one's interlocutor. For Strindberg, the self is dissolved or frittered away in speech; the speaker does not commit himself to his utterance but dissipates himself in the impermanence of the spoken word; hence he prefers to withdraw from social intercourse and reappropriate the presence that eludes him in speech in writing, most immediately in what that experienced man of letters, Samuel Richardson, calls, 'the converse of the pen. The pen that makes distance, presence; and brings back to sweet remembrance all the delights of presence; which makes even presence but body, while absence becomes the soul'.[5] Thus 'Strindberg prefers the solitary, secondary, invented mode of writing, which arrests, fixes, abstracts from, and supplements experience, a mode of communication which eschewes the immediacy and disorder of dialogue, and which is characterized by a double absence, or occultation, wherein the reader is absent from the writing of the book and the writer from its reading, to what is regarded, if only because of the anteriority of speech to writing in the individual's life and in history, as the primary, natural, even divine mode of communication in which the voice, borne by the breath, and guaranteed by facial expression, gesture, tone and inflection, signifies the presence of the speaker and his companions to himself and to others, in an interlocutory situation that binds voice and ear in the here and now.'[6] As he tells Schering three days later, when he is still seeking to justify his absence from Berlin, 'Mina skrifter är jag!' (My writings are myself) and any attempt to exhibit himself in public would be a form of 'prostitution' (XIV, p. 223).

The private letter, which straddles the gulf between presence and absence, is thus Strindberg's preferred genre, alongside the theatre in which the interlocutory situation described here may be realized by proxy. And consequently his reluctance to visit the theatre, which several of his biographers have chronicled, does not mean (as they sometimes argue) that he showed little concern for the practicalities of performance, or even that he was so out of touch with what could be staged that he wrote such theatrically impossible works as *Ett drömspel* (A Dream Play) and *Spöksonaten* (The Ghost Sonata). Indeed, the dominant trend of Strindberg studies has been so preoccupied with questions of biography and literary history that the theatrical dimension, and in particular its practical aspect, has frequently been lost.

In fact, alongside the *Öppna brev till Intima teatern* (Open Letters to the Intimate Theatre),[7] where characteristically he appears before his theatre company in print rather than in person, Strindberg's letters provide a valuable corrective to this point of view. Certainly, there are periods when he has little or nothing to do with the theatre, and several volumes in his correspondence (5, 11, and 12, for instance) feature no letters to actors or directors.[8] But just as he wrote more plays when there was a possibility of having them performed so he normally wrote to actors and directors only when they performed in them or were considering putting them on stage. As he tells August Falck, in 1910: 'Blir verkligen en ny teater vid Birger Jarlsgatan, så bli nog nya stycken också, om så behöfves' (XIX, p 12 – If a new theatre really does come off at Birger Jarlsgatan there will doubtless be some new plays, should they be needed). For much of his life Strindberg was essentially his own agent and P.R. man; he did not wish to write superfluously; and it is hardly surprising, therefore, that the majority of these letters should be written to the moment, when there was the prospect of performance or he had a new work that he was seeking to place. With the exception of a few items to Frans Hedberg, Ludvig Josephson, and August Lindberg in the 1870s and early 1880s there is thus little before a flurry of activity in 1888-89 when he sought to establish his Scandinavian Experimental Theatre in Copenhagen, a further group around the turn of the century when he has a whole new drama to be performed and certain works, *Till Damaskus I, Gustav Vasa,* and *Erik XIV*, enter the repertoire, and thirdly, and most especially, the long sequence of letters that he addressed to August Falck and the company of the Intimate Theatre between 1907 and 1910 when he is occupied with theatre business of all kinds, from ticket prices and the requisitioning of props to the staging, decor, costuming and acting of his plays. Then, quite literally, he gives notes to the cast in the form of notes, and we may thank his reluctance to appear in person for many of his most perceptive comments on the theatre. For as he writes to the young actor, Anton de Verdier: 'Vill Ni låta Era kamrater läsa detta, så slipper jag repetera mig. Det finns kanske några observationer som andra kunna draga nytta af! Jag är ingen talare, derför skrifver jag!' (XVII, p. 22 – If you would let your comrades read this, that would save me repeating myself. There are perhaps some observations [here] that others might find useful! I am no speaker, therefore I write).[9]

Although he is on a friendly footing with a number of the actors to whom he writes, and some, like August Lindberg, Tore Svennberg, or Ivar Nilsson, even become familiars at his Beethoven evenings in Blå tornet and elsewhere, these letters do not have the introspective quality of his correspondence with (say) Torsten Hedlund during 1895 and 96 (and it is important to remember that such a correspondence as the one he conducted with Hedlund need not be with someone who is a close personal friend: Strindberg, of course, never met Hedlund); nor do they share in the intellectual adventure of his exchanges with Leopold Littmansson during the 1890s or the burlesque humour that characterizes several of his letters to Carl Larsson, the energy of his correspondence with Verner von Heidenstam, the range of the confessional letters that he addressed to Bjørnson, or even the pathos regarding money matters in many of his letters to Albert or Karl Otto Bonnier. Only when he is writing to Harriet Bosse do his letters to a performer attain this kind of level, but then it is rarely to the practising actress that he addresses himself: it is rather the unfolding drama of his private life that generally concerns him here, not the drama as such, and the same applies to his later correspondence with Siri von Essen or their second daughter, Greta, who was likewise an actress, but where theatre business also becomes only an occasional topic of importance.

Nor does he normally allow the personal peccadilloes that enliven much of his correspondence to interfere with his advice to a performer. It is therefore exceptional when he writes to the Danish playwright and actress, Nathalie Larsen: 'Men nu spela Fröken Julie så som den skall spelas – icke som en sentimental prestgårdsmamsell utan som emanciperad (= prostituerad) modern dame af verld. Visa Era passioner, om Ni har några, eljes: spela dem!' (VIII, p. 210 – But play Miss Julie as it should be played – not as a sentimental vicarage miss but an emancipated (= prostituted) modern woman of the world. Show your passions, if you have any, otherwise: act them), or when he instructs Siri von Essen to perform *Den starkare* (The Stronger) 'så att Pontoppidan och Fru Nansen få blåskatarrh' (VII, p. 263 – so that Pontoppidan and Fru Nansen get cystitis). Indeed, he rarely devotes much space even to the ideas informing the work he is discussing. In writing to actors or directors, he is more concerned with a play's structure or its effectiveness as theatre, and in particular how the individual parts should be realized. Thus, as soon as he hears that August Falck the elder is to play the Captain in *Fadren* (The Father) at Nya Teatern in 1887 he immediately sends him a letter full of practical advice, a great deal of which is derived from his experience of the play's Danish première earlier that year, with Hans Riber Hunderup in the title role. Although he disclaims any practical expertise and expresses an unwillingness to interfere in the actor's domain – 'Som Du vet från fordom har jag just icke mycket begrepp om scenens detaljer, och jag stör ogerna skådespelarens arbete med att ingripa' (As you know from times past, I haven't much idea of scenic detail, and I'm reluctant to disturb the work of the actors by interfering) – his comments have great practical relevance. Beginning with a general observation, that the style of the play is 'icke tragedi, icke komedi, utan något midt emellan' (not tragedy, not comedy, but something in between), and that it should therefore be performed 'som Lindberg låtit spela Ibsen' (as Lindberg performed Ibsen), he focuses on the tempo ('Ta icke tempot för fort... Låt det snarare krypa fram stilla, jemt, tills det ökas af sig sjelf mot sista akten' – don't take too fast a tempo... Rather let it creep forward quietly, evenly, until it gathers momentum of its own accord towards the last act) and on character, stressing that 'ryttmästaren är icke en rå soldat; utan en lärd, som står öfver sitt yrke' (the Captain isn't a coarse soldier, but a scholar who has risen above his profession). And as with the reference to Lindberg's Ibsen style he feeds Falck the names of several Stockholm figures who might be used as templates in preparing the role: 'Tänk, utan att kopiera, på ryttmästarne aflidne P. v. Möller ledamot af Vitterh. Hist. och Antiqvitetsakademien; v Holst målaren, v Kock, filantropen etc.' (Think, without copying him, of the late Captain P. v. Möller, a member of the Academy of Letters and History; the painter v. Holst, the philanthropist, v. Koch, etc.). He also gives detailed instructions for the Captain's entry in Act Three, which is precisely visualized ('när han kommer in i tredje akten är han i skjortärmarne (Jaegerskjorta), har böckerna under ena armen och sågen under den andra' – when he enters in the third act, he is in his shirt sleeves (woollen shirt), has his books under one arm and the saw under the other) and supplies Falck with 'ett tacksamt moment' for Laura 'i 3^e Aktens I^a Scen, då hon sitter vid samma chiffonier-klaff der Ryttmästarn förut satt. Om hon der upprepar eller imiterar någon gest ryttmästarn haft (t.ex. att fatta pennan med läpparne och säga en replik så, förutsätt att ryttmästarn begagnat verkligen den gesten) så får man en fin kontrastverkan' (a rewarding moment in Act 3, Scene 1, when she sits at the same secretaire at which the Captain was sitting earlier. If she repeats or makes some gesture of the Captain's (e.g. putting the pen between her lips and saying a line with it there, always assuming the Captain really used that gesture), the contrast will make a fine effect). Here, the notion of 'hjärnornas kamp' (the battle of the brains) and the unconscious influence of one mind upon another, which the play as a whole explores, is deftly absorbed into a piece of stage business.

Elsewhere in the letter he tips Falck on how to manage the lamp throwing episode at the end of the second act ('Här var lampan af korgverke; glaset och kupan fästas med kitt så att lampan kan lyftas utan att glaset ramlar af; kastas förbi hufvet på Laura ut genom dörren, först sedan hon dragit sig baklänges ut, så att åskådaren lemnas i okunnighet om hurudvida den träffat eller ej' – Here we used a wicker lamp; the glass and shade can be fastened with putty so that the lamp may be lifted without the glass falling off, and thrown past Laura's head out through the door, but not before she has exited backwards, so the spectator is left in doubt as to whether or not it has hit her) and he is particularly perceptive about the casting of Laura's role. 'Om Laura spelas af en yngre dam med skönhet [he observes] bör hon vara hård, ty utseendet mildrar, och hennes inflytande på mannen motiveras derigenom; spelas hon af en äldre, måste det moderliga mera fram och det hårda sättas undan något' (VI, pp. 337-8 – If Laura is played by a younger and beautiful woman, she should be hard, for her appearance will soften the effect, and her influence over her husband will be motivated in that way. If she is played by someone older, the maternal aspect must be stressed, and the hardness somewhat underplayed). And so aware is he of the way in which an actor's appearance can influence the audience's reception of a role that six days later (this time in a letter to the publisher Claës Looström), he advances the candidature of his old friend Hilma Frankenfeldt over a certain Fru Gardt in Laura's role because her type will actually counterbalance the impact of his writing: 'Hilma F[rankenfeldt] skulle bli utmärkt! Den der kallhamrade, snåla, lögnaktiga Lauras karakter, skulle hon med sin skönhet och elegans adla opp, och i motsats till Fru Gardt göra sannolikt att hon vore en ryttmästares fru, och att hon genom sina qvinliga behag kunnat haft detta inflytande på mannen' (VI, p. 349 – Hilma F would be excellent! The hard-boiled, mean, mendacious side of Laura's character would be ennobled by her beauty and elegance, and in contrast to Fru Gardt she would be believable as a Captain's wife, someone who through her feminine charms could have exerted such an influence on her husband). Taken together with his advice to Manda Björling concerning the protagonist of *Kristina* (Queen Christina), namely that 'Äfven der Kristina är rå, måste Ni vara behagfull' (XVII, p. 43 – Even when Kristina is coarse, you must be charming), Strindberg here touches upon Stanislavski's dictum that an actor should always seek the opposite aspects of the role he or she is playing – the young man in the old, for example, or the good woman in the wicked.

What is characteristic in this letter to Falck is Strindberg's attention to detail and the ready confirmation that in thinking about his plays he was also visualizing them. In this respect casting is certainly one among several of his recurring preoccupations, not least because, unlike much nineteenth-century theatre practice, he knows that 'en rol kan aldrig tidigt nog lemnas ut! Derigenom vexer den fram sakta och ger mogen frukt' (XIII, p. 338 – a role can never be distributed early enough. In that way, it develops slowly and ripens well). 'Jag ville skrifva ett helt kapitel om rolfördelning, som är Direktörns pröfvosten' (I could write a whole chapter about the distribution of roles, which is the touchstone of a director), he tells August Falck's son, and his collaborator with the same name at the Intimate Theatre: 'Att kunna se i en blick skådespelarens naturell och ställa in honom på det rätta rutan!' (XVI, p. 302 – To be able to recognize an actor's aptitude at a glance and place him in the right slot). In his first major letter to an actor, written in 1871 to his friend August Dörum, who was to play Orm in the forthcoming première of *Den fredlöse* (The Outlaw), he questions the wisdom of much of the other casting, and has the temerity, at this early stage in his career, to seek through Dörum to influence the Royal Theatre and its dramaturg, Frans Hedberg, regarding the disposition of roles. Sometimes, however, his concern is opportunistic. In 1910, for example, he writes temptingly to the great French director of symbolist theatre, Aurélian Lugné-Poë, to offer him 'Reine Christine! Voici un beau rôle pour [votre femme] Suzanne Després' (XIX, p. 218) and in 1900 he approaches the current director of the Stockholm Royal

Theater, Nils Personne, with a somewhat disingenuous 'ord om flickans (Eleonoras) rol [i *Påsk*]! Du känner min svaghet för Fröken Bosse. Den fond av poesi och "Allvor" som hon eger, saknar jag hos hennes Kamrater; och hennes barnsliga gestalt lämpar sig väl för en flicka med fläta på ryggen' (XIII, p. 335 – word about the girl's (Eleonora's) role [in *Easter*]! You know my weakness for Fröken Bosse. I miss in her colleagues the wealth of poetry and 'Seriousness' which she possesses; and her childlike figure is well-suited for a girl with a pigtail down her back). Likewise, the following year he remarks to the director Emil Grandinson, apropos *Kronbruden* (The Crown Bride), that 'Mitt enda vilkor är, som jag skrifvit Personne, att Fröken Bosse får Kersti' (as I've written to Personne, my only condition is that Fröken Bosse gets Kersti). And then, remembering Bosse's slight stature, he adds, with disarming good sense: 'För att få vackra proportioner mellan figurer menade jag Fröken Sjöberg skulle spela Brita' (XIV, p. 49 – in order to obtain nice proportions between [their] figures I had in mind Fröken Sjöberg for Brita). However, once Bosse comes to play a central role in Strindberg's life, as well as in his stage works, certain parts are out of bounds to her. Although she created the role of The Lady in the première of *Till Damaskus I* in 1900, her subsequent assumption of the role of Strindberg's third wife made it impossible for her to take the same part in a production of *Till Damaskus II* or, indeed, in any revival of Part I: 'Jag har ingenting emot att den spelas, men ber att min hustru bli förskonat från "Damen", likasom hon äfven ber, i händelse af repris, få slippa samma rol i Del I' (XIV, p. 99 – I have nothing against it being performed, but request that my wife be spared 'The Lady', just as she also asks to be excused the same role in Part I, should it be revived).

Normally, however, Strindberg's concern is to match 'skådespelarens naturell' to his conception of the role. Thus, in a long correspondence with Grandinson and one of Personne's successors at the new Royal Dramatic Theatre, Knut Michælson, concerning *Siste riddaren* (The Last Knight), he is greatly agitated by whom to cast as the younger Sten Sture. Rejecting both the experienced Anders de Wahl and Gösta Hillberg, he argues for August Palme, 'om han är smal om lifvet' (if he's got a slim waist) or Ivar Nilsson, 'om han kan vara mjuk' (XVII, p. 45 – if he can be tender), and for a moment he even has the 'befängd idé...att Sturen skulle återges af – Julia Håkonsson!' (XVII, p. 70 – ridiculous notion...that Sture should be portrayed by – Julia Håkonsson), who was best known for her performances in Ibsen's dramas of contemporary life, from Lona Hessel in *Samfundets støtter* (The Pillars of Society) to both the principal women's roles in *John Gabriel Borkman* and Maja in *Når vi døde vågner* (When We Dead Awaken). Not surprisingly, Grandinson failed to run with this last idea.

However, if the vicissitudes of casting have now lost their urgency for all but the theatre historian, many of Strindberg's other instructions to his actors and directors remain pertinent, both in the immediate context of how his plays might be staged and (as Gösta Bergman has rightly indicated),[10] as part of the general theatrical revolution that took place around the turn of the century. For, like Gordon Craig, Fuchs, Appia and Meyerhold, Strindberg was then engaged in developing a new, post-naturalist language of the stage which was exclusively and uniquely theatrical. These instructions do not amount to anything like the system that Stanislavski was currently uncovering in Moscow, nor do they argue a single-minded theory of acting as (say) Diderot does in *Le paradoxe sur le comédien*: they are too diffuse and written to the moment. Nevertheless, fragmentary as they are they suggest that if Strindberg visited the theatre only rarely, he made good use of his time there.

He is, for example, aware from the outset that theatrical performance involves a collaboration between performers and audience, and that the actor needs to find ways of entering into a 'rapport med dem hon talar för' (XIV, p. 174 – a rapport with those before whom she is speaking). The actor must be in 'oupphörlig korrespondens med publiken' (III, p. 12 – continuous contact with the public), he tells Siri von Essen in 1882, and in the previously quoted letter to Dörum on *Den fredlöse*, he makes a serious point in jocular fashion when he advises the latter:

...spela inte för mycket! Förstå mig – åskådaren är en lathund som vill ha allt klart för sig med ens – han ids inte tänka långt för sig – behöfver han det då gäspar han och det är tråkigt! Men han är road af antydningar – ty så här går det till – gör Du en liten gest en obetydlig nuance i minspelet så förstår han det godt – bara han behöfver tänka litet – då blir han förtjust öfver sin egen qvickhet i uppfattningen och det är då han vänder sig till sin granne med en knuff i sidan ... hvilken knuff skall betyda "förstod *Du* det der".

(I, p. 81 – ...don't overact! Understand me – your spectator is an idle dog who wants everything explained to him straight away – he can't be bothered to think very much for himself – if he has to, he starts yawning and gets bored! But he's amused by hints – this is how it works: if you make a slight gesture, a mere nuance of facial expression, he'll understand it well enough – as long as he only has to think a bit – then he'll be delighted with himself for being so quick on the uptake, and that's when he turns to his neighbour and digs him in the ribs – as much as to say, 'did *you* get that?')

The audience must be engaged in the performance, and the long, one-act form of drama which Strindberg favoured from *Den fredlöse* to *Fröken Julie* (Miss Julie) and the Chamber Plays is in fact a ploy to gain and retain its attention. In a long play like *Till Damaskus I*, for example, he argues that the audience need to be kept in their seats for as long as possible: 'Låter man dem gå ut och räsonnera, och väpna sig till medvetet motstånd så kan spelet förloras' (XIII, pp. 322-3 – let them out to discuss things, and arm themselves for conscious resistance, and we can lose the play), he tells the director, Grandinson. Hence 'Omdekoreringarne ända dit [i.e. the central asylum scene, following which an interval is permissable] få ske i mörker; men intet ridåfall. Så snart ridå faller, ruskar publiken på sig och säger nej' (p. 323 – the scene changes up to that point must take place in blackout, but without a curtain. As soon as the curtain comes down, an audience gives itself a shake and rejects what it's seen). On the other hand, where the performers experience technical problems even in a relatively short play, such as *Bandet* (The Bond) Strindberg recognizes the need to assist them with an interval. Following a dress rehearsal of the play at the Intimate Theatre, he wrote to Falck: 'Förmiddagens resultat: Ni måste ta entre-akt i Bandet, ty Du tröttnar, Fröken Flygare tröttnar, publiken tröttnar! Men med entre-akt kan Du och Fr. Fl. *tala långsammare* publiken uppfatta bättre, och stycket vinna' (XVI, p. 165 – As a result of yesterday morning: you must have an interval in *The Bond*, for you will tire, Fröken Flygare will tire, the audience will tire! But with an interval you and Fr. Flygare can *speak more slowly*, the audience catch what is said better, and the play will profit by it).

Although the way in which the playwright has constructed his play may assist the actor, it is the latter who is immediately responsible for gripping the audience's attention. Most of Strindberg's advice is therefore directed to him. And while he could, on occasion, be cavalier (thus to the inexperienced Viggo Schiwe, who was to appear as Herr Y in the Scandinavian Experimental Theatre's production of *Paria* (Pariah), and in desperate need of some direction, Strindberg merely advised: 'Spela på ingifvelse – improvisera som Italienarne – och låt oss se om stycket bär sig! ... Tänk Er in i rolen så kommer hon ut sjelf på föreställningen men ej förr' (VII, p. 269 – act with some inspiration – improvise like the Italians – and let us see if the play holds! ... Think yourself into the role and it will come of its own accord in performance but not before)), he was generally specific and pertinent. Even his seemingly casual remark to Schiwe is given some sense when placed alongside a later comment to the more experienced Manda Björling, to whom he writes: 'öfva in rolen i minnet först, sedan kommer af sig sjelf uttrycket och stämningen. Att "studera" en rol har jag aldrig riktigt förstått, ty i en studerad rol syns arbetet och afsigten' (XVI, p. 191 – rehearse the role in your memory first, then the expression and the mood will come by itself. I have never understood what to 'study' a role means, because in a studied role the work and design are visible). What he, like Stanislavski or any good modern director, was seeking to avoid was the slentrian and the mechanical; the question was how to assist the actor in finding his or her character in a well-written role.

To this end Strindberg argued from an early stage in favour of what Stanislavski codified as affective, or emotion, memory. He asks Dörum to 'bed [Alfred Hansson] leta i sitt minne efter något djup sorg – riktigt djup, om han haft lyckan att ega en sådan – [och] bed honom ställa den för sig när han säger detta enda "Gunlöd"' (I, p. 80 – ask [Alfred Hansson] to cast about in his memory for some deep sorrow – really deep, if he's been fortunate enough to experience such a thing – and ask him to call it to mind when he says the word 'Gunlöd'!). The actor, in short, shall bring his or her own experience to the role, and find in memory the appropriate key with which to inform the part at a particular moment. At other times, in a theatre that was only now freeing itself from the collation of individual parts at the expense of the play as a whole, he would (like Ibsen)[11] tell an actor to 'se efter hvad de andra rolerna säga om Er; de gifva ju karakteristiken' (XVI, p. 173 – see what the other roles say about you; after all they give you your character), a point which is of even greater relevance in a drama like Strindberg's, where character was presented as multiple and relationships between the characters shifted according to their knowledge of each other.

Again like Stanislavski he was aware of the importance of concentration, and the need for ensemble playing. Thus, he advises Svea Åhman, who was to appear as the wife in *Leka med elden* (Playing with Fire) to: 'Kryp in i rolen, men äfven i den stämning som råder i scenen der Ni skall in; / Derför att godt att [sic!] i kulissen vänta repliken, höra de innevarandes tonfall, gripa stämning och ton; och så in på scenen; men icke ur klädlogen och småpratet direkt' (XVI, p. 171 – creep inside the role, but also into the mood which prevails on stage when you make your entrance; that's why it is a good thing to wait for your cue in the wings, listen to the intonation of those on stage, catch the mood and tone; and then make your entry; but not straight out of the dressing-room and its small talk). He even tells Falck, apropos his production of *Påsk* (Easter), to encourage a kind of hypnosis, a form of concentration in which one character continues to exert an influence over his fellow performers even when he is not on stage:

Än en gång; vårda sortierna. Den som schasar ut, tar någonting med sig af de innevarandes stämning: men han skall lemna något qvar af sin rol. Och när han är ute, skall han icke afklippa tråden genom att prata eller göra annat. Har han hufvudrol, får han absolut icke släppa kontakten, när han är utanför. Han skall hålla tankarne qvar inne på scenen, och utifrån leda; hans själ skall stanna inne fastän kroppen går ut. Det qvararande känna detta på sig, och när De tala om honom skall publiken liksom se honom.

(XVI, p. 278 – Once more: pay attention to the exits. An actor who rushes out takes with him something of the mood of those still on stage: but he should leave something of his role behind. And when he is off stage, he should not cut the thread by talking or doing something else. If he has a principal role he should absolutely not lose contact while he is off stage. His thoughts should remain on stage and lead the action from without; his soul should remain there although his body exits. Those who remain feel this, and when they talk about him the audience should seem to see him.)

Strindberg also authorizes the actor to play against what might appear the dominant tone of the text. Thus, Hunderup in the role of Gustav in *Fordringsägare* (Creditors) is instructed to 'spela nu hela rolen lekande godmodigt, såsom den öfverlägsne kan ... så att de blir sanning i Teklas ord: att hon finner Gustaf "så fri från moral och predikningar".... Alltså: Gustaf såsom katten lekande med råttan innan han biter honom! Aldrig ond, aldrig moralisk! aldrig predikande!' (VII, p. 259 – now act the whole part playfully and good naturedly, as someone who is superior can ... so that there is some truth in Tekla's words, when she finds Gustaf 'so free from moralizing and preaching'. ... Therefore: Gustaf as the cat playing with the mouse before he bites him! Never nasty, never moral! never preaching!). Likewise, Harriet Bosse as Damen in *Till Damaskus I* gets the important note: 'Det var stort och vackert (Damaskus) ehuru jag tänkt mig figuren något ljusare, med små drag af skalkaktighet och med mera expansion. Litet af Puck! – det var mitt första ord till Er! och blir mitt sista!' (XIII, p. 337 – It was great and beautiful (Damascus), although I had imagined the character somewhat lighter, with little touches of mischief and with more expansiveness. A little of Puck! – Those were my first words to you! and will be my last!). In every case he stresses the individual over the stock character, and is insistent on the avoidance of cliché. Svea Åhman, for example, is given copious advice on how to play the wife in *Leka med elden*, ending with the assurance, 'Ett djerft grepp till, och Ni är räddad: Slunga den röda peruken från 1870, och tag svart Cléo de Mérode-hår...och Ni skall känna Er som en annan menniska i rolen!' (XVI, p. 168 – One further bold trick, and you will be saved: Throw away that red wig from 1870, and have black Cléo de Mérode hair ... and you will feel like another person in the role) while Falck, who is appearing in *Paria*, is told: 'Tag icke rödt skägg och hår i Paria, det är för starkt att karakterisera med (= landsort). Bofvar äro sällan rödhåriga. Tar heldre ett urvattnadt blondt (smutsigt). ... [men] behåll cigarrstumpen och tumma den, tugga den' (XVI, p. 186 – Don't wear a red beard and hair in *Pariah*, as characterization it's over the top (= provincial). Villains seldom have red hair. Better take a wishy-washy blond (dirty) ... but keep the cigar-end and thumb it, chew it).

Above all, however, Strindberg is concerned with movement and speech, and in particular those moments when they are in symbiosis. Obvious clumsiness on stage is always to be avoided. Thus Nathalie Larsen is told not to walk with her feet splayed (VII, p. 254) and he is severe on anyone whose arms hang limply by their sides. In this respect, as when he tells Greta Strindberg to 'Vårda gången; elasticera sulan från hål till tå, och lyft icke foten oböjlig rätt opp. Springa aldrig, vagga icke på kroppen ... och trippar inte på scenen' (XVIII, pp. 195, 228 – Pay attention to your walk; elasticate the sole from heel to toe, and don't lift the foot straight up rigidly. Never run, don't waddle ... and don't mince on stage), he recalls Goethe's concern with stage propriety in his notes to his Weimar actors: certain things are simply not done on stage, as when he tells Manda Björling, to avoid being 'vresig' (cross) in *Herr Bengts hustru* (Sir Bengt's Wife) since it is unbecoming a woman (XVI, p. 191)! More significantly, however (and this is an observation unusual in a non-practitioner), Strindberg is aware that 'När hela varelsen har rolen i sig, så lefver den i hvarje muskel, nerv och sena. Med ordet följer gesten af sig sjelf; inte en muskel är liflös....händerna följa munnens rörelser om orden komma från hjertat, så att man icke tänker på't' (XVI, p. 278 – When your whole being has the role in it, it lives in every muscle, nerve and sinew. The gesture follows automatically with the word; not a muscle lacks life. ... the hands follow the movements of the mouth if the words come from the heart, so one doesn't think of it). And again, this time to Helge Wahlgren: 'ät Er in i rolen, så att gesten föds med ordet' (XVII, p. 87 – eat yourself inside the role, so that the gesture is born with the word), a remark that perhaps unfairly implies precedence to the word over gesture when, as the practising actor is aware, it is generally more a case of speech accompanying or following on from gesture and movement. What characterizes the actable script, like *Fadren* or *Fröken Julie*, is its 'potential gesturality',[12] a linguistic text with these gestures and movements implicit in it.

It is here, where voice and speech are concerned, that Strindberg appears to be at his most conventional. Or certainly, at his most prescriptive. And yet appearances may mislead. When writing to his daughter Greta or to members of the Intimate Theatre he is evidently concerned with what would once have been called their elocution, and therefore takes them to task over their *'frasering, eller musikalisk interpunktion det är framhäfvande av vigtigare ord och undanhållande af ovigtiga samt en rigtig uppdelning af frasen; nyansering eller iakttagande af höjning och sänkning, accelerando (påskyndande) och ritardando (återhållande), pausering, legato och staccato'* (XVII, p. 18 – *phrasing* or musical punctuation, that is the stressing of the more important words and the withholding of unimportant ones together with a proper dividing up of the phrase; *modulating* or observation of raising and lowering, *accelerando* (speeding up) and *ritardando* (slowing down), pausing, *legato*, and *staccato*). The musical terms employed here are typical of the period (Meyerhold, for example, uses a similar vocabulary to describe *The Cherry Orchard*),[13] and 'legato' ('Det stora legato' (XVI, 166 – the great *legato*), as he describes it to Falck) and 'staccato' become Strindberg's shorthand for the desirable and the undesirable. In everyday conversation speech becomes careless and jerky, and this cannot be transferred to the stage, even in the interests of realism, without detracting from the performance and its reception by an audience. As he tells Greta, *'Prata* inte, utan tala, stort, bredt; bind (sjung) ord och perioder, och hacka inte (staccato)!' (XVIII, p. 167 – Don't *chat*, but speak, on a big scale and with breadth; bind (sing) words and periods, and don't chop (*staccato*)). One must practise either by speaking 'soigneradt i hvardagslag' (XVI, p. 327 – carefully in everyday use) or, as in British drama schools some thirty-five years ago, by verse speaking. Thus, when confronted by poor articulation, Strindberg's recurrent recommendation is the poetry of Esaias Tegnér (1782-1846). 'Bed Prinsen i *Svanehvit* läsa Tegnérs vers hvarje dag, så han får legatot' (XVI, p. 135 – Tell the Prince in *Swanwhite* to read Tegnér's poetry [aloud] every day, then he'll get the *legato*), he tells Falck; even Manda Björling is advised to 'Sök opp igen Er naturliga stämma, håll fast vid den, odla den med vokaliser på vers (Tegnér)'

(XVI, p. 191 – Find your natural voice once more, hold on to it, cultivate it by vocalizing poetry (Tegnér)) while his inexperienced protegée, Fanny Falkner, is encouraged to 'Öfva rösten hvar dag på vers; t.ex Tegnérs *Asatiden*' (XVII, p. 112 – Exercise your voice everyday with poetry; e.g. Tegnér's *Asatiden*) and similarly Alrik Kjellgren: 'Vill Ni lära Er Tegnérs *Aolsång* utantill och komma och läsa den för mig, så skall jag säga Er talets hemligheter ... Ni är en utmärkt skådespelare, född till banan. Men nu skall Ni bli fullkomlig! Ni säger sakerna rigtigt, i ton och stämning, men det ska klin[ga] vackert!' (XVI, p. 332 – If you will learn Tegnér's 'Aolsång' by heart and come and recite it for me, I shall tell you the secrets of speech ... You are a splendid actor, born to the stage. But now it's time you became perfect! You speak properly, where tone and mood are concerned, but it must sound beautiful). But in almost every instance here he is, of course, writing to inexperienced and even untrained performers, whose voice control is likely to have been their weakest point. Pedantic and old-fashioned as these remarks appear, it is therefore hardly surprising that audibility and articulation should be of such concern to Strindberg, and he rarely comments on his speech when writing to an experienced performer like Falck.

He, on the other hand, is taken to task because in *Pelikanen* (The Pelican) he '"skrek och lefde", spelade för starkt, det är det man kallar landsort ... Modern eller ny skådespelarkonst det är: att icke gestikulera och icke skrika....Men vara inne i rolen, inne på scenen, i stämningen' (XVI, p. 111 – 'shouted and made a racket', went over the top, it's what one calls provincial ... The modern or new art of acting is: not to gesticulate and not to shout. ... But to be inside the role, behind the proscenium, keeping the mood [of the performance]). Here Strindberg touches upon what has become, with Stanislavski, a key notion of acting in the modern realistic theatre, namely the so-called mystical gulf that separates the stage, on which the actor appears to have no knowledge of the audience, from the auditorium. In this theatre the art of acting resides in concealing its art so that the actors appear to behave quite naturally. Thus, the performer in a play like *Fröken Julie* must appear oblivious of the public and yet, as Stanislavski also knew, must operate in circles of concentration that admit a lateral awareness of an audience that would otherwise be excluded from the action, and lost. As any practitioner knows, the dividing line is a fine one, and Strindberg draws it with some precision in a long letter to Falck, in which he defines the difference between a performance that crudely draws attention to itself, one that loses itself in introspection on stage, and one that finds the appropriate balance:

Nu har jag slutligen upptäckt att största illusion åstadkommes om man icke tänker på publiken, utan spelar i scenen. Det gjorde Kjellgren i Benjamin, och Falck som Lindqvist. Flygare måste ibland tala med ögonen utåt, då orden icke räckte, och det gjorde hon bra. Rydell gaf ett tag ett nummer, eller dedicerade sina ord till parketten; det verkade gammalt och bröt ut henne ur ramen. De Werdier var lagom. Man kan vända ansigtet utåt salongen utan att "tala till folket". Det gjorde W.; han gaf ut, utåt, men höll sig sjelf innanför ridån; det är saken.

(XVI, p. 279 – Now I have finally discovered that maximum illusion is achieved if one does not think of the audience, but acts [within the framework of] the stage. That's what Kjellgren did as Benjamin and Falck as Lindqvist. Flygare sometimes had to speak with her eyes directed out front, when the words did not suffice in themselves, and she did that well. For a while Rydell put on an act, or played to the gallery; that appeared old-fashioned and she became detached from the frame. De [V]erdier was just right. One can turn one's face towards the auditorium without 'speaking to the audience'. That's what W. did; he directed his performance outwards, but kept himself behind the curtain; that's what matters.)

Or, as he tells Manda Björling, as if it were the simplest thing in the world, '...tala till folkmassan derute på samma gång Ni är inne i scenen, på scenen' (XVII, p. 12 – speak to the mass of people out there at the same time as you are within the scene, on the stage). What, of course, he does not say, presumably because he does not know, is how to do this; that remains the prerogative of the true practitioner.

However, what is admirable about Strindberg's correspondence with actors and directors is his flexibility and his willingness to learn. For example, although he argued for the primacy of the spoken word ('"I begynnelsen var ordet!" Ja, ordet, det talade är allt!', XVI, p. 304 – 'In the beginning was the word!' Yes, the word, the spoken word is everything!), he was generally prepared to adapt his texts in the light of experience. Thus, having at last seen *Mäster Olof* (Master Olof) staged, he acknowledged that it needed shortening and wrote at once to his director, Ludvig Josephson, to suggest that he cut part of the tavern scene at the beginning of Act Two, the nobleman's harangue in Act Three, and the churchyard scene at the beginning of Act Five (II, p. 340). Regarding the Swedish première of *Fadren* he gave August Falck some cuts and told him, 'Stryk mer om ni vill. Ni hör nog på repetitionen hvad som stöter' (VI, p. 337 – Cut more if you want. You will no doubt hear during rehearsal what jars) while during rehearsals of *Den starkare* in 1889 he told Siri von Essen to 'ändra om det fins fraser som icke falla bra' (VII, p. 263 – change any phrases that don't come naturally). Thus, although the text for Strindberg was crucial and the theatre he finally acquired in 1907 was a playwright's theatre, devoted almost exclusively to his own works, he was ready to adapt to prevailing circumstances and take the exigencies of staging into account. Indeed, the latter sometimes encouraged him to break with current practice and experiment. For example, anticipating problems with *Stora landsvägen* (The Great Highway) he writes to Falck, in January 1910:

Om Du är rädd för barnets scen i *Landsvägen* eller barn förbjudes, så stryk icke, utan gör så här; begagnande monodram-metoden.
    Du säger: "Här kommer härskarinnan – " [Hon kommer icke i detta fall.]
    Derpå säger Du: "Denna scen har jag varit med om – förr – någonstädes – Hon kommer – och säger: Gå tyst etc."
    Derpå säger *Du* hela scenen, dels som Du tänker Dig den skola ske, dels som "Du" upplefvat den!...
    Detta är en resurs, förstår Du, och frågan är, om scenen i absoluta ensamheten icke skulle verka bättre, större, mera mystisk.

(XVIII, p. 272 – If you are afraid of the scene with the child in *The Great Highway* or children are forbidden, then don't cut it, but proceed as follows; using the monodrama method.
    You say: 'Here comes the sovereign –' [As it happens she doesn't come.]
    Then you say: 'I've experienced this scene – before – somewhere – She comes – and says: Go quietly, etc.'
    Then *You* speak the entire scene, partly as you think it should take place,

partly as 'You' have experienced it!
This is an expedient, you see, but it's debatable whether the scene [with you] entirely on your own shouldn't work better, have a greater, more mystical effect.)

Monodrama attracted considerable attention around the turn of the century; indeed, Strindberg had already toyed with the genre himself as a vehicle for Harriet Bosse, for whom he set out to adapt a number of works, including Schiller's *Maria Stuart*, as monodramas.[14] But it is in his search for this 'mera mystisk' form of staging that he is at his most revolutionary. And again, as so often happens during the emergence of the modern theatre, it is the need to resolve the problems posed by the practical limitations of the situation in which one is working that occasions the development of new theatre practice. The premises of the Intimate Theatre at Norra Bantorget had room for 161 spectators and the stage itself was a mere 6 metres broad and 4 metres deep. Nor was there room in the wings to store any amount of scenery or the possibility of flying new sets in from above. (Not the least of the theatre's founding problems had to do with health and safety, and in particular the fire regulations.) Thus Falck and Strindberg were soon confronted by technical as well as artistic problems (as if, in the theatre, the two are separable!), and Strindberg's response, which he urged upon his sometimes doubting co-director, derived a great deal from his knowledge of developments elsewhere in Europe – in, for example, the ideas of Edward Gordon Craig, whose *On the Art of the Theatre* Strindberg had first read in 1905 (XV, p. 135), and Georg Fuchs' *Die Schaubühne der Zukunft* (XVII, p. 238) – and something from his reading about past methods of staging in Herman Ring's *Teaterns historia från äldsta till nyaste tid*. It was, for example, in Ring that he found the idea for what he called the Molière stage (in reality Abr. Bosse's widely reproduced picture of the farce actors at the Hôtel de Bourgogne in 1630) where a pair of balustrades on either side of the acting area could be used to indicate time and place, and a change of scene by the removal or addition of one or another decorative prop placed upon them.[15]

But his principal source of inspiration was in fact the practice of working in the theatre itself, of, for instance, seeing for himself how a four-square solidly built set could be replaced by drapes in heavy velvet, on which the lights could play in various colours to achieve both a different sense of perspective and/or the impression of a change of scene. Hence his enthusiasm for staging *Spöksonaten*, again without an interval, but on a 'dematerialized' stage where a heavy and cumbersome setting has been supplanted by curtains: 'Mumien t. ex. sitter i springan af fonddraperiet såsom garderob. Det skulle lyfta stycket opp till dess plan, som icke är materialplanet' (XVII, p. 322 – 'The Mummy, e.g., sits in an opening in the rear curtain as in a closet. It would raise the play up to its plane, which is not the material plane). As he developed his ideas it was therefore continually in the direction of such greater simplicity that he moved, sensing that it was there that he would achieve the impression of 'dematerialization' that was implicit in dramas like *Ett drömspel* and *Spöksonaten*, and which was undermined by the kind of staging conventional in larger theatres at the turn of the century. Seeking to dispense with what he calls 'allt detta teaterbjäfs, som nu översvallar scenen' (all these theatrical gee-gaws which nowadays engulf the stage)[16] at the Royal Dramatic Theatre in Stockholm, he therefore urges on Falck the adoption of a 'stående dekoration, som ger unitet, fordras enkelt möblemang; några få nödvändiga pjeser – i *ton*, så att det inte svär! Börja vi soignera möbler och reqvisita, då äro vi på gamla stråten igen ... Ett bord och två stola! Idealet!' (XVI, p. 232 – permanent set – in the right tone so that it doesn't clash! If we go in for elegant furniture and props, we'll be back on the beaten track again ... One table and two chairs! That's the ideal!). This is a recipe that recalls his description of *Fordringsägare*, at the height of his naturalistic period, as 'bättre ändå än Fröken Julie, med tre personer, ett bord och två stolar, och utan soluppgång!' (VII, p. 105 – better even than *Miss Julie*, with three characters, one table and two chairs, and no sunrise!), and in such a simplified staging he argues that even *Fadren* will 'lyftas ut ur sin tunga hvardagssfer, och bli en tragedi i högre stilen; menskorna sublimeras, anobleras, och verka från en annan verld. ... Vi har sjunkit [he tells Falck] tillbaka till det som kallades Molander, eller realismen, naturalismen, hvilket allt är förbi' (XVI, p. 236 – be raised out of its heavy everyday sphere and become a tragedy in the high style; the characters will be elevated, ennobled, and seem to come from another world. ... We have sunk back to what was called Molander, or realism, naturalism, all of which is over and done with), and consequently lost the immediate, uncluttered, dematerialized playing style at which they should be aiming. For, according to Strindberg, the gains for the performer as well as the dramatist in adopting this meticulous but unfussy form of staging are immeasurable: 'Med enkla dekorationer kommer hufvudsaken fram: personen, rolen, talet, minen, åtbörden. ... "I begynnelsen var ordet!" Ja, ordet, det talade är allt!' (XVI, p. 304 – With simple sets what matters stands out: the character, the role, speech, expression, gesture ... 'In the beginning was the word!' Yes, the word, the spoken word is everything!). As Gösta Bergman remarks, of this declaration, 'Strindberg was far removed from Appia's and Craig's speculations about the rhythm of movement and mimic force. In the beginning was the word, *not* the dance or rhythmic movement.'[17] And yet, like the plays that he had already written for a theatre that was so far unable fully to accommodate them, these letters, notes and sketches to his fellow theatre workers between 1907 and 1910, indicate that in his thinking about the practicalities of staging, Strindberg had indeed crossed the threshold from the nineteenth to the twentieth-century stage.

Notes

1. *August Strindbergs brev*, edited by Torsten Eklund and Björn Meidal (Stockholm, 1948-97), XIV, p. 220. Future references to this edition will appear in parenthesis after a quotation, with the volume number in Roman numerals. References to Strindberg's *Samlade Skrifter*, 55 vols (Stockholm, 1912-20), are distinguished in parenthesis as SS followed by the volume and page number in Arabic numerals, and the ongoing series of *August Strindbergs Samlade Verk*, by SV with volume and page number, also in Arabic.
2. *Œuvres intimes* (Paris, 1982), pp. 452, 536.
3. For more detailed discussions of Strindberg as a letter writer and his epistolary aesthetic in particular, see Kerstin Dahlbäck's major study on Strindberg as a letter writer, *Ändå tycks allt vara osagt. August Strindberg som brevskrivare* (Stockholm, 1994), and in English, Michael Robinson, 'Life, Plots and Letters', *New Comparison*, 4

(1987), pp. 107-20, and the Introduction to *Strindberg's Letters*, Selected, edited and translated by Michael Robinson, 2 vols (London, 1994), I, pp. vii-xvi. The letters to Siri von Essen, Elisabeth Strindberg and Emil Schering quoted here are translated in full in these volumes.
4. In fact this comment from *En blå bok* echoes comments in a letter he addressed to his third wife, Harriet Bosse, on the subject of letters and letter writing: 'Orden och tungan äro ju så orenade att de icke förmå uttrycka det högsta; det skrifna på det hvita papperet är renare! (XVI, p. 251 – Words on the tongue are so sullied that they are unable to express the highest things; what is written on the white paper is more pure).
5. *The Correspondence of Samuel Richardson*, edited by Anna Laetitia Barbauld (London, 1804), III, p. 246.
6. Michael Robinson, *Strindberg and Autobiography* (Norwich, 1986), p. 62. But see chapter three, 'Writing, not Speaking: Strindberg, Language and the Self', pp. 47-84, passim.
7. Translated Walter Johnson (Seattle: University of Washington Press, 1968). These letters and memoranda take the place of the book on acting that Strindberg sometimes considered writing, for example in a letter to Tore Svennberg: 'Jag ämnar skrifva en bok om Skåderspelarkonsten, 40 års iakttagelser och reflexioner' (XVII, p. 245 – I intend to write a book about the Art of Acting, 40 years observations and reflections).
8. But one might also observe that throughout 1895-6, when his correspondence is otherwise prolific, there are no letters at all to any of his Swedish publishers, and only three during the whole of 1894.
9. One is again reminded of Richardson who, in the latter part of his life 'was rarely seen among his workmen, sometimes not twice a year, and, even when he was in town, gave his directions by little notes.' Mrs Barbauld, quoted in Malvin R. Zirker, Jr., 'Richardson's Correspondence: The Personal Letter as Private Experience', in Howard Anderson, Philip Daghlian, and Irvin Ehrenpreis, *The Familiar Letter in the Eighteenth Century* (University of Indiana Press, 1966), p. 73.
10. Gösta Bergman, *Det moderna teaterns genombrott 1890-1925* (Stockholm, 1966), pp. 264-310 and 'Strindberg and the Intima Teatern', *Theatre Research International*, 9:1 (1967), pp. 14-47.
11. See, for example, Ibsen's letter of 25 March 1887 to Sofie Reimers about Rebecca's role in *Rosmersholm*: 'The only advice I can give you is to read the whole play several times through very carefully, and pay particular attention to what the other characters say about Rebecca. Our actors often used to make the mistake, in earlier days at

any rate, of studying their parts in isolation and without paying sufficient regard to the character's position in relation to the whole work.' *Henrik Ibsen: A Critical Anthology*, edited by James McFarlane (Harmondsworth, 1970), p. 92.
12. Keir Elam, *The Semiotics of Theatre and Drama*, 2nd edition (London, 1988), p. 142.
13. See Edward Braun, ed., *Meyerhold on Theatre* (London, 1969), p. 28.
14. See e.g. XV, p. 169-70: 'Om Du vore här skulle jag skrifva monodramer åt Dig! Eller anrätta Macbeth och Schillers Maria Stuart m. fl. till monodramer....Med tre personer skall jag fournera en teater och spela med skärmar och en båge. Tänk på det!' (If you were here I would write monodramas for you! Or serve up *Macbeth* and Schiller's *Maria Stuart*, etc., as monodramas!).
15. See Herman Ring, *Teaterns historia från äldsta till nyaste tid* (Stockholm, 1898), p. 220.
16. *Svenska dagbladet*, 21 January 1899, quoted in Gunnar Ollén, *Strindbergs dramatik*, 4th edition (Stockholm, 1982), p. 275. Ollén makes clear that Strindberg has in mind the heavy, elaborate, Meininger-style staging then in fashion at the Royal Dramatic Theatre.
17. Bergman, 'Strindberg and the Intima Teatern', p. 31.

8

A Romantic Novel:
The Correspondence between Alexander L. Kielland and the Drewsen Family

edited and with a commentary by
Tor Obrestad
Stavanger

Foreword

The correspondence between Alexander Lange Kielland and Louise (née Collin) and Viggo Drewsen, which extends over the years 1881-1905, can be read as a narrative of the lives of two married couples, an epistolary novel about human passions and life's complications, which also contains several subplots. It is presented here as an unfolding drama, together with comments by the central characters drawn from other contexts, and by other members of the families who were involved.[1]

The letters have wandered from Drewsen's daughter Gerd to Kielland's granddaughter Pernille Smitt-Ingebretsen (née Krag). Her daughter Mette Bjerke passed them to Gerd's grandchildren. With the kind help of Uffe Lange, and especially Eivind Lange, who has the originals, almost sixty of these letters have recently been made available to the public for the first time. The letters from Louise and Viggo Drewsen are in the manuscript collection of the Royal Library in Copenhagen, and have also been made available to the public for the first time. The collection is supplemented by letters that have been published in Johs. Lunde's four-volume *Collected Letters* and in Kielland's son's *Collected Letters* from 1907. Thus, the forthcoming edition will be a complete representation of all the existing correspondence. The originals of some letters no longer exist, and have, most likely, been destroyed. As we can see from Drewsen's invitation of September 1881, the couples became acquainted at the beginning of Kielland's long stay in Denmark. Kielland lived here during his first years as a writer (from the summer of 1881), and probably met the Drewsens through Edvard Brandes' radical circle of acquaintances.

There soon developed a warm friendship between the two couples, a friendship that would span the rest of their lives. Sten Drewsen, the son of the house, would later become a journalist. In his memoir, *En kværulant ser tilbage* (A Querulous Man Looks Back, 1937), he describes Kielland:

Der var f'resten en rigtig nordmand med, han hed Kielland, og han var meget mere spænd og talte sådan et flot sprog og så' aldeles grinagtig ud, for han var blank i hele ansigtet og havde vandkæmmet hår ved ørene, men ellers slet ingenting og lignede en rigtig laps skjønt han var rødmosset i hele hovedet. Knebelsbarten den stod ud som to vridbor, og han gik med lommekam som han sad og trommede med i bordet fordi det ikke var så morsomt at høre de andre tale, som at snakke selv. Han var vældig modig – midt medens en anden sagde noget, turde han godt sidde og gør nar og lave ansigter hen til børnene – han var også den vittigste i hele selskabet, han vilde aller helst drille far, bare for spøg, og når han fik sagt noget som far ikke straks svarede på fordi han naturligvis vilde tænke sig rigtig om først, så fløj den norske op og tog den lange papirkniv og satte sig overskrævs på den og red sejrsridt rund i stuen, og så lo de.

(There was a real Norwegian there as well, called Kielland, and he was much more interesting and had such an elegant turn of speech and looked really comical, because his face was all shiny and the hair round his ears was slicked back, but otherwise there was nothing there at all and he looked like a proper dandy although his face was ruddy all over. His moustache stood out like two gimlets, and he carried a pocket comb which he sat and drummed on the table with because it wasn't so amusing listening to other people talking as it was to be able to talk himself. He was very bold – in the middle of somebody else's speech he actually dared to sit and make fun of them and pull faces for the children – he was also the wittiest person in the room, and he wanted most of all to tease father, just for fun, and when he thought of something to say father didn't answer immediately because of course he wanted to think it over properly first, the Norwegian sprang up and picked up the long paperknife and sat astride it and rode round the room in triumph, and then they all laughed.)

Louise and Viggo Drewsen were cousins who belonged to the inner intellectual circle in Copenhagen. Her brother, the zoologist Jonas Collin, had established a friendship with Hans Christian Andersen, and was married to Benedicte Knudtzon, the daughter of a wealthy Copenhagen merchant. Her sister Bertha became Georg Brandes' great and life-long (extramarital) love. The Drewsens were very close to Georg Brandes. Among other things, he was given use of their apartment whenever he visited his homeland from his exile in Germany.

Viggo Drewsen was born on 15 November 1830 and died on 8 November 1888. His wife Louise was born Louise Collin on 20 February 1839 and died on 6 December 1920. The couple had four children: Svend, Sten, Gerd, and Jonna. Viggo's father Adolph Drewsen was a judge and Konferensraad. Viggo's mother Ingeborg (née Collin) was the sister of Edvard Collin, Louise's father. He was a lawyer, and later departmental director, and State Councillor. Her mother was Henriette O. Thyberg. The couple had other relatives who were public officials.

Louise Drewsen

It is Louise's voice that lends depth to the letters. She found a communion with the celebrated Norwegian author that few experienced, even though many reached a kind of self-awareness through his writing. Her biography is somewhat lacking in facts, but is rich and exciting in its content, its inner life. She was a housewife, had four children and lived for her family. However, she was a person who could draw on a deep experience of life.

In order to create an image of this woman, we begin with some quotations from letters she wrote to Bjørnstjerne Bjørnson on the topic of Krøyer's bust of Kielland. Kielland had first given it to the Drewsens, but later presented it to Bjørnson; it had not been displayed prominently enough in the Drewsens' home. She writes of this in her letters of 31 January, 18 March, and 11 December. As is usual for her, she omits to include the year. It is probably 1892.

Ærlighet er *det* af alt, jeg mest forlanger af mig selv.

(Honesty is the thing above all others which I demand of myself.)

I min ungdoms lange brydefulle kamp med den mand, jeg elskede, manglede jeg saa tidt evnen til at gjøre mig forstaaelig.

(In my long and onerous struggle in my youth with the man I loved, I so often lacked the ability to make myself understood.)

Jeg mente noget andet, jeg vilde noget andet end ham.
(I thought differently, I wanted different things than he did.)

Sten Drewsen creates an image of his mother in his memoirs. In 1895, he is eighteen years old. He has a job, and wants to move out on his own. She is concerned and attempts to say what she cannot demonstrate: 'i den familie kyssede de aldrig hinanden' (in that family they never kissed each other). However, she does manage to voice some objections.

The son moves out, and does not do as his mother says. He even falls in love with an actress older than himself. Constantly worried, Louise writes to her son:

Min egen kære dreng!
Vil du først og fremmest love, at det jeg skriver nu, ikke må skille dig fra mig?
 Jeg kender dig godt nok til at vide, at du straks går aldeles ud af dit gode skind, og at alt det onde nu vil fare op i dig; men så puf det ned igen! Kan du huske de røde legetøjsdjævle i et glas med et stykke skind over, og naar man trykkede paa skindet, maatte djævlene ned til bunden – prøv nu, om du kan tvinge dit første raseri mod mig helt ned i maven, og naar du ikke mere ser rødt, tænk saa paa, at det dog kun er noget godt jeg vil sige dig; thi hvorfor skulde jeg vilde andet.

(My own dear boy!
Will you promise me first of all that what I'm going to write to you won't cause a rift between us?
 I know you well enough to know that you will flare up straight away, and all the badness in you will rise to the surface; but just push it all down again! Can you remember those red toy devils in a jar with a piece of leather over the top, and when you pressed the leather it made the devils drop down

to the bottom – just try and see whether you can't push your first fury against me right down into your stomach, and when you don't see red any longer, then try to think that all I want is to help you; how could I want to do anything else.)

This very woman of course, fuels her concerns. They have been observed together at a café. His reputation could be *damaged*:

Hvis en dame ses aften efter aften paa offentlige steder og lader sig traktere af en ung fyr med 60 kroner om maaneden, saa er det daarlig smag. (---) jeg advarer dig, det er min hjerteangst, der faar mig til et fortvivlet forsøg. (---) jeg føler en angst i mig for, at denne kvinde kommer til at gøre dig ondt. Men selv om du bliver rasende nu, saa glem aldrig, at du har en mussa, som du altid kan stole paa, og som elsker dig, og som aldrig vil lade dig i stikken. Betro dig til mig, saa længe du har mig.
Mo'er.   P.S. Send endelig snart vasketøj. Vi vadsker paa fredag.

(For a lady to be seen night after night in public places and to let herself be paid for by a young man with 60 kroner a month, is in bad taste. ...I am warning you, it is my deep fear which makes me make this desperate effort. ...I feel so afraid that this woman will do you harm. But even if you are furious now, you must never forget that you have a mamma you can always rely on, and who loves you and will never leave you in the lurch. Confide in me for as long as you have me.
Mother.   P.S. Make sure you send your washing now. We wash on Friday.)

However, Mother's concern carries no weight. The son continues as before. One day his landlord comes to say that his mother has arrived. She wants to know if it is a good time to visit:

Der stod hun, tæt indenfor døren, som om hun ikke vilde gaa for langt.
    Hvad kom hun da for? Hvorfor sprang hun ikke lige løs, hun der blev modigere end alle, så snart det var alvor? Men da så' jeg et ansikt som slet ikke var kampberedt; de tunge, tunge øjenlåg hvælvede sig ikke engang over bekymringer – hun smilede snarere, eller prøvede vist, men hun blev måske lidt genert; vi havde slet ikke set hinanden så længe.
    Herregud, hvor hun dog var lille. Og i den samme grå kåbe som altid – også jeg kom alligevel til at føle at det var lang tid siden; jeg vilde gerne række hånden – men man må være på sin post!
    Heller ikke hun trådte et skridt nærmere eller tog mindste tilløb til dét hun vilde sige mig; hun slog bare øjnene modigt op, da hun sagde det:
    – Jeg har fået et brev i dag. Om dig og din veninde.

Veninde! Hvad mente hun? Hvorfor brugte hun pludselig et venligt ord om en, hun helst vilde se død?
 - Et anonymt brev, fortsatte hun, og det så ud som hun et øjeblik fik kvalme. Men så sagde hun ganske naturligt:
 - Jeg vilde bare spørre dig, min dreng --- og nu smilede hun som venner smiler:
 - Trænger du til nogle penge?

(There she stood, just inside the door, as if she didn't want to go too far.
 What had she really come for? Why didn't she just launch into it, she who was braver than anyone else when it really mattered?
 But then I saw a face which was not at all ready for combat; the heavy, heavy eyelids were not even covering over her worries – rather she was smiling, or at least trying to, but perhaps she was feeling a little shy; it was so long since we had seen each other.
 Good Lord, how tiny she was after all. And in the same grey coat as always – I too came willy-nilly to feel that it was a long time ago; I wanted to reach out my hand – but one has to be on one's guard!
 She didn't take a single step forward either, or take any time to get round to what she wanted to say; she just looked up courageously as she said it:
 'I had a letter today. About you and your girlfriend.'
 Girlfriend! What did she mean? Why did she suddenly use a friendly word about someone else she would rather see dead?
 'An anonymous letter,' she continued, and for a moment it looked as if she felt sick. But then she said in a normal voice:
 'I just wanted to ask you, my boy' – and now she smiled just as friends smile:
 'Do you need any money?')

Viggo Drewsen

Viggo Drewsen studied law for some years, but never took the exam required for civil servants. After his service as a volunteer for the Customs and Excise Service, in 1859 he became assistant to the Finance Minister. During the Dano-Prussian war of 1864, he voluntarily enlisted. He was seriously wounded and taken prisoner at Dybbøl. It was then that he developed his 'stiff leg'. He worked as an archivist in the Finance Minister's Office from 1866-70 and then Administrative Assistant until 1873. That same year he was hired as a manager in the Insurance and Welfare Department, where he worked until his death. From 1882 he was Director of the department, and from 1886 he served on the board of Copenhagen's Savings Bank. In other words, Viggo Drewsen was a pillar of his society with philosophic and literary inclinations, but with radical sympathies.

Drewsen's Philosophy

Viggo Drewsen participated in the literary life of Denmark by cultivating, anonymously, a philosophic writing career. He 'was amongst those who work quietly', writes Harald Høffding, the Danish philosopher, in his obituary. Both his modesty and his privileged social position explain his choice of anonymity. However, he involved himself in events. He especially involved himself in the great debate on sexual morality that swept the Nordic countries in the 1880s. From his optimistic stance, he attempted to formulate his views on philosophy and conduct.

Experience and common sense were, in his view, mankind's only guidance in the attempt to understand one's existence. One must accept 'der er sat en grænse, ud over hvilken den menneskelige viden ikke evner at nå, og at det derfor er ørkesløst at søge at overskride den' (there is a barrier beyond which human knowledge is not able to reach, and therefore it is fruitless to try to cross it). As a result, he rejected metaphysical and religious explanations for life's riddles. Taking in psychological and evolutionary considerations, he put forward a theory that an individual can only satisfy his need for self-fulfillment and experience selflessness in a marriage rooted in 'true' love – a marriage where both partners love each other. Through this relationship, the individual will find recognition and affirmation of his or her own individualism. Since the marriage is only valid with the power of love's 'truth', it can 'undvære både kirken og staten og naboers og gjenboeres sanktion' (dispense with both church and state and the sanction of the neighbours next door and the neighbours opposite).

He put forth these views in several anonymous articles in the 1880s debate, along with three books: *En Livsanskuelse grundet paa Elskov* (A Philosophy Based on Love) from 1881, *Forholdet mellem Mand og Kvinde, belyst gennem Udviklings-Hypothesen* (The Relationship Between Man and Woman, As Seen Through Evolutionary

Theory), from 1884 and *Grænser for Kønsfriheden. Uddrag af et ufærdigt Arbejde* (Limits for Freedom of the Sexes. Excerpts from an Unfinished Work) from 1888.

In the first of these books, he states that the need to be oneself and the need to be selfless reach their truest and deepest reconciliation in a loving relationship and in marriage. For the author, marriage and family were the priority of human existence – it becomes his religion. Høffding makes no comment on Drewsen's opinions here, but writes that, in his eyes, Drewsen has 'givet et af de alvorligste og bedst gjennemtænkte indlæg i striden om ægteskabets og familiens betydning for det menneskelige liv' (made one of the most serious and considered contributions to the debate about the significance of marriage and the family in human life).

Drewsen was also a controversialist, and his attack on Georg Brandes over two issues of *Tilskueren* in 1885 deserves mention: 'Om en reaksjon mod den moderne stræben efter større sexuel sædelighed' (Concerning a Reaction against the Modern Striving for an Improvement in Sexual Morals). Viggo Drewsen was an author who was well-acquainted with and inspired by Søren Kierkegaard's thoughts and writings. He also knew Hans Christian Andersen.

Drewsen voiced opinions that, in our time, have become quite common. A sexual relationship and a shared life between two people are things in which no one else should interfere. It is as binding as any other contract entered upon and ratified by the state. It appears that his wife Louise more than shared his opinions. Alexander L. Kielland also must have found an echo of his own thoughts on these questions. Both men wished to distance themselves from the Brandes brothers who, at that time, were quite provocative in their views and personal conduct.

How to read the letters?

There are many ways in which these letters can be read. There must have been many personal traits of the participants that created a special chemistry between them – points of contact that made it possible for such reciprocal love and which opened, to such a great degree, a very close friendship. The letters can be read as messages between people, between friends who have an active interest in one another's wellbeing. These messages record moments of existential choice among the everyday joys and vexations that allowed the friendship to develop.

Letters of this sort can also be a method of expressing sides of one's self that would otherwise remain dormant. The secret behind this method is that the letter allows an outlet for the psychic energy of the soul that is also liberated in art. By addressing 'hiin Enkelte', the special person in an intimate conversation, one finds a channel that provides access to this energy, and releases it, especially during periods when these creative areas of the personality are not so easily reached.

Read in this way, there are a series of levels of consciousness in a letter from Alexander to Louise. For example, a letter that is written to Louise alone is written with the consciousness that Viggo will read it, and it is also a letter to 'the inner reader' in himself, i.e. a letter to the future reader, and an explanation and inspiration for the poet.

One can also read the letters as a picture of the time when the literary left became a concept. Here is a series of sketches from the circle around Georg and Edvard Brandes. These were people who contributed to the development of the political and literary debate, and who stood up for their point of view. For several years Georg Brandes collected a stipend of 4,000 crowns, which compensated him for the refusal to appoint him to a position at the University of Copenhagen and enabled him to lecture there without economic dependence on the public hierarchy. The letters mirror the tone of the intellectual circle: gossip and prejudices, philosophy and banality. At the time, a letter was a way of expressing oneself publicly – a sort of half-public channel for communication. It was also a way in which to manipulate the public. Georg Brandes, for example, could write one letter to his mother and say that he was on his way to Prague, knowing full well that the entire circle would immediately be informed of his destination. In reality, he was in Berlin together with his lover.

One can also read the letters as a contribution to Kielland's biography. It is rare that he opens up on personal issues as he does here. The communications with the Drewsens become a channel for encountering aspects of his personality that otherwise are somewhat difficult to discern. The letters to Drewsen demonstrate the urbane Kielland, he who could have been the centre of the social scene in Copenhagen. The tone can be frivolous, uninhibited, even what in our own time would be considered offensive and inappropriate. Many of these letters have a coded language. It is a raw and direct style that can only exist between people who are sincerely and lovingly tied to one another.

The letters are also engaging as a written expression of the elegance, intensity and depth of communication between Nordic intellectuals of the time. They mirror some of the social forms of the intellectual circle; jocular, provocative, and inspired. All three principals have a special understanding of the style and the special history of the letter as a genre. The authors are conscious that their correspondence must also be exploited publicly, at a later date, when history will be written. The letters, at that time, were also an economic investment in the children's future. When most of the players had gone from the stage, the letters could describe the daily lives and being of some of the most central players of the time. They could, therefore, be a source of insight for later generations.

All the additional information given by a letter of this sort must be mentioned here, information that disappears with the printing of the handwritten text. Something of the letter's total atmosphere is lost in the printed version; the optical and graphic image the writing conveys, the ink stains, the paragraphs, the marginal comments.

Finally, and this method of reading is the basis for the presentation of this material, these letters can be read as a novel, a story about the relationship/relationships between the parties involved. This presentation will emphasize this method of reading. However, the reader must not focus exclusively on the private relationship between the people. One must begin with the whole discussion of love, sex and morality that occupied the Scandinavian intellectuals during those years. The letters can also be read as a romantic novel of the time, or as a love triangle between a woman and two men who are tied to each other on several levels as seen through the eyes of a fourth individual in the background.

The Book Read as a Novel

Letter novels of this kind were a literary genre in the middle of the eighteenth century, established by Samuel Richardson with his novel *Pamela* (1740-1742). According to Tore Brøym in his foreword to his presentation of Kielland's letters 'Tre brev og fire billetter' (Three Letters and Four Notes), the idea behind a novel in epistolary form is an increased feeling of realism and an increased level of intimacy. The novel's overture can be read in a note from September 1881, with Kielland's inscription from 1886. Here, it states, amongst other things: 'baade Beate og jeg fandt, at fru Louise var en liden ubetydelig dame – optaget af husstel og fjollet forresten: Senere har vi mange gange leet af dette selskab, hvor vi, som dog skulde blive saa gode venner, gik omkring hinanden uden forstaaelse og ligesom i mørke' (both Beate and I found that fru Louise was a small insignificant woman – preoccupied with household matters and silly into the bargain. Later we have laughed many times about this occasion, where we, who were after all to be such good friends, walked around each other without any understanding and as it were in the dark).

Preliminary skirmishes follow, along with invitations to parties, and a battle between the two male rivals over national territory. It was a meeting between two warriors. It ended with a new understanding and a deeper friendship. Nearly two years had passed. At this time, Kielland returned to Stavanger as the celebrated and successful author. He would build a mansion overlooking Hafrsfjord and live comfortably from his book sales and penmanship. In the two years, his relationship to the Drewsens had become of great significance to him. Through many social gatherings and meetings, discussions and conversations, they had developed a depth of reciprocal fondness. What these conversations were about, we can only guess. They begin with a devotion and interest between friends which expands (and narrows) through their correspondence.

Not until their separation, when the Kiellands returned to Stavanger in the summer of 1883, does the woman, the main character, begin to have her say. That is – Beate has also taken part in the formation of the novel, but her contribution from this time is presumably lost. It cannot be traced through the letter collections of the various universities. Thus, she becomes a present but anonymous character who must be treated with the courtesy and respect that is due the poet's wife, and nothing more. In this way, history is pitiless. Therefore it is debatable as to whether this is a correct image, since Beate never contributes a word to the actual text. She only reads it.

We begin the story in the spring of 1883. Kielland finished the first draft of his novel *Gift* (Married) on 31 March, 1883. The book was published in June, and the author and his family returned to their hometown. Meanwhile, Kielland had collaborated with Edvard Brandes on a dramatization of his novel *Garman & Worse*.

Louise Drewsen's first proper letter is dated 8 August. She rarely included the year in her letters, but we can assume the date to be 1883. This is where the novel's action really begins. Kielland's response of 14 August is missing. Most likely, it was too forward, because Louise writes frankly in return. It was written from the couple's summer home at Ellekilde. Here, she holidays with the children while her husband works part-time in town.

It is in this letter that she first introduces what will become a recurring theme in the letters, a theme that is an undercurrent throughout their correspondence: 'The Dream of Norway'. The Drewsens have been invited to Norway. The invitation is repeated over and over again, and is the subject of intense and serious consideration. Will they travel to Norway, or won't they? The question remains. The exact nature of the question varies in the future. However, neither Louise nor Viggo ever make it to Stavanger. Why?

The letters indicate how much has transpired between the two characters. She writes that because she has not written, he must assume that she is dead! Further, she says that her life is empty. She is despondent: life there is 'mere beregnet paa det legemlige end paa det aandelige velvære' (more suited to bodily than to spiritual wellbeing). She needs peace, she says. When her husband is away, the sun shines. When he comes home, there are storms. 'Vi strider med næb og klør om deres [barnas] oppdragelse' (we are fighting tooth and nail about their [the children's] upbringing). The strife is so bitter that they will part, according to her letter. She has never met a person as grand as Kielland, she says, and ends the letter with heartfelt words about herself: 'Det, hun mangler er lykke, og den finder hun aldrig' (what she lacks is happiness, and that she will never find). Finally she declares that she will soon write to Beate – 'Hvad nu? Standser alt, fordi vi ikke ses?' (What now? Will everything stop because we never meet?).

Again, we will never know what Kielland answered to this outburst from an obviously unhappy woman trapped in an existence that she perceived as suffocating; so openly, so directly did she turn to him. Vulnerability and longing flood her next letter, where she nevertheless declines once again the invitation to Stavanger. Kielland repeats the invitation in a letter from the end of September: 'De skal Fanden gale mig herop, om saa Deres dyd er tyk som pap' (You damn well will come over here, even if your virtue is as thick as cardboard). In this same letter, he implies something of his own marital sorrows. Viggo Drewsen's response to the invitation is prompt and portentous. On a postcard dated 1 October, he writes only: 'Naar døden kalder, kommer vi' (When death calls, we shall come).

Fru Louise sends a long letter on 16 October. Her perception of his use of living models in *Gift* is so clear that she speaks of her husband as Professor Løvdahl. Alexander Kielland had dedicated the novel to Louise Drewsen. It is noteworthy and rather telling that Johs. Lunde, in his detailed discussion of the model for Wenche Løvdahl, never mentions this clue. But it was all quite obvious to the Drewsens.

The situation for Viggo could not have been easy. We are dealing with a man whose whole value system has been tied to the sanctity of marriage. He has a wife who feels that she is trapped within that marriage. She confides in a third person. This person responds positively and emotionally to her intimations. And he is a writer. In an undated, and rather aggressive, uncontrolled letter from Viggo Drewsen to his wife during that time (Kielland, judging by the inscription, received the letter in 1895) he refers to an episode from the Copenhagen circle's social agenda that summer. Drewsen heard Georg Brandes' father say that Drewsen's position in the triangle was that of a 'jordmoder-mands' (lit., male midwife). Whether this was true or not, it had become a question of honour. Drewsen writes – 'Thi hvad andet er jeg for ham, hvis jeg fulgte Dig op til Norge i sommer, end en jordmoders-mand, en taalt existens, et nødvendig onde' (For what else am I for him, if I accompany you up to Norway this summer, than a male midwife, a tolerated individual, a necessary evil)?

Nor does he refrain from saying what he really thinks of the Norwegian Kielland, alias the engineer Mordtmann:

jeg kan dog ikke lade være at konstatere, at det land, som han mener er skabt til at føde fribaarne mænd, efter hans eget sigende er beboet alene af fallenter.

Vil Du hilse hans elskelige hustru Beate Kielland, født Skrefsrud eller noget lignende fra mig.

(I can however not refrain from pointing out that that country, which in his opinion was created to bring forth freeborn men, is by his own admission populated solely by bankrupts.

Will you convey my greetings to his sweet wife Beate Kielland, née Skrefsrud or something like that.)

Now the cat is out of the bag, and the real reason that a visit to Norway remains only a dream is apparent: the man was jealous.

Louise and Alexander continue steadily with their correspondence. He expands on his views of sexual morality in his well-known letter of 29 October. Here, he lays out his true feelings on Bjørnson's "hanskepreken" (lit. glove-sermon) and his piously chaste sister: '(Det er ikke mere dyd i den forstand, vi tiltrænger; men vi trænger til slappere tøiler for begge kjøn. Fruentimmerne skulde ikke lære at overvurdere sin jomfruelighed, og mændene skulde være tilfreds med – nuvel) derved blir livet friere og elskoven sundere. — Puh! – lad pigerne more sig! – det er min moral' (It's not more virtue in that sense that we need; what we need is slacker reins for both sexes. Women should not be taught to overvalue their virginity, and men should be content with – oh well) in that way life would be freer and love healthier. – – Ha! – let the lasses enjoy themselves! – that is my morality). Moreover, in this same letter, he writes for the first time of her husband as 'The Inescapable', and regrets that he must have been given access to her letters.

She is provoked and made nervous by such matter-of-fact

speech. She writes that she had not expected such contemptible behaviour from him. She does not elaborate on this here – that comes later – but she crosses into another theme of the novel: a sketching of the circle around the Brandes brothers' tribulations. Amalie Skram gets a comment too. It was around this time, or soon after, that Drachmann's departure from the Brandes' crowd caused ripples on the duckpond.

At the same time as being both a love story and a love triangle, the correspondence functions as messages from one *family* to another. Furthermore, we can register both a collective and individual reception. Kielland is especially exact in addressing the one or the other individually. He writes both to the wife and, later, to her husband. He recommends that they read Garborg's novel *Bondestudentar*, for example: 'det er en virkelig god bog' (it is a really good book). The expression of friendship is renewed and strengthened. This special genre, with its contradictory signals from the author, on both a conscious and unconscious level, opens the reading of the texts to various and interesting interpretations. The messages contain both word games and direct speech. Deeply serious – and literary. Play, and threatening, existential reality. All three are well acquainted with Kierkegaard and his theories of human existence. For example, in one of Louise's undated letters from about this time, she writes that she would love to speak to Kielland face to face. It states:

Men hvis vi nogensinde mødes i Norge en dag ude paa landet, Viggo og Beate i det fjærne som to smaa prikker, saa maaske! Og jeg som i Dem saa en mand, der ved sit livs renhed og maaske ved sit lands friskhed havde beholdet sin tro paa mennesket! – maa jeg spørge skal smaapigerne deroppe opdrages paa det ny princip «lad pigerne more sig»? Oho, javist! Nej, hvad vedkommer moralen og opdragelsen hinanden. Edv. B. omgjærder sine børn med kristd. og selv praktiserer han sin moral paa andre folks døtre – men nu er jeg og lige ved at gaa over stregen.

(But if we were ever one day to meet in Norway, out in the country, with Viggo and Beate in the distance like two small dots, then perhaps! And I who saw in you a man who through the purity of his life and perhaps through the vigour of his country had preserved his belief in mankind! – may I ask whether the little girls up there are going to be brought up according to the new principle: 'let the lasses enjoy themselves'? Aha, there we have it! No, what do morality and upbringing have to do with each other. Ed[vard] B[randes] fences his children in with Christianity, and he himself practises his morality on other people's daughters – but now I too am about to go too far.)

It is in his reply to this invitation that Kielland tells her: 'jeg var tidligt og altid ideelt anlagt og saare samvittighedsfuld i elskov som i venskab; alt er gaaet stille af' (I was always, from early on, inclined to idealism and deeply conscientious, in love as in friendship; all has passed off quietly). At the same time, he comes with a confession: 'en enkelt gang, hvor jeg har gjort stor skade, var forholdet aldeles rent og ærbart. Er det da noget ravgalt i dette? – jeg forstaar ikke, hvad De græder over; er jeg Dem mindre værdt, fordi jeg som et langt tyndt spøgelse en og anden gang har listet mig opad en trap, som ikke maatte knirke?' (one single time, when I did great harm, the relationship was completely pure and honourable. Is there anything so terrible in that? – I don't understand what you are weeping about; am I of less worth to you because I on one or two occasions, like a long thin ghost, have had to creep up a staircase which must not creak?) At the same time, he repeats his credo: 'Jeg tror at kydskheden er overvurderet hos den kvindelige ungdom og jeg venter, at den langsomt vil synke i pris, medens den for mændene vil stige, indtil der naaes en passende, gjensidig fordragelighed' (I believe that chastity is overvalued amongst young females, and I am waiting for the price to drop slowly, whilst that for men will rise, until we reach a balanced mutual tolerance).

This letter concludes the first chapter of the novel. This is followed by two interludes that we can categorize under the titles 'J. P. Jacobsen's Sickness and Death', and 'The Brandes Brothers' Tribulations and Danish Politics'. But this does not hinder Kielland from uttering new declarations of love. For example, on 29 February 1884 he writes:

Er det ikke besynderligt, hvoredes den Gud, som vi ikke tror paa, har bragt os to nær og dog saa langt fra hinanden! Den 20. februar var De – med skam at melde; 45 aar og den 18. februar var jeg 35; vilde det ikke været rørende, om jeg nu kunde forære Dem 5 aar, saa vare vi lige, og saa skulde vi envoyer l'inevitable se promener paa stive fod.

(Is it not remarkable how that God in whom we do not believe has brought us two close and yet so far apart! On 20 February you were – forgive my rudeness – 45 years old, and on 18 February I was 35; would it not be touching if I could make you a prsent of five years, and then we would be the same, and then we would 'envoyer l'inevitable se promener' on stiff legs.)

On the same day, he writes a letter to her husband on the topic of Norwegian politics!
And she replies. On 9 March, she changes her greeting, which has always read Kjære (Dear) Kielland, to K-K-? She repeats that there will be no trip to Norway and says: 'Kun ét. Det er ikke at Viggo og jeg skal skilles. De kunde jo have grund til at tro det efter de mange med sikker haand førte beviser, De har givet meg for at jeg egentlig er ulykkelig gift' (Just one thing. It is not that Viggo and I are going to separate. You might have reasons to believe that after the many convincingly argued proofs you have supplied to the effect that I really am unhappily married). He responds on April 13, with 'E.L!' [Elskede Louise]: 'Jeg skrev saa muntert E.L. over brevet, fordi De skriver: K.K.; og min hensigt var at være uhyre vittig og skarp' (I began my letter so cheerfully with B.L. [Beloved Louise], since you wrote: K.K.; and my intention was to be amazingly witty and sharp). From here, he launches into a confession and apology for disrupting their marriage. This is the first time that he speaks directly of these things in a letter. He writes of Beate with her 'dry, sober mind' not understanding him. She can thoughtlessly annoy him: 'ja pine mig med tusind smaating, uden at hun har anelse derom' (even torture me with a thousand little things of which she has not the slightest idea).
Furthermore he says that: 'hvad der kunde forstyrre min ligevægt i det elskovsagtige ved ægtestanden, har jeg forvundet – ialfald paa det nærmeste; jeg er bleven gammel' (what might have disturbed my equilibrium as regards the sexual side of marriage I have got over – almost, at least; I have grown old). And then: 'Lad mig snart høre fra Dem og tilkast den Uundgaaelige en haanlig hilsen' (Let me hear from you soon and throw The Inescapable my scornful greetings), he says in closing. This time, six months pass before she replies. During this time, Beate travels to Copenhagen on a retreat, and stays with the Drewsens. Now the 'male midwife'

enters the scene. He sends Kielland two of his books. He has published these books anonymously. Most likely, Kielland was unaware that Viggo Drewsen was writing philosophical essays. Drewsen cannot contain himself and attacks his competitor with sarcasm. Norway cannot get the better of Denmark, he says. 'Norge har ej heller været ganske vel beregnende i sin politik. --- fra begyndelsen har det for meget ladet sin bagtanke skinne gennem' (Norway has not been very clever in its politics either....from the start it has allowed its ulterior motives to be too apparent). A new chapter begins.

Kielland finds himself in a pinch. How will he manage this? In the first place, it is not certain that he succumbs to the Kierkegaard-inspired thought that is present in these letters – ornate and embellished as they are. Secondly, how is Kielland to position himself in relation to their content? What will he remark on this Professor Løvdahl when he begins to preach? Will he scorn the man (because of the disparity between philosophy and life), or will he approach him seriously, or both? The matter concerns a friend and a rival who together make up a contact which is becoming vital to Alexander L. Kielland.

Take, for example, an exert from *En Livsanskuelse, grundet paa Elskov*, a book of 176 pages. Here, in the sixth paragraph of a chapter entitled 'Elskov og det derpaa grundede Ægteskab' (Love and the Marriage Based on Love), Drewsen writes: '... *fuldbaaren elskov kender ikke skindsyge.* – Forholder det sig saaledes, at hvor elskov er født af en helstøbt trang der vil ny elskov være en umulighed, fordi hvert gran af elskovstrang alt er stillet, maa de tvende, der have fundet troen paa deres gensidige bestemmelse for hinanden, være absolut sikre indbyrdes. Enhver skinsygens tvivl vilde være vantro paa selve grundvolden for forholdet, mistro til bestemmelsen, og derfor tegn paa, at elskoven var ufuldbaren' *(fully realized love knows nothing of jealousy.* – If it is the case that where love is born of an unalloyed need, new love will be an impossibility, because every particle of loving need is satisfied, then those two who have come to believe that they are mutually destined for each other must be absolutely secure together. Every jealous doubt would be heresy against the very foundations of the relationship, lack of faith in destiny, and therefore a sign that the love was not fully realized).

He goes on to suggest a fundamental law: '*hvor elskov er hel, maa de elskende begære at blive til ét væsen*' (*where love is whole, the lovers must desire to become one being*). This leads to a further fundamental law:

Ere de elskende forenede til ét væsen, ville de føle samme glæde over det gode og samme sorg over det mulig daarlige i de elskendes væsner som hvis det fandtes i deres eget; og de ville da gensidig være hinandens samvittighed.
– Hvad der har bundet de tvende sammen er netop glæden over hos hinanden at have fundet det store og sande menneskelige og derved at have vundet tro paa slægten og paa deres medeje i disse slægtens egenskaber. Jo rigere de elskende møde det herlige hos den elskede, des inderligere ville de glæde sig, og glæden vil være som var den over dem selv, fordi jo ypperligere den elskede er, des større andel tør de tro at have i det gode, eftersom hin jo kun formaar at genelske dem gennem det, hvori de ere hinanden lige. Men til gengæld ville de elskende rammes af sorg, hvis det skulde hænde, at de traf noget daarligt i den elskedes væsen, der, om det end ikke helt maatte omstøde, saa dog kunde forstyrre det billede, de havde af denne, og de vilde sørge som var det i deres eget væsen.---
Ere de elskende blevne til ét væsen, maa den fuldeste aabenhed herske mellem dem.

(*If the lovers are united as one being, they will feel the same joy about the goodness and the same sorrow about the potential badness in the beloved's being as if it were present in their own; and they will then be each other's conscience.* – What has bound the two together is precisely their joy at having found in each other what is greatly and truly human, and thereby having gained a belief in humanity and in their common ownership of human qualities. The more richly the lovers meet what is glorious in the beloved, the more deeply they will rejoice, and their joy will seem like joy in themselves, because the more superior the beloved is, the greater part do they themselves believe that they have in what is good, since the former will only be capable of loving them in return by virtue of that in which they resemble each other. On the other hand, the lovers would be struck down by grief if it should happen that they found something bad in the beloved's being, which, though it might not completely destroy, yet might distort the picture they had of the latter, and they would grieve as though it were in their own being.

If the lovers have become one being, the fullest openness must reign between them.)

What does Kielland do about this challenge? The strategy is outlined in his comment written on the letter Drewsen sent with the books: 'besv. spøg 29 april' (repld. joke 29 April). This letter begins thus: 'Ak – kjære ven! – at jeg ogsaa i literaturen maatte møde den uundgaaelige rival!' (Ah, my dear friend! – that I should meet the inescapable rival in literature too!) Here, the tone has been set. One can sense a whiff of alcohol in these letters. He wriggles around the subject by being jocular. The humour is so effective that Drewsen's response reads: 'Jeg maate læse det 3 gange højt for Louise og i 3 dage mødte vi hinanden paa trappen og i stuerne, smaaklukkende af latter og citerende nu et, nu et andet sted af brevet' (I had to read it out loud to Louise three times and for three days we met each other on the stairs and in the living room, chuckling with laughter and quoting first the one and then the other passage from your letter). Kielland answers with a new burlesque, farcical and lavish letter in which he makes fun of the academic tone in Drewsen's books. He adroitly implies that they are ornate and boring, but concludes thus: 'Jeg er endnu for mat til at kunne udtale mig om bogen, men jeg forbeholder mig ret til at komme tilbage – nei, pennen steiler! – jeg frafalder min ret!' (I am still too weak to be able to pronounce on your book, but I reserve the right to return to it – no, my pen revolts! – I renounce the right!).

Drewsen writes back in the same tone. However, behind the laughter, are claws and aggression. Kielland is mocking: 'for at udgrine hvad De højagter, for at bespytte hvad De aner er sandhed, for at korsfæste Deres overmand, den anonyme forfatter!' (in order to poke fun at what you respect, to spit on what you suspect to be true, to crucify your superior, the anonymous author!).

He notices that Kielland has reserved the right to come back to the books, and with that thought, his pen stops. But according to Drewsen there is no help for it, : 'De vil stadigt komme tilbage til bøgerne. De vil hvile som en mare paa Dem; De vil stirre derpaa som paa et blændende lys, og Deres tanker ville dreje sig om dette nye pust fra nu af' (You will continually come back to the books. They will haunt you like a nightmare; you will stare at them as though at a blinding light, and your thoughts will circle around this new breath from now on). The fact that Kielland never takes up the challenge and gives a proper response to Drewsen's writings is a part of this chapter. It stands in sharp contrast to the way Drewsen criticizes the books that Kielland later writes.

It is from Louise, on 30 August, that Kielland first has news of his wife's visit. Louise begins with a rather practical characterisation of Beate: 'Sød naturligvis, medgjørlig og fordringsløs; udmærket flink som husmoder, omhyggelig moder. Sund og forstandig i sin dom, grundærlig overfor sig selv og andre. Lys og let af natur, absolut utilbøjelig til at tro paa eller indlade sig i strid med modgang' (Sweet of course, cooperative and undemanding; extremely skilled as a housewife, a painstaking mother. Sound and sensible in her judgements, uncompromisingly honest towards herself and others. Light and easygoing nature, completely disinclined to believe in or defend herself against adversity). She continues in a direct manner:

Var der udsigt til at jeg virkeligt kom til at tale med Dem, saa vilde jeg gjærne begynde i breve; men hvad kan dette blive til. Jeg har en saadan bunke liggende som der skulde tales om, og nu vilde jeg kunne tale med Dem. Men skrive <u>kan</u> jeg ikke. Først vilde jeg fortælle om ham – den gang lastefuld, men ikke stivbenet, nu stivbenet, men ikke lastefuld. Og saa vilde jeg -- ja, og saa og saa -- men da jeg aldrig kommer til det.

(If there were any prospect of my being able to talk to you in real life, I would happily begin in letters; but what is the point. I have such a weight of things which I need to talk about, and now I would be able to talk to you. But I *cannot* write it. Firstly I would talk about him – formerly dissolute, but not stiff-legged, now stiff-legged, but not dissolute. And then I would – yes, and then and then – but since I will never be able to –)

She concludes the letter by pleading: 'Hvorfor blev De dog ikke hernede, hvorfor kommer De ikke igjen!' (Why did you not stay down here, why do you not come down again!).

This letter inspires Kielland to write one of his most famous letters. On 7 September 1884, he speaks out about the principles underlying his correspondence and friendship. 'Et brev er for mig et venskabeligt ord eller et uvenskabeligt – et haandtryk eller et dolkestød – bestemt for en eneste bestemt person solo' (A letter is for me a friendly word or an unfriendly one – a handshake or a dagger-thrust – intended for one single individual alone). Anything other is for him 'noget i retning af fælles tandbørste' (something more like a shared toothbrush). There is a path from heart to heart 'det er lyden om at gjøre, lyden af et venskab langt borte, bevidsheden om, at man færdes i hinandens tanker – -. Det beste brev er ikke det dybsindigste, men det oprigtigste' (it is the sound that matters, the sound of far-off friendship, the awareness that you are present in each other's thoughts – -. The best letter is not the most profound one but the most sincere).

This letter is one of the novel's high points. Now things cool off for a time. Of course 'Uncle Viggo' and his 'nephew' exchange news and gossip, but life makes demands on them both. Drewsen's father dies. Kielland is occupied with a new project – staying sober – a project for which he must endure much ridicule, but which in reality is a heroic effort. He no longer writes. He admits that he has drunk too much. But the demands of those nearest to him, and his accumulating debt is taking its toll. His debt to Gyldendal is over 12,500 kroner. It is during this time that he and his friends attempt to secure a poet's 'stipend' for him. A venture that ends in temporary defeat and affects him much more than history has recorded. At this point, he flees to the Mediterranean on one of his cousin, Andreas Sømme's cargo ships.

Louise doesn't write. He makes a new attempt to contact her in a letter from 28 July 1885. In it he appears half-sentimental, and half-cynical. He remembers her eyes and writes: 'de var graa og temmeligt trætte til hverdags; mine ere nu helt grønne med gule reflexer' (they were grey and rather tired most days; mine are now quite green with yellow lights). He begs for a letter: 'saavidt jeg kunde vide, vi vare gode venner – det er da bitterdød ikke sexuelt!' (just so that I could know that we are friends – there is nothing sexual about it, by God!), and looks at her portrait. He is on the defensive: 'jeg tror, det er hans skyld – den gamle overscaponneuren, De er gift med' (I believe it is his fault – that old overchaponneur you're married to).

Drewsen's texts have had their desired effect.

Ida Aalberg

At the end of October 1885, Kielland travels to Copenhagen again and stays until December. He cannot write and is fairly desperate, with thoughts of suicide in his head. He is warmly welcomed at the Drewsens' house. Once again Louise Drewsen takes things in hand. This time, it is for her 'chosen son'. Kielland has fallen in love with the Finnish actress Ida Aalberg. In order to have contact with her, he asks the Drewsens to invite her to a party. Louise agrees, but Viggo has his reservations. His wife writes: 'Han spurgte om jeg egenlig ikke fandt det forræderi med Beate at jeg gik ind paa dette. Først sagde jeg noget med højhed om at jeg ikke var forpligtet til at passe paa Beates mand, men senere kunde jeg ikke blive af med en vis uhyggelig fornemmelse' (He asked whether I did not really think it was betraying Beate to go along with this. First of all I said rather haughtily that it was not my duty to keep an eye on Beate's husband, but later I could not rid myself of a certain unpleasant feeling).

In the end, the actress is invited and the rest of the story has become a part of literary history, without anyone ever having noticed this story's links to the important and desperate play *Tre Par* (Three Couples). The short letters to and from Drewsen that follow are an excellent accompaniement to the notes that Kielland sent to the Finnish lady. Louise takes on the role of mother, even though in a later letter Kielland accuses her of being jealous. Viggo Drewsen was enjoying himself – if not royally, then in a manner appropriate to an old second lieutenant. Oh, how he enjoys the whole story at length! Read his exceedingly witty letter from Christmas day 1885, for example. It is a time for farce and scandals. This is also the same time that that dirty man, the 'chimney sweep' Georg Brandes is around, covering himself with soot (that is, rolling in his own scandals), all to the great applause of a greedy, prying Copenhagen. Bertha Knudtzon, the merchant's daughter – well really!

At the same time, Kielland gets what's coming to him. 'Uncle' Viggo makes fun of his open letter to the liberal Students' Association. Kielland replies: 'dette forknuste menneske, hvis hjerte hænger smaafillet nedover leveren – synes De, tror De, jeg holder taler -; fester!! for studenter!!! – O Moses! – O Potifar!' (this crushed individual, whose heart is shredded into ribbons over his liver – do you think, do you believe, that I am making speeches -; parties! for students!!! – Oh Moses! – Oh Potiphar!), and says that he has told the entire story of the Finnish siren to Beate.

On 11 March 1886, Kielland receives a letter from Louise Drewsen. The letter expresses deep longing. 'Hvem skulde tro at jeg holder saa meget af Dem, som jeg gjør' (Who would believe that I am so devoted to you as I am), she writes, and signs, for the first time, 'Deres til døden trofaste Louise Drewsen' (Your eternally faithful Louise Drewsen). Kielland answers immediately, but his letter is uninspired. When he moves to Aarre in May 1886, he once again invites the Drewsens to Norway. Fru Louise responds: 'De kan ikke tro, jeg ler ved tanken om at bo i de to smaa rum paa Jædderen. Jeg kan i øjeblikket ikke tænke mig *noget* jeg heller vilde. Men det er saa umuligt som ingensinde før' (Don't think that I would laugh at the thought of living in those two small rooms in Jæren. At the moment I cannot think of *anything* I would sooner do. But it is impossible as never before).

Then she tells of her son Svend, who having read the story of Joseph in the Old Testament, asks her what chastity is. 'Saa lagde jeg haanden paa mit hjærte og sagde: Svend, jeg véd det ikke længer. – Der er i det hele saa gruelig meget jeg ikke véd længer, – menneskene er saa forskjællige at jeg er nær ved at tro med Brandes at baade kjærligheden – ja at den hele moral bør være hvers private sag' (Then I placed my hand on my heart and said: 'Svend, I don't know that any longer.' – There is altogether such a fearful amount that I don't know any longer, – people are so different that I am close to agreeing with Brandes that love – indeed that morality in general ought to be every person's own private affair).

This kind of realization would not have been possible for Louise at the beginning of the novel. Kielland reacts to the chilly tone he feels in the letter. The salutation especially upsets him. '"Kjære venner!" – hvem er det? – er det en passende tiltale til mig, som er saa enestaaende aparte for mig selv alene privat og hemmeligt forelsket i Dem?' ('Dear friends!' – who is that? – is that a suitable salutation for me, who am so uniquely solely on my own privately and secretly in love with you?).

During this time, there are literary discussions with Viggo.

One could call this chapter 'Kielland's Literary Development'. Viggo, with his close contacts to the Royal Theatre, follows the treatment of *Tre Par* from the ringside. He makes some wise comments on the play, which he thinks is first-rate. In July he does travel to Norway. More precisely, he travels to Maridalen, where his brother lives. He has been there only a few days, when he becomes homesick and writes to his wife: 'vi har slidt det samme gulv, indaandet den samme luft, og talt om det samme og det samme i en halvhundrede aar' (we have worn the same floor, breathed in the same air and talked about the same thing over and over for half a century).

The Kiellands move to Cernay la ville, and for the first time, Alexander addresses a letter to them both. He actually gives in. 'Kjære Onkel og Louise! – jeg kan jo ligesaagodt tage Eder begge for mig i tanken, da dog intet formaar at adskille Eder – hverken spot eller formaning!' (Dear Uncle and Louise! – I might just as well address you both in my thoughts, since nothing succeeds in separating you – neither mockery nor exhortation!).

In November, Viggo writes down his opinion of *Sne* (Snow) which was published in 1886: 'Jeg læste og læste og syntes ikke rigtigt om den' (I read and read and didn't really think much of it). He gives reasons for this, saying that he still has not heard any discussion of the book, nor read a critique. Viggo Drewsen was well read, and a good friend and critic. We know nothing of Kielland's reaction to this critique. However, from their continued correspondence, we can assume something of his reaction. Kielland learns that the couple has been invited to dine with the 'enemy' Holger Drachmann, and he telegraphs immediately, 'Avez vous diné chez Mr. Drachmann[?]' The answer arrives promptly: 'Oui, et j'espère qu'il dinera ici'. The telegram is interpreted as a termination of their friendship, writes Louise, and Kielland sits in his cold atelier and writes with stiff fingers his most humble letter in the hope of saving their friendship. His joke had been too coarse. Explanatory letters follow, and the friendship is deepened and strengthened. Louise praises *Sne*: 'det var en lise for mit syge sind. Det er en fin og ren og klog bog' (It was balm for my sick mind. It is a fine and pure and intelligent book).

She is concerned about the change in the Kiellands and is

anxious for them to return from abroad, 'ind til liv og varme. Jeg fik en fornemmelse af noget mørkt og tungt, som aldrig skulde være over Jer' (in to life and warmth. I had a feeling of something dark and heavy, which should never oppress you two). This letter, dated 1 January 1887, is the last letter we have from her.

The chapter on Holger Drachmann, which is really about supporting or opposing Georg Brandes, ends with an intense, emotional moment between the two writers. Viggo writes several letters discussing the new literature. In March 1888, Kielland says, in connection with the discussion of his novel *St. Hans Fest* (Midsummer Festival), 'Jeg skriver nemlig altid saa at sige under Søren Kierkegaards øine, af hvem jeg har lært baade allegorien og gjentagelsen' (I always write as it were under the eyes of Søren Kierkegaard, from whom I have learnt both allegory and repetition).

Viggo Drewsen dies in the beginning of November 1888. Immediately prior to that, Kielland had sent Louise a letter about longing. He longs to sit an evening in her home: 'saa meget, der skulde været delt med vennerne, saa meget taushed, der skulde været udvexlet, saa meget kjægl, der skulde været udkjæglet. Naar man saa endelig tager fat paa et brev, saa er man saa fattig, somom man skulde binde kranse af visnede blomster' (so much, which should be shared with friends, so much silence, which should be exchanged, so much argument, which should be argued through. When you finally get started on a letter, you are so poor, as if you were to make a wreath of withered flowers). Then Viggo dies. On 16 November Alexander writes to the widow: 'Vor kjærlighed til ham og til Dem og ham sammen er af de bedste og dybeste følelser i os – Beate vilde sige det lige saa vist for sin part; og min bedrøvelse ved tanken om, at han ugjenkaldelig er udslettet af livet, kunde ikke være større og bitrere, om han havde været min kjødelige broder' (Our love for him and for you and him together is among our best and deepest feelings – Beate would say it just as surely for her part; and my sadness at the thought that he is irrevocably obliterated from life could not be greater or more bitter if he had been my own brother).

Louise bestows her husband's ring on Alexander, and he wears it. This is the end of the novel. Why is it over? Should not the hero and heroine finally be united? Should not there be a resolution, now that the triangle is dissolved? Why does the relationship not develop? Was Viggo necessary for that? This is not a romantic novel – this is life as it really is. The 'Novel' is written. The presupposition was that all the characters had complex relationships with one another. When one main character falls away, the foundation of the story is gone. It was, and should have been a story, not something to be realized as life.

Epilogue

The rest is epilogue; gloom, melancholy, tribulations fill Alexander's monologue. Louise no longer answers. Now come long complaints about the children. Kielland's daughter Baby heads to Copenhagen for a long stay with fru Louise. Gerd, Louise's daughter, stays for some time in Stavanger. Here are some of Alexander's final notes:

21 May 1889: 'Kjære fru Louise! Livet er forbi, naar det bare bliver til pligtdanse; og jeg vilde ønske, at jeg havde en, som kunde tale mig tilrette og holde mig tilbage fra den glidning nedover, som jeg er begyndt paa' (Dear fru Louise! Life is over when it is reduced to going through the motions, and I wish that I had someone who could tell me off and hold me back from the downward slife on which I have begun).

28 June 1892: 'Man fylder ikke ustraffet et fint hoved med en hel bys kloaksystem; det begynder med, at man modstræbende tager imod, indtil man formelig interesserer sig for gaderegulering, fattiggaard, sygehus og pest! – Beklag, men glem ikke Deres til døden Alexander L.K.' (You can't fill a fine head with the sewers of a whole town without suffering for it; at the beginning you are reluctant to take it in, but with time you actually become interested in road regulations, poor houses, hospital and plague! Have pity on but don't forget your eternally faithful Alexander L.K.).

29 November 1895: '... med aarene tager sentimentaliteten til i uklædelighed. Og dessuden maatte vi nu egentlig helst tale med hinanden — Alderen gjør nemlig saa store forandringer, at ved saa lange adskillelser som vor, kan brevene igrunden ikke helt hjælpe, man maa se hinandens øine igjen og høre stemmen, for med et igjen at være á jour og have hele glæden af hinanden' (... over the years, sentimentality is less and less becoming. And in any case we really ought to talk with each other – Such great changes come with age that in the face of a separation as long as ours, letters don't

really help very much, you have to see each other's eyes again and hear each other's voice in order to be *à jour* again and have real joy of each other).

14 September 1897: 'Jeg vilde bare fortælle Dem, at Beate og jeg har det ondt' (I just wanted to let you know that Beate and I are unhappy).

7 September 1902: 'Dem holder jeg af som i de gode dage, og jeg vilde give meget for at sidde hos Dem igjen og føle det gamle trofaste venskab og lyden i Deres stemme og Deres kloge ord -og hvis jeg endnu kunde faa Dem til at le!
– De husker, jeg gaar hver eneste dag med onkel Viggos ring, og De maa tro, at den mangfoldige gange lokker mig ind i fantasier og erindringer fra den tid, som dog maa have været uhyre lykkelig, – uden at vi kanske netop var os saa bevist, at den var saa solbeskinnet; – siden fik vi vide det.

De var altid tung, og jeg var altid lek, vi burde altid været hinanden saa nær, at vi kunde balanceret hinanden; De kan tro, jeg har gjort meget dumt, som De kunde forhindret, – eller som De ialfald kunde leet af – og De ler altfor sjældent; – hvor kunde jeg nu tage fat og fortælle Dem disse lange aars ringe indhold, hvor langt jeg kom bort fra alt det, som fordum bevægede sig i vore samtaler.

(I am fond of you as I was in the good days, and I would give so much to sit with you again and feel the old loyal friendship and the sound of your voice and your wise words – and if I could still get you to laugh!
– You remember that I wear Uncle Viggo's ring every single day, and you must believe me that it many a time entices me into fantasies and memories from that time that must after all have been richly happy, – without us perhaps being so aware of the fact that it was so sunny; – later we discovered it.

You were always heavy, and I was always playful, we should have been so close that we could have balanced each other; you can be sure that I have done many stupid things which you could have prevented, – or which you at least could have laughed at – and you laugh all too rarely; – how I could set to now and tell you about the scant achievements of these long years, how far I have moved away from everything which previously filled our conversations).

31 October 1905: 'Men hvorledes et menneske kan forandres – nu mener jeg Beate! eller kanske er det mig selv? – ak om vi nu havde havt Onkel Viggo til at tage mig af dage! – jeg er saa ensom. Men ellers var livet her noget for Dem; om De nogensinde kunde flygte, skulde Deres siste aar finde fred i en natur saa deilig som i digternes drømme fra Deres ungdom; blandt en landsbys fredelige befolkning – saadan som der var i Deres ungdom langt

ud ad Strandvejen; det samme trofaste hav skyller ogsaa her op med stranden, og De kunde gjøre Deres livs regnskab op, mens solen gaar ned, fordi vi alle ere trætte af den'

(But how changed a person can become – I mean Beate! or perhaps it is me? – Oh if we only had Uncle Viggo here to make an end of me! – I am so lonely. But otherwise this life would be something for you; if you ever could get away, your last years would find peace in a nature as lovely as it was in the poets' dreams of your youth; amongst the peaceful population of a country town – just as it was in your youth far out along Strandvejen; the same faithful sea washes up on the shore here, and you could draw up the accounts of your life whilst the sun goes down, because we are all tired of it).

What an adventure this must have been. It was a story of friendship and of passion, of the soul's hunger for its mate and for solidarity approaching bliss. I think that we, in our time, need to listen to stories like this one – practically devoid as they are of sexuality, lewdness or indiscretions. There is so much reductionism in our time. One reduces mankind's yearning for one another, yearning for the immortal space, yearning for the merciless sun of truth. Stories from our time are often cluttered with gossip, or the blindness that is our time: the paparazzi photographers' false images of 'real' life. We cling to these letters because they describe the freshness and pride of people who once were here, and deserve to remain here, forever.

Note

1. Since this material was presented in Norwich, the letters have been published with an introduction and commentary by Tor Obrestad: *To par. Brevvekslingen mellom Alexander L. Kielland og Louise og Viggo Drewsen* (Oslo: Cappelens Forlag), 1998.

9

'French Fungi':
Some snooping in Holger Drachmann's letters

Henk van der Liet
University of Amsterdam

The Danish author Holger Drachmann (1846-1908), whose literary life fits precisely within the framework of this book, made his official debut in 1872,[1] and was productive until he died in January 1908. During most of this period he regarded himself, as did his contemporaries, as *the* national Danish poet – a *skald* 'equal to the most distinguished in our classical literature', as he himself once put it.[2]

In the eyes of his contemporary countrymen, Holger Drachmann was Denmark's answer to such great Nordic writers as Bjørnstjerne Bjørnson (1832-1910), Henrik Ibsen (1828-1906) and, in part, also August Strindberg (1849-1912). But in contrast to most of these colleagues, Drachmann was never able to make an international breakthrough as they had done. The enthusiasm evinced for Drachmann's work by his contemporaries did not last long; the reckoning with it began immediately after his death and in histories of literature he is generally portrayed in less flattering terms.[3] Today most of Drachmann's work has fallen into oblivion. The fact that Drachmann's name, nevertheless, is still alive is to some extent due to his affiliation with the literary movement of which Georg Brandes (1842-1927) was the central figure, the so-called 'Modern Breakthrough'. This is not least demonstrated by the fact that Drachmann was one of the principal writers Georg Brandes dealt with in his epoch-making book *Det moderne*

Gjennembruds Mænd (Men of the Modern Breakthrough) from 1883. It is well known that the relationship between Brandes and Drachmann was a problematic one. The content of Drachmann's works, especially his poetry, often stands in contrast to the idiom of the Modern Breakthrough, as it reveals a strong preference for more regressive, romantic and bourgeois themes – such as the idyllic portrayal of women and national and historical topics – that hardly fit the image of an author who ostensibly stood so close to the Brandesian movement. I shall return to this ambiguity later in the context of Drachmann's correspondence with Georg Brandes.

Another reason why Drachmann is still remembered nowadays, and still appeals to the imagination of contemporary Danes, is his much-discussed bohemian life style and tempestuous love-life. These non-literary circumstances made him appear in the eyes of the public as *the* modern radical poet of his time, and this glamorous image must have been so strong, that it outlived the author and is still alive today.

Looking at Drachmann's *oeuvre* from a quantitative perspective, it is easy to see that it is one of the most voluminous in Danish literature in the nineteenth century, probably only surpassed by the work of N. F. S. Grundtvig (1783-1872) and Søren Kierkegaard (1813-1855). There were approximately sixty books of Drachmann's work published during his life-time, and in a wide range of genres: poetry, drama, novels, stories, travelogues, journalism, translations and so forth. There is hardly any genre he did not turn to at some moment in his career. Furthermore, Drachmann often illustrated his own works, as he was trained as a painter.

The most comprehensive bibliography available – Johannes Ursin's *Bibliografi over Holger Drachmanns forfatterskab* (Bibliography of Holger Drachmann's Work, 1956) – enumerates some 778 separate publications during Drachmann's life, as well as 60 posthumous publications. And even in more recent years a number of hitherto unknown writings, especially from Drachmann's early years, have been identified as his work.[4] According to an inventory that was recently carried out by the Danish Society for Language and Literature (DSL),[5] Drachmann's collected works would comprise approximately 50 volumes of 250 pages each, that would make a total of 12,500 pages, not including his letters. It is difficult to make a reasonable estimate, but looking at the more than 1,000 letters that have been published, and at the Danish Royal Library's catalogues of acquired manuscripts,[6] one may roughly estimate that Drachmann wrote more than 2,500 letters of more than just private interest, which would require at least fifteen volumes of about 250 pages each – if they were ever to be published.

The Sources

It is hardly surprising that not all of the letters by Drachmann that we know of have appeared in print, and not all of them will have literary and historical value. But the sources that are at our disposal – apart from the original letters in the Danish Royal Library's archives – are rather easy to survey. All in all some 1,000 letters by Drachmann are available in print in a limited number of collections.

The most important and most reliable of these anthologies is, without doubt, the one edited and commented by the esteemed philologist Morten Borup, *Breve fra og til Holger Drachmann* (Letters to and from Holger Drachmann), which was published in 1968 and 1970.[7] These four volumes contain 889 letters, of which by far the most have been written by Drachmann. In a number of cases, however, relevant letters by others have been added, to render the individual letters and the correspondence as a whole more comprehensible.

Next to the Borup collection – which is the lion's share of the material I shall take into account here – a number of other Drachmann letters have appeared. The first collection of Drachmann letters that was ever published, appeared in 1932, and was edited and commented by Drachmann's half-sister, Harriet Bentzon (1861-1945), entitled *Holger Drachmann i Breve til hans Fædrenehjem* (Holger Drachmann in Letters to His Parental Home). This work was not a strict edition of letters, but an attempt to write a Drachmann biography. With the help of a large number of inserted letters to his relatives, Harriet Bentzon basically illustrated and strengthened the biographical opinions and explanations she put forward. Furthermore, the ninety-two letters involved cover only a limited span of time, essentially the period between 1860 and 1887, and they have a limited scope, owing to the fact that only a small number of intimate addressees is involved. It is clear that this book was generated for a particular reason. As a member of the family, Harriet Bentzon wanted to put an end to the many rumours and speculations that still hovered over Drachmann's reputation and the negative image of their family-life that had been given in some biographical studies after Drachmann's death.[8]

Harriet Bentzon's somewhat awkward *genre-mixte* of a biography-cum-collection-of-letters was, by the particular nature of her mission, focused on the letters Drachmann sent to his parental home and next of kin. The definition of her subject-matter resulted in the fact that none of the letters written by the addressees themselves was recorded. The reason for this omission is obscure, because she no doubt had access to them, and they might have clarified some of the issues involved.[9] Nevertheless, this collection contains a number of interesting letters, and it urged the later Drachmann-scholar, professor Paul V. Rubow, to write the first article on Drachmann's correspondence a few years later.[10] Rubow put forward the question of why no proper biography of Drachmann that covered more ground than the Bentzon book did, had yet been written. Furthermore, Rubow made a passionate plea for the publication of more of Drachmann's letters. Not surprisingly it was Rubow himself who wrote the first comprehensive biography of Drachmann. We know that Rubow started his research in the Drachmann material in the early 1930s and in the review article on the Bentzon collection he neatly makes it clear that he is planning to continue to work on it. And in 1940 the first volume of his biography on Drachmann appeared, in which he included a large number of citations from Drachmann's correspondence and even reproduced quite a number of letters in full.[11]

Apart from the large Borup collection and the family letters edited by Bentzon, a number of stray letters and smaller collections of them are also available.[12] Some letters too, are spread over various biographies, such as the ones by Paul V. Rubow and Johannes Ursin, as well as in other studies. This material, however, will play only a minor role here.

Although Holger Drachmann was the most productive and well-known Danish writer of his day, it took considerable time to publish a reliable collection of his letters. The first reason for this has undoubtedly been the author's quite turbulent private life. Thus, particular precautions had to be taken towards a great many individuals who were addressed or otherwise involved in the material. One of the things that strikes the (modern) reader of the Borup collection for instance is the fact that none of Drachmann's letters to his lover, Amanda Nilsson (1866-1953) were selected, notwithstanding the fact that she played a considerable role in Drachmann's private and literary life.[13] This is all the more puzzling if one bears in mind that the Danish Royal Library, as early as 1947, acquired approximately 850 letters from Drachmann to this woman, known as 'Edith'.[14] These letters were, for no apparent reason, excluded from the Borup collection and later served as the main source for a book by Margrethe Loerges, *Edith – en skæbne i et bundt breve* (Edith – A Destiny in a Bundle of Letters, 1983). Margrethe Loerges had earlier used quite a number of private letters, mostly ones that had been exchanged between Holger Drachmann and his many female acquaintances and lovers, in her book *Drachmanns Muser* (Drachmann's Muses) from 1981. Unfortunately, although these two books are basically the only printed sources of this particular material at our disposal, the editorial principles of these works are not of a standard that they can be dealt with as solid scholarly material.

A second reason why the Drachmann letters were not published earlier, may be the fact that Drachmann's reputation as an artist deteriorated rapidly in the years after his death. His literary fame dwindled and it is not far from the truth to say that Drachmann's works, are, with the exception of a few poems and plays,[15] now largely forgotten. Thus, there were only few and feeble forces in literary and academic circles which advocated an edition of the correspondence by Drachmann. Even when the Danish Society for Language and Literature commissioned the publication of the first two volumes of Drachmann's letters in 1968, it was uncertain whether or not any further volumes would appear. Fortunately, two years later the remaining two volumes came out. Thus, eventually, four sturdy volumes with letters by Drachmann edited by Morten Borup, entitled *Breve fra og til Holger Drachmann*, are available today.

The Borup collection is designed with the following formal guidelines in mind: the first two volumes deal with Drachmann's letters between the years 1862 and 1883, and thus end at the moment when Drachmann broke with the literary and political current that he, until then, had been a part of, the Modern Breakthrough. The last two volumes contain letters from the year 1884 until Drachmann's death in 1908, and focus mainly on the aftermath of this conflict and Drachmann's subsequent literary *Alleingang*.

The letters: a part of Drachmann's literary legacy?

A fair number of Drachmann's letters are accessible, but an important issue is the function that these letters had for Drachmann. Or to put the question more precisely: To what extent are these letters to be regarded as private documents, and to what extent are they to be taken as public material and, thus, as part of Drachmann's literary legacy?

That the concept of privacy played a quite different role in Drachmann's time than in our own, goes without saying. It is clear as well, that the growth of his fame must have influenced the balance between the public and private character of his various correspondences. Over the years, he became an increasingly public figure and he understood – probably better than anyone else in his day – that a fundamental ingredient in his success was the neverending turmoil around his private life and his omnipresence in the media. I think that the particular balancing-act between public and private was a typical problem of the period 1870 to 1910 – at least, this is a hypothesis that the Drachmann letters seem to support. At this time the role of the press, as well as that of literature, was in a process of transformation, and the social position of authors, and artists in general, was in transition. The awareness of living in a period of fundamental cultural change was not least expressed by, and mirrored in, the political tensions of this era, the so-called 'Provisorietid' (The era of provisional legislation). The movement towards a democratic society with its institutions, such as a modern press and universal suffrage, had started around the turbulent year 1848 and, in Denmark, culminated in 1901, the year of the so-called 'systemskifte' (change of system). From a cultural perspective, authors and public cultural personalities in the widest sense of the word played an important role as forerunners of the political and social transition of this era. Thus, a great deal of attention was given to them, partly by a press they themselves worked for as reporters and journalists.

Furthermore, in the eyes of the general public, authors had to be 'interesting people', they were, so to speak, role-models of a new era, who were rewarded for their probing of new ways of social (and anti-social) behaviour and their exploring of the border lines of morality. Authors, actors and so on, tested new, more liberal, life-styles in a society that still was dominated by conservative and Victorian behaviour and ideas.[16] The 'market-value' of a writer was not only determined by the aesthetic quality of his works, but also to a considerable extent by the ways in which he (in public) was recognizable as 'different' from both the traditional bourgeois cultural elite, as well as from 'the man in the street'. Examples such as Herman Bang (1857-1912), Peter Nansen (1861-1918), Georg Brandes and Edvard Brandes (1847-1931), and women writers such as Agnes Henningsen (1868-1962), Thit Jensen (1876-1957) and Amalie Skram (1846-1905) come to mind.

This public interest in authors' private correspondence, and the difficulty in drawing a clear line between private and public letters is also demonstrated by the fact that writers, such as Drachmann, let a great number of letters appear in magazines and papers. I think that the status of letters in this period is reflected in the status of a similar genre, namely the *hyldestdigt*, a poem in which homage is paid to someone. This is also demonstrated in Drachmann's letters, for example, in a letter to his friend Otto Borchsenius (1844-1925) from 1879, where he gives an overview of the *literary* publications he plans for the near future. Drachmann states here that he is working on six books, as well as: 'et Par smaa Lejligheds-Lystspil, Skitser, Brevsamlinger, løse Digte, Udkast osv' (*HDB* I, p. 5 – a few minor occasional comedies, sketches, collections of letters, odd poems, drafts, etc.). It would seem, therefore, that at least some kinds of letters were also regarded as a public literary genre.

Nevertheless, from the earliest stage of his career as a writer, Drachmann was conscious of the fact that, at some moment in the future, his letters might become the object of public scrutiny. As early as 1873, for example, he asks an addressee to destroy a letter after reading it,[17] a request that does not occur often, but which is repeated every now and then,[18] and one of Drachmann's notorious 'new-year letters' to the publisher Frederik V. Hegel (1817-1887) is specifically marked 'private', and contains the request to return the letter after reading.[19]

Although more than a century had passed between the date of the first letters of Drachmann and their publication in the Borup collection, the editor asks the reader to show some indulgence towards the author, because Drachmann never had a tendency to weigh his words with care. He was an impulsive writer, or, as Borup formulates it, the letters 'are conceived in the whim of the moment and must therefore not be taken too literally' (*HDB* I, p. 10).

This remark throws an ambiguous light on this collection. It is certainly true that Drachmann's letters, in fact, have a very loose and free-flowing associative style, and that the ideas and points of view that the author expressed in them over the years were often, and rapidly, subject to change. In every sense of the word, Drachmann was an unusually 'mobile' personality. On the orthographical level though, if one studies the original manuscripts, the letters show but few erasures and other signs of sloppiness and haste, at the moment of their conception, although Drachmann was rather often imprecise in dating his letters.[20]

It may seem to be an empty phrase, but Drachmann actually liked to write, and he did so frequently and with great ease; his letters are eloquent and mostly written in a straightforward manner. Once, he even pointed out that, for him, writing a letter was always the first step to writing fiction.[21] In the later years of his life though, he became a more hectic letter writer, which is visible in the manuscripts by an increasing number of underlinings, exclamation marks, dashes, dots, recurring phrases, and so forth.[22]

Drachmann's letters clearly show too, that he was no modest

man. He was not afraid of glorifying his own work and justifying apparent weaknesses but, knowing the facts of his life and the strain under which he had to make a living as a writer in Denmark, a great portion of this bravura must be seen in the light of his dependency upon his publishers. Publishers had to be continually convinced and assured that the risks they took by supporting him would be covered and reimbursed by the 'magnificent' works that he was to produce. Drachmann's lack of self-criticism meant that he and his friends, literary and otherwise, at some point in their relationship, inevitably came to loggerheads. He had long-lasting and violent quarrels with some of his closest friends, and several relationships were never repaired.

It would hardly make any sense to sum up all the individuals that Drachmann corresponded with. They were essentially all the major Scandinavian writers and cultural personalities of his day, especially the ones affiliated with the circle around the Brandes brothers. There are also a great number of letters to his main publisher, Frederik V. Hegel. Among the earliest addressees were his schoolmates, Erik Skram (1847-1923) and Edvard Brandes. By family ties Drachmann was also in close contact with some of the most influential political and cultural personalities of his time, among them people like the journalist and politician Viggo Hørup (1841-1902), who was his nephew, and the philosopher Viggo Drewsen (1830-1888), his brother-in-law.[23]

The Brandes brothers

Without any doubt the correspondence with the two famous Brandes brothers, Edvard and Georg, is the most interesting of all. Drachmann had been a classmate of Edvard Brandes at von Westens Institut and, in the early 1870s, he was one of Drachmann's main literary confessors and helped him with his first literary attempts. As a matter of fact, Edvard Brandes and Holger Drachmann had their unofficial stage-debut together, with a short play – a so-called *revy* – entitled *Nytaarsaften* (New Year's Eve).[24]

During the early years of Drachmann's first marriage to Vilhelmine Erichsen (1852-1935, later Mrs Hilarius-Kalkau) – a marriage that only lasted for five years, from 1871 to 1876 –

Edvard Brandes and Holger Drachmann were on intimate and friendly terms with each other. But this situation did not last. The discrepancy between Drachmann and Edvard Brandes became distinct during the divorce negotiations, negotiations in which Brandes played an ambiguous role.[25] Immediately, tension between them grew and culminated when Drachmann, in 1878, wrote an unpleasant caricature of Edvard Brandes. From then on, they avoided each other's company, and their correspondence becomes rare.

The first signs of coolness in their correspondence is, significantly enough, found in a letter to Georg Brandes, written in Paris on New Year's eve 1877.[26] It is hardly an exaggeration to say that in the mind of Drachmann, Edvard Brandes gradually developed into some sort of personal demon, whom he thought haunted him everywhere, in his private as well as in his literary existence.[27]

The break with Edvard Brandes culminated soon after, in the spring of 1878, and Drachmann wrote, as a result of this, (again) to Georg Brandes: 'Til Edv. hverken *kan* eller *vil* jeg tale. Han har selv umuliggjort mig det' (*HDB* I, p. 351 – To Edv. I neither *can* nor *will* talk. He has himself made it impossible for me), and a few days later Drachmann even declared, in another letter to Georg: 'nu er Krigen erklæret' (*HDB* I, p. 358 – now war has been declared). Although Edvard Brandes and Drachmann kept away from each other as much as possible, they still had mutual business affairs and thus had to maintain some kind of contact, basically by means of short messages, in which they kept to a rather reserved and chilly tone.[28]

Drachmann possessed a remarkable capability to fall out with all his friends. For shorter or longer periods he quarrelled with virtually everybody. Correspondence would stop and sometimes break off entirely, but mostly reconciliation would follow and contact be established again.[29]

Of course Drachmann's relationship to Georg Brandes, which started around 1871, was affected by the tensions between Edvard and Drachmann. But after the breach in the relationship with Edvard, Georg Brandes initially took over the position of his younger brother as the literary confidant of Drachmann. The correspondence between Drachmann and Georg Brandes, continued throughout the seventies, came to a halt in the 1880s, and picked up again in the early 1890s, continuing until Drachmann's death.

Thus, both Brandes brothers were at odds with Drachmann in the 1880s. The conflict with Georg Brandes originated from a violent clash between them in 1882 and reached its climax in 1883, the year in which Brandes published his book *Det moderne Gjennembruds Mænd*, in which a substantial and quite critical chapter is dedicated to Drachmann.

The real reason for this conflict, however, was an improvised poem that Drachmann wrote during a visit to Aulestad in Norway, on the occasion of the celebration, in 1882, of Bjørnstjerne Bjørnson's fiftieth birthday, as well as the twenty-fifth anniversary of his literary career.[30] This poem, called *Til Aulestad* (*To Aulestad*) was not intended for publication but, nevertheless, it fell into the hands of a journalist who was present at the party and who subsequently published it in the magazine *Verdens Gang*. The reason why Georg Brandes was so infuriated by the poem, was a line in the second stanza, which runs as follows: 'vi kom hertil halvt kritisk-jødisk-franske' (we came here half critical-Jewish-French).[31] Georg Brandes was offended by these words and made this clear to Drachmann in various ways, both private and public. Brandes even accused Drachmann of anti-Semitism.[32]

It goes without saying that the relationship between Georg Brandes and Drachmann suffered tremendously from the ever-deteriorating aggression between Drachmann and Georg's younger brother, and eventually Drachmann saw both Brandes brothers as bloodsucking 'demonic' characters: 'Jeg har aldrig tænkt paa at sigte Georg for andet, end hvad jeg skal staa ved hele mit Liv: for, i Samarbejde med sin Broder, at have været den aandelige, kritisk-negative Vampyr, der har suget *mit* Blod, min Følelse, mit Hjærte etc, ligesom jeg nu ser, at de suger videre ned efter igennem Ungdommen' (*HDB* II, p. 271 – I have never thought of accusing Georg of anything but what I shall maintain for the whole of my life: that, together with his brother, he has been the intellectual, critical, negative vampire that has sucked *my* blood, my feelings, my heart, etc., just as I now see that they are going on sucking the blood of the young).

The question of whether or not Drachmann was an anti-Semite can not be definitively answered within the limited framework of this chapter. Nevertheless, it is interesting to take a closer look at Drachmann's letters to see what role anti-Semitic notions play in them.

'French fungi'

The editor of the Drachmann-letters, Morten Borup, was well aware of the fact that anti-Semitic views were expressed in them. Nonetheless, he brushed the issue aside by simply claiming in his introduction to the third volume: 'Hans gentagne grimme Udfald mod Jøderne behøver man næppe at tage for alvorligt, da alle hans Gerninger viser, at han ikke var Antisemit og adskillige af hans nære Venner var Jøder' (*HDB* III, p. 13 – we hardly need to take his repeated ugly attacks on the Jews too seriously, as all his actions show that he was not antisemitic and several of his close friends were Jews). This is the only remark made about this issue and, naturally, statements like these arouse one's scholarly curiosity. Is this really all there is to it?

The first time anti-Jewish expressions appear in Drachmann's correspondence is in the period when Drachmann's conflict with Edvard Brandes broke out, in the year 1876. The literary and political breach with the Brandes brothers, especially with Edvard, was there for everyone to see after the publication of the journalistic and polemical book of essays, *Derovre fra Grænsen* (Across the Border), in 1877. The conflict reached its zenith and now also involved Georg, when *Skyggebilleder fra Rejser i Indland og Udland* (Shadows from Journeys at Home and Abroad) appeared in 1883 – a book that, by a twist of fate, appeared on the very same day as Brandes's *Det moderne Gjennembruds Mænd*. In *Skyggebilleder*, there was one particular polemic travel story, entitled 'Ostende-Brügge', which clearly aimed at scorning the modern ideas of the Brandesian movement, including, to some extent, those which Drachmann had himself been advocating since the early 1870s.[33]

At first, Drachmann's conflict with Edvard did not affect the relationship between Drachmann and Georg Brandes. They kept in close contact and Drachmann even started one of his letters to Georg – containing extremely negative words about Edvard Brandes – by saluting him as 'Kære Ven og Broder' (*HDB* I, p. 357). In this letter from April 1878, which Drachmann calls a 'kind of literary testament', he describes the conflict with Edvard with the following remarkable words: 'Det er saaledes en Slags Racekrig – jeg benytter stedse hans egne Udtalelser – der kommer til at føres mellem ham og mig, og samtidig er det en Borgerkrig som mellem Syd- og Nordstaterne i Amerika; des mere haardnakket vil den blive' (*HDB* I, p. 360 – it is thus a kind of racial war – I am all the time using his own statements – that is to be waged between him and me, and at the same time it is a civil war like that between the southern and northern states in America; all the more dogged it will become). Shortly after, Drachmann, in a letter to his colleague, Sophus Schandorph (1836-1901), refers to Edvard Brandes in the plural, by saying 'Jøderne har vist mig Døren' (*HDB* I, p. 370 – the Jews have shown me the door).

Drachmann's discontent with the role that Edvard Brandes played turned into open hatred when Brandes tried to intervene in a parliamentary discussion about an increase in Drachmann's annual Government grant. Now Drachmann struck below the belt by referring not only to the fact that Edvard Brandes had married a wealthy wife, but also to his Jewish background: 'Arrogance kan undertiden tilgives Genierne, meget nødigt Andenhaands-Literater, og allernødigst jødiske Andenhaands-Literater' (*HDB* II, p. 219 – geniuses can sometimes be forgiven for arrogance, but second-rate scribblers less easily, and Jewish second-rate scribblers least of all).

Of course remarks like these, in the end, also led to a conflict with Georg Brandes. Their disagreement started with the Aulestad poem from 1882 and turned into a feud that lasted for nearly a decade. As a result, both Georg and Edvard Brandes did their best to avoid any contact with Drachmann, and it was not until the funeral of Drachmann's highly respected father, A. G. Drachmann (1810-1892), that Georg Brandes and Drachmann shook hands again and buried their differences.[34]

But what happened after the Aulestad-episode? The very first letter of Drachmann recorded by Borup after his return from

Norway is to his friend Victorinus Pingel (1834-1919). This letter makes it clear that Drachmann placed the Aulestad-affair in an anti-Jewish context.[35] In this letter, Drachmann counters the attacks on him as a result of the Aulestad poem by describing his opponents as 'Edv. Brandes med Drabanter ... og tillige hele det fæle, skvalrende, taktløse Parti af unge Jøder à la Cantor etc' (*HDB* II, p. 170 – Edv. Brandes and henchmen ... and then all that dreadful, prattling, tactless crowd of young Jews *à la* Cantor, etc.). Drachmann's vocabulary became increasingly indelicate and Pingel and others actually warned him that the language and ideas he was using were quite uncivilized.[36] Thus, Pingel suggested that he take precautions: 'Skaan fremfor alt Jøderne imellem os og kald dem høist Gallomaner' (*HDB* II, p. 240 – in particular spare the Jews among us and call them at most Gallomanes). Some months later Drachmann assured Pingel indirectly, that he by no means wanted to be associated with the strong anti-Semitic currents in Central Europe at that time.[37]

As it turns out, Drachmann accepted Pingel's idea of replacing the word 'Jew' with the word 'French'. And in a great many of the following letters, sentences can be found such as: 'hvor vanvittigt det er, at denne lille gallo-hebræiske Klike skal dominere herhjemme i Literaturen' (*HDB* II, p. 266 – how crazy it is that this little Gallic-Jewish clique should dominate literature here in Denmark), and so on. But, when anger runs away with him, he expresses what he really meant with the euphemism 'French': 'Der maa være *en* Digter i dette Land, og han maa i sig optage alle Kunstgrene – og alle *Hjærter* (dem, som Jøderne spotter over)' (*HDB* II, p. 270 – there must be *one* writer in this country, and he must absorb all branches of art within him – and all *hearts* (those the Jews ridicule)).

In any event, this is the background for the fact that Drachmann – although he keeps using the word Jew in a negative sense every now and then – as an alternative applies the word 'French'. The first time this interesting combination of interchangeable terms appears is in a draft-letter to Georg Brandes that was never sent. Here Drachmann wanted to give Georg Brandes an explanation for his Aulestad poem: 'Vi var alle meget "idealistisk" opsatte paa at udrense af Nordens fremtidige

Fremskridtsparti ... netop alle hine Udvæxter, der saa stærkt kom frem gennem det *daarlige* Franske og det *daarligt* Jødiske hos din Broder' (*HDB* II, p. 205 – we were all very 'idealistically' intent on cleansing the future progress party of the North ... of all those excrescences so very clearly visible in the *bad* French and the *bad* Jewish qualities in your brother).

In a letter to Frederik V. Hegel, it becomes clear what Drachmann meant by the term 'French'; meticulously avoiding the word Jew, there is no doubt what he is aiming at, when he exclaims: 'Front imod det Franske, Front imod Pessimismen. Frem med det Sunde, det Nedarvede, det Oprindelige!' (*HDB* II, p. 208 – turn against the French, turn against pessimism. Forward with what is healthy, inherited, original) and, four days later, he writes to Pingel: 'den sygelige Sensibilitet, som Sems Efterkommere selv ere i Besiddelse af' (*HDB* II, p. 210 – the unhealthy sensibility of which Sem's descendants themselves are in possession).

If one scrutinizes Drachmann's letters, dozens of anti-Jewish remarks can be found, either in French disguise or straightforwardly anti-Semitic. On 6 January 1884, he writes to Otto Borchsenius about his literary and political visions of the future and the battle he is fighting against certain tendencies of these days: '*imod* den atheistiske, negative, skeptiske og hovmodige Periferi, der nu bestaar af saa mange blandede Elementer, baade "klare" og "uklare" Hoveder, omskaarne og uomskaarne Individer' (*HDB* III, p. 40 – *against* the atheistic, negative, sceptical and arrogant periphery which is now made up of so many mixed elements, both 'clear' and 'unclear' heads, circumcised and uncircumcised individuals). In the same letter he also tells his friend about a disease that his wife Emmy (née Culmsee, 1854-1928) had recently caught, apparently while eating mushrooms: 'er det ikke som et mærkeligt Symbol, at Emmy, den mest rationelle af os to, den, som længst har holdt igen paa min Haand, at hun ... bliver forgivet af *franske Svampe?* Skade at det ikke var hendes Mand! – hører jeg hele Kobbelet gø' (*HDB* III, p. 44 – is it not a somewhat strange symbol that Emmy, the more rational of us two, the one who has longest held back my hand, should ... be poisoned by *French fungi*? Do I hear the entire pack baying, 'What a pity it was not her husband'?). Here Drachmann draws an obvious parallel between 'French fungi' and the Brandes brothers, a metaphorical representation he also uses the next day in a letter to Karl Gjellerup (1857-1919).[38]

France and French culture encompassed everything that in Drachmann's opinion was detestable, and thus, when he came in conflict with the Brandes brothers, he joined the words 'French' and 'Jewish' in one semantic unit. That Drachmann had a negative, and a kind of ethno-psychological image of the French, is clear as early as 1877. At that time Drachmann's career had barely begun, and he had only been in France a little while, but nonetheless he writes in a letter from Paris to his father:

Hele Betragtningsmaaden af Livet og af Kunsten er mig fremmed her; i denne Henseende har Poeten fine Nerver, og jeg *vil* ikke, saaledes som Heiberg f. Ex., krænge min Natur om, forat optage galliske Partikler, som jeg bagefter ikke vil kunne fordøie; eiheller *kan* jeg, saaledes som Brødrene Brandes, gøre det sine culpa, i Overensstemmelse med en Race, en Natur, der er den galliske meget mere beslægtet end vor germaniske....[39]

(The entire way of looking at life and art here is alien to me; in this respect the poet has sensitive nerves, and I *will* not, like Heiberg for instance, turn my whole being inside out in order to absorb Gallic particles which I will then not be able to digest; nor *can* I, like the Brandes brothers, do it *sine culpa*, in keeping with a race, a nature, that is far more related to the Gallic than our Germanic ...)

Seven years later, when the conflict with the Brandes brothers is at its height, Drachmann returns to this French-Jewish contamination. In a letter to his current publisher, Jacob Hegel (1851-1918) and his wife Julie (née Bagge, 1857-1924), he writes on Christmas Eve 1884, from Vienna:

jeg beder Jer begge to, kære Venner, have jer Opmærksomhed rettet imod selve Arnestedet for al denne modbydelige Oversvømning med Pikanteri og Analyse og Gemenhed – selve Paris! Her [in Vienna] er blandt alle bedre Forfattere og Kunstnere en nagende Uvilje mod de 'skrivende Jøders' formalistiske Tyranni. Den evropæiske Jødedom skal tage sig lidt i Agt. Den lever jo hovedsagelig af Affaldet fra Frankrig, som den iøvrigt véd at tilberede paa den pikanteste Maade.... saa maa baade de tyske og de skandinaviske Jøder og Jødevenner til at tage Reb i Sejlene, og saa ... og saa

... ja ja, det er store Spørgsmaal.

(I ask you both, dear friends, to have your attention directed to the very source of this repugnant flood of piquancy and analysis and coarseness – Paris itself! Here [in Vienna], among all better-class authors and artists, there is a gnawing aversion to the formalistic tyranny of 'writing Jews'. European Jewry must watch itself a little. Of course, it is living mainly on the garbage from France, which, incidentally, it is able to prepare in the most piquant manner ... then both German and Scandinavian Jews as well as their friends watch their step ... and then ... yes indeed, these are major issues – *HDB* III, p. 227.)

Later, Drachmann continues this manner of reasoning by referring to Brandesian thought as 'denne fransk-norsk-israelitisk-epigrammatiske Fricassé' (*HDB* III, p. 239), as well as by writing:

Her ude i det store Evropa, her samler alle de hæderlige, begejstringsdygtige kristne eller i hvert Fald ikke-jødiske Kræfter sig til en afgørende Kamp – vel at mærke *ikke* mod de hæderlige orthodokse Jøder, der lever et stille, beskedent Liv, heller ikke mod en stor Del af de indifferente Semiter, som i alle haande borgerlige Stillinger gøre Gavn og respekterer baade skrevne og u-skrevne Love – men sandelig, sandelig mod den literære Jødedom, der paa lidt nær regerer hele Fastlandets Presse, og som konsekvent nedbryder alle ærværdige, noble og ridderlige Traditioner ved en ætsende Kritik, der til Slutning lægger os alle forsvarsløse for Anarkiets Fødder.

(*Here* in a wider Europe, here, all honest Christians capable of enthusiasm, or at all events all non-Jewish forces are gathering for a decisive battle – *not*, it should be noted, against the honest orthodox Jews, who live quiet, modest lives, nor against a large proportion of the indifferent Semites who are worth their salt in all kinds of respectable posts and respect both written and unwritten laws – but in truth, in truth, against the literary Jewry that is close to dominating the entire Continental press and quite consistently demolishes all venerable, noble and courtly traditions by means of acid criticism which will finally submit us all, defenceless, to anarchy – *HDB* III, p. 248.)

It would be quite boring to quote all of Drachmann's letters containing expressions like 'alle de smaa fanatiske Rabalderjøder, som jeg dog engang *maa* tage et afgørende Tag i...' (*HDB* III, pp. 65-6 – all those fanatical noisy little Jews with whom I really *must* do decisive battle one day), but there are dozens of them. I will only offer a few significant examples of them, such as: 'Jeg har reddet min Sjæl og mit Hjærte, min religiøse Grundtone og min Fædrelandskærlighed ud af det Skibbrud, hvori vore hjemlige Jøder og Fritænkere i det mindste til Dels havde Skyld da jeg selv endnu var ubefæstet og vaklende' (*HDB* III, p. 199 – I have saved my soul and my heart, my fundamentally religious tone and my patriotism from the shipwreck for which our Jews and freethinkers here in Denmark were at least partly responsible when I myself was still weak and vacillating), 'jeg *er* denne Overgangstidens Dobbeltnatur: Romantikeren, der har Afsky for "Politik", "Jødedom" og "Atheisme" – og paa samme Tid den moderne Mand, der fuldt vel kender til "Livet"...' (*HDB* III, pp. 159-160 – I *am* the dual nature of this transitional time: the Romantic who loathes 'politics', 'Jewry' and 'atheism' – and at the same time the modern man who well knows what life is about ...), 'Der er i dette Øjeblik 79 mindre og større, omskaarne og uomskaarne Strindberger i Norden. Bort fra *dem*; – tilbage til *Naturen!*' (*HDB* III, p. 143 – There are at this moment 79 lesser and greater, circumcised and uncircumcised Strindbergs in the North. Let us get away from *them*; back to *nature*!), 'hele den "Opposition" af Mænd og Fruentimmer, som nu grupperer sig om Koalitionen Jøder og Socialister derhjemme – den bringer Danmark aandelig talt til Undergang' (*HDB* III, pp. 226-227 – all this 'Opposition' of men and women now grouping themselves around the coalition of Jews and socialists at home – they will intellectually speaking be the ruin of Denmark) and:

Det vil nemlig gaa mig i en Række af Aar saaledes, at 'man' (det vil sige den fransk-jødisk-evropæisk-unationale-radikal-fandenivoldsk-liderlige Retning derhjemme) vil grine eller trække paa Skuldrene ad saadanne Arbejder som 'Der var engang', ... midt i vor moderne Sump af Raffinerthed, Frivolitet og raat Atheisteri i det mindste sidder *én* Digter, der ikke lader sig hverken sjælelig eller legemlig omskære til Fordel for den Alliance mellem Jøder og Intransigente, der truer 'Folkets' virkelige Kærne over alle de germanske Lande.

(For a number of years I shall suffer seeing 'people' (that is to say, the French-Jewish-European-unnational-radical-irresponsible-lascivious persuasion at home) laughing or shrugging their shoulders at such works as 'Det var engang' ... in the midst of our cesspit of sophistication, frivolity and raw atheistery there is at least *one* writer who refuses to allow himself to be either physically or spiritually circumcised to the advantage of the alliance of the Jews and intransigent figures threatening the true essence of 'the people' throughout the Germanic countries – HDB III, p. 158.)

It seems clear that anti-Jewish sentiments played a significant role in Drachmann's world-view and, thus, in his letters as well. At the same time, it is clear too, that he used the word 'French' as a semantic disguise. This interesting juxtaposition has its ideological roots in the ethno-psychology that was very potent in this era as a whole.[40] Even in a letter from Drachmann to Edvard Brandes himself, it shows how strong these notions were. In 1880 he wrote, evaluating their ongoing disagreement: 'Kun Et vil jeg lægge Dig paa Sinde: Folk med Naturer som min (hvoraf der er en Del i vor Kreds) have, i Modsætning til romanske og asiatiske Mænd, ikke saa meget deres Anskuelser, Meninger eller Principer gennem en klar, logisk Tænkning, der da, udadtil, drager en bestemt Rettesnor for Individets Optræden eller Viljesact' (HDB II, p. 32 – only one thing I would exhort of you: people with characters like mine (of whom there are a number in our circle) do not, in contrast to Romance and Asiatic men, so much have their views, opinions or principles as the result of clear, logical thinking which, at least outwardly, draws up a specific guiding principle for the individual's behaviour or conscious acts).

The relationship between Holger Drachmann and Edvard Brandes was never restored to its former shape. When Edvard Brandes became editor of the daily Politiken, they found common ground again, but they kept their contacts at a strictly business-like level.[41]

Drachmann's letters – Impulse as strategy?

Finally, I return to Morten Borup's two casual, but central statements: (a) that Drachmann was an impulsive writer, and (b) that his anti-Jewish remarks therefore should not be taken too seriously.[42] The question that may be asked then is, had Holger Drachmann simply such an extremely impulsive personality that he blindly threw himself into the arms of false ideas and objectionable movements in the society he lived in, such as anti-Semitism? Was his really such an uncontrollable mind?

In part, judging from his letters, this appears true. One must conclude that Drachmann was not a great philosophical thinker, a streak in his character that he himself was well aware of. Drachmann knew that he was easily led by others and subject to changing moods, things that made him change ideas and sides very often and very easily.

But – and here is one of the striking observations that can be made – at the same time Drachmann was a strategic genius in turning this weakness into one of his advantages. This phenomenon is, among others, supported by a number of letters to his father and stepmother, his publishers Gyldendal and Schubothe,[43] but also by some curious letters to bishop H. L. Martensen (1808-1884), to Vilhelm Topsøe (1840-1881)[44] and to the Maecenas, J. C. Jacobsen (1811-1887), the founder and director of the Carlsberg breweries. In these letters he tried to portray himself as a neutral political figure and as a pious and respectable private person, a real family-man.[45] Therefore, it would be wrong to deny Drachmann strategic intelligence, not to say cunning, in numerous letters, where he pursued a specific goal. In some cases, he meticulously planned the sequence of letters to get a delicate point across, or to make people act in favour of him.

Cunning or, in any event, a subtle strategic talent is also displayed by Drachmann in some instances where he would rather speak to a person in the flesh, instead of putting his message in writing. This is the case, for example, when he discusses financial matters with his publishers. Whereas Drachmann once exclaims 'Ak dette Brevskriveri – hvorved man i Grunden faar sagt saa lidt!' (*HDB* IV, p. 57 – alas, all this writing of letters – whereby one fundamentally manages to say so little), the publisher Jacob Hegel makes it clear to him that some business agreements have to be put on paper, by saying: 'Du maa ikke tage mig det ilde op, at jeg ved disse Linier berører vort pecuniaire Mellemværende, det er det behageligste for begge Parter, at vi ordner denne Sag skriftligt' (*HDB* IV, p. 155 – you must not take it amiss that in these lines I touch on our financial relations, it is best for both parties that we should settle this matter in writing).

On a personal, but also on an aesthetic level, Drachmann

eventually found himself at loggerheads with realism and naturalism. He was more and more taken up with an aesthetics and an authorial role with its roots in Romanticism, rather than the Modern Breakthrough. He found a temporary ally in Karl Gjellerup, who broke with Brandes more or less at the same time as he himself did, but Drachmann was not looking for allies; he wanted to stand alone, as the sole heir of Jens Baggesen (1764-1826), Adam Oehlenschläger (1779-1850) and J. L. Heiberg (1791-1860). In striving for this goal, he felt obstructed by these two other great Danes of his time, Edvard and Georg Brandes.[46]

It is clear that in the early 1880s Drachmann endeavoured an ideological *tour de force*, that consciously aimed at finding a literary and politically unique position for himself. On the one hand, he sought to single himself out from the Modern Breakthrough, while on the other, he tried to stay out of the arms of the still strong conservative literary circles. Drachmann's more or less desperate search for a unique position in the Danish cultural landscape of his time led him into a fantasy about being the leading figure of a new national movement which he christened 'Den danske Bevægelse' (The Danish Movement). The concept of this movement was inspired by the so-called Flemish Movement in Belgium, a current in Belgian literature and politics aimed at cleansing Flemish culture from Francophone influences.[47]

To reinforce this idea, Drachmann, in quite a number of letters, used military metaphors. That is, he refers to himself as a 'one-man army' who uses poetry as his 'cavalry', stories as his 'infantry', and dramatic works as his 'artillery'.[48]

In many letters he refers to the idea of 'Den danske Bevægelse', but it is never made clear what the content of this concept precisely is. One thing is clear, though, and that is that this so-called 'Danish Movement' was nourished by one basic sentiment: in his opposition to the Brandesian ideas, Drachmann turned to a revaluation of Christianity, to which, as a matter of fact, he gave a clear anti-Jewish orientation. This conclusion can also be drawn from the fact that, simultaneously with the appearance of the concept of the 'Danish Movement', for the first time in Drachmann's letters the word 'Jew' is applied in a negative sense, and subsequently exchanged for the word 'French'.[49]

Drachmann's widespread use of anti-Semitic modes of expression is the more surprising because a number of his closest friends and acquaintances were Jews. And it must be stressed that Drachmann's letters to Georg Brandes and Harald Christensen (1847-1919) for example[50] – both being of Jewish origin – are among the most caring and sincere he wrote.

Drachmann was – no doubt – a vain, unbalanced and probably arrogant personality.[51] And at the same time he was Denmark's national poet, who found himself in a constant, but vain, struggle to achieve world-fame. The tremendous strain this ambition caused, led him astray in embracing anti-Semitism[52] as a tool to reach his goals, and in this respect, he did not stand as alone as he always claimed, as a great number of encouraging responses to his anti-Semitic expressions so unfortunately demonstrate. Throughout Europe, anti-Semitic notions became *en vogue* from the late 1870s on and reached Scandinavia soon afterwards, turning into a potent cultural current in European, as well as Scandinavian, *fin de siècle* literature and culture.[53] Holger Drachmann was never a theoretician of any kind, and his anti-Semitism must be seen as an expression of his instant enthusiasm for new and nationalistic currents in contemporary cultural thinking. When, in the late 1890s, he heard about what had happened to Albert Dreyfus (1859-1935) in France as a result of this growing anti-Semitism, he was outraged and did not hesitate to write a poem in defence of Dreyfus and in support of Émile Zola (1840-1902).[54] From a late twentieth-century perspective this was a much more reasonable attitude, which, fortunately, is also to be found in this versatile writer's letters.[55]

Notes

1. In April 1872, with the collection of short-stories *Med Kul og Kridt* (With Charcoal and Chalk), and later that year, with a volume of poetry entitled *Digte* (Poems).
2. Harriet Bentzon, *Holger Drachmann i Breve til hans Fædrenehjem* (Copenhagen, 1932), p. 247 [nr. 89, letter from Drachmann to his father, 19 November 1884].
3. See, for example, Johannes Jørgensen, *Geschichte der dänischen*

Literatur (Kempten and Munich, 1908), p. 152; Hans Brix, *Danmarks digtere. Fyrretyve kapitler af dansk digtekunsts historie i billeder* (Copenhagen, 1925), p. 358; Paul V. Rubow, *Holger Drachmann 1878-1897* (Copenhagen, 1945), p. 223.
4. One of the latest discoveries is a series of lyrical contributions from his school-years. See: Mogens von Haven, *Holger Drachmann – hans ukendte digterdebut og tegninger fra 1864* (S.l., 1996).
5. Henrik Andersson, Flemming Conrad, Per Dahl and Jørgen Hunosøe, *Udgivelse af danske litterære tekster efter 1800. En redegørelse for behov, problemer og perspektiver* (Copenhagen, 1996), pp. 68-73.
6. Lauritz Nielsen, *Katalog over danske og norske digteres originalmanuskripter i Det kongelige Bibliotek*, I (Copenhagen, 1943), pp. 79-98; Birgitte Possing and Bruno Svindborg, *Det kongelige Biblioteks Håndskriftafdeling. Erhvervelser 1924-1987*, I (Copenhagen, 1995), pp. 187-189.
7. The publication of the first two volumes of Morten Borup's collection made a number of people aware of letters they had in their possession. As some of this material would have made his collection more comprehensive and interesting, Borup then published some of this subsequently discovered material in a separate article: Morten Borup, 'Holger Drachmann og "Sorte". Træk af et venskabs historie', *Nordisk Tidskrift*, XLV (1969), pp. 9-22. See also for recently discovered letters: Torben Nielsen, 'Hilsen fra Amanda', *Magasin fra Det kongelige Bibliotek*, 8 (1993), nr. 2, pp. 63-68.
8. From a scholarly perspective the Bentzon book is not completely unreliable as a source, not least because the author/editor had expert help from her brother, Professor A.B. Drachmann, the well-known philologist, who was one of the editors of the first two editions of *Søren Kierkegaards Samlede Værker*, I-XIV (Copenhagen, 1901-1906; 1920-1936).
9. That these letters were not lost is shown by Morten Borup's selection of 29 letters in his 'Holger Drachmann og hans fader. Breve fra A.G. Drachmann til sønnen 1875-1890', *Fund og Forskning*, XV (1968).
10. See: Paul V. Rubow, *Smaa kritiske Studier* (Copenhagen, 1935), pp. 57-82.
11. This three-volume work, which appeared in the years 1940, 1945 and 1950, is interesting enough in its own right, and might be subject of a little study, not least because the interest in Drachmann's personal life and literary work takes a quite surprising turn in the last volume. Barely hidden for the reader, it becomes clear that Rubow had become tired of his project and hastily brings it to a close, making some very peculiar editorial choices in the final volume.
12. Borup, 'Holger Drachmann og hans fader', (1968); Borup, 'Holger

Drachmann og "Sorte"', (1969); Nielsen, 'Hilsen fra Amanda', (1993); Margrethe Loerges, *Drachmanns Muser* (Copenhagen, 1981); Margrethe Loerges, *Edith – en skæbne i et bundt breve* (Copenhagen, 1983).

13. One of Borup's criteria was that the letters should have obvious literary and artistic value. But, just in passing, he nevertheless points out, that 'a selection of letters that casts light on the private life of the author could also be desirable', Morten Borup, *Breve fra og til Holger Drachmann*, I (1968), p. 5.
14. Drachmann met the twenty-year younger singer in 1887. The relationship between them led to the break-up of Drachmann's second marriage and continued until 1897 or 1898. See also: Nielsen, 'Hilsen fra Amanda', (1993), p. 63.
15. Exceptions are, for example, *Strandby Folk* (1883, *Beachtown Folk*) and *Der var engang* (Once upon a Time, 1885).
16. See, for example, Agnes Henningsen's autobiographies, which appeared in eight volumes in the years 1941 to 1955.
17. *HDB* I, p. 103 [nr. 35, to Edvard Brandes, 8 September 1873]. See also a remark in a letter to Georg Brandes in the previous month, *HDB* I, p. 97 [nr. 34, to Georg Brandes, 13 August 1873], as well as: *HDB* III, p. 444 [nr. 626, to Jacob Hegel, 23 November 1890]; *HDB* IV, p. 143 [nr. 754, to Jacob Hegel, November 2 1900] and p. 283 [nr. 864, to Viggo Lachmann, 2 October 1906].
18. *HDB* I, p. 464 [nr. 236, to Georg Brandes, 27 December 1879]. See also: *HDB* II, p. 148 [nr. 332, to Otto Borchsenius, 20 January 1882], in which Drachmann wrote: 'Det er godt, at jeg efterkom din Anmodning i dit Brev, om at brænde det; derved sattes jeg ud af Fristelsen til at kaste det i Ansigtet paa Dig. Af alle fornærmelige Breve – raadgivende eller dømmende – som jeg har modtaget, er dette det fornærmeligste' (It is a good thing that I did as you asked me in your letter, and burned it; I have thereby removed from myself the temptation to throw it in your face. Of all the insulting letters – giving advice or expressing condemnation – which I have ever received, this is the most insulting).
19. *HDB* I, p. 290 [nr. 142, New Year's Eve 1877]. See also: Niels Birger Wamberg, *Digterne og Gyldendal* (Copenhagen, 1970), p. 135.
20. An interesting example of this is a letter dated 31 June, which of course is an impossibility, as June tends to have only thirty days. See Rubow (1945), p. 68.
21. He states in a letter to Otto Borchsenius in 27 September 1878: 'Det er dog altid en Begyndelse til literair Beskæftigelse'. See: *HDB* I, p. 378 [nr. 184].
22. At the same time, he was forced to write in a bigger handwriting, due to

his diminishing eyesight.
23. Also his second and third wives, Emmy (née Culmsee, 1854-1928) and Soffi (née Lasson, 1873-1917), came from influential circles.
24. Performed in the Casino theatre in December 1873. See Paul V. Rubow, *Holger Drachmanns Ungdom* (Copenhagen, 1940), pp. 78-79; Robert Neiiendam, *Casino Oprindelse og Historie i Omrids* (Copenhagen, 1948), p. 44; Johannes Ursin, *Holger Drachmann. Liv og Værker*, II (Copenhagen, 1953), pp. 55-56.
25. See Kristian Hvidt, *Edvard Brandes. Portræt af en radikal blæksprutte* (Copenhagen, 1987), pp. 97-103; Rubow (1940), p. 59.
26. *HDB* I, p. 301 [nr. 143, New Year's Eve 1877].
27. In the first year of their feud, Drachmann also felt himself burdened by the fact that he had borrowed money from Edvard and the third Brandes brother, Ernst (1844-1892).
28. *HDB* I, p. 389 [nr. 191, 12 November 1878].
29. An intense correspondence that was completely broken off was the one with Otto Borchsenius. For many years, no letters were written between them and the first sign of reconciliation was a note from Borchsenius sent on the occasion of Drachmann's sixtieth birthday in 1904. Another example, but of an entirely different nature, is the correspondence with the Norwegian writer, Alexander Kielland. Kielland formally terminated the relationship with Drachmann [*HDB* II, pp. 273-74, nr. 399, 1883]. Nevertheless, Drachmann wrote to him again in 1894. The answer from Kielland, however, came two years later, and even then Kielland had not forgotten the reasons why he, more then a decade earlier, had put an end to their correspondence.
30. This was the occasion on which Erik Skram met his future wife, then Amalie Müller. See also: Rubow (1945), pp. 94-96.
31. Rubow (1945), p. 94. Actually Rubow has a very accurate and ironical description of the entire poem: 'Digtet er fremragende slet og stilløst, noget ganske forfærdeligt Seminarie-Pøjt, minder ikke saa lidt om *Vadums Harpe* eller Sørensen-Fugholms Poesier' (The poem is excrutiatingly awful and without any sense of style, dreadful training-college rubbish, somewhat reminsicent of *Vadums harpe* or Sørensen-Fugholm's poetastery), Rubow, (1945), p. 95. The particular stanza goes as follows: 'Det skulde synes sært – især det sidste, / og navnlig for det danske Kontingent, / men dersom noget kan Gemyttet friste / til sligt – saa har Patentet du fortjent; / vi kom hertil halvt kritisk – jødisk – franske, / halvt pessimistiske, halvt Troens Folk: / du har erobret for os selv os ganske – / ved Manden, som er dine Tankers Tolk' (It would seem strange – especially the latter / and in particular for the Danish contingent, / but if anything

can tempt dispositions / to such things – you have deserved the patent for it; / we came here half critical-Jewish-French, / half pessimistic, half people of faith: / you have completely conquered us for ourselves – / through the agency of the man who is the interpreter of your thoughts). From Emmy Drachmann, *Erindringer. Barndom og Ungdom til 1883* (Copenhagen, 1925), p. 174.

32. For an account of this period see Emmy Drachmann, (1925), pp. 173-182.
33. See also Rubow (1945), p. 126.
34. *HDB* III, pp. 452-453 [nr. 632 and 633; 15 October 1891 and 3 November 1891].
35. See also: Rubow (1945), pp. 94-101; Ursin (1953), I, pp. 184-190 and pp. 208-214.
36. As he did in a letter on 27 August 1882 and another on 5 March 1883. See: *HDB* II, pp. 176-178 and pp. 246-247 [nr. 345 and nr. 379; both letters from V. Pingel].
37. See, for example, Georg Brandes, 'Bevægelsen mod Jøderne i Tyskland', in *Berlin som tysk Rigshovedstad, Erindringer fra et femaarigt Ophold, 1885* [written between 1878 and 1883]. Also in Georg Brandes, *Samlede Skrifter*, 14 (Copenhagen, 1904), pp. 278-285.
38. *HDB* III, p. 52 [nr. 403, 7 January 1884].
39. Bentzon (1932), pp. 156-157 [nr. 67, 4 January 1877].
40. They even occur in a letter from Georg Brandes to Drachmann, where there is a reference to a critic who had claimed that Brandes was a 'romansk' personality, whereas Drachmann was called a 'germansk' character. See *HDB* I, p. 265 [nr. 128, 14 December 1877].
41. It is significant that Drachmann's first letter to *Politiken*, the paper Edvard Brandes was editing, is addressed to the editorial staff, and not to Edvard Brandes in person, although he no doubt was the intended addressee.
42. Also the esteemed Drachmann-biographer Paul V. Rubow is of the opinion that Drachmann's anti-Jewish rhetoric was caused by his personal dislike of Edvard Brandes, and a profound contempt for French art of the era. See Paul V. Rubow (1945), p. 169.
43. See: *HDB* I, p. 162; p. 247; p. 308; p. 354, as well as: *HDB* II. pp. 11-15. See also Georg Brandes, *Levned*, I (Copenhagen, 1905), p. 267.
44. The last two aiming at getting permission to remarry after his divorce from his first wife.
45. To Martensen: *HDB* I, p. 283; p. 285; p. 286, as well as: *HDB* II, p. 67. To Topsøe: *HDB* I, p. 416, pp. 450-451, as well as: *HDB* II, p. 75.
46. He felt that he had nothing to fear from J. P. Jacobsen (1847-1885) who had a very poor physical constitution, nor from Herman Bang (1857-1912), who was too excentric to be of any importance as a

competitor in this race for the favour of the general public. The only real competitor he saw, at the end of his life, was the 'robust' up-and-coming-man Johannes V. Jensen (1873-1950).
47. See Rubow, (1945), p. 125. See also Alex Bolckmans, 'Holger Drachmanns reisherinneringen uit Nederland en België', in *Album Prof. dr. Frank Baur. Den jubilaris bij zijn zestigsten verjaardag als huldeblijk aangeboden door collega's vakgenoten en oud-leerlingen*, I (Antwerp, Brussels, Ghent, Louvain, 1948), pp. 90-98; Victor Claes, 'Holger Drachmann en Vlaanderen. Een klerikale vergissing uit het jaar 1912', *Tijdschrift voor Skandinavistiek*, 9:1-2 (1988), pp. 31-40.
48. See, for example, *HDB* I, p. 187 [nr. 79, 27 April 1876]; p. 171 [nr. 73, 28 March 1876]; *HDB* II, p. 171; p. 175 [nr. 344, 26 August 1882]; p. 239 [nr. 375, 21 February 1883].
49. The first time there is a reference to Jews is in 1877, but here the word is only used in a neutral sense. See *HDB* I, p. 250 [nr. 120, 18 November 1877].
50. Probably the ship-broker Harald Christensen, son of Wulff Nathansen, was Drachmann's most intimate friend. They met in the early 1870s and remained friends throughout their lives. He was referred to as 'Sorte' (Blacky), because of his dark complexion. See Morten Borup, 'Holger Drachmann og "Sorte"', 1969, pp. 9-22.
51. In the curious little biography by Lauritz Nielsen, *Holger Drachmann. Hovedtræk af en tragisk Digterskæbne* (Copenhagen, 1942), which is a kind of a psycho-pathological study of Drachmann's character structure, this trait of vanity is discussed from a psychiatric point of view. But this analysis does not take into account that the driving forces behind all of this were not so much Drachmann's psychological particularities but much more socially stimulated kinds of behaviour.
52. The term 'anti-Semitism' was coined by the German agitator, Wilhelm Marr in 1879.
53. See, for example, the case-study by Robert Fuchs, *Ola Hansson – Antisemitismus und Kritik an der Moderne* (Berlin, 1997).
54. The poem was entitled 'Bravo Zola', and printed in the daily, *Politiken*, on 15 January 1898. See Morten Borup's commentary in *HDB* IV, p. 426.
55. See, for example, *HDB* IV, p. 107 [nr. 734, to Jacob Hegel, 11 February 1898].

10

Henrik Pontoppidan's Correspondence with Scandinavian Writers 1880-1910

Elias Bredsdorff
Copenhagen

In October 1997, 548 letters from the Danish novelist Henrik Pontopiddan were published in Denmark, selected and edited by myself and my colleague, Carl Erik Bay, Research Librarian at the Royal Library in Copenhagen. This is the first time that unabridged letters from Pontoppidan have been made available, and Carl Erik Bay and I were given permission by Pontoppidan's heirs to publish his correspondence. They are published in two volumes, covering the period 1880 to 1943, the year he died. But in this essay I shall limit myself to the period between 1880 and 1910.

Pontoppidan's first work was published in 1881, and two years later he spent the summer at Skagen in the company of the Danish artists Michael and Anna Ancher and P. S. Krøyer and the Norwegian artist and writer Christian Krohg. In a letter to Michael Ancher, written in February 1884, he wrote that he had felt it strange to listen to discussions among people who believed in *l'art pour l'art*, whereas to him the concept of Kunst (art) 'kun får værdi ved at være det højeste Udtryk for et bestemt individuelt Livssyn og derigennem at have et bestemt praktisk Formål: at bibringe andre dette Livssyn' (the concept of art is valuable only by being the highest expression of a clearly defined view of life and thus by having a definite practical purpose: to impart to others that view of life).

In 1886 Pontoppidan's novel *Mimoser* (Sensitive Plants) was published as a contribution to the discussion about sexual morality, sparked off in Scandinavia by Bjørnson's *En hanske* (A Gauntlet). Edvard Brandes, who reviewed the book in *Politiken*, summed up the main idea of the novel in these words: 'Han (Pontoppidan) tvivler, om det er nyttigt at gøre Kvinderne til yderst følsomme Mimoser, så længe Naturen har skabt Mændene af så skrøbeligt Stof' (He doubts whether it is advisable to make women into oversensitive mimosas, as long as nature has created men from such a fragile material). And in a private letter he asked Pontoppidan to explain publicly what he intended with the book. But Pontoppidan replied: 'At oplyse Verden nu, hvad jeg har ment med *Mimoser*, synes mig at ville smage vel meget af – enten en Falliterklæring eller Reklame, og jeg kan det så meget mindre, som jeg vedvarende betvivler, at Bogen – fornuftig læst – overhovedet lader sig misforstå' (to inform the world now what I intended to say with *Mimoser* seems to me a little too much of – either an admission of failure or self-publicity, and I am the less inclined to do it since I still doubt whether the book – rationally read – is at all capable of misinterpretation).

In the autumn of 1887 a number of Swedish and Finnish writers – August Strindberg, Axel Lundegård, Victoria Benedictsson, Ola Hansson and K. A. Tavaststjärna – came to live in Copenhagen for a period. Henrik Pontoppidan, who was otherwise reserved and shy, made friends with all of them, as did Edvard Brandes. Indeed, Pontoppidan and Axel Lundegård became intimate friends and kept up a correspondence for many years, while much later, in a letter to Georg Brandes, Pontoppidan reported a conversation he had had with Strindberg at that time: 'Jeg husker en lang Samtale med Strindberg, som dengang også var omkring de Fyrre og netop havde skilt sig ved en af sine Koner. Han var ikke impotent, men han koketterede med, at han ønskede at være det, længtes efter at blive det, "for at økonomisere med sin Tid og sin Kraft". Hjernen var i de År den Afgud, han vilde ofre hver Dråbe af sit Blod' (I remember a long conversation with Strindberg, who was then also about forty and had just got rid of one of his wives. He wasn't impotent, but he flirted with the idea that he wished to be so, longed to become impotent 'in order to make economies of time and strength'. In those years his brain was the idol for which he was prepared to sacrifice every drop of his blood).

The first of Pontoppidan's many letters to Axel Lundegård is dated 8 August 1888. After Victoria Benedictsson's suicide he wrote to Lundegård: 'Jeg havde ikke troet, at Ernst Ahlgren bar på en så dyb Melankoli, en så grundig Tro på Døden som den eneste Læge. Men dine sidste Fortællinger i *I Gryningen* får nu mere Klarhed over sig; nu forstår jeg bedre både den og hende' (I had not believed that Ernst Ahlgren [Benedictsson's pseudonym] was inflicted with so deep a melancholy, such a fundamental belief in death as the only cure. But your last stories in *At Dawn* make more sense to me now; now I understand more clearly both your book and her).

His support for other writers is evident in many of his letters. When in the spring of 1889 Amalie Skram asked Pontoppidan to support her application for a Norwegian literary grant, he did so with a statement from which I quote the following words: 'Blandt Deres Fædrelands mange betydlige Skribenter indtager De, mener jeg, allerede nu en fremskudt Plads, og Deres Talent er så ungt og frodigt, Deres Energi så beundringsværdig, at man, får De blot Lov at arbejde under gunstige Vilkår, sikkert tør spå Deres digteriske Virksomhed en smuk og rig Fremtid' (Among the many important writers of your native country you already hold, in my opinion, an important place, and your talent is so young and fertile, your energy so admirable that it seems safe to foresee a fine and rich future for your literary activity provided you are allowed to work under favourable conditions).

In 1890 Pontoppidan's political stories about 'provisorietiden', the period when Denmark was governed according to provisional Finance Acts, were published under the title *Skyer* (Clouds). The publisher, Gyldendal, objected to two things in the manuscript, firstly, the subtitle, in which the word 'statskup' (coup d'état) was used, and secondly, a comment by a fictional character about Estrup (who was at the time still the Danish Prime Minister), in which he employed a derogatory expression which Gyldendal's director identified with Pontoppidan's own views. We do not know the exact word used, for neither the original manuscript nor the proof sheets survive. Pontoppidan objected to what he considered censorship, and it was decided to appoint Alexander Kielland and Holger Drachmann to act as arbiters. Both their verdicts are still extant, and both agreed that the word 'statskup' should be omitted in the subtitle, and that the invective should be modified. The title now reads 'Skyer. Skildringer fra Provisoriernes Dage' (Clouds. Sketches from the Time of the Provisional Government).

Also in 1890 there was a legal case brought against Ernst Brandes (Georg and Edvard's younger brother) for articles in *Kjøbenhavns Børs Tidende*, which Ernst Brandes edited. But the articles had been written by Pontoppidan, who immediately acknowledged their authorship. He wrote to Edvard Brandes in December 1890: 'Jeg vil hellere sidde fire Måneder i Fængsel (dersom det er sådan noget det drejer sig om) end jeg vil være Skyld i, at Deres Broder sidder der i fjorten Dage' (I would rather spend four months in prison (if it is something like that which is in prospect) than be the cause of your brother being imprisoned for a fortnight).

The outcome was that Ernst Brandes was found guilty of blasphemy and ended by committing suicide, and Pontoppidan, who had not been charged, lost his government grant of one thousand kroner for one year.

Before this happened, in February 1891, Pontoppidan had written to Georg Brandes from Berlin:

Jeg har ventet med at skrive for at kunne fortælle Dem noget om Ibsen i Berlin; men så bad forleden Deres Broder mig om at skrive derom i *Børstidende*, og dertil har jeg nu sendt et par Småbreve om Opførelserne i Lessing-Teatret. Det er for mig kun grumme lidt at sige om sligt. Jeg forstår mig for lidt på Skuespilkunst. – Jeg havde tænkt at gøre Ibsen en Visit, men jeg fik ikke Mod dertil, da det kom til Stykket, fordi jeg ikke vidste andet at sige ham, end at han vistnok var en grumme stor og dristig Digter, men en temmelig lille og frygtsom Skribent, det aldrig havde villet eller vovet at sætte sin Autoritet ind på noget til Fremme for en Sag eller en Person. Jeg véd kun at have set, at han en Gang offentlig i Aviserne anbefalede – et Pensionat et Sted i Syden. I den Henseende priser jeg Bjørnson; han satte dog sin egen Statsunderstøttelse ind på at skaffe Kielland en. Men når de få 'Europæere', der endelig vinder Ære og Uafhængighed, kryber i et Musehul og roligt ser på, at deres Forbundsfæller plukkes, kan man ikke undre sig over Nederlagene. Det havde været mere værd, om Ibsen i Stedet for at udgive *Hedda Gabler* havde skrevet blot ti Linjer i en Avis, hvor han trådte i Skranken for en eller anden Sag som f. Ex. Deres Broders Blasfemi-Sag eller Deres egen Hædersgave.

(I have been waiting to write in order to be able to tell you something about Ibsen in Berlin; but then the other day your brother asked me to write something about it in *Børstidende*, and I have now sent him a few short letters about the performances at the Lessing Theatre. As far as I am concerned there is very little to say about this. I am not an authority on play-acting. – I had intended to pay Ibsen a visit, but my courage failed me at the crucial moment, because I could not think of anything else to tell him than that he might well be an extremely great and courageous *poet* but a pretty small and frightened writer who had never wanted to or had the courage to use his own authority in support of a cause or a person. I remember only once seeing him publicly recommend [anything] – a boarding house somewhere in the south of Europe. In that respect I admire Bjørnson; he staked his own government grant in order to obtain one for Kielland. But when the few 'Europeans' who at long last have obtained honour and independence creep into a mousehole and quietly watch their fellow artists being robbed, one cannot be surprised at the defeats. It would have been more valuable if, instead of writing *Hedda Gabler*, Ibsen had written just ten lines in a newspaper in which he took up the cudgels for some cause, such as for instance your brother's blasphemy case or an award to you in acknowledgement of your services.)

After Ernst Brandes had been found guilty of blasphemy because of one of the articles that Pontoppidan had written, the Danish government asked the latter to give a detailed explanation of what his intention had been in writing the article. Pontoppidan refused to give any such explanation and added:

For øvrigt skal jeg tillade mig i Ærbødighed at bemærke, at en sådan Dom, fældet af en juridisk Domstol, under ingen Omstændigheder kan være afgørende for mig som *Forfatter* eller afgive nogen Rettesnor for mig med Hensyn til min fremtidige Produktion. Jeg handler som Skribent efter den urokkelige Overbevisning, at al Kunst har sine egne Love, og at det er en Forfatters Pligt at efterkomme disse Love, selvom det skal ske med Fare for at komme i Strid med Tidens herskende Smag og med den deraf afhængige Opfattelse af bestående Lovparagraffer.

(In addition I shall take the liberty of remarking that such a sentence, pronounced by a court of law, can under no circumstances be decisive for me as an *author* or give any guidance to me as far as my future production is concerned. As a writer I act on the unshakeable conviction that all forms of art have their own laws, and that it is the duty of an author to obey these laws, even though there may be a danger of him coming into conflict with the ruling taste of the period and with the consequent interpretation of existing paragraphs of the law on that account.)

It was also in response to this demand from the government that Pontoppidan wrote to Edvard Brandes, who was then a Member of the Danish Folketing, in December 1892: 'Det var åbenbart Ministeriets Mening, at jeg skulde skrive et Tiggerbrev, hvori jeg skulde bede mange Gange om Forladelse og love aldrig at gøre det mere – men det vilde jeg ikke. Jeg holder meget af Penge, men man kan dog også bukke sig for dybt' (It was obviously the intention of the ministry that I should write a begging letter, in which I should ask for forgivenesses and promise never to do it again – but that I wouldn't do. I am very fond of money, but you can also bow too low).

On the same topic, Pontoppidan wrote a significant statement in December 1893, in a letter to a Danish literary critic, C. E. Jensen: 'Der, hvor Lidenskaben koger, må Poeten sætte sin Gryde over, og jeg er ikke langt fra et mene, at al stor Kunst i vore Dage må have været i Berøring med den politiske Ild og have en lille sveden Bismag af den' (Where passion is on the boil the poet must place his cooking-pot, and I am disposed to believe that in our time all great art must have been in touch with the fire of politics and have a little scorched after-taste of it).

Two years later, in 1894, he wrote again to Edvard Brandes: 'Jeg ønsker inderligt, at vi atter kunne komme bort fra den Ibsenske Lære-Digtning. Folk i vore Dage er nær ved at forlange, at enhver Bog skal være en Slags Katekismus, og Følgen bliver, at det er Seminaristerne, der i Publikums Øjne skriver de bedste Bøger' (I do wish we could get away again from Ibsen-influenced didactic literature. People in our time more or less demand that every book must be a kind of catechism, and the result is that, in the public's opinion, it is the half-educated people who write the best books).

In 1898, Professor Valdemar Vedel asked a number of Danish authors, 'what influence have Ibsen's works had on you?' I quote Pontoppidan's reply in extenso:

Om det Indtryck Ibsens første Bøger gjorde på mig erindrer jeg intet. I det hele mindes jeg ikke under selve Læsningen at have følt nye Himle – eller nye Afgrunde – åbne sig for mig; men det vilde sikkert være ganske urigtigt, om jeg deraf sluttede, at jeg ikke vilde have været synderligt anderledes, end jeg nu er, dersom jeg aldrig havde læst en Bog af Ibsen. Ibsens Bøger virker, synes det mig – så blændende de i mange Henseender er – ikke netop som Lyn, men ejer med deres Livsvisdom en egen stille Trolddomsmagt, der først lidt efter lidt tager Sindet fangen. Den omfattende Diskussion hver enkelt af dem har rejst – og endnu til Stadighed fremkalder – har vel også bidraget til at give dem en endnu større Betydning end man oprindelig havde tiltroet dem.

Således er det ihvertfald gået mig. Straks, under Læsningen af hans Bøger, har der altid været 'noget, der vendte sig i mig'. Jeg tror at hans Digtninge har været for ujordiske, særlig i Bertragtning af at de dog ikke behandlede overjordiske Ting. Ibsen er jo nok bleven Realist, men man mærker tydeligt, at han begyndte sin Digterflugt i Højdernes tynde Luft. Der er, synes mig, noget bastardagtigt over mange af hans Skikkelser. Hans kvindelige Gæs får Ørnevinger (Nora), hans mandlige Får rejser pludselig en Løvemanke (*Rosmersholm*). Desuden er hans Emner jo – som ofte fremdraget – ikke videre dramatiske. Han har måttet vride og vende dem på Dramaets Prokrustes Seng (der hos ham mange Steder tilmed knirker fælt) og ofte vanskabt dem på det slemmeste. – Og dog! Efter kort Tids Forløb glemmer jeg alle sådanne Ting, der under Læsningen har stødt, ja fornærmet mig; og lidt efter lidt vokser Dramaets Skikkelser ligesom lutrede op for min Erindring; hvad der i dets Bygning syntes mig vrangt og vredent, retter sig ud, og jer ser dets lille Verden for mig i dens Sammenhæng, omfatter og gennemtrænger den med et eneste Blik, således som jeg indbilder mig, at Ibsen i sine inspirerede Øjeblikke selv har set den. Dette er, synes mig, det særegne Trylleri ved Ibsens senere Digtning, at han ligesom delagtiggør sin Læser i den Undfangelsens Glæde han selv må have følt, da Værket opstod i hans Tanke. Naturligvis beror dette på et Selvbedrag. Men hvad er Poesi andet?

Et Ibsensk Skuespil bevares derfor altid i min Erindring som en Helhed, aldrig (hvad ellers i Almindelighed er Tilfældet) stykkevis, en enkelt Scene, nogle enkelte Figurer o.s.v. Jeg tror ikke jeg har læst mange af dem mere end én Gang; og dog står de – ikke i Detailler men i Omrids – hver for sig ganske levende for mig. Det er denne hans Værkers Helstøbthed, jeg navnlig beundrer. I Sammenligning hermed synes næsten al moderne Digtning mig løst sammenflikket Stykværk (særlig flyder jo den danske Poesi mere og mere ud i lyrisk Journalistik).

Hvilken Indflydelse Ibsen har haft på mig som Menneske ser jeg mig ikke i Stand til at udrede. Derimod ved jeg bestemt, at hans kunstneriske Mesterskab, hans enestående Evne til billedligt at udtrykke, hvad der rører sig i ham, har virket i høj Grad ansporende og æggende på mig, skønt jeg jo arbejder i en Digtart, der ikke er hans.

(Concerning the impression that Ibsen's first books made on me I have no recollection. On the whole during the reading itself I do not remember having felt new heavens – or new chasms – opening themselves to me, but it would undoubtedly be quite wrong if I concluded from that that I would not have been much different from what I am now if I had never read one of Ibsen's books. Ibsen's books do not, it seems to me, have the effect of lightning shafts, however dazzling in many respects they are, but with their vital wisdom possess a quiet fascination which only gradually takes possession of their reader. The extensive discussion each of them has given rise to, and even now still gives rise to, has probably also contributed to making them even more important than they were originally given credit for.

That at least is what happened to me. My immediate reaction on reading his books has always been that there was something I couldn't stomach. I think his writings have been too unworldly, especially when one considers that they did not deal with supernatural things. It is true that Ibsen has become a realist, but one feels clearly that he began his poetic flight in the thin air of the heights. There is, it seems to me, something hybrid in many of his characters. His female geese get eagle's wings (Nora), his male sheep suddenly raise a lion's mane (*Rosmersholm*). Furthermore, his subjects aren't really dramatic, as has been frequently maintained. He has had to twist and turn them on the Procrustes-bed of drama (which in his plays in many cases creaks badly) and often deformed them terribly. – And yet! After a short while I forget all such things which hurt or even insulted me whilst I read; and the characters of the drama gradually take form, almost purified, in my memory. That which in its construction seemed to me to be wrong and distorted now straightens out, and I see with my inner eye its little world in all its coherence, take it in and penetrate it in a single glance in the way I imagine Ibsen himself saw it in his inspired moments. This, it seems to me, is the special magic of Ibsen's later works, that he almost lets his reader share in the joy of conception that he himself must have felt when the work arose in his mind. That, of course, is a delusion. But what is poetry other than that?

A play by Ibsen is therefore always preserved in my memory as a complete whole, never (which is otherwise usually the case) in bits and pieces, a single scene, individual characters, etc. I do not think I have read many of them more than once, yet all the same they are for me – not in detail, but in outline – each of them entirely living. It is this ability to create a unified whole I particularly admire. In comparison almost all modern literature seems to me loosely tacked together patch-work (Danish poetry especially dissolves more and more into lyrical journalism).

I am not able to express what influence Ibsen has had on me as a person. However, I am certain that his artistic mastery, his unique talent for expressing in images what agitates his mind, has had a highly stimulating and inciting effect on me, even though I am working in a field of literature which is different from his.

It is worth adding that on the occasion of Ibsen's seventieth birthday Valdemar Vedel wrote a short book of some sixty pages entitled *Ibsen og Danmark*. In it he compared Dr Relling in *Vildanden* (The Wild Duck) with the principal character, Dr Levin, in Pontoppidan's *Den gamle Adam* (The Old Adam), and Emanuel Hansted, the central character in *Det forjættede Land* (The Promised Land), with Hjalmar Ekdal. Vedel sent his book to Pontoppidan, who replied in September 1898:

Det er mig umuligt at forstå, hvad den kynisk-materialistiske Dr. Relling kan have mere end Doktortitlen tilfælles med Dr. Levin, denne bedragne Ægtemand, der i Angst for den gamle Adams Magt har søgt sin Tilflugt til Filosofien, til den blotte Tanketilværelse, gjort sig til Discipel af Epiktet og i hans Ånd priser 'det Sjælens stille Planteliv, hvorunder Menneskeånden opfylder sin Bestemmelse og når sit Endemål: Klarhed og Fred'.

Endvidere: hvorledes *Det forjættede Land*s Emanuel, der godtroende, men højsindet ofrer alt indtil sit inderste Selv for det, han anser for sit Kald, hvorledes denne helt igennem tragiske Skikkelse kan minde en forstandig, endsige en intelligent Læser om den egoistiske, helt igennem småtskårne, tragikomiske Nar Hjalmar Ekdal, det er også en af de Gåder, som en nærsynet Kritik bestandig giver Forfatterne at løse.

(It is impossible for me to understand what the cynical and materialistic Dr Relling can have in common, apart from the title of doctor, with Dr Levin, that deceived husband who for fear of the power of the Old Adam has sought refuge in philosophy, in the life of the mind alone, has made himself into a disciple of Epictetus, and in his spirit praises 'the quiet plant-life of the soul in which the human spirit fulfils its destiny and reaches its goal: clarity and peace'.

Furthermore: how Emanuel in *The Promised Land*, who credulously but generously sacrifices everything including his innermost self for what he considers to be his calling, how this altogether tragic character can remind a clever, not to say intelligent reader of the selfish, altogether small-minded tragi-comic fool Hjalmar Ekdal – that is also one of the riddles which a short-sighted criticism continually requires authors to solve.)

In 1898 the first instalment of Pontoppidan's novel *Lykke-Per* was published. Otto Borchsenius, who was the first Danish editor to publish a novel by Pontoppidan, saw *Lykke-Per* as an attempt to portray the Danish people in the nineteenth century. But Pontoppidan wrote to him in July 1898:

Når jeg har samlet Skildringerne omkring Lykke-Pers Person, er det for tillige at give noget mere. Jeg har søgt for mig selv at efterspore og klarlægge Grundene til, at Halvfjerdsernes såkaldte Gennembrudsbevægelse, trods alt, *måtte* mislykkes, i hvert Fald i første Omgang, idet den stødte an mod de evige Love, hvorefter Menneskeskæbner og Tidsskæbner styres. – Også om Lykke handler Bogen; thi at Titlen skal forstås ironisk er ikke ganske rigtigt (jeg er i det hele ikke nær så ironisk som jeg desværre nu engang har fået Ord for at være), – men Ordet har i mine Øren en melankolsk Klang; og 'Moralen' i denne Bog er ganske den samme som i min forrige Roman, hvor den tydeligt og ganske uironisk er udtrykt i de Ord: 'at Lykken her i Livet består i at fæste Rod i egen Jordbund og vokse i Lyset af den hjemlige Himmel', hvor sort denne så er.

(The reason why I have grouped the descriptions around the person of Lucky Per is also to give something more. I have attempted for my own satisfaction to trace and clarify the reasons why the so-called Movement of the Modern Breakthrough of the seventies *had to* fail in spite of everything, at least to begin with, since it clashed with the eternal laws according to which human destinies and destinies of time are governed. – The book is also about good fortune or happiness; for it is not quite correct to say that the title should be understood as being ironic (altogether I am not quite as ironic as I am generally believed to be), – but the word has in my ears a melancholy ring, and the 'moral' of this book is precisely the same as in my previous novel, in which it is clearly expressed, and entirely without irony, in the words: 'that happiness in this life consists in taking root in one's own soil and growing in the light of one's native sky', however dark that sky may be.)

In continuation of this life of thought, Pontoppidan wrote to Edvard Brandes in 1904: 'Jeg var i sin Tid for ung til at komme med i Halvfjerdsernes Stormkolonner. Jeg har nu tænkt mig, at jeg kunde være brugbar ved Dækningen af Tilbagetoget' (In those days I was too young to join the storm troops of the seventies. It seems to me now that I might be useful in covering the retreat).

His disillusionment with Danish – and Norwegian – literature can also be seen from a letter to Axel Lundegård: 'Jeg længes efter igen at læse noget svensk Litteratur. Nordmændene keder mig. Selv Bjørnsons nye Skuespil (*Paul Lange og Tora Parsberg*), som jeg læste forleden, interesserer mig ikke. Det er Præstepræk og Degnelyrik. Herhjemme fremkommer der heller ikke meget som man kan glæde sig ved. Der er mellem de yngste en Mand, der hedder Johannes Jensen. Falder du over en Bog af ham, skal du læse den; han er vild og stærk' (I am longing to read some Swedish literature again. I am bored with the Norwegians. Even Bjørnson's latest play (*Paul Lange and Tora Parsberg*), which I read the other day, does not interest me. It is a clergyman's preaching and a parish clerk's poetry. Here in Denmark little worth enjoying is being published. Among the youngest writers there is a man called Johannes [V.] Jensen. If you come across a book by him, you should read it; he is wild and strong).

Over the years a close relationship developed between Pontoppidan and Georg Brandes. As early as February 1899, Pontoppidan wrote to Brandes: 'Jo ældre jeg bliver, des stærkere føler jeg mig knyttet til Dem ved en Taknemlighedsgæld, der daglig beskæftiger mig' (The older I get, the more strongly I feel attached to you through a debt of gratitude which is in my thoughts every day).

Pontoppidan sent Georg Brandes each new instalment of *Lykke-Per* as it was published. Like Borchsenius, Brandes also thought the title was ironic, but Pontoppidan corrected him in a letter of January 1900: 'Titlen skal ingenlunde forstås ironisk. Men hans Skæbne bliver i en vis Forstand tragisk, fordi den Lykke han har attrået og virkelig vundet, ikke passer for ham; han har ikke hjemme i de Regioner, hvori Jacobes kærlighed fører ham op' (The title must in no way be understood as ironic. But in a certain sense his destiny becomes tragic, because the good fortune he has coveted and truly won, is not the right one for him; he does not belong in the regions into which he is taken by Jacobe's love). And he continued: 'Men mon man forresten ikke i vore Dage for interesseret spørger om "Meningen" med en Bog, og mon ikke de Digterværker, der – som det hedder – bygges over en Ide, gerne bliver de magreste? Man ser for sig en Række Billeder,

Menneskeskikkelser, Situationer, og man gør en Bog af dem i Tillid til, at der er så megen Sammenhæng i ens Tankeverden, at hvad der såes som et Kaos ganske af sig selv samler sig til et Hele. Er det der ikke, nytter det dog vist næppe, hvor ivrigt man end knytter og binder med "røde Tråde"' (I wonder whether we are not in our days too eager to ask for the 'intention' of a book, and I wonder whether the literary works which – as we say – are constructed around one idea, do not have a tendency to become the most meagre ones? One sees in one's mind a number of images, human destinies, situations, and one makes a book out of them, trusting that there is enough cohesion in one's imagination so that what was seen as chaos automatically forms itself into a whole. If there is not such cohesion, no good will come of it, however eagerly one ties up and binds with 'red threads').

On the occasion of Georg Brandes' sixtieth birthday, in February 1902, Pontoppidan wrote:

De har i disse Dage ikke Tid til at læse Breve. Jeg vil da nøjes med kort og godt at lykønske Dem til Fødselsdagen, og bringer Dem dertil en fattig Tak for alt, hvad De har været for mig både til godt og ondt. De var jo for os alle det Kundskabens Træ, hvoraf vi plukkede både søde og bitre Frugter, indtil vi erkendte vor Nøgenhed. Gid De endnu længe må blomstre iblandt os, vi har Dem stadig hårdt behov.

(During these days you have no time to read letters. I shall therefore content myself with a brief congratulation on your birthday, and in addition convey to you a poor thank you for everything you have been for me both for better and for worse. For all of us you were the tree of knowledge from which we picked both sweet and bitter fruits until we realized our own nakedness. I hope you will continue to blossom for a long time among us, we still need you badly.)

In the summer of 1902 Pontoppidan had sent Georg Brandes the latest instalment of *Lykke-Per*, the volume entitled *Lykke-Per og hans Kæreste* (Lucky Per and his Fiancée), which Brandes then praised in a letter to Pontoppidan, who replied: 'Det ville jo være Skaberi af mig at fragå at jeg ved Skildringen af min Bogs Dr. Nathan specielt har haft Deres Virksomhed i Tankerne, og skønt jeg naturligvis ikke mener, at De i mindste Måde skulde have godkendt mit Tilløb til en Karakteristik, håber jeg dog i Deres venlige Brev at måtte se Vidnesbyrd om, at De ikke har misopfattet den Følelse eller den Hensigt, der har affødt mit Forsøg' (It would be an affectation on my part to deny that in the description of Dr Nathan in my book I had particularly had your activities in mind, and though of course I do not think that you should have approved my attempt at characterization in the least, I hope in your kind letter to be allowed to see evidence of the fact that you have not misunderstood the feeling or the intention on which my attempt is based).

Over the next few days these remarks led to an important exchange of letters. Brandes protested against certain statements about Dr Nathan if, indeed, the latter was intended as a true portrait of himself, and although Pontoppidan agreed with one of his objections, he remained firm where the others were concerned.

In this context I cannot help quoting a characteristic statement in a letter from Pontoppidan to Peter Nansen, another contemporary Danish novelist: 'Det er aldrig min Hensigt at såre. Kan jeg derimod se mit Snit til at dræbe, gør jeg det gerne' (It is never my intention to wound. Yet if I can see the chance to kill, I will seize it gladly).

In 1903 Herman Bang celebrated his twenty-fifth anniversary as a writer, and Pontoppidan sent him the following letter, which I quote in full:

Modtag også min Lykønskning og Tak. Den beundrende Hyldest, der i Dag vil lyde op mod Dem allevegnefra, er så meget mere betydningsfuld, som den langsomt er aftvunget et forudindtaget, modvilligt Publikum. Det er det bedste Bevis på Deres Kunsts Magtfuldhed, at den har formået at overvinde selv den største Uvilje mod Deres Person. At en sådan urimelig Uvilje har eksisteret adskillige Steder, har De næppe kunnet undgå at mærke. Med det i bedste Forstand kvindelige Drag i Deres åndelige Fysiognomi var De så grundforskellig fra det danske Idealmandfolk, der altid var af Slagterstatur. Selv hos den, der bestandig har æret både Deres Kunst og Deres Karakter, tit måske den sidste endnu højere end den første, – selv hos dem risikerede De undertiden at vække Anstød. Nu hører De til vore laurbærkronede Mænd og ser kun begejstrede Venner og andagtsfulde Elever om Dem. Om andre femotyve År vil Folket feste om Deres Statue.

(Please also accept my congratulations and thanks. The homage of admiration that will reach you today from all sides, is so much more important as it has been drawn slowly out of a prejudiced, antagonistic public. That is the best proof of the power of your art that it has managed to vanquish even the strongest dislike of your person. The fact that such an unreasonable antagonism has existed in many places is something you have hardly been able to escape noticing. With the – in the best sense – female streak in your spiritual physiognomy you were basically so different from the Danish masculine ideal, who always had a butcher's stature. Even in those who have constantly admired both your art and your character, perhaps the latter even higher than the former – even among them you ran the risk of sometimes causing offence. Now you are one of those crowned with laurel wreaths and see only enthusiastic friends and devoted pupils around you. In another twenty-five years people will gather around your statue to celebrate you.)

A Danish literary feud had its origins in 1905, following Professor Vilhelm Andersen's reduction of Danish naturalism to a melancholy and sad period in his book *Bacchustoget i Norden*. Pontoppidan, who identified himself with Naturalism, reacted sharply in the Preface to a new edition of one of his early works, *Fra Hytterne* (From the Cottages), where he called Andersen 'Borgerskabets anerkendte Smagsdommer for Tiden' (the respected arbiter of taste for the bourgeoisie). Andersen was unhappy about both the tone and the substance of Pontoppidan's reply and admitted that it would have been perfectly possible to measure Danish naturalism by another yardstick than the Dionysian one. He concluded by saying: 'Men hvad der gør mig overordentlig ondt er, at De håner mig. Jeg har den Forfængelighed, at jeg vil nødig hånes netop af Dem' (but what hurts me a great deal is that you sneer at me. It is my vanity that I feel a reluctance to be scorned by you of all people).

Pontoppidan replied in a personal letter to Andersen, which ended with the following words: 'Jeg ønsker Dem alt det Solskin, hvortil De er født. Vi er i Forvejen nok, der kun trives i Skyggen. Men netop på Grund af den overordentlige Autoritet, De har vundet overalt i Landet, kan vi, der føler os forurettet af Dem, ikke lade Deres Ord stå uimodsagte, og trods al min Beundring for Dem, vil De rimeligvis altid finde mig blandt Deres Modstandere' (I wish for you all the sunshine for which you were born. There are already enough of us who thrive only in the shadow. But just because of the extraordinary authority you have won everywhere in this country we, who feel unjustly treated by you, cannot pretend that you did not say what you said, and in spite of all my admiration for you, you will probably always find me among your antagonists).

However strange it may sound, this sharp exchange of views was the introduction to a warm and close friendship between the two men, a friendship which lasted until Pontoppidan's death in 1943.

Pontoppidan was pleased and proud when in 1906 Martin Andersen Nexø dedicated the first volume of his novel *Pelle Erobreren* (Pelle the Conqueror) 'Til Mesteren Henrik Pontoppidan' (To the Master, Henrik Pontoppidan). Time and again Pontoppidan had called himself 'en folkelig Forfatter' (a popular author), a term which Sven Lange, a conservative Danish literary critic, had regarded as an expression of praiseworthy modesty. In Pontoppidan's letter to Andersen Nexø, in which he thanked him for having dedicated *Pelle Erobreren* to him, he remarked of Sven Lange:

Den Slags Folk forstår ikke, at der for en Skribent, som dog vil regnes til Digterlavet, kan være noget større Mål end at blive optaget i de litterære Rangklasser. – Men tager jeg fejl i, at det just er i denne Folkelighed, at Fællesskabet mellem os to ligger? Vi har begge været med til at skabe en Litteratur, der kunne bidrage til at udvikle, hvad man har kaldt Levekunsten, den største og vanskeligste af alle Kunster, – en Litteratur, der (og det er netop det nye ved den) ikke udelukkende kan måles med den æstetiske Målestok. At ville gøre dette, er som at ville bestemme Musikken i en Flok Skovarbejderes Øksehug ved Hjælp af en Stemmegaffel.

(People of that sort do not understand that for a writer who wants to be reckoned among the Guild of *Digtere*, there can be any greater aspiration than to be enrolled in the literary ranks. – But am I wrong in assuming that it is exactly this *folkelighed* that is common to both of us? We have both of us shared in creating a literature which may contribute to develop what has been called the art of living, the greatest and most difficult of all arts, – a literature which (and that is exactly what is new in it) cannot be measured by means of the aesthetic yardstick alone. Wanting to do that is like wanting to identify the music caused by the strokes of the axes of a group of lumberjacks by means of a tuning fork.)

When the editor of *Politiken*, Henrik Cavling, asked Pontoppidan in 1909 to send a greeting to the newspaper on the occasion of its twenty-five years' jubilee, Pontoppidan replied:

Kære Ven! Tænk, at *Politiken* nu er bleven så gammel, at den kan holde Jubilæum! Jeg har jo nok observeret, at det på den sidste er bleven svært bred og fed og desuden passende kristelig; men jeg havde dog ikke tænkt mig Jubelåret og Dommedagen så nær. Nu ønsker du, at også jeg skal være med til at blæse i Basuner på Festdagen, når Fortiden skal genopstå af Graven. Men jeg frygter for, at der herved ville overkomme mig en upassande Længsel efter den Tid, da Bladet var ungt og dets Borgerskab endnu i Himlen, at der i det hele vilde undslippe mig et Suk, som netop ved den Lejlighed ikke bør høres. Lad mig derfor være udenfor.

(My dear Friend, Incredible that *Politiken* has become so old that it can celebrate a jubilee! I have observed, of course, that recently it has grown broad and fat and in addition suitably Christian; but I had not thought that the jubilee year and the day of judgement could be so near. Now you want me too to take part in the blowing of trumpets on the festive day when the past is supposed to rise from the grave. But I fear that this would provoke in me an unsuitable longing for the time when the paper was young and its citizenship still in heaven, and that altogether there would a sigh would escape me, which at that very time ought not to be heard. Please, therefore, let me stay out of this.)

In November 1909 Georg Brandes delivered his first lecture on Goethe in Berlin, and after his return to Denmark he was taken ill and admitted to hospital in Copenhagen. In a letter to Brandes Pontoppidan wrote: 'Jeg håber oprigtigt, at det ikke skal vare længe, for De igen står på Katedret og jeg ved Deres Fødder med en beklemmende Følelse af, at Deres Ord er rettet til mig personlig, noget en god Tilhører vel forresten altid har overfor Dem. Jeg har nu også en Grund til at være særlig lydhør, den at jeg, skønt Goethe-døbt, ikke er noget helt pålideligt Medlem af Menigheden og kan have godt af at blive bestyrket i Troen. Geheimeråden er mig noget for meget af en Duksenatur. Jeg får undertiden – på Fuksemaner – Lyst til at vrænge af ham, hvad jeg naturligvis bør skamme mig over' (I sincerely hope that it will not be long before you will stand at the lectern once more and I at your feet with an oppressive feeling that your words are aimed at me personally, something a good member of the audience always feels about you, I think. I also have a reason to be especially attentive, namely that, although Goethe-baptized, I am not a reliable member of the congregation and may need to be strengthened in the faith. The *Geheimrat* is slightly too smug for my liking. Sometimes – in the manner of a dunce – I feel a desire to mock him, a desire of which I ought to be ashamed, of course).

In January 1910 Georg Brandes wrote and told Pontoppidan that he intended to read a paper on him to the students in Christiania. Pontoppidan replied on 28 January: 'Det var både Stolthed og Ydmyghed, der greb mig under Læsningen af Deres Brev. At være Emne for et Foredrag af Georg Brandes – det er den danske Nobelpræmie, og skønt jeg naturligvis inderst inde bærer på meget overdrevne Forestillinger om min Betydning for Nutid og Efterslægt, så skal jeg ikke nægte, at jeg endnu bæver lidt ved Tanken. Da De sidst holdt Foredrag, var det om Goethe. Jeg erkender her en Forskel' (I was filled with both pride and humility on reading your letter. To be the subject of a lecture by Georg Brandes – that is the Danish Nobel Prize, and though of course in my innermost soul I have very exaggerated ideas of my importance for the present and for posterity, I shall not deny that I am still slightly atremble at the thought. When you gave your last lecture, it was about Goethe. I acknowledge a difference here).

Brandes delivered the lecture on Pontoppidan at the Student Society in Christiania in March 1910. A month later he gave the same lecture in a slightly different form at the Kasino concert hall in Copenhagen. On the very day the lecture was given Pontoppidan wrote to Brandes:

I dette Øjeblik står De på Katedret i Kasino og holder Dom over mig, og skønt ingen kan være dybere interesseret i denne Sag end jeg, sidder jeg herhjemme. Jeg havde, da det kom til Stykket, ikke Mod nok til at overvære Eksekutionen, og det skønt jeg jo godt ved, at det ikke er nogen Dødsdom De fælder over mig. Men på Operationsbordet kommer jeg dog; mine indvendige Dele, både de 'ædlere' og de mindre ædle, bliver fremdraget til Beskuelse, og jeg, for hvem det jo på en vis Måde gælder Liv og Død, måtte for de mange fremmede Øjnes Skyld lade som ingenting. Jeg trøster mig nu med, at Foredraget vel nok engang bliver trykt, og dermed må jeg lade mig nøje.

(At this very moment you are standing at the lectern in Kasino, passing judgement upon me, and even though no one can be more profoundly interested in this matter than I, here I am at home. In the end, my courage failed me so that I dared not attend the execution, although I know very well that it is not a death sentence you are giving me. Even so, I shall be placed on the operating table; my inner parts, both the 'nobler' and the less noble will be produced to public view, and I, to whom it is a matter of life and death in a way, taking into account the many strangers' eyes, I would have to behave as if nothing was happening. My consolation is that some time it will probably be published, and this must be enough for me.)

Henrik Pontoppidan lived for another thirty-three years, but the letters he wrote between 1910 and 1943 fall outside the period under discussion in this volume.

11

Knut Hamsun and Denmark

Harald Næss
Kristiansand

Knut Hamsun was not a racist, but he had strong feelings – some may say prejudices – about nations. He wrote a whole book denouncing the United States, he harboured a life-long aversion to England, disliked France, despised Switzerland, while approving of the Kaiser's Germany, a country he had only visited briefly and whose language he did not understand. But Germany by 1910 had translated and published all his books – twenty-three titles – many of them in the same year as their original Norwegian publication, while in those same twenty years England had produced only a single book by Hamsun.

Within Scandinavia, Hamsun had little sympathy for Sweden. He visited the country in 1892 and told his Danish publisher 'jeg hadde tænkt at rejse over til Gotland, men jeg vender om allerede idag. Nej, jeg er bleven paavirket mere og mere antipatisk efterhvert som jeg er kommet frem i dette Land. Jeg kunde aldrig leve her nogen Tid' (I had thought of going over to Gotland, but I have decided to turn back today. No, I became more and more antipathetic to this country as I went on. I would never be able to live here for any length of time, KHB 1, p. 271).[1] But he found it difficult to live even in Norway. Back in Kristiania after three years in America and Denmark, he wrote to his publisher in Copenhagen: 'Jeg er halvt ødelagt. Her er et Helvede for mine Nerver. En Vært, der dræber mig Led for Led med sit Prat...Gud bevare mig for nogensinde at rejse til Norge mer, hvis jeg engang kommer ud herfra nu' (I am a wreck: it is sheer hell here for my nerves. A landlord who is destroying me limb by limb with his chatter...God save me from ever coming to Norway again if only I can get away this time, KHB 1, p. 129). Ten years later Hamsun spent several months in Helsingfors, where he met poets, writers, critics, editors; many of them became his friends and some of them for life. Finally about Denmark, he told a Danish author in 1910: 'Mit Forhold til Danmark! En eneste Tak og Lovprisning til Danmark. Av al sin rike Kultur har det ogsaa drysset litt paa mig, og jeg har nytt godt av den *Hjærtets Dannelse,* som intet Folk jeg kjender har Maken til' (My relationship to Denmark? Thanks and praise to Denmark. Of all its rich culture it has also sprinkled a little on me, and I have profited from the *wisdom of the heart,* that no other people I know have in the same degree, KHB 3, pp. 308-9).

Hamsun saw Denmark for the first time briefly in 1879, however, between the years 1888 and 1905 he visited the country more than twelve times, staying from three to eight months on each occasion, and – apart from a winter on the island of Samsø – always in Copenhagen. Here, as also in Helsingfors, he met writers and publishers who became his friends, but Copenhagen was different from Helsingfors in being the city that launched Hamsun on the literary scene. Here he published a section of his first novel *Hunger,* here he lectured for the first time to university students and had his lectures accepted for publication, here he was invited to the homes of critics and writers. Like Byron he awoke one morning and found himself famous, and though his sudden fame and growing arrogance soon provoked attacks from certain Copenhagen critics, Hamsun never forgot that it was in Denmark – and thanks to Denmark – that he made his literary debut.

From the period under discussion – 1870-1910 – we have about two hundred letters from Hamsun to Danes, most of them to his Danish publishers and to his Russian translator P. E. Hansen. To his colleagues in the writing business there are a number of single letters – to Herman Bang, Marie Bregendahl, Sophus Claussen, Holger Drachmann, Agnes Henningsen, Johs.V. Jensen, Sven Lange, Karl Larsen, Viggo Stuckenberg – showing that he knew these people quite well, but the letters do not indicate a close friendship of the kind that sometimes results in an extended correspondence. Like other great writers, Hamsun reveals his literary dreams and ambitions mainly in his early letters. The young and unknown are more willing to share their innermost thoughts, while the middle-aged writer – after some recognition or perhaps even fame – sees less need to confess or seek advice. And so Hamsun's later correspondence – where it does deal with literary matters – often takes the form of public statements, such as letters to the editor or articles printed in newspapers and journals. The most remarkable example of this latter category is a letter from Hamsun to his Danish colleague and friend Johannes V. Jensen, published in 1908 in the periodical *Tilskueren* (The Spectator) under the heading 'Bondekulturen. Brev til Johannes V. Jensen' (Peasant Culture. Letter to Johannes V. Jensen).

In June 1888 Hamsun sailed from New York on the ship *Thingvalla* and arrived three weeks later in Copenhagen, where a pawnbroker gave him six kroner for his raincoat so that he could rent an attic room in St. Hans Gade. He had little to eat, but even so he wrote to an American friend: 'Hvor dette Land er mig behageligt! Jeg forsikrer Dig, den hele Væren – Livsordning her er i den inderste Harmoni med mit Sind, min Natur! Her er Europa, og jeg er Europæer – gudskjelov' (How comfortable I feel in this country! I do assure you, the whole nature of things, the way of life here is essentially in harmony with my mind and my nature! This is Europe, and I am a European – God be praised!', KHB 1, p. 78). Hamsun was working on two projects, one a characterization of the Norwegian poet and immigrant pastor Kristofer Jansen and the other a section of what later became his novel *Hunger*. Both pieces were eventually printed in the new periodical *Ny Jord* (New Soil), but in the meantime Hamsun lived the life of the *Hunger* hero, and was rescued by the editor of *Politiken*, Edvard Brandes, who later told a friend: 'Et mere forkomment Menneske har jeg sjelden seet. Ikke bare at hans Klæder var fillede. Men det Ansigt! Jeg er ikke sentimental, som De ved, men det Ansigt greb mig' (I have rarely seen a more destitute person. It was not only that his clothes were ragged. But that face! As you know, I am not sentimental, but that face touched me).[2] Brandes also recommended the young Norwegian to the publisher Gustav Philipsen, who offered Hamsun the considerable sum of one hundred kroner. We only have one letter from Hamsun to Edvard Brandes, although it is a very interesting one, and I shall come back to it in due course. But Edvard Brandes is often referred to in Hamsun's letters to other Scandinavians, and, like other newspapermen, he soon became one of Hamsun's pet enemies.

Although Edvard Brandes had indeed helped Hamsun financially and otherwise, he must have felt that Hamsun lost his innocence and modesty a little too soon, a feeling shared by the American Minister to Copenhagen, Rasmus Andersen, who in his autobiography tells of a dinner given by Erik and Amalie Skram to honour 'this street-car driver from Chicago, a man who...a few days before had been at the point of starvation in the garret of St. Hans Torv. And how conscious he was of his own importance! He walked among the other guests and talked with them with the greatest assurance as if he had been to the manner born and had a ready made opinion on every question under the sun'.[3] Edvard Brandes reviewed Hamsun's book about America as well as *Hunger* and *Mysteries*, and though Hamsun found his tone cold and mocking, he did not at first take the reviews too seriously. 'For Edvard Brandes faar jeg herefter skrive fornuftige Husholdningsromaner', he told his publisher Philipsen (For Edvard Brandes I had better, from now on, write sensible popular fiction, KHB 1, p. 177). But he realized that Brandes, as editor of *Politiken*, was a powerful man and that he himself was not invulnerable. He noticed in particular how Brandes' characterization of him as a publicity-seeking Yankee was more and more generally accepted, and decided to seek a rapprochement. From Paris he sent Brandes a copy of Wedekind's *Frühlingserwachen* (*Spring Awakening*) and asked politely for his opinion of the work. When this ploy seemed not to work, he begged a trusted friend to intercede and soon regretted it:

skjønt jeg er mærkelig lidet sjæleligt frisk nu, saa vilde jeg ikke alligevel have forledet, bedt, dig, Bolette til at sende Brandes det Brev nu. Fraregnet, at det nok ikke hjælper – nej, jeg er saa sikker paa som jeg sidder her, at det er forgæves – saa var det min første jammerlige Streg dette med at forsøge paa at tilsmugle mig en Overbærenhed, som man ikke har tiltænkt mig. Og nu kan jeg heller ikke sige til mig selv: du har *aldrig* bedt om Naade. Nej, for jeg har faktisk gjort det én Gang.

(but though I am in remarkably poor mental health, all the same I wouldn't now have cajoled you, begged you, Bolette, to send that letter to Brandes. Apart from the fact that it's probably not going to help – indeed, it's as certain as I am sitting here that it will be in vain – that business of trying to sneak for myself an indulgence which hadn't been intended for me was my first miserable ruse. Nor can I now say to myself: you have *never* asked for mercy. Because I have in fact done it once, KHB 1, p. 366.)

Edvard Brandes did not review Hamsun's next novel but gave it to his colleague Peter Nansen to write about. Of Nansen's review Hamsun wrote in an English letter to his German publisher: '*Neue Erde* was criticized in *Politiken* by Peter Nansen, and that was the most brutish, most horrible critic I ever got in any paper, in any country. He insinuated that I have wrote my book only for making money from the merchants, he said right away that I had no talent, that I was no artist, nothing, only a humbug-maker, speculating in making reklame' (KHB I, p. 435). Strangely, Peter Nansen gradually became one of Hamsun's best friends, but of Edvard Brandes Hamsun said many years later, 'that man has never liked me', and his assessment of the situation was probably right.

With Edvard's brother Georg, Hamsun had a more complicated relationship. In Georg Brandes he sensed an aristocratic disposition; his connections with the press and, particularly, with the Danish Folketing, were less obvious and Hamsun had spoken contemptuously of the parliamentary mind of his brother Edvard. During the second of Hamsun's two lectures on the intellectual life of modern America, Georg Brandes was present and spoke approvingly of what he had heard; he later invited Hamsun to his home, and he reviewed the lectures when they finally appeared in book form. Hamsun wrote to thank him for his remarks after the lecture, and later for the book review, in which he found sympathy and understanding. With his critical instinct Georg Brandes had also touched on something essential in Hamsun's style, 'som trods Forfatterens uophørlige Udfald mod det amerikanske, paa Grund af hans ubevidste nervøse Paavirkelighed af Omgivelserne, er bleven rent amerikansk, springende, skjærende, humoristisk overdrivende, jagende efter Effekt og i Regelen findende Effekten' (which, despite the author's unceasing assault on everything American, on account of his unconscious, nervous impressionability has become altogether American, cursory, cutting, with exaggerated humour, striving for effect and, usually, finding it).[4] But once again Hamsun was getting too eager for his Danish benefactors. He asked Georg Brandes to write a foreword for a planned German edition of his America book and was in for a surprise. He told Philipsen: 'Jeg forstaar ikke, at man i København begynder at blive uvelvillig mod mig nu, saa hjærtelig gode alle Folk har været før. Et Kort fra G.B. er simpelthen ufatteligt. Selv Deres Brev er saa strængt' (I can't understand why people in Copenhagen should begin to be so hostile to me now, when earlier everybody was so extremely kind. One card from Georg Brandes is simply incomprehensible. Even your own letter is so stern, KHB 1, p. 145). And, as Hamsun was getting more aggressive, so Georg Brandes seemed to lose some of his original enthusiasm for the young Norwegian. He found Hamsun's new novel *Sult* (Hunger) monotonous, and Hamsun retorted 'Min Bog maa ikke betragtes som en Roman. Der er nok af dem, som skriver Romaner naar de skal skrive om Sult – fra Zola til Kielland. De gør det allesammen. Og er det Mangelen paa det Romanagtige, som kanske gør min Bog monoton, saa er jo det bare en Anbefaling, eftersom jeg simpelthen havde bestemt mig til *ikke* at skrive en Roman' (My book must not be regarded as a novel. There are enough people who write novels when they want to write about hunger – from Zola to Kielland. They all do it. And if it is the lack of this novel-type quality which perhaps makes my book monotonous, then that is simply a recommendation, since I had determined quite deliberately *not* to write a novel, KHB 1, p. 161).

We know that Georg Brandes felt snubbed, though he put on a good face. 'Jeg har truffet Brandes', Hamsun wrote two years later to friends in Bergen. 'Han er lige elskværdig med at bede én komme op til sig, og naar han driver paa Gaden, strør han endnu lige sorgløst de mest storartede Ting udover den, der gaar sammen med ham' (I have met Brandes...He is just as kind about asking me to call in on him; and when he walks along the street he quite happily pours out the most marvellous comments to the person who is accompanying him, KHB 1, p. 250-51). In March 1893 Hamsun lectured once more to the students in Copenhagen, this time on modern literature. Georg Brandes was present and in the following discussion tore Hamsun and his ideas apart. Brandes afterwards called the lecture a bunch of trivialities and told others privately that Hamsun's immature behaviour could be explained by the fact that he was completely without schooling. But Hamsun already regarded Brandes as passé. When Ibsen's *Lille Eyolf* (Little Eyolf) appeared and Brandes was less than enthusiastic, Hamsun wrote: 'Georg Brandes vil ikke kritisere Ifsen længer, bare takke. Ja, hvorfor skulde Brandes kritisere Ifsen? Han er den Generations, GBs Generations største Navn, og hvorfor skulde han slaa ned sit største Navn? Men det forpligter ikke os, mig, Generationen senere. Gud bevare os, hvor «Eyolf» er daarlig, hvor den er tynd og kedelig' (Georg Brandes does not want to criticize Ifsen any longer, simply thank him. Well, why should G.B. criticize Ifsen? He is that generation's – GB's generation's – greatest name, and why should he bring down his greatest name? But this does not bind us, me, the later generation. God save us, but how bad *Eyolf* is, how thin and boring, KHB 1, p. 444).

As with Edvard Brandes earlier and with Bjørnson later, Hamsun tried to patch up his friendship with Georg Brandes, and did so in a curious way. When Christen Collin attacked Georg Brandes in a newspaper article and Brandes defended himself in *Politiken*, Hamsun felt Brandes should not have dignified Collin and other nobodies with an answer. He wrote: 'De slaar [de stræbende og modige X'er fra Gaden] ned med Deres Haan og Foragt, men De har dog beskæftiget Dem med dem...naar man som De, i over tyve Aar kun har værdiget de Fornemste Deres Svar, saa kunde De nok i tyve Aar til undlate at svare...Collin. Og havde jeg været i København, da dette foregik, vilde jeg ha gaaet til Dem, – ringet paa og med Hatten i Haand bedt Dem om at lade det være' (You strike them [the busybody Xes from the streets] down with your scorn and contempt, but they have succeeded in engaging your attention...But when someone, like yourself, has for over twenty years considered only the most distinguished people worthy of a reply, surely over the next twenty years you could refrain from answering...Collin. And if I had been in Copenhagen when all this happened, I would have come to your house, rung the bell and with my hat in my hand would have begged you to let things be, KHB 1, p. 492). Three years later Hamsun did – figuratively – come to

Brandes with his hat in his hand. His novel *Victoria* had been attacked by Nils Vogt, who claimed Hamsun did not really know the ways of aristocratic women and should not write about them, which Hamsun took to be – among many other things – an attack upon his wife Bergljot, who had earlier been divorced. He wrote to ask Brandes for his views of Hamsun's work, and Brandes must have answered with a friendly letter, though not concealing that Hamsun had earlier been less than receptive to his criticism and furthermore that Hamsun's lack of conventional culture was undeniable. Hamsun's reply – distressed and revealing – was written in Helsingfors on Christmas Eve 1898 and is well known. He defends himself against those who accuse him of arrogance, he admits that he is without Brandes' conventional culture, but maintains that he is striving to attain instead that wisdom of the heart – hjertets dannelse – which he later claimed many Danes possessed. The tone of the letter – sentimental and deferential – is sustained to the end: 'Det er Juleaften iaften. Jeg husker med Tak, at jeg for ni Aar siden var i Deres Hus Juleaften. Meget har forandret sig siden dengang; jeg er dog saapas langsom af Hoved, ogsaa saapas uomskiftelig af Natur, at min Beundring for Deres Flammesjæl er den samme' (This evening is Christmas Eve. I recall with gratitude that nine years ago I spent Christmas Eve in your house. Much has changed since then; nevertheless my mental processes are so slow, and my nature is so unchangeable, that my admiration for your fiery soul is the same, KHB 2, p. 111). Brandes responded in a way Hamsun apparently never got to know: for a Russian edition of Hamsun's collected works, he wrote a preface, in which he gave a very positive analysis of Hamsun's work from *Sult* to *I æventyrland*.[5]

After 1910, their very occasional and brief encounters were in the daily press or in letters to other people. On his seventieth birthday in 1912, Brandes read the following words by Hamsun in the pages of *Politiken*: 'Saa ung er han endda at han fremdeles vil være det store Eksempel for de endda yngre' (He is still so young that he will remain the great example for those still younger). During World War I Brandes accused Hamsun of being paid by the Germans, which made a furious Hamsun resort even to anti-Semitic slurs. However, in 1917 he told an American journalist: 'Med hensyn til Brandes, saa er han all right; han er en fører for oss alle. Vi har alle lært av ham, skjønt han er en av de mænd som læser 99 bøker og paa grundlag herav skriver den 100de' (As regards Brandes, he is all right; he is a leader for all of us. We have all learned from him, though he is one of those men who read 99 books and on the basis of that write the 100th, KHB 4, p. 124-5). When Hamsun received the Nobel Prize for literature, Brandes was somewhat less generous. He wrote to Selma Lagerlöf:

Ja, Selv Hamsun forekommer det mig lidt komisk saaledes at udmærke. Jeg har kendt ham nøje, da han kom som forhenværende Sporvognsconducteur fra Amerika, har omgaaedes ham flere Aar af hans Ungdom. Han har tappert efterlignet Dostojevski, og har et utvivlsomt Talent, *men end ikke en Nuance af Dannelse, end ikke Begreb om Dannelse.* Da jeg havde forklaret ham Nietzsche og han vidste, at jeg som ung havde elsket Stuart Mill, fik han den Proletar-Idé at Stuart Mill betyder *Fortid og Reaktion,* Nietzsche Fremtid og Fremskridt, og udviklede denne dybsindige Tanke i et taabeligt Drama, *Livets eller Rigets Port* troer jeg, det hed. Slige Folk bør gaa i Skole, kan ikke lære andre.

(Yes, even Hamsun I think it is somewhat strange to honour in this manner. I knew him quite well when he came as a former tramcar conductor from America, met him often during several years of his youth. He has imitated Dostoevsky untiringly and undoubtedly has talent, *but not even a smattering of culture, not even a concept of what culture is.* When I explained Nietzsche to him and he knew that as a young man I had loved Stuart Mill, he conceived the proletarian idea that Stuart Mill means *the past and reaction,* Nietzsche the future and progress, and developed this profound idea in a silly play, *The Gate of Life* or *of the Realm* I believe it was called. Such people need to go to school, they cannot teach others – *Nordisk tidskrift* 1996, no. 3.)

As a 'young man', Brandes says, he had loved John Stuart Mill. And it was as a young man in his formative years that Hamsun loved Georg Brandes. When Brandes died, Hamsun wrote in *Politiken*: 'Jeg sidder og tænker paa de faa Gange, jeg traf ham. Han var fuld af Godhed, han tog mig med hjem, skænkede mig sin Tid og talte, talte fra sin vide Alverden. Jeg husker jeg gik fra ham som i Rus' (I sit here thinking of the few times I met him. He was full of generosity, invited me to his home, gave me of his time and talked, talked about anything in his wide universe. I remember leaving him as if in a trance).[6]

We have only nine letters from Hamsun to Georg Brandes but twenty-one to Erik Skram. Erik and Amalie Skram opened their home to the newcomer from America, and his first letters to them are full of gratitude. Hamsun admired his older colleague, who had served as a volunteer in the Dano-Prussian war and later studied philosophy and aesthetics. To Hamsun he became more than a friend, rather a comrade with whom he could go hiking in the Danish countryside and share his innermost secrets. His letters to Skram contain details of his sexual dreams in America or of his erotic adventures with Mrs Winkel Horn in Copenhagen. And, Skram being also the literary critic, Hamsun the literary artist sent him his progress reports. 'Jeg agerer ren Kulturhistoriker for nærværende. Det er dette græsselige Amerika, der skal ud som Bog' (At the moment I am sitting here pretending to be a veritable cultural historian. It's this frightful America which is to be brought out as a book, KHB 1, p. 108). And three months later: 'Nu er der ikke noget videre tilbage af Amerika, jeg har lagt det næsten øde. Hvilket jeg vilde' (Now there is not much left of America, I've almost totally destroyed it. Which is what I wanted, KHB 1, p. 120). A year later, when *Sult* had appeared and not received the kind of approval Hamsun hoped for: 'Godt, saa skriver jeg en ny Bog! Jeg skal Herren straffe mig skrive det maanelyst for de fire store Profeter herhjemme. Jeg er fuld, pæreful af Stof og stærk som en Løve' (Very well, I'll write a new book! I will – God help me – write clear as moonlight for the four great prophets here in this country. I am full – tight as a drum – with material and strong as a lion, KHB 1, p. 170). Three months later, after hearing from a reviewer of *Sult* that the scene with Ylajali proved the author was himself incapable as a lover, Hamsun writes from Lillesand 'Jeg gaar og tumler med noget, som Gud straffe mig skal blive noget af det stejleste, der til dato er skrevet paa Jorderig ... Jeg skal Fan tørke mig skrive en Kærlighedens Lovsang, saa Allah og Bjørnson skal bæve!' (I'm now trying my hand at something which – so help me – will be one of the boldest things ever attempted on this earth ... Damn me if I don't write a hymn to love to make both Allah and Bjørnson quiver! KHB 1, pp. 183-4, 186).

Skram and Hamsun dropped titles after only a year – not so common in Denmark a century ago. But Skram was married to Amalie Skram, whose impetuosity scared Hamsun. And being herself a writer, she belonged to a class of women of whom Hamsun did not approve. Only a few weeks after meeting her for the first time, he criticized the use of dialect in her books, claiming it was not natural to her but something she had picked up from bad people. During his lecture tour of West Norway in the spring of 1891, he also criticized writers who gave their characters some form of *faculté maitresse* and, as an example, mentioned Amalie Skram's extensive use of the word 'altså' (so then) as an emphatic filler word. In May 1892 Hamsun wrote to a friend in Kristiansund: 'Jeg tror, Skrams er lidt sure paa mig, ikke han, men Kærringa. Det maa være fordi hun har hørt om, at jeg i et af mine Foredrag har omtalt et Par af hendes Bøger som 'Altsaa' Literatur. Gud, hvor lidet man taaler ogsaa! Men Skram er – saavidt som han tør for hende – den samme gilde Mand' (I think the Skrams are a bit sore at me – not he but his wife. That must be because she's heard that in one of my lectures I called a couple of her books 'so then' literature. God, how little one tolerates! But Skram is – as far as he dare in front of her – the same splendid man, KHB 1, p. 256). But six months later the tone is also less cordial in a letter to Skram, who had recently reviewed *Mysterier*:

Du er den fine, indtryksømme Mand. Naar du gør mig til større Poet end Tænker, vil du forresten nok – naar jeg sender dig min næste Bog – forandre den Opfatning, eftersom jo akkurat det stik modsatte er det rette. Det lille jeg er, er jeg Hjærnemennesket, Reflektatoren ... [Tak] for den Hilsen fra Fruen. Hun er mig ikke huld mere, men hvis hun vidste, hvor lidet det er, som har bevirket Omslaget, saa var hun mig immer huld. Jeg er ingen – ikke paa noget Felt – en Forræder, men jeg slaar for *min* Sag. Jeg har i Sinde at knække Ryggen for den og, om fornødent, miste de et Par Venner, jeg har. Punktum.

(What a discriminating, sensitive man you are. When you make out that I'm a greater poet than thinker, you will, I'm sure – when I send you my next book – want to change your opinion, since the very opposite is the correct view. What little I am, I am a cerebral person, a reflective type...[Thanks] for those greetings from your wife. She is no longer loyal to me; but if she knew how little the thing was that caused the change-over, she would still be loyal to me. I am – in no way – a traitor, but stand up for what I believe in. For that I would be prepared to break my back, and if necessary lose the few friends I have. Full stop. KHB 1, p. 284.)

In September 1893 Edvard Brandes's colleague in *Politiken*, Peter Nansen, reprinted extracts from an article that Hamsun had written for a French journal about Norwegian literature in the 1870s and pointed out that Hamsun had not mentioned Arne Garborg, Amalie Skram, and Gunnar Heiberg. Hamsun defended himself by saying he had 'mentioned' them, but that the realistic movement of the 1870s would have achieved the same results without them. The incident, however, spelt an end to what had once been a warm friendship. Three years later, in December 1896, Hamsun sent his last letter to Skram:

Kære Skram, Din Kone har sagt i et Selskab i Bergen, at jeg er perfid. Jeg ved ikke, hvad der ligger til Grund for din Kones Ord, og det faar i Guds Navn være, hvad det vil. Men det er disse Ord som har gjort, at jeg ikke har skrevet til dig i flere Aar og ikke sendt dig mine Bøger, som det altid var mig en Ære og en Glæde at sende. Naar jeg hos Jær blev holdt for en perfid Mand, saa vilde jeg ikke bringe mig i Erindring. Jeg skrev senere i *La revue des revues* en Artikel om norsk Litteratur. I sit Angreb paa den Artikel i *Politiken* siger Peter Nansen at jeg ikke har nævnt din Kone og Garborg. Peter Nansen løj. Og hvis han i det hele Taget betød noget, den Mand, saa skulde jeg offentlig kalde ham en Løgner...Og saa har Tiden gaaet. Jeg skulde ikke have skrevet idag heller, men et Brev fra København, hvori du var nævnt, slog en Gnist af mig og drev en gammel Varme til mit Indre. Din hengivne Knut Hamsun.

(Dear Skram. Your wife once said in company in Bergen that I am perfidious. I don't know what lies behind your wife's words; let it be what it will, in God's name. But those words are the cause of my not having written to you for several years and not having sent you my books – something which was always an honour and a joy for me to do. If I was considered in your household to be a perfidious man, I had no wish to remind you of me. Somewhat later I wrote an article in *La revue des revues* about Norwegian literature. In his attack on this article in *Politiken*, Peter Nansen says that I made no mention of your wife or of Garborg. Peter Nansen lied. And if that man had been of any significance at all, I would publicly have called him a liar...And so time has passed. I wouldn't have written today, but for the fact that a letter from Copenhagen mentioned you by name and struck a spark in me which kindled an inner glow as of old. Yours sincerely, Knut Hamsun.)

To no other Dane did Hamsun send more letters than to Gustav Philipsen, his Danish publisher from 1889 to 1895. Although their social and political views differed – Philipsen was a liberal like Edvard Brandes, and later a member of the Folketing with a special interest in social legislation – Hamsun always liked his old publisher and respected his good sense, his equanimity and fair-mindedness. Many of the fifty-seven letters naturally deal with money matters, but Hamsun's road from apprentice to master is also well illustrated here and sometimes better than in letters to close friends, including, for instance, the fact that Hamsun once hoped to spend some time in prison. In connection with the novel *Redaktør Lynge*, in which Hamsun had used Olaf Thommessen as the model for his antihero, many reviewers accused him of cowardice, and Hamsun asked Philipsen about printing the following note in *Dagbladet*: 'I Anledning af gentagne Skriverier om min Bog «Redaktør Lynge», erklærer jeg herved, at jeg selvfølgelig overtar Ansvaret for alt, hvad jeg deri har sagt. Min Model opfordres derved til at træffe de Forføjninger, han ønsker mod mig, jeg skal intet fragaa, intet fordølge' (Because of repeated mentions of my book *Editor Lynge*, I hereby declare that I of course accept the responsibility for everything I have said. Hence my model is encouraged to take whatever steps he deems desirable against me, I shall disclaim nothing, conceal nothing). And he turned again to Philipsen: 'Nu spørger jeg Dem ogsaa: da jeg intet vil bevise, ikke engang der, hvor jeg kan, saa blir jeg vel dømt for Bagvaskelse. Men kan man sone Bagvaskelse med Fængsel? For hvis jeg blir dømt til Pengebøde, saa er dé det værste som kan hændes mig. Kan man ikke ogsaa sone en Pengebøde med Fængsel?' (I am now asking you as well: since I intend to prove nothing, even where I would be able to, I shall probably be sentenced for libel. But can you serve a sentence for libel in prison? For if I am sentenced to pay a fine, then that's the worst that can happen to me. Couldn't you also pay a fine by serving time in prison? KHB 1, p. 310, 309). Philipsen did not think a note in *Dagbladet* or a week behind bars was a good idea, and two weeks later Hamsun agreed: 'Da den værste Hede gik af mig, syntes ogsaa jeg, at det er bedst at lade Erklæringen ligge hos mig. Edvard Brandes og Garborg kunde ellers beskylde mig for Reklameri' (As soon as the worst excitement subsided, I too thought it would be best to let the declaration stay right here. Edvard Brandes and Garborg might otherwise accuse me of self-promotion, KHB 1, p. 314). Hamsun's publishers had great difficulty satisfying his desire for publicity. When newspapers did not mention his books, he asked Philipsen to write to them. And when he did, that too was sometimes wrong. Hamsun's shortest letter to Philipsen reads: 'Er det Dem, som har underrettet Gadebladet «Politiken» om at jeg «snart skal udgive et Drama»?' (Are you the person who has informed that gutter press paper *Politiken* that I 'will soon be publishing a play'? KHB 1, p. 459). The letter was not even signed and Philipsen for once lost his temper, as we can see from Hamsun's answer five days later:

Naturligvis er ikke De forpligtet til at modtage min Mening om et Blad, og jeg beder Dem om Undskyldning. Undskyld ogsaa velvillig, at jeg i det hele taget skrev Kortet og spurgte mit Spørgsmaal. Politisk har, trods alle dets gamle og nye Slingringer, vedkommende Blad ogsaa min Sympati. Jeg har derimod ingen Forpligtelse paa mig til at elske det eller endog at agte det...Saa daarligt og fattigt og bondeagtigt, som det visselig er med mig i mange Retninger, jeg tror dog ikke, at mit personlige Liv er mindre rent end Edvard Brandes' og Peter Nansens. Jeg har aldrig solgt mig, og det Blad, der beskylder mig derfor, er i min inderste Sjæl et Gadeblad. Men jeg beder atter om Undskyldning for at have krænket Dem ved at sige det.

(Of course you are not obliged to receive my opinion of a newspaper, and I ask your forgiveness. Kindly forgive me also for having written the card at all and asked my question. Politically speaking, despite all its old and new turnabouts, the newspaper in question has also my sympathy. But I am under no obligation to love or even respect it...Though I am undoubtedly in many ways both poor and plebeian, I still believe my conduct is no less honourable than that of Edvard Brandes and Peter Nansen. I have never sold myself and a newspaper that accuses me of having done so is in my innermost soul part of the gutter press. But once more I ask your forgiveness for having offended you by saying so, KHB 1, p. 459, 460.)

Hamsun's regular correspondence with Philipsen ended in 1895. Philipsen's company merged with Nordisk Forlag and later with Gyldendal, but Hamsun always remembered him with gratitude. 'De har været mig en overmaade elskværdig Kreditor' (To me you have been a wonderfully generous creditor, KHB 2, p. 56), he wrote in 1897, and 'jeg er den Dag idag bedrøvet over, at De ved at sælge Deres Forlag skilte os ad og sendte mig ud til andre Forlæggere' (to this day I am very sad that, by selling your publishing firm, you made us part company and sent me to other publishers, KHB 2, p. 50). Ten years later he wrote in his last letter to Philipsen: 'Tusind Tak for Brevet; – jeg forsikrer Dem, det kendes som i gamle Dage naar jeg fik Brev fra Dem om et nyt Manuskript. Jeg har savnet de Breve, de støttet mig og der var Deltagelse for mine Skridt i dem' (Thanks for the letter, – I assure you, it felt like the old days when I received a letter from you about a new manuscript. I have missed those letters, they helped me and showed sympathy for my undertakings, KHB 2, p. 359).

Some of Hamsun's enemies later became his best friends, like the Danish writer and critic Peter Nansen, who had reviewed Hamsun's novel *Ny Jord* and accused Hamsun of selling his literary talent to the Kristiania business community. In 1896 Peter Nansen joined the Gyldendal Publishing Company and in the following twenty years gained a reputation as one of Denmark's greatest publishers. Hamsun had a lot to do with him and very soon looked upon him as a trusted friend. Nansen was not only a business man, but himself a writer with full understanding of a writer's many needs, and he was generous with money and with his time when it came to discussing books and reviews. Beyond their pleasant business relationship, Hamsun and Nansen agreed on many issues – from literature and film rights to Germany and the first World War. And when Fredrik Hegel took over Gyldendal and deposed Nansen, Hamsun supported Nansen and threatened to leave his old firm. His last letter to Nansen ends with the following words: 'Hjærtelig Hilsen fra mig. Ja jeg holder av Dem. De var en Mand man kunne komme til med sine Bekymringer. Ak Gud, De skulde være alle Forfatteres Forlægger eller Disponent, Løn 50 Tusen og frit Slot' (Heartfelt greetings from me. Yes, I am fond of you. You were a man a person could come to with his troubles. Oh God, you should be all writers' publisher or manager, salary 50 000 and a free palace, KHB 4, p. 192-3).

Finally, let me return to the letter I mentioned earlier, from

Knut Hamsun to Edvard Brandes, which I shall use as a footnote to the difficult question, 'what may Hamsun have learned from Denmark'? In his interview with an American journalist in 1917, Hamsun said of Georg Brandes, 'We have all learned from him.' Brandes claimed that Hamsun had imitated Dostoevsky untiringly, and Hamsun would certainly have agreed that Dostoevsky was an influence. To the end of his days he kept a picture of the Russian master in his bedroom. But he also had another picture there, of Goethe, who, like Brandes, represented the other – the classical – side of Hamsun. Hamsun shared with Dostoevsky a sense of the abnormal. He writes to his friend Erik Skram: 'Jeg kunde Gud straffe mig skrive en Verden om desperate Sindsbevægelser. Men naar man ansér Dostojewsky for gal, saa kan jo ikke jeg komme nogen Vej. Ti hvad Dostojewsky har meddelt af Forunderligheder i de tre Bøger jeg har læst af ham – jeg har ikke læst flér – det gennemgaar jeg daglig Dags, og langt, langt besynderligre Ting, bare jeg gaar en Tur nedad Gothersgade' (I could, so help me, create a whole world about desperate states of mind. But if people look upon Dostoevsky as mad, then I am not likely to get anywhere. For the kind of oddities Dostoevsky has written about in the three books by him I have read – and I haven't read more – is something I live through daily. I only have to take a trip down Gothersgade to find far far more peculiar things, KHB 1, p. 99).

Hamsun's books tell us of fantastic things, but these things are in most cases personal experiences, and the importance of their connection with the real world is something Brandes may have taught the young Hamsun. In the autumn of 1888, Hamsun – just back from the United States – wrote for Edvard Brandes, editor of *Politiken*, a short article on the American public speaker Robert Ingersoll. Edvard Brandes complained that the article contained too many foreign words, and Hamsun answered in a letter dated 17 September 1888, from which I quote a number of passages:

Der var nok uden Tvivl formange fremmede Ord i mit Stykke...Med Hensyn til de unorske Vendinger, erkjender jeg ogsaa, at *de* er der. Og *de* er i alt, jeg prøver at skrive. Jeg har med Forsæt aldrig *bestræbt* mig for at være norsk. Og det ligger mig ikke i Blodet at være det. Bjørnsonpartiets 'Norskhed' i Sproget støder mig mér end faktiske Fejl...Jeg har sét et Sted, at den største Digter (Skribent) skulde være den mest nationale. Om jeg ikke mindes fejl, er det Deres Broder, som har sagt det – denne Mand, som har lært mig simpelthen det lille, jeg kan. Men her er jeg ude af Stand til at forstaa. Og jeg beder Dem om engang, jeg træffer Dem, at være saa venlig at retlede mig lidt. Denne Lære forrykker virkelig hele min Stilling...Jeg har tænkt meget paa Deres Broders Ord; mit Blod har opponeret mod dem...Den Bog, jeg arbejder paa, er desperat lidet norsk, og jeg er ikke ligegyldig for dens Skjæbne. Jeg havde ikke villet skrive for Nordmænd – der er ikke et Stednavn i den hele Bog – jeg har villet skrive for *Mennesker* hvorsomhelst de fandtes.

(Doubtless there were too many foreign-sounding words in my piece...With reference to the un-Norwegian turns of phrase, I do acknowledge that *they* too are there. And *they* are there in everything I try to write. I have deliberately never *striven* to be Norwegian. And it isn't in my blood to be so. The 'Norwegian-ness' in the language of the Bjørnson faction offends me more than actual mistakes...I saw somewhere that the greatest poet (writer) is held to be he who is most nationalistic. If I am not mistaken, it was your brother who said it – the man who quite simply has taught me what little I can do. But here I am incapable of understanding. And I beg you, if any time we should meet, to be kind enough to give me some guidance. It is a doctrine that really upsets all my ideas...I have thought much about your brother's words; my blood opposed them...There is so desperately little of Norwegian in the book I am working on, and I am not indifferent to its fate. I hadn't wanted to write for Norwegians – there isn't a placename in the whole book – I wanted to write for *people* wherever they found themselves. KHB 1, p. 80-81.)

The book Hamsun was working on was presumably a version of the novel *Sult*, part of which was printed in the November 1888 issue of the periodical *Ny Jord*, while the completed novel did not appear until June of 1890. In the meantime Hamsun published a piece called 'Hazard', set in the Balkans, perhaps in Rumania. The story has curious geographic names like Damvaz, Verenjib, the Fugomihol Sea, names that confused the German translator, Marie Herzfeld, who was told not to worry. 'Jeg er kendt paa det Sted, hvor Historien foregaar' (I myself know the locality where the story takes place, KHB 1, p. 191), Hamsun wrote, though by that time he had not been south of Hamburg. The publication of 'Hazard' was unfortunate in that it led to Felix Hollander's accusation that Hamsun had plagiarized Dostoevsky, but it was, I believe, also fortunate in that it may have taught Hamsun that places as well as place names need to be real. And so when the final version of *Sult* appeared, it was very much a Kristiania novel, and full of place names – Grænsen, Slotsbakken, Pilestrædet, St. Olavs plass, Ullevålsveien, Youngstorvet, Toldbodgaten, Tomtegaten 11, etc. It is also worth noting that all of Hamsun's novels thereafter have a Norwegian setting, be it a coastal town in South Norway, a sanatorium in East Norway or – as in most cases – some North Norwegian community. This complete turnabout from an international to a more national mentality, then, could be the result of Hamsun's discussion with the Brandes brothers and an example of many things Hamsun had in mind when he later said of Denmark: 'it has also sprinkled a little on me of all its rich culture.'

Notes

1. KHB: all references are to Harald Næss ed. *Knut Hamsuns brev I-IV* (Oslo: Gyldendal, 1994-97) with translations in many cases by James McFarlane from the two-volume *Selected Letters* of Hamsun, edited by Harald Næss and James McFarlane, Norvik Press, 1990-1998.
2. Axel Lundegård, *Sett och känt* (Stockholm, 1925), p. 100.
3. *Life Story of Rasmus B. Anderson* (Madison, 1915), p. 317.
4. *Samlede Skrifter*, Vol. 17 (Copenhagen, 1906), p. 279.
5. See Martin Nag, *Edda* 1990, pp. 115-127.
6. *Politiken*, 20 February 1927.

12

'Why do Norwegians hate Denmark so much?': National Consciousness in Amalie and Erik Skram's Correspondence

Janet Garton
University of East Anglia

The exchange of letters between Amalie and Erik Skram covers a period of seventeen years, from 1882 to 1899. It can be divided into two main periods, the first lasting just over one and a half years, from August 1882 to March 1884, and the second from 1885 to 1899. The first period covers the time when Amalie Müller was living in Kristiania and Erik Skram in Copenhagen, beginning shortly after their first meeting on the occasion of Bjørnstjerne Bjørnson's 'dikterjubileum' at Aulestad in August 1882, and following the course of their growing acquaintance and love until Amalie moved to Copenhagen in 1884 and they got married. During this time the letters were very long – at least eight pages was what Amalie considered acceptable – and very frequent; almost half of the nearly six hundred letters which have been preserved were written during these eighteen months.[1] The correspondence from the second period is more sporadic; as they were now living together, they wrote to each other mainly when they were apart for some reason, when Erik was travelling to collect information for a newspaper report or for his study of Sønderjylland, or when Amalie was in Norway trying to finish a novel. (Amalie did also on occasion write to Erik when they were both in the same house, when she found it too difficult to confront him in person.) These letters follow the course of their married life and their careers, the birth and early years of their daughter, their growing conflicts and eventual separation in 1899. The letters then cease, and there are no more before Amalie's death in 1905.

From the point of view of an editor and of a literary historian, the first period of the correspondence is the more satisfactory, and the one on which I shall concentrate in this article; the letters form a continuous dialogue, when Amalie and Erik were, as they told each other, getting to know each other through writing. After their first meeting in August 1882, they spent six days together in December 1882, then part of July and most of August 1883, and finally most of November 1883 – and that was all until Amalie moved to Copenhagen at the end of March 1884. They explained themselves and explored each other by letter – with all the dangers that involved, as they were both well aware, of idealization and distortion of their perception of each other. Their letters were also a forum for debate of a more general kind; both were fully involved in the cultural life of their respective capitals, and the letters are full of news and opinions about the latest books, theatre performances, political and literary debates and gossip.

Their letters reveal both many similarities and many contrasts in their opinions and attitudes. In broad terms they shared the same cultural standpoint. The early 1880s were a time of political ferment in both countries, with the new radical left-wing parties struggling for power against the entrenched conservatism of the old establishment, and both writers unequivocally supported the left. In religious and literary matters too they were both radicals. When they decided to get married, neither wanted a church ceremony; Erik had long ago declared himself no longer a member of the state church, and Amalie, though she had not taken the same official step, had also come to regard herself as a freethinker. Both were ardent supporters of the literature of the Modern Breakthrough, and wrote enthusiastically of Bjørnson and Brandes, Jacobsen and Ibsen, Garborg and Kielland. *And* they were in love, and with that had an endless source of delight in each other's appearance, habits, background, opinions, and all the little details of each other's daily lives.

Once all that is given, however, it is the contrasts in their correspondence which emerge more forcefully and are the more revealing of personality and convictions. Their differences can be summarized under four main and related headings which will be considered in this article: their approach to writing, their positions in the debate on sexual morality, their temperaments and their national allegiances.

As writers, Amalie and Erik were very different. In a purely physical way, this can be seen from the letters themselves; Amalie's are impulsive, dashed off, variable in size and script according to the intensity of her emotions, whereas Erik's are neat, closely written and carefully worded. He complained how long it took him to write a letter and how little time he had; she retorted that it *could* only take half an hour (this with reference to letters of eight pages or more). When they began their correspondence, they were at very different stages in their writing careers. Erik had published two novels (*Herregårdsbilleder*, 1877, and his best novel, *Gertrude Coldbjørnsen*, 1879) and was a regular contributor to Morgenbladet; Amalie had published several reviews, but no fiction. She wrote glowingly to him about her admiration for his novels, which criticism had so underrated; before she knew him, she confessed, she was half in love with the author of *Gertrude Coldbjørnsen* – a man with enough psychological insight to understand how a girl could be persuaded into marriage with someone she did not care for, and how damaged she could be as a result (A to E, 5/10/82).[2] At the same time she could not resist criticizing parts of the novel where motives and relationships were too relentlessly explained; more, she felt, should emerge from the telling itself. Erik, for his part, knew that Amalie had made her first unpublished attempts at writing fiction when they met, and in one of his first letters asked her to send him what she had written – he wanted to get to know her as a writer too. But she resisted; it was not until after her short story 'Madame Høiers Leiefolk' was published early in 1883 that she finally sent him some other stories she had written. His response was positive but critical, and the exact opposite of hers; in the short story which was to develop into the novel *Constance Ring* (1885), he told her, she did not explain enough: 'det er ikke et *helt* Billede man får. Jeg vil vide, *hvorfor* Fru Ring keder sig så gudserbarmeligt. Du har præsenteret hende straks om jeg så må sige på for nært Hold. ... der mangler et Kapitel' (We don't get a *complete* picture. I want to know *why* Fru Ring is so excruciatingly bored. You have presented her, if I may say so, too close up straight away... A chapter is missing (E to A, 26/3/83)). She protested in the next letter that she could not be bothered to change the story, but she did in fact revise and expand it, and the resulting novel takes note of his comments; if Erik could not develop his own literary talent further, there is no doubt that he helped Amalie to develop hers.

(It is interesting to note that in their fiction after their marriage in 1884, the differences in their writing became more rather than less pronounced; Erik's play and two novels published in the years 1895-99 are very short, delicate, concentrated studies of love, jealousy and sexual morality among the upper middle classes, whereas Amalie expanded into a fuller format, painted with a broader brush, created a study of a whole society from the bottom up. Erik maintained that it was reading Zola which stopped him writing fiction after 1879, when he realized what a dilettante he was in comparison; Amalie's *Hellemyrsfolket*, on the other hand, is the closest Scandinavian literature comes to Zola's 'Rougon-Macquart' series.)

Sex was a burning topic in 'den store nordiske krig om sexualmoralen' (the Great Northern War of sexual morality), which was at its most intense during this period;[3] and it could be said that Amalie and Erik fought the whole battle in their letters. They began from diametrically opposed positions. Amalie was still recovering from her traumatic experience of marriage to a man she did not love, and the shock of a meeting with sexuality for which she had been totally unprepared; her marriage, like Gertrude Coldbjørnsen's, had been a rape. She had been through breakdown, separation and finally (as late as May 1882) divorce; she was finished with men, despised the declarations of passion to which her notorious beauty continually exposed her, and had decided that sexual love was not worth pursuing; she wanted to be left in peace to study and bring up her sons. Erik was, in his own words, 'en Mand, der har levet som andre Mænd' (a man who has lived like other men (E to A, 10/12/82)); he made no pretence of celibacy, but told her in one of his very first letters that he had a mistress – an admission which nearly finished the relationship there and then.

Confronted with Amalie's violent reaction, Erik set about persuading her, first verbally and then physically, that she was missing an important part of life. In October 1882 he spent a week writing a 16-page letter (later often referred to by both as 'formeringsbrevet' (the reproduction letter)) to explain why she should not turn her back on love. It is a mixture of a biology lesson about the facts of life and a prose poem about the joy of sex, extolling its delights as the source of all human creativity:

Det er Selvhengivelsen, de to nøgne Menneskers dybe og inderlige Forening, den forunderlige Taben sig selv og Finden sig igen, det er Sansernes og Tankernes usigelig mættede Fryd, Naturens virkelige Lykke. Der gives ingen anden, som er hel...Og at Naturen har samlet det finest udviklede af sin glædefrembringende Evne i Kærlighedslysten, i Trangen hos Kvinden til at give sig hen, og i Ønsket hos Manden om at blive taget til Nåde og være Beskytter tillige, hænger simpelthen sammen med Naturens hele store Livsøkonomi, at Livets bevaring og Udvikling kun kan bygges på det Glædefrembringende. Kun *det* er frugtbargørende, kun i virkelig Glæde eller ud fra dens oprindelige Grund spirer Livets Kræfter og de Tanker som bære fremad. Børnene fødes efter Mødet på Elskovslejet, og også kun der fødes Poesi, Kunst og Moral.

(It is self-abandonment, the deep and intimate union of two naked human beings, the marvellous loss of one's self and finding one's self again, it is the indescribably satiated joy of the mind and the senses, nature's true happiness. There is no other which is complete ... And the fact that nature has concentrated its most finely developed talent for creating joy in the desire for love, in the woman's urge to give herself fully, and in the man's wish to find favour with the beloved and to protect her at the same time, all this is simply a part of nature's great economy, that the preservation and continuation of life can only be built on what creates joy. That alone gives rise to fertility, only in real joy or from its original source do the forces of life spring, and those thoughts which carry us forwards. Children are born after the lovers' meeting, and there too, and only there, are born poetry, art and morality (E to A, 1/10/82).)

At their meeting in December 1882, he put his theories into practice; physically and intellectually seduced, she capitulated.

Yet both of them were children of their time, and although there is little doubt that each was the great love of the other's life, the contrasts and conflicts remained, and emerged at intervals in their correspondence and later in their marriage, eventually destroying it. Amalie was jealous of Erik's past, of the women he had loved before her, and always ready to suspect that he was involved with someone else; and Erik gave her cause for suspicion, concealing things from her and refusing to reassure her. Her old prejudices were given new fuel, and he poured oil on the flames. They each brought out both the best and the worst in the other; their marriage is a study in the tragic effects of the double standard.

Their differences in temperament, like their sex, were an attraction when things were going well, a problem when they were not. Expressed in succinct terms, Erik was too slow, Amalie too quick. 'Jeg er så langsomt et Menneske' (I am such a slow person (E to A, 2/9/82)) is a constant refrain in Erik's letters; he learns to love slowly, but when he loves, he is tenacious. On the positive side, this quality leads to an infinite patience in his wooing of Amalie; he never gives up, but waits and hopes as she announces on several occasions that all is over between them, and is prepared to explain his convictions and declare his love again and again. On the negative side, he can sulk for an extended period, and can demonstrate a stiffness and inflexibility in the latter part of their relationship which are hard for Amalie to bear. She, on the other hand, rushes at life; his reproach to her on the first occasion when she breaks off their relationship: 'Amalie, Du har dømt hurtig, for hurtig' (Amalie, you have judged quickly, too quickly (E to A, 10/9/82)) sounds again and again in his letters. She knows at once what she thinks about a man, a book, a picture, a political event; she scandalizes conservative ladies and fascinates radical men by her outspokenness. Erik takes her to task in his letters and she complains about his harshness: 'Du skjænder så græsseligt på mig....Jeg er tilmode som en skolepige der er sat i skammekrogen og ikke slipper ud før hun beder om forladelse' (You tell me off so dreadfully....I feel like a schoolgirl who has been made to stand in the corner and who won't be let off until she asks forgiveness (A to E, 22/9/82)); but she listens and revises her opinions, not only about sex but also about Jews, for example – he makes her think about her irrational anti-Semitism. *Her* impulsiveness moves their relationship along: it is she who suggests they meet in Göteborg in 1882, she who travels to Copenhagen on impulse in November

1883 after they have quarrelled, she who proposes marriage when Erik dare not take the financial risk. But her outbursts become as much a problem for Erik as his sulkiness does for her, as their later letters bear copious witness. What had been a bridge becomes a barrier.

Finally, there is the difference of nationality, which is the main focus of this essay. Amalie was Norwegian, Erik was Danish – a fact which can be perceived both as similarity and as contrast. From the point of view of a non-Scandinavian observer especially, the similarities are striking; they were formed by the same history, shared common values and preoccupations and a common cultural inheritance, perhaps particularly strongly felt during the period of the Modern Breakthrough. And they shared – almost – a common language; a matter of great importance to writers so conscious of their craft. Both could write in their own tongue without being misunderstood more than was amusing. In their own perception, however, it was the contrasts which were more apparent.

Consciousness of their nationality was important both to Amalie and to Erik. In 1864, at the outbreak of the Dano-Prussian war, Erik had been a schoolboy; he had run away from school before his seventeenth birthday to join the Danish army as a volunteer and had been seriously wounded at the battle of Als. His early experience of the reality of war was a formative one; he revisited the area in later life, and twenty years later wrote an engaged account of his experiences and of the fate of those who lived in what was now German territory.[4] *His* consciousness of nationality, like that of many Danes, was sharpened by reference to Germany: 'Tyskerne kan gøre, hvad de vil, hjemme i vort Land bliver de ikke, alene fordi de har haft Magt til at besætte det', he declared in 1887 (the Germans can do what they like, they won't belong in our country just because they have had the power to occupy it).[5] Before his death in 1923, he had the satisfaction of seeing the border redrawn largely along the lines he had suggested in 1887.

Amalie's point of reference, on the other hand, was Denmark. It is well known that by the end of her life Amalie had embraced Danish culture and the Danish people; and that in her pamphlet *Landsforrædere* (Traitors), published in 1901, she wrote that she wished to be regarded as a Danish author: 'Og så har mine bøger ... her i Danmark fundet den smule forståelse, den smule anerkjendelse, der gjør at et menneske får mod til at arbejde videre... Norsk *er* og *blir* jeg til min dødedag. Men norsk *forfatter* er jeg ikke' (And then my books ... have here in Denmark found that little bit of understanding, that little bit of recognition, which gives a person courage to go on working.... Norwegian I *am* and will *remain* until my dying day. But a Norwegian *author* I am not).[6] In the early 1880s however, in her letters to Erik, she was very far from this position.

There is considerable discussion in their early letters about the nature of Danishness and Norwegianness; in general terms, Amalie is positive about being Norwegian and sceptical about Danes, whereas Erik is practically apologetic about being Danish. This is apparent whether they are discussing language, landscape, politics or national characteristics.

Amalie picks Erik up on his language as early as October 1882; she objects to his use of the plural forms of Danish verbs: 'kan du ikke tjene mig i at skrive dine præsenser i singularis, selv om subjektet er pluralis. Jeg kan ikke for min død fordrage vi 'ere', de 'høre', vi 'komme'...' (Can you not please me by writing your present tenses in the singular, even when the subject is plural. I can't for the life of me stand forms like 'vi ere', 'de høre', 'vi komme'...) – though the only reason she can find for her objection is 'det er, – ja, det er så 'dansk'' (it's – oh, it's so 'Danish' (A to E, 21/10/82)). Erik makes no reply to this, although he does use fewer plural forms in later letters. As these plural forms were dropping out of use in written Danish at this time (and were officially abolished in 1900), it is unclear whether this is to please Amalie or simply a result of linguistic change. She is irritated when he uses words she is unfamiliar with. In October 1882 he tells her of his plans to write a play, and that it will divert his concentration from her: 'når jeg begynder mit Skriveri, kommer Du på Aftægt, hvis Du kender det Ord. Det er mig da ikke muligt at skrive synderlig meget eller synderlig ofte til Dig' (When I begin writing, you will be put out to grass, if you know that expression. It won't be possible for me to write to you very much or very often (E to A, 29/10/82)). She does not understand – or cannot read – the phrase 'Du kommer på Aftægt', and asks him more than once to explain it. His eventual response is evasive: 'Det Ord, som jeg har brugt en Gang, og som har plaget Dig, er ikke aflægs, men Aftægt. Det betyder – nej det er altfor langt at forklare. Det er også altsammen lige meget, der sker intet, før jeg har talt med Dig' (The expression which I used once, and which has worried you, is not 'aflægs', out of date, but 'Aftægt'. It means – oh, it would take too long to explain. It's all irrelevant anyway, nothing will happen before I have talked with you (E to A, 17/11/82)). Since the expression was normally used about the custom of building a little cottage on a farm for the old folk to retire to when they were no longer fit for work, it is perhaps not surprising that he did not want to explain it.

Amalie's use of Norwegian words, however, is a constant source of delight to Erik. He exclaims over phrases like 'å pyt!' (pooh!), 'her har været slig sjau' (there's been such a to-do (A to E, 25/10/82)) and 'jeg går på strømpelæsten' (I walk in stockinged feet (A to E, 7/11/82)) – 'er det nu ikke til at forgå af Henrykkelse over at høre Dig sige det. Ja det kan Du måske ikke forstå, men en sød Kvinde, der er norsk, er det to Gange' (it's enough to make you die of delight just hearing you say it. You may find it difficult to understand, but a sweet woman who is Norwegian is twice as sweet (E to A, 3/11/82)). He wishes he could speak Norwegian, and confesses that he positively seeks out people from Bergen in order to listen to the melody of their language: 'Jeg bryder mig ikke rigtig om det østlandske norsk, de skal snakke som Du, for at det skal være Musik for mig' (I'm not very fond of Eastern Norwegian, they have to talk like you before it sounds like music to me (E to A, 17/11/82)). The written language, however, is a different matter; when she later sends him an article she has written for possible publication in Denmark and he 'corrects' her language, changing her plural 'sin' to the Danish 'deres', she crossly demands it back: 'jeg kan umulig være tjent med at du skriver den om' (It can't possibly be a help to me if you rewrite it (A to E, 19/1/84)).

Erik feels apologetic about the Danish landscape too, in comparison to the Norwegian. In September 1883, when they have just agreed to get married, he goes out into the Danish countryside and looks around somewhat anxiously to see whether it is an environment that he can in all honesty ask her to come and live in.

He is reassured and seeks to reassure her too:

Jeg var rasende angst for, at det altsammen skulde være grimt nu, efter at jeg havde levet mig ind i den norske Natur... Du Elskede, jeg var så bange for, hvad Du vilde sige til dette flade Land, som jeg har lokket Dig ned til. Du elskede, elskede Ven, tro mig rolig og sikkert, når jeg siger Dig, at her er til at leve. Landskabet var fint og af en egen blid Ynde, der så ved Søen i den friske Kuling med Skum og Sprøjt fik en tilstrækkelig Tilsætning af Kækhed og Kraft. Du elskede, Du vil kunne være glad her nede, det er ikke dumt og flovt og ækelt og grimt det Sjælland Du skal bo på – Tankerne kan gå viden om her, og de lave bølgende Høje med Korn eller Skov i vekslende Lys efter Skylagets Beskaffenhed lå så venlige der, så stilfærdig indbydende: Kom ud til os, slå Dig til Ro her, lev Dig ind i vort Liv, Du skal se, der er Fred og Hygge her og Finheder, som gør en Sjæl godt. Det ser lidt Småt ud, det vi byder på, men Vennen min, det er ikke ubetydeligt det, som sker her.

(I was really worried that it would all look ugly now that I have acclimatized myself to the Norwegian landscape... My love, I was so concerned about what you would think about this flat countryside which I have enticed you down to. You can believe me, my dearest darling, when I tell you that it is possible to live here. The landscape was fine, with its own gentle charm, and down by the sea was a strong fresh wind, with froth and foam, which gave it a sufficient seasoning of strength and spirit. My love, you will be able to be happy down here, it isn't stupid and nasty and dreadful and ugly, the Zealand where you're going to live – there is room for thoughts to wander here, and the low curving hills of corn or forest in changing light under the moving clouds looked so friendly, so modestly inviting: Come over to us, settle down here, live your life in tune with ours, you'll see, there is peace here and comfort, and fine qualities which nourish the soul. It doesn't look like a lot, what we have to offer, but my darling, it is not insignificant, what happens here.)

Amalie blithely accepts his reassurances, – though it is apparent from her reply that it is more because she is in love than for any real affection for the Danish landscape:

Du er så sød med din bekymring for at dit land ikke skal være skjønt nok. Du kan være ganske rolig, jeg skal nok komme til at elske det, det er jo det land som har formået hvad Norge ikke kunde: give mig min elskede og mit livs lykke. Og desuden jeg har altid havt Danmark kjær, i altfald fra jeg kom til sjæls år og alder; som barn og ganske ungt menneske gik jeg og hadede det, men jeg blev omvendt lidt efter lidt. Og nu, – der er ikke tale om andet end at jeg er glad i det, og vil finde mig vel der, bedre der end nogetsteds i verden, fordi det er dit hjem, og fordi det er der, jeg skal få være hos dig.

(You are so sweet with your worries about whether your country is going to be beautiful enough. You can set your mind at ease, I shall love it all right, it is the country which has succeeded in doing what Norway could not: giving me my beloved and my life's happiness. And in any case I've always been fond of Denmark, at least since I was old enough to be discriminating; as a child and very young woman I actually hated it, but I was gradually converted. And now, – there's no question that I love it, and will thrive there, better there than anywhere else in the world, because it is your home, and because it is there that I shall be with you (A to E, 19/9/83).)

Despite Amalie's seeming certainty here, however, there is a problem about the relationship between Denmark and Norway, on both a personal and a general level, which surfaces again and again in their letters. In October 1882, Erik was invited to dinner by Alexander Kielland, who was living in Denmark at the time and who expressed his contempt for all things Danish in no uncertain terms. Afterwards Erik wrote to Amalie in some perplexity:

Er det virkelig så, at *Forbitrelsen* mod Danmark holder sig, måske endog tager til med Selvfølelsen i Norge og ikke tager af, at man t.Ex. i Norge betragter Jammerligheden under de Oldenborgske Konger som særlig Uret mod Norge og ikke som en Fællesplage og -nød? At man i det Hele i Norge er så instinktmæssig vis på, at det er Foreningen med *Danmark*, der har holdt Udviklingen tilbage og ikke lægger Mærke til, at Danmark i visse Måder holdtes endnu mere nede under det Regimente, der i lang Tid førtes, og at Norges Stillestående også må tilskrives den politiske Svaghedstilstand i Norge, som overhoved havde ført de to Riger sammen? Det forekommer mig, at Spørgsmålet er et ganske roligt Kundskabs- og Skarpsindigheds-spørgsmål; men er det kun fordi jeg er dansk og altså har mine Instinkter fra det Land, det sikkert nok i Foreningstiden følte sig som det overlegne og vel tildels endnu pukker på sin 'finere' Intelligens?

(Is it really the case that the *bitterness* towards Denmark persists, is perhaps even growing with Norway's self-esteem instead of decreasing, that people in Norway for example regard the misery under the Oldenborg kings as a particular injustice against Norway and not as a shared torment and grief? That people in general in Norway have such an instinctive certainty that it is the union with *Denmark* which held up progress and do not notice that Denmark in many ways was even more held back by the regime which was in charge for so long, and that Norway's stagnation is also due to the political weakness in Norway which brought the two kingdoms together in the first place? It seems to me that it is quite simply a question of knowledge and intelligent reasoning; but is that simply because I am Danish and therefore derive my instincts from the country which no doubt during the time of the union felt itself to be superior and to some extent still insists on its 'finer' intelligence? (E to A, 29/10/82).)

To assume, as Erik does here, that a question about national feeling can be decided calmly and rationally argues a certain naïveté on his part, as does his assertion later in the same letter: 'Jeg holder så inderlig af Norge – også uafhængig af min Kærlighed til Dig – jeg deler gerne ud til det af min Fædrelandsfølelse' (I am so deeply fond of Norway – independently of my love for you – that I gladly extend my patriotism to it too).

In her reply, Amalie tries to explain both why Norwegians have felt bitter towards Denmark because of the humiliations of the past (although many, including her, have now got over that stage), and why the attitude of the Danes towards the Norwegians still causes resentment:

Man er ikke 'forbitret' på Danmark heroppe, men jeg tror der i det store hele er bleven siddende en uvillie igjen mod danskerne ikke fordi man endnu går og harmes over vor underkuelsestid, men fordi man idelig og altid pånyt mærker hvorledes danskerne er tilbøielige til at overse os norske... Det vilde jo være unaturligt, hvis den lange fornedrelsestid under hvilken Danmark foer frem mod os (lad være at det var styrelsens skyld), på en oprørende måde, – (skjøndt nei, det er mere oprørende at vi fandt os i det) ikke skulde have sat mærker i sindene, der vil gå i arv endnu gjennem nogle generationer. Og jo mere vor selvstændighed voxer, jo større, ser vi, har uretten været. Det er langt lettere for en dansk at holde af Norge og 'dele ud til det af sit fædrelandssind' end for en norsk ligeoverfor Danmark. Danskerne var jo dem, der gik af med fordelen på alle områder, var de overlegne, de styrende, de undertrykkende. Og alt hvad der duede i Norge tog jo Danmark og slugte, alt, alt uden undtagelse.

(People are not 'bitter' about Denmark up here, but I believe that there has survived a general anti-Danish feeling, not because we are still nursing a grievance about the time of our oppression, but because we time and again are made to feel how the Danes have a tendency to overlook us Norwegians... It would be unnatural if the long years of humiliation, during which the Danes acted towards us (admitted that it was the fault of the government) in an outrageous manner, – (although it is more outrageous that we were prepared to put up with it) had not left traces in our minds which will be passed on for several generations to come. And the more our independence grows, the greater, we realise, was the injustice. It is far easier for a Dane to be fond of Norway and 'extend his patriotism to it' than it is for a Norwegian to Denmark. It was after all the Danes who had the advantage in all areas, they were superior, the rulers, the oppressors. And anything that was any good in Norway was taken and swallowed up by the Danes, everything, everything without exception (A to E, 1/11/82).)

This is an interestingly inconsistent reply. Although Amalie begins by asserting that there is no bitterness in Norway against Denmark because of the past, the more she talks about it, the more the bitterness surfaces. In her statements as in Kielland's, there is an emotional reaction against Danish attitudes which she cannot explain rationally, although Erik asks her, with increasing plaintiveness as the correspondence goes on, to try to help him to understand: 'hvad Nordmænds Had til Danmark egentlig er for noget' (... what Norwegians' hatred of Denmark is really about (E to A, 17/12/83)). Her statements about the relative merits of the countries are often emotional in the extreme. Norwegians are 'så brav, så beskeden, så *lidt* fordervet' (so solid, so modest, so unspoilt) compared with Denmark, where the cultural leaders get short shrift from her: 'Når jeg tænker på dem af det literaire venstre jeg kjender personlig og af omtale, så er de alle simple, Georg Brandes med, – jeg tænker på Schandorf, Dr.mann, Borchsenius ...' (When I think of the men of the literary left whom I know personally and by reputation, they are all coarse, Georg Brandes included, – I'm thinking of Schandorph, Drachmann, Borchsenius (A to E, 15/3/83)) – all except Erik, that is. Norway's cultural leadership is simply in a different class from Denmark's, as Bjørnson is in a different class from Edvard Brandes:

Brandes er en præst, men B.B. en profet af det stof hvoraf de gamle lavede sine guder. At Norge frembringer profeter men Danmark bare præster er et tegn på at Norge *er* mere, *magter* mere, står mere for tur til at føre det store ord end Danmark; men det vil i virkeligheden sige at Norge står tilbage. Det vil sige – *der* hvor Danmark *er*, må Norge desværre også komme. Desværre, desværre.

(Brandes is a priest, but B.B. is a prophet of the same stuff of which people in the old days created their gods. The fact that Norway produces prophets but Denmark only priests is a sign that Norway *is* more, can *do* more, is more capable of making great pronouncements than Denmark; but that means in actual fact that Norway has still to catch up. That is to say: where Denmark *now* stands, Norway must alas also come. Alas, alas (A to E, 5/6/83).)

It was not only Kielland during these years who shared Amalie's negative feelings about Denmark; this was made abundantly clear when Amalie finally plucked up courage to tell her friends that she was going to move to Denmark and marry Erik. That the men she knew, several of whom were in love with her, were upset that she was getting married, is in itself not surprising; but the fact that she was marrying a Dane does seem in some cases to make their rejection more wounding. Erik warned her in a letter in December 1883 that they would not like it (E to A, 3/12/83), but was taken aback by the violence of the reaction. Later that month Amalie described the scene which occured with one of her admirers, the geologist Amund Helland, when she announced her plans:

'Det har vi ikke fortjent af dem' – sa'e han omsider, – 'gifte dem når de virkelig elsker, – det er en ting, men gå til Danmark, til dette forbandede, flade, forhadte 'jyteland', der ligger os alle iveien, og er enhver skikkelig og retskaffen nordmand en forsmædelsens torn i øiet... Det er en national forhånelse, værre end om statsråderne ikke blir dømt, – en offentlig forsmædelse, – et ubegribeligt forræderi, – en spytten på os alle lige i vort åbne ansigt. Nei at det skulde overgå os, – sådan en skjændsel, en danske, en jyte, sådan en skam og spot, og så at folk skal sige at vi står igjen med lange næser.'

('We have not deserved that of you' – he said finally, – 'to get married when you are really in love, – that is one thing, but to go to Denmark, to that damned, flat, hateful 'land of Jutes', which gets in the way of all of us, and is an ignominious thorn in the flesh of every decent and right-thinking Norwegian... It is a national insult, worse than if the cabinet ministers are not found guilty, – a public disgrace, – an unimaginable treachery, – spitting straight in our faces. Oh, that this should happen to us, – such dishonour, a Dane, a Jute, what shame and mockery, and people will say we stood there with long faces' (A to E, 13/12/83)).

This was no doubt one of the more extreme reactions, but it has a certain echo in Amalie's own thinking. In February 1884, only a few weeks before she moved to Copenhagen to join Erik, she was seized with doubt as to whether she could actually live in Denmark. This was part of her last-minute panic about whether marriage was a good thing at all – were they not both too settled in their ways, too independent, too old, and was not she at least too intolerant of any restrictions on her freedom to be prepared to demonstrate the flexibility that would be necessary if the marriage was to be a success? But beyond this, she wondered, could they actually understand each other? 'Jeg frygter også for at det at vi tilhører forskjellige nationaliteter skal blive os en *stor* og måske uryddelig anstødssten.... Vi ser forskjelligt på så mange ting, og vi opfatter og bedømmer forskjelligt, for det meste' (I am afraid that the fact that we belong to different nationalities might become a great and possibly insuperable stumbling block... We see so many things differently, and understand and judge differently in most things (A to E, 1/2/84)). The following day she was still worrying about it: 'min frygt for at vor forskjellige nationalitet skal gjøre os måske ulykkelige i samliv. Havde du vært norsk, eller jeg dansk *vilde* det vært bedre, derom er ingen tvil' (My fear that our different nationalities might make us unhappy in our life together. If you had been Norwegian or I Danish, things *would* have been better, there is no doubt (A to E 2/2/84)).

A couple of weeks later she returned to the same topic, complaining that Erik always asked her to justify what to her were obvious truths, and that that was because he was Danish; no Norwegian would dream of challenging her on such matters. Erik was always so sure that he was right! (A to E, 12/2/84) Even culinary habits became a problem; Amalie intended to bring her icebox with her to Copenhagen, and could not see that any self-respecting household in Denmark could manage without an icebox – everyone in Kristiania had one! Erik had much difficulty convincing her that a) there was no room for an icebox in their small flat and b) no-one in Copenhagen used them anyway; if she did bring it with her, there would be no ice to put in it. Finally, reluctantly, she agreed to leave it behind.

Erik's patience was somewhat tried by these last-minute flurries of panic which expressed themselves in such chauvinistic terms. In his best pedagogic manner he sat down with her, 'min blide lille Hustru' (my sweet little wife), in his next letter and set out for her how she ought to view the matter:

Tal til din Kammerat om din Frygt for vor forskellige Nationalitet, tag ham blidt om Armen og sig, at Du stoler på ham. Se ham ind i Øjet: danske Dreng, Du skal hjælpe mig at se til Bunds helt ned i det Gode ved jert danske Væsen, hvad er det, som gør jer til brave Folk, hvad får Landet til at blomstre? Jeg er en norsk Jenteunge med alle mine Forestillinger hamrede ind fra Barnsben med norske Spiger, jeg er blød af Sind, jeg ønsker ikke at have en eneste Forestilling spigret fast, som gør Uret imod nogen. Og jeg vil være sammen med Dig, Gut, og Du er dansk og jeg er norsk, og Du har ikke rusket i en eneste af mine Spigre og sagt, at den ikke duede, fordi den var norsk, Du har pillet ved og rykket i så den og så den fasthuggede Forestilling, men Du har ladet mig i Fred med min Norskhed. Sig mig Dreng, som jeg elsker, er der da ikke noget af det, Du vil have rettet ved mig, som Du fører tilbage til min Nationalkarakter, og som Du er bange for?

(Talk to your comrade about your fears about our different nationalities, take his arm gently and tell him that you trust him. Look him in the eye: Danish boy, you must help me to see right through to the goodness in your Danish character, what is it that makes you into good people, what makes the country bloom? I am a Norwegian girl with all my ideas hammered in from infancy with Norwegian nails, I have a gentle disposition, I don't want to have one single idea nailed fast which contains injustice to anyone. And I want to be together with you, boy, and you are Danish and I am Norwegian, and you haven't pulled at a single one of my nails and said it was no good because it was Norwegian, you have picked and tugged at one or two of my firmly fixed ideas, but you have left me in peace with my Norwegianness. Tell me, boy, whom I love, is there not anything of what you would like to put right in me, which you can trace back to my national character, and which you are worried about? (E to A, 13/2/84).)

This imaginary monologue continues for another whole page, in a tone that might well strike a modern-day reader as endearing but also somewhat patronising. Amalie seemed to find it unequivocally endearing, however; in her next letter she thanked him: 'at du har været udmærket klog og god og elskelig i din måde at behandle denne uenighed på' (for being so exceptionally clever and good and kind in the way you handled this disagreement (A to E, 16/2/84)), and she was thenceforth silent on the subject.

It is not surprising that nationality was more of a problem for Amalie than it was for Erik. Danish independence might have been threatened in the nineteenth century, both by the English and by the Germans, but it had never been lost, and Copenhagen was secure in its position as a cultural capital. Norway, on the other hand, was still struggling for independence in the 1880s, still defining what the national character was, and Kristiania was physically and mentally a small town, many of whose writers and artists derived their cultural inspiration from Copenhagen, Paris, Berlin and Rome. Amalie's suspiciousness, sharpened by her nervousness at burning her bridges and beginning a new life in another country, was not untypical of her circle. Once she had moved to Copenhagen, however, it ceased to be a problem, insofar as one can tell from her letters; whatever went wrong with the marriage, they neither of them ascribed it to national origin. It was in Copenhagen that Amalie found the cultural environment to which she later gave the credit for her literary achievement, although she had to return to Norway for inspiration and consultation; in that sense she derived the best from both countries, though it was not achieved without considerable anguish, as can be seen from her later letters. Paradoxically and in defiance of her own opinion, one might say that it was in Denmark that Amalie Skram became a Norwegian author.

Notes

1. The correspondence is deposited in the Royal Library in Copenhagen.
2. References to the letters are given in the form 'A to E' or 'E to A' with the accurate date of the letter. (NB some of the letters in the Royal Library have been wrongly dated.)
3. See Elias Bredsdorff, *Den store nordiske krig om sexualmoralen.* (Copenhagen, 1973).
4. *Hinsides Grænsen*, (Copenhagen, 1976 (originally published as part of L. M. Galschiøt: *Danmark – i Skildringer og Billeder af danske Forfattere og Kunstnere*, 1887)).
5. Ibid., p. 69.
6. Amalie Skram, *Landsforrædere* (Copenhagen, 1901), pp. 7, 19.

13

Amalie Skram's Talking Cure Revisited

Judith Messick
Northwestern University

On 28 December 1896, the Norwegian novelist Amalie Skram wrote her first letter to the Danish politician and writer Viggo Hørup. She was fifty years old and her life was spinning out of control. Her brother Ludwig was mortally ill in Kristiania; her writing career was stalled on the unfinished fourth volume of *Hellemyrsfolket* (The People of Hellemyr), and most unsettling of all, she had learned that her husband Erik was having an affair.[1] She may have chosen Viggo Hørup as a confidant because she knew he had been having troubles too. The fifty-five-year-old editor of *Politiken* had suffered both political and personal losses in recent years, particularly the deaths of his son and his close friend Henriette Steen.[2] Hørup travelled in the same literary circles as Amalie and Erik Skram, and he had written a favourable review of her novel *Professor Hieronimus*. Amalie Skram's reasons for approaching Hørup can be inferred from the letters: he was known to her, he was a successful writer, and he was a man of the world who could perhaps help her understand herself and her situation. During the first three months of 1897, the most intense period of their correspondence, Amalie Skram and Viggo Hørup exchanged twenty-three letters in which they established and then negotiated the terms of their relationship.[3]

The letters are important because they show two literary imaginations at work in the process of creation and self-creation. The writers are working in an interactive medium – an exchange of letters – in which both parties use their literary skills to control the relationship. They try to shape their interaction in three ways: 1) they create personas for themselves and each other – masks that shift throughout their epistolary exchanges; 2) they employ different verbal strategies to reveal or conceal their feelings; and 3) they joust for control of the literary product of their collaboration – the physical objects of the letters themselves.

Patient and therapist

What Amalie Skram originally had in mind was a talking cure. In *Professor Hieronimus*, the novel she wrote about her mental breakdown and treatment by Dr Knud Pontoppidan in the Copenhagen City Hospital, her surrogate Else Kant finds relief in writing about her feelings to Dr Hieronimus. Unable to speak to him directly, she unburdens herself in a letter that expresses her anger and feeling of betrayal. It may not be too fanciful to suggest that in her letters to Viggo Hørup, Amalie Skram tries to rewrite the therapeutic relationship she experienced with Knud Pontoppidan in 1894. This time she turns for her talking cure to a very different kind of therapist: a 'klog mand' (a wise man) who smiles instead of frowns, who listens, talks, and kindly advises.[4]

The letters between Amalie Skram and Viggo Hørup play variations on the theme of the talking cure. Amalie Skram initially defines her role as that of a needy patient who exposes her feelings and actions to the ministrations of her analyst. Viggo Hørup initially defines his role as that of a dispassionate analyst of her marital and emotional troubles. But as the correspondence develops during the winter and spring of 1897, the relationship changes. Amalie Skram wants more from her therapist. She pushes the boundaries of the original roles; Viggo Hørup resists. The letters are a series of influence attempts in which the nature of the relationship is negotiated both overtly and covertly – in the manifest content of the letters and in the forms and formats of their language.

Persona creation

In the letters that pass back and forth in the early months of 1897, both parties create surrogate selves to motivate each other, to express aspirations, to conceal feelings. The motivational function can be seen in Amalie Skram's first letter to Viggo Hørup. Her letter of 28 December creates a scenario of need: she invents two personas separated by a gulf of pain: the Olympian deity and the earth-bound sufferer.

De, om hvem alle mennesker siger, at De står på overlegenhedens højeste tinde, at intet bider på Dem, at De har et olympisk smil kun, for alt og alle – *De* altså – kan og vil De ikke hjælpe mig til at bli ligedan?
 Jeg har jo ikke stor anden ret end den rent medmenneskelige til at be Dem om nogenslags hjælp. Men jeg gjør det alligevel. Det er min kummer jeg vil af med, hjælp mig, snak mig fra den! Jeg mener bare, at De skal svare paa dette, skrive til mig, være lidt af en ven for mig. Hvordan det har sig, *véd* jeg ikke, men den tanke at De kunde hjælpe mig, snakke mig op og ud over det hele, har jeg i to år gåt med.

(You are, everybody says, a person who stands at the highest peak of excellence; you are proof against anything; you, with your Olympian smile at everything and everyone – can't you, won't you help me be like that, too? I have absolutely no right, except as a fellow human being, to beg you for any kind of help. But I am doing it anyway. I have to get rid of this sorrow – help me, talk me out of it!
 I mean only that you should answer this, write to me, be a bit of a friend to me. How it came to me I don't *know*, but the thought that you could help me, talk me over and through the whole thing, has been with me for two years.)[5]

By talking to Hørup, or more precisely, by writing to him, she hopes to master her sorrow about the disintegration of her marriage and gain control of her behaviour toward Erik. The relationship she proposes to Hørup is thus cast in the familiar, and stereotypical, framework of masculine rationality and female emotionality. His God-like smile – a sign of wisdom, detachment, and control – promises relief from the emotional storms that have buffeted her throughout her life and marriage to Erik Skram.
 Two days later on 30 December, Viggo Hørup responds, surprised and flattered by her request. He agrees to play the Olympian role she has created for him, yet the whiff of ambivalence is evident. He begins by expressing his shock at her

directness, then by offering to help in any way he can: 'Hvis De kan bruge mig til Noget, tilmed noget Alvorligt, er der Ingen, jeg hellere vil være nyttig end Dem' (If you can use me for anything, even something serious, there is no one I would rather be useful to than you, p. 306). He assures her that he will keep her confidences to himself:

En Ting kan De stole paa: Jeg forraader ikke Mennesker. Af Vane og Tilbøjelighed er det mig imod. De kan rolig tage mig som en Krukke med Laag, hvor Laaget er det bedste. Hvad De vil fylde i mig af Deres Overflod paa Mismod – og Synd er det, at De skal have mere, end De selv har Lyst til at bære – det ligger godt gemt...

Men Kuragen skrumper ind og bliver lille som jeg selv, naar jeg tænker paa at skulle sige Dem noget Nyttigt, et stort, underligt og beundringsværdigt, uroligt og altid pønsende Menneskebarn som De og dertil saa erfaren og klog paa Mennesker og trods alt saa kæk, for det var alligevel kækt at skrive det Brev - jeg har ikke den Tillid til Mennesker.

(One thing you can rely on, I do not betray people. By habit and inclination, that is repugnant to me. You can confidently regard me as a crock with a lid – a tight lid. If you want to fill me with the overflow of your misery – and it's a pity that you have more than you can deal with yourself – it will stay well hidden...

But my courage fails me when I think of saying anything useful to you, a great, wondrous, praiseworthy, restless and always thoughtful child of humanity like you, who is also so experienced and wise about people, and above all, so brave, for it was indeed brave to write that letter – I don't have that much confidence in humanity, pp. 306-7.)

The letter shows his esteem and compassion for her, as well as his artful way of describing their roles. She will be the 'child of humanity' who pours her troubles into the 'crock' with a 'tight lid' – a welcoming, if inert, receptacle for her sorrows.

The next day, 31 December, she fires back a response that expresses her relief at his answer and makes her expectations more explicit: The request that he be 'lidt av en ven' (a bit of a friend) in her first letter becomes 'helt min ven' (wholly my friend, p. 308) in the second. From desiring a sympathetic listener and adviser, she has moved to desiring that he speak to her without disguise or restraint:

Jeg er slet ikke så klog og erfaren, som De tror. Jeg er inderst inde en liden stakker, som ved og forstår så meget, og som dog er helt og holdent hjælpeløs. Det var det, jeg vilde be Dem om, at De skulde hjælpe mig. Ved at snakke med mig uden maske på. Jeg tror, De *kan*.

(I am not as wise and experienced as you think. In my inmost soul I am a poor creature, who knows and understands a good deal, and who nevertheless is completely helpless. That is what I wanted to ask you about: If you would help me. By talking to me without a mask. I believe you *can*, p. 307.)

The passage introduces an important image in their correspondence: the mask. Her formulation suggests that there are only two states: masked and unmasked. But the reality is more complex. As we have seen, both Viggo Hørup and Amalie Skram wear masks in their correspondence – they invent personas and hide behind their assumed roles of doctor/patient, teacher/pupil. They discuss each other's inventions. But the masks do not always stay put. They slip and provide tantalizing glimpses of emotions beneath.

Amalie Skram's mask of compliant patient is difficult for her to keep in place. When Hørup describes her as 'experienced and wise' she rejects that persona and casts herself as a 'a poor creature' who is 'helpless' to deal with her sorrows herself. Although she insists on her weakness, she repeatedly challenges his choice of words. When he tells her he's had to master himself in order to respond, to write in as 'uforbløffet' (unperturbed, p. 306) a fashion as possible, she responds:

Jeg liker ikke det ord: 'uforbløffet'. Hvorfor skulde De bli forbløffet fordi jeg vilde Dem noget. Det er liksom De sætter en ære i at være 'uforbløffet'.... Uf, bare De havde skrevet tydeligere! Der er ord i Deres brev, som jeg ikke *kan* læse.

(I don't like the word 'unperturbed'. Why should you be perturbed because I want something from you? It's as if you make a point of honour to be 'unperturbed'.... Uf, if only you had written more legibly. There are words in your letter that I *can't* read, p. 308.)

This first exchange of letters is fraught with portent for their future interaction. We see many of the themes that will recur in the correspondence: the masks; the flattery; the focus on words and their meanings; the pressure to expand the boundaries of the relationship. And as an omen of the difficulties ahead, Hørup's words as well as his feelings are sometimes hard for Amalie to read.

Accepting his therapeutic role Hørup gets right to his task. In his letter of 9 January,[6] he offers his diagnosis: 'De skulde sige saa højt, at det hørtes i hele Deres morsomme lille Stue, de to rædsomme Ord: Skinsyg Kone! Og hvis det ikke hjalp, skulde De se i Spejlet, om det var Noget for Dem' (You should say out loud, so it could be heard throughout your charming little sitting room, two terrible words: jealous wife! And if that doesn't help, you should look in the mirror and see if that works, pp. 308-9). He then tells her a cautionary tale about his ninety-year-old mother, whose jealousy has tortured the soul out of her husband throughout their married life. Hørup sweetens his dose of bitter medicine by adding the balm of flattery:

Men De kan ikke, hvor megen Lyst De end har, thi dertil hører endnu en Naturens Goldhed og Egenkærlighed, som er det Modsatte af Deres Natur. Det lykkes kun at omsætte hele sin Kærlighedsævne i Misundelse, naar man har meget smaa Midler, det lykkes ikke for en Nabob som Dem.

(You won't become like that, however much you might want to, because to be that way you have to have a sterile and selfish nature, which is the opposite of your nature. You can only transform your whole capacity for love into envy when you have very few resources – and that's not the case with a nabob like you, pp. 308-9.)

This mixture of tough talk followed by praise is his standard form of discourse with her. He repeatedly juxtaposes contrasting identities for her to examine and choose between.

In his role of therapist Viggo Hørup repeatedly suggests behavioral strategies for dealing with an unfaithful husband. His advice is astonishing: a virtual handbook for the wives of errant husbands. The overriding theme is 'Stand by your man'. In his letter of 9 January, his imaginative entry into Erik Skram's consciousness seems informed by his own experience of dealing with a wife and mistress. He delivers his mixture of advice and flattery in a tone of passionate involvement: on this topic we see something of the man behind the mask of therapist:

...saa maa De erobre Deres Kongerige tilbage.... Und ham Livet og prøv at bjærge Dem over i det Venskabelige forat begynde forfra i det. Sæt ikke de pinefuldt forskræmte Øjne paa ham, som gør et Menneske helt hjærtesyg paa Deres Vegne, men se med de kloge og gode Øjne, De har for Deres Venner og som er saa rundeligt bedaarende. Hvorfor vil de tvivle om, at De er fuldt vel værd et Kongerige og at De kun behøver at ville det forat tage Deres eget i Besiddelse? De skal spille den Rolle at være lykkelig. En Rolle kan ethvert Menneske spille, end sige da et Fruentimmer, som er skabt til det. Det vilde være naragtigt at sige til Dem: De bør være lykkelig; men spille den Komedie, det kan De da, naar det er nødvendigt. Og naar det er saa vigtigt, som De tror, kan De naturligvis spille den brilliant.

Men hvis de slet ikke vil gøre noget Klogt, fordi det ikke morer Dem, saa maa De ogsaa nok lade være og for denne Gang nøjes med at læse denne Vennesnak til Tidsfordriv. Saa har jeg dog ud af det for en halv Times Tid, hvad den liden David havde ud af at lege for den tungsindige Saul.

(Then you must win your kingdom back.... Allow him his own life, and assume the safe ground of being friendly. Don't look at him with tortured eyes that make a person heartsick on your behalf; but look at him with the wise and tolerant eyes you use with your friends – and that are so utterly fascinating. Why would you doubt that you are worthy of a kingdom and that you only need to want it in order to take possession of it. You must play the role of being happy, a role anybody can play, especially a woman who is created for it. It would be foolish to tell you: You should be happy; but put on an act, that's something you can do if it's necessary. And when it's so important, as you believe, of course you can play it brilliantly.

But if you absolutely will do nothing wise, because it doesn't amuse you, you can refrain, and for the time being content yourself with reading this friendly advice to pass the time. Then perhaps for half an hour I've accomplished what little David accomplished when he played for the melancholy Saul, p. 309.)

However much she appreciated his subtle flattery – turning himself into the youthful David serving the regal Saul – it could not have escaped her notice that this instruction on traditional gender roles is not so different from the advice that the heroine of Skram's novel *Constance Ring* receives from Pastor Huhn when she wants to leave her unfaithful husband.[7] It is the woman's responsibility to keep the home intact. Answering Hørup the next day, Amalie

Skram does not overtly challenge his masculine perspective; she does object to the way he makes her situation ordinary. Point by point she goes through his advice and rejects it:

Nej det er vist ikke skinsyge, der piner mig. Det er *sorg* over at ha forspildt noget godt, som aldrig kommer, og aldrig *kan* komme igjen. Ja, det tror jeg da.
　　Jeg nærer f.eks. ikke spor af uvilje mod hende den anden. Tværtom. Hun er mig meget sympathetisk, og fortjener også at være det.

(No, it's certainly not jealousy that tortures me. It's *grief* at having thrown away something good, that will never come, never *could* come back again. Yes, that's really what I believe.
I don't nurse any ill will toward her, the other one. Quite the contrary. I feel great sympathy for her and she deserves it, p. 311.)

Part of her suffering comes from the knowledge that she has not been a good wife to Erik. But she cannot translate sorrow into action:

Nej. Jeg vil *ikke* forsøge på at erobre noget tilbage. Jeg ejer ikke det tålmod, den ydmyghed, den fra dag til dag fortsatte og uforanderlige ydmyghed, som skulde til. Og så har jeg i mit hjærte ingen tro på, at det vilde lykkes. Når der i hans hjærte er begyndt et nyt, og rigt og lykkeligt liv, så må det liv ha sin vækst og udfoldelse.... Jeg skulde spille komedie, siger De, lade som jeg var lykkelig. Man jeg *kan* ikke spille komedie! Umulig, umulig kan jeg det...

(No. I will *not* attempt to win anything back. I don't have the patience, the humility – the day to day unchanging humility that is necessary.... And in my *heart* I have no confidence that it would succeed. If in his heart he has begun a new, rich, and happy life, then this life must have its growth and development... I should put on an act you say, laugh, as if I were happy. But I *cannot* put on an act! Impossible, impossible for me to do it, p. 312.)

But though she refuses to accept the role of the militant wife, fighting for the sanctity of her home, she at least wants Hørup to know that she's making progress. At the end of the letter she writes:

Ja, nu ser det kanske ud som at jeg ingen nytte har havt af Deres så elskværdige brev. Men sådan er det ikke. Tværtom. Kuren ar allerede begyndt. Jeg har således, siden jeg fik Deres brev, tænkt *meget mere* på Dem og brevet end på det andet. Nej, jeg har ikke tat fejl af 'min mand'. Sikrere end nogensinde er jeg nu på, at De kan hjælpe mig. De og ingen anden.

(Perhaps it may seem that your very kind letter has done no good, but that is not the case. Quite the contrary. The cure has already begun. Since I received your letter I have thought *much more* about you and the letter than about the other matter. No I have not been mistaken about 'my man'. I am more sure than ever that you can help me, you and nobody else, p. 312.)

The flattery implicit in her statement is one of her primary strategies for maintaining the relationship. By assuring him that she is benefiting from his therapy, she affirms her continuing need for a service only he can provide.

Five days later, on 15 January, Hørup returns to his subject of managing an errant husband. In his role of therapist, he continues to deliver pointed instruction in traditional nineteenth-century gender roles. He begins by creating a compelling persona for her – an angel in the house:

Men tag Dem i Agt for de uskyldige Spørgsmaal! Gud forbarme sig at spørge ham, om hun var med, som efter det Selskab. Og det kalder De uskyldigt! De skal aldrig spørge om Noget, som De har den fjerneste Mistanke om, at han ikke kan svare paa. Og De skal ikke undre Dem over Noget, hverken over, at han kommer eller gaar, sent eller tidlig. Hvorfor gøre Deres Stuer til et Fængsel med en Gendarm, eller en Forhørssal med en Inkvisitor ved Protokollen, det vil sige et Helvede. Lad ham søge sit Helvede udenom og hos Dem et altid lige trygt Asyl med en Fredens Engel. Den er ikke Ydmyghed, kan De da se, men den højeste kvindelige Stolthed.

(But beware of those innocent questions! Good Lord! Asking him if she was there, like you did after that party. And you call that innocent! You must never ask him anything you have the slightest suspicion he can't answer. And you must not be surprised about anything, whether he comes or goes, early or late. Why make your sitting room into a jail with a gendarme or an interrogation room with an inquisitor of protocol – in other words, a Hell. Let him seek his Hell elsewhere and in you always find safe asylum with an angel of peace. This is not humiliation, you see, but the highest womanly pride, p. 313.)

Empathizing with the husband, Hørup commends her for not

taking the affair as 'et Indgreb i Deres lovlige velerhvervede Ejendomsret' (an incursion into spousal rights of ownership, p. 314). In cool third-person terms he summarizes her situation. The persona he now presents is that of a capricious, destructive woman:

Tilfældet er dette:
 Hun har i tre – 3 – Aar ladet ham gaa for Lud og koldt Vand. Hun har Intet givet og Intet modtaget. Af Intet kommer Intet. Det er et Kærlighedsforhold, hvis Ild er brændt ned til den sindigt ulmende Glød, hvis hele Varme er en lunken Tilfredshed over, at han er der og ikke er gaaet andet Steds hen. At hun er *glad i ham* vil kun sige det eneste Ene, at hun ønsker at have ham staaende med Gevær ved Foden paa den ham af Guds og hendes Naade beskikkede Post. Ellers vil hun ham ikke Noget, slet ikke Andet end at holde ham in Ruhestand...
 Saa gaar han naturligvis hen og forlieber sig. Hvad i Verdens Riger og Lande skulde han ellers gøre? Naturligvis. Og saa forgaar hun af Kummer.
 Dersom hun flammede op ved at se Andre brænde for ham, var det endda respektabelt. Dersom hun saa sin Verden synke i Afgrunden og styrtede efter forat redde, vilde alle gode Ønsker følge hende. Men ingenlunde. Hun kedes ved Tanken om at erobre ham tilbage, hun ved ikke, hvad hun skulde gøre med ham, hvis hun fik ham. Hun vil kun det, at hans Hjærte ikke maa blomstre...
 Det er hverken tragisk eller komisk, men rent ud skandaløst. Det er den ægte, skinbarlige fruentimmerlige Skinsyge, som intet honet *Kvindfolk* kan være bekendt og som vor Herre aldrig et Øjeblik har tænkt paa, at De skulde fordybe Dem i.

(The case is this: She has for three years – 3 – neglected him. She has given nothing and accepted nothing. From nothing comes nothing. This is a love relationship in which the fires have burned down to a steady smouldering glow, whose entire warmth is a lukewarm satisfaction that he is there and hasn't gone anywhere else. That she loves him means only this single thing: that she wants him standing at attention, at the post God and she have appointed him to. Otherwise she wants nothing, absolutely nothing from him except to keep him on hold....
 So naturally he goes off and falls in love. What in the world else should he do? Naturally. And then she perishes of grief.
 If she were to ignite when she saw someone else's passion for him, that would be still respectable. If she saw her world falling into an abyss and dashed off to save it, all good wishes would follow her. But it's nothing like that. She's bored by the thought of winning him back. She doesn't know what she would do with him if she got him. The only thing she wants is that

his heart must not bloom...
It's neither tragic nor comic, but flat-out scandalous. It's a pure female jealousy incarnate that no respectable woman should admit to, and one in which our Lord never for a moment could imagine you would wallow, pp. 314-5.)

He ends this astringent analysis with an exhortation:

Derfor ranker De Dem naturligvis op over dette, saasnart Deres sanddru Øjne har set tvært igennem Deres Tilfælde og set, hvad det er indeni. Saa kaster De det fra Dem og er igen fri for det Onde, det vil sige glad.
 Nu har jeg bevist Dem, at De aldeles ingen Kummer har. Kom nu og modbevis det, hvis De kan.

(So of course you will straighten your shoulders about this, as soon as your truthful eyes have looked right through your circumstances and seen what is inside. Then cast it aside and be free of that evil. In other words, be glad.
 Now that I've convinced you that you have absolutely no grief at all, come on and argue against it if you can, p. 315.)

The vigour of his admonitions is softened by a humorous twist at the end. He dips her into the chilly waters of his criticism, then pulls her up, pats her dry and sends her on her way.

As the letters pass back and forth in January, Amalie Skram attempts to expand the boundaries of their roles. Increasingly she wants greater physical and emotional access to her therapist. She makes demands on his time, asking to see him more often, to visit his home, to visit his office. In her letter of 17 January, the emphasis has clearly shifted from her problems with Erik to her interest in being in Hørup's company:

Men jeg forstår ikke, at De ikke kan finde på noget, som naturlig kan bringe mig hver dag i Deres nærhed. De skulde bare se, at jeg alligevel ikke skulde overhænge Dem. Næsten ingen tanke i verden er mig mere imod, end den, at være påtrængende. Hvad gjorde det at folk lo af det. Af *mig* ler de jo alligevel fordi jeg er en 'skinsyg stakkels kone', og De, De er da stor nok til at kunne knipse af latteren.

(I don't understand why you can't find some means that will bring me into your company every day. You would see that I wouldn't pester you. Nothing is more repugnant to me than being intrusive. So what if people laugh about it. They laugh at *me* anyway for being a 'poor jealous wife', and as for you, you are great enough to be able to shrug off the laughter, p. 316.)

In pursuit of her goal of greater access, she creates scripts for her social visits to his home:[8]

Når vi ses – ja når blir det? De må skrive og sige mig hvilken dag jeg skal gjøre visit i Deres hjem, og så må De ha lov at udsætte det sålænge som De har hjærte til det. Men ét *må* De love: at ta mig med, når De går. Når De siger: 'ja, nu må jeg desværre afsted,' så rejser jeg mig og siger: 'ja, det må jeg også.' Når så de andre derhjemme siger, at jeg endelig må bli siddende, og jeg siger at det *kan* jeg ikke, fordi jeg har så meget at udrette, så må De støtte mig og sige, at det forstår De så godt, og at nu er det bedst, vi slår følge. Hører De! Går De fra mig, og lar mig sidde der igjen, blir jeg fortvilet.

('When we see each other' – when will that be? You must write and tell me which day I should come to see you at your home, and then you can postpone it for as long as you have the heart to do so. But you *must* promise me one thing: to take me with you when you leave. When you say, 'Well, I have to be off now, unfortunately', I'll stand up and say, 'Yes, I have to leave, too'. When the others say that I really must stay and I say that I *can not* because I have so much to do, then you *must* back me up and say that you understand and that the best thing will be if we go together. Do you hear? If you go off and leave me sitting there again, I'll be in despair.)

Later in the same letter she makes her feelings explicit:

Mine fleste tanker drejer sig nu om hvorledes det skal la sig gjøre for mig at være det mest mulige sammen med Dem uden at det vækker opsigt. Når jeg nu mærker at samværet med Dem kurerer mig, er det da så underligt? Har De selv ingen opfindsomhed i den retning?

(Most of my thoughts now revolve around figuring out how I can be with you as much as possible without arousing any attention. When I notice that being with you cures me, is it so strange that I want to be with you as much as possible? Don't you have any ingenious ideas in that direction?)[9]

One can almost hear the mask of patient snapping into place, concealing inadequately the increasingly personal nature of her appeal to him.

Verbal Strategies

In the letters between Amalie Skram and Viggo Hørup, the conflicting impulses to push and to withdraw are enacted at the margins of the letters: the salutation and signature. The beginnings and endings of the letters become metaphorical spaces in which the nature of their relationship is debated. As their intimacy increases, Amalie Skram becomes dissatisfied with the standard forms: by her fourth letter, she has dropped 'Kjære hr. Hørup!' (Dear Mr. Hørup!, p. 305) and has begun to personalize the openings of her letters. On 17 January, she begins: 'Kjære, velsignede menneske! Slig må jeg nok vel få lov til at kalde Dem, siden De allerede har gjort mig så meget godt' (Dear, blessed person! I trust I can be permitted to address you that way, since you've already done me so much good, p. 315). On the 19th, she skips the formal salutation entirely and begins: 'Ja, nu sidder jeg her min kjæreste, bedste "kloge mand", og skriver til Dem igjen' (Here I am, my dearest, best 'wise man' writing to you again, p. 320). On 24 January she begins: 'Nej, jeg *vil* ikke skrive "kjære hr. Hørup", og Deres "hengivne". Det er det, som alle mennesker skriver til hinanden. Så må hellere mine breve være ganske uden overskrift' (No, I will *not* write 'Dear Mr. Hørup' and 'Yours sincerely'. That's the way all people write to each other. I'd rather my letters be without a salutation, p. 324). On 31 January she makes a small concession to convention, 'Jo, jeg vil alligevel skrive kjære, hvis jeg får lov til at kaste hr.et bort' (All right, I'll write 'Dear' if I have permission to get rid of 'Mister', p. 328).

In contrast, Hørup insists on standard forms of address. From the beginning to the end of their correspondence he opens his letters, 'Kjære fru Skram!' (Dear Mrs. Skram). The ends of his letters are also conventional. On 23 January he writes, 'Hvad er der at tænke ved "hengivne"? Kan ikke De være hengiven uden at blive Filosof og tænke Noget ved det, saadan ganske simpelt ud af Landevejen som, Deres hengivne, V. Hørup' (What is the issue about 'sincerely'. Can't you be sincere without being philosophical and meaning something by it? – Therefore, rather simply, in the usage of the land, Yours sincerely, V. Hørup, p. 324). When she offers to send him the first three volumes of *Hellemyrsfolket* he agrees, but insists on buying them himself. Writing back to her on the 26th, he pokes fun at the verbal sparring about their forms of greeting:

Men om Bøgerne vilde jeg sige, at De ikke maa købe dem til mig, som er meget rigere end De, men at jeg vil være glad, hvis jeg faar Lov at købe dem og De saa vil skrive Deres Navn i dem – Deres – f.Eks. 'hengivne – Amalie Skram'. De skal se, De finder ikke paa noget Bedre.

(But about the books, you mustn't buy them for me, because I have much more money than you, but I would be very happy if I were permitted to buy them and if you would write your name in them – 'Yours', for example, 'sincerely, Amalie Skram'. You'll see that you won't be able to come up with anything better, p. 328.)

Clinging to the standard forms is a way of emphasizing the limitations and propriety of the relationship. Viggo Hørup insists on conventional openings and closes: Amalie Skram wants something personal and unique.

If her increasing desire to control him is particularly evident at the margins of the letters, it can also be seen in the tension between direct and indirect forms of expression. In her letter of 19 January, she addresses his penchant for disguised forms of language:

De er så sød, når Deres ansigt er alvorligt, og når De snakker til mig uden den ironiske mine, som er bleven Deres naturlige måde at snakke på. Gjør en undtagelse ligeoverfor mig, vær uden maske altid, bestandig. Jeg – som selve altid er uden maske. Altid. Altid.

(You are so sweet when your face is serious and when you speak to me without an ironic expression, which is your natural way of speaking. Make an exception for me, be without a mask always – forever. As for me, I am always without a mask. Always. Always, p. 320.)

This naked appeal for intimacy presents a problem for Hørup. How does he continue to provide support without being pulled deeper into the relationship?

Hørup's strategic use of indirection is particularly evident in his letter of 18 January. He gently fends her off, artfully depersonalizing the erotic potential of their relationship by creating a series of metaphorical identities for her to consider. His images are reductive: they shift him from the role of powerful physician and teacher into a series of lesser identities.

Kære Fru Skram! De maa ikke sige saa mange Lovord og snakke om Taknemlighed og sligt, De gør mig jo flov som en lille Pige og forfængelig som en Konfirmand, der ikke er vant til at høre saa meget Godt. Naar jeg tænker paa, hvor tidt jeg allerede har sagt: 'De skal' og 'De maa ikke' and andet ligende Pædagogisk, maa jeg le af mig selv over, hvor strunkt et Mandfolk rider, straks et Kvindfolk faar sat ham paa den høje Hest. Men jeg ved da nok, at jeg blot er den Springstok, som De i Øjeblikket har Brug for til at komme over en besværlig Passage og at det er Dem selv, der springer.... Og i Dem er der lykkeligvis Spændstighed nok til at springe højt og sætte over en bredere Grøft end den, der nu synes Dem et Svælg.

(Dear Mrs. Skram, You mustn't say so many words of praise and speak about gratitude and the like. You make me as embarrassed as a schoolgirl and as vain as a confirmand who is unaccustomed to hearing so much goodness. When I think about how often I have already said 'You must' and 'you must not' and other similar pedagogical things, I have to laugh at myself over how upright a man rides as soon as a woman places him on a high horse. But I know well enough that I am just a vaulting pole that you need to use for the moment to get across a difficult passage and it is you yourself who will do the vaulting ... And in you, there is luckily spring enough to vault high and get across a broader ditch than the one that now seems like a chasm to you, p. 317.)

Hørup's dizzying flood of images continues throughout the letter. He compares himself to 'en Østers in sin Skal' (an oyster in its shell, p. 318) that clamps shut instinctively to protect its soft interior. In his reductionist mode, he transforms his 'klog Mand' (wise man, p. 318) persona into a quack: 'Kommer der saa En, der virkelig lider ilde, maa man ikke fortænke en retskaffen Kvaksalver i, at han ser til sine Krukker og Salver og siger: "Kæreste, Bedste, jeg er kun en Kvaksalver, vi Medicinmænd er allesammen Kvaksalvere" (When someone appears who really suffers badly, one must not blame the upright quack for looking at his crocks and salves and saying: 'My dear, I am only a quack, we medicine men are all quacks', p. 318). He ends the letter with his second reference to the terrifying directness of Norwegians:

Gud forbarme sig, hvor I Norske er direkte! Naar I siger: 'Jeg kunde gaa i Ilden for Dem' siger vi paa Dansk: 'Det er længe siden, jeg har set Dem'. Paa Dansk siger jeg: Jeg glæder mig til at se Dem i Morgen, og jeg venter at se Dem som en rolig overlegen, forstandig Østers i sine to Skaller, saaledes som De ynder at tænke Dem Deres hengivne V. Hørup.

(Good Lord, how direct you Norwegians are! Where you say 'I would go through fire for you', we say in Danish 'It's been a long time since I've seen you'. So in Danish I'm saying, I look forward to seeing you tomorrow. I'm expecting you like the calm, composed, sensible oyster within its two shells that you like to imagine me. Yours sincerely, V. Hørup, p. 319.)

By clothing his rejection in humour, Hørup keeps his distance yet allows her to maintain face.

In his letter of 23 January, he lightly warns her that she is making a spectacle of both herself and him:

Men af Papir har jeg ellers fra Dem to lyserøde Billetter, hvorom jeg intet Ondt vil sige, kun saa meget, at jeg gærne vilde bede Dem, naar De skriver paa Lyserødt, om De saa ikke ogsaa nok vil parfymere det, forat Redaktionen og alle Medarbejderne straks kan lugte, hvad det er og ikke behøver Allesammen at fingerere ved Redaktørens Billetter forat gætte, hvad det kan være.

(Speaking of paper, I've received two pink letters from you, about which I have nothing bad to say, except that I would like to ask you, when you write on pink paper, if you won't also perfume it, so the editors and all my colleagues can immediately smell what it is, and they all won't have to finger the editor's letters to try and figure out what's going on, p. 324.)

Hørup's irony does not fully mask the unease he feels about the incursion of pink paper, with its claim of intimacy, into the business offices of *Politiken*.

The stress of the relationship becomes increasingly evident in the metaphorical pairs that Hørup uses to describe their interaction. In his letter of 23 January, the two are no longer doctor and patient, teacher and pupil, but lamb and vulture:

...medens jeg er sagtmodig og ydmyg af Hjærtet, som det Lam, jeg er, og Dem lige god, uforanderlig lige god, enten De slaar ned som en Grib og sætter Deres Klør i Ulden og gaar til Fjelds med Deres Rov, eller De slipper

Amalie Skram's Talking Cure

og lader Lammet falde gennem Rummet og selv sidder og kikker fra et Bjerg og funderer paa, om det stødte sig.

(...while I am meek and humble at heart as the lamb I am, and you, just as good, unalterably as good, whether you swoop down like a vulture and set your claws in the wool and take off for the mountains with your prey, or you drop it and let the lamb fall through space while you peer from the mountain and ponder whether it hurt itself, p. 322.)

He piles on other images of masculine impotence:

Tror De ikke, jeg véd, at De blæser denne Skolemesterremse et langt Stykke og at De ikke giver en Bønne for denne Gammelmandssnakk? Men saadan er vi Mandfolk, altid skal vi rette af og opdrage paa Jer og disse Dumheder, selv om vi véd, at en Kvinde altid er 'en Vild' i egne Anliggender, og at selv en Kulturkvinde, om hun er kommet aldrig saa højt op, dog bestandig bevarer en Rødhuds Hjærte under Korsettet.
    Saa det var med Overlæg, at De kom forsent. Ja, snild som en Slange er De.

(Don't you think I know that you make fun of this schoolmasterly rigmarole, that you don't care a bean for this old man's chatter. But that's how we men are, always correcting and educating you and these follies, even though we know that a woman is always a 'savage' in her own affairs and that within even a cultured woman, however elevated she becomes, there's always the heart of a Redskin under the corset.
    So it was deliberate that you came late. You're as clever as a serpent, p. 323.)

This is the second time he has called her a serpent. It is hard to avoid the impression that Viggo Hørup is thinking of the garden of Eden and the tempting female who led the rational Adam astray. But characteristically he clothes this allusion in a garb that will not offend her. As a temptress and a wild woman, she can feel her own power.
    In her letter of 24 January, Amalie Skram somewhat ruefully tells him that his humorous admonitions have had the desired effect: they have cheered her up.

Altid når det er som ondest for mig, minder jeg mig om det, De har sagt, og oftere og oftere hjælper det. De skal se, De tildidst får ære af mig. Men hvor

De dog bespotter mig og gjør nar af mig i Deres sidste brev! Var det ikke fordi jeg ustanselig må le over det, fordi det er så – jeg havde nær sagt – djævelsk morsomt – vilde jeg blet sint for det. Nu tænker jeg: kanske at le er den hurtigste kurmethode.

De er dog et storartet menneske. Men noget lam er De ikke. Man skal bare komme Dem for nær! Se, hvor jeg får for mine lyserøde billetter, som burde vært parfumerede.

...Og nu har De to gange kaldt mig slange. Det *kan* jeg ikke like, likså lidt som fruentimmer.... Bare jeg kjendte Dem rigtig nøje! For jeg *kan* ikke sikkert se om der bag al ironien i Deres brev er andet end ironi.

(Always when it's the worst for me, I think about what you have said, and more and more often that helps. You'll see, you'll be proud of me yet. But how you slander and make fun of me in your last letter. If it hadn't made me laugh so hard because it was – I could almost say, devilishly funny – I would have been angry about it. Now I'm thinking perhaps laughter is the quickest cure.

You really are a splendid man. But a lamb you are not. Just try to get too close to you! Look what I get for my pink notes that ought to be perfumed.

... And that's twice you've called me a serpent. I do *not* like that a bit – almost as little as 'female.' ... If only I knew you really well! For I can't tell for sure if behind the irony in your letters there's anything else but irony, p. 325-6.)

A writer and creator of masks herself, she recognizes his distancing strategies: irony, humour, and metaphor.

By early in February, Amalie Skram seems to have accepted the fact that she is not going to get the deeper relationship with Viggo Hørup that she desires. The frequency of the letters declines and the tone shifts. On 8 February she sums up their relationship in elegiac terms:

...Kjære Hørup, jeg håber at jeg ikke har trættet Dem mere end at De kan bli ved at tænke med godhed og velvilje på mig. Husk på hvor oprevet og nødlidende jeg var. Og husk *bestandig* på at De i mig har en *ven*. Kanske bryr De Dem ikke om at ha en sådan ven. Men man kan aldrig vide. – Jeg forsørger nu at gjøre som De sidst bød. Jeg sletter ud, hvad jeg kan, og *hvor* jeg kan. Jeg siger at jeg har det godt og at alt er udmærket. Deres altid taknemmelige, Amalie Skram.

Husk på at De har lovet mig at brænde det blyantskrevne brev!

Amalie Skram's Talking Cure

(...Dear Hørup, I hope that I have not exhausted you so much that you can't still think of me with kindness and good will. Remember how disturbed and needy I was. And remember *always* that you have a *friend* in me. Perhaps you don't care to have such a friend. But you never know. – I will try now to do what you ordered the last time. I erase what I can and where I can. I say that I am doing well and that everything is fine. Yours always gratefully, Amalie Skram.
Remember you promised to burn the letter I wrote in pencil, p. 330.)[10]

There is another flare-up of emotion in her letter of 13 May 1897:

De snakker aldrig som en ven til mig, bare som en venlig læremester....Jeg har vært så ubegrænset åben ligeoverfor Dem. Jeg syntes at til *Dem* kunde jeg sige *alt*, og så var alt dog ikke nok....å ja, mange ganger, når jeg har snakket med Dem har jeg havt en ubændig trang til at kaste mig ind til Dem, til at græde ud, og få den trøst som gode og kjærlige ord kan gi. *Det* og *intet* mere har jeg ønsket mig. Men De er så tilknappet, så fornem og fjern. Og dog så god, så fin og stille.

(You never speak to me as a friend, just as a friendly schoolmaster... I have been so boundlessly open toward you. I thought that to you I would be able say *everything*, and then everything wasn't enough.... Oh yes, many times when I've talked to you I have had an uncontrollable need to throw myself in your arms and weep, and receive the comfort that good and loving words can bring. *That* and *nothing* more have I desired. But you are so aloof, so dignified, and remote. And yet, so good, so refined and quiet, pp. 335-6.)

There is a tone of resignation as she accurately describes the contrast between their verbal styles and the degree of emotional involvement in the relationship. The next day she writes back and apologizes for the product of her 'nattestemning' (night mood, p. 336), and asks for her letter back. The struggle to possess him, shifts to a desire to possess the tangible traces of her emotion and their relationship, the letters themselves.

Control of the letters

Early in their correspondence they wrote about the subject of confidentiality, when she asked him to burn a letter she considered incriminating.[11] Hørup replied that her short story 'Post festum', had already made Erik's affair a public matter.[12] In his letter of

9 January, Hørup mocked her obsession with secrecy in terms that reverberate uncomfortably to the modern reader:

Hvad De er for et Fruentimmer! Jeg mener, hvor fuldkomment et Fruentimmer, De dog er. Nu er De den største Intelligens paa Spindesiden in disse Riger og Lande, men at netop det Brev skulde brændes, forat Efterverdenen ikke skulde finde det og opdage Deres Hemmelighed, det havde intet Mandfolk fundet paa.
 Tror De ikke, at vi ved det? Saa skulde De ikke skrive offentligt om det.... Det Brev kan De meget trygt aflevere til det kgl. Biblilotek, forat Deres Biograf eller en anden Borchsenius kan brede sig over det en Gang, naar De er død. Derved kommer saamænd ingen Hemmelighed ud i Verden.

(What a female you are! I mean, how completely female you truly are. You are the greatest intelligence in the distaff side of the kingdom, but the letter must be burned so that posterity will not discover your secret – no man could have thought that up.
 Don't you think we know about it? Then you shouldn't write about it publicly.... That letter you can quite safely deliver to the Royal Library so your biographer – or some Borchsenius or another – can sprawl over it some time after you're dead. No secrets will get out that way, pp. 308-9.)[13]

On January 10 she replied in horror:

De må ikke skræmme livet af mig ved at snakke om det kgl. bibliothek. Det brev *skal* og *må* brændes. Jeg *vil* netop ikke ha at nogen Borchsenius efter min død skal sidde og frådse i det dokument. Hvad man kan læse og slutte sig til ud af en forfatters bøger, blir dog kun altid slutning og gjætning. Men en egenhændig nedskreven bekjendelse, det er dog noget andet. Og jeg påstår hårdnakket at *ingen ved* noget. Ingen uden altså nu De.

(You mustn't scare the life out of me by talking about the Royal Library. The letter *shall* and *must* be burned. I will absolutely not have some Borchsenius sprawling over this document after my death. What a person can read and embrace in an author's books is only deduction and guesswork. But a written confession in one's own hand, that's quite another thing. And I declare vehemently that *nobody knows* anything. Nobody aside from you, pp. 309-10.)

In May, her passionate involvement with Hørup waning, she returns to the subject of privacy and asks him to return her letters. On 20 May she writes: 'Jeg *kan* ikke forstå at der enten på norsk eller

Amalie Skram's Talking Cure

dansk kan være noget råt i at sende en dame hendes breve tilbage når hun selv ber om det. Jeg vilde heller ha dem tilbage end se dem brænde. Jeg liksom ikke nænner at være med til at brænde dem' (I *can* not understand, either in Norwegian or Danish, how there can be anything crass about sending a woman her letters back when she asks for them herself. I would rather have them back than have them burned. I can't imagine being a party to burning them).[14] Significantly, they argue about *how* to return the letters. Amalie Skram asks him to send them back through the mail. He replies that only a lout would return a lady's letters through the mail. If she must deprive him of the pleasure of keeping her letters, he will bring them to her in person. But the letters remain in his possession.

During their sporadic correspondence of the next few years she repeatedly asks him to return her letters. On 19 April 1898 she writes to remind him:

De skrev engang til mig at *jeg* var herre over når de brever, jeg har sendt Dem, skulde brændes. Nu *bér* jeg Dem om at brænde dem, og jeg *ved*, at jeg ikke bér forgjæves.... Kjære, kjære Hørup, tak for alt. Brænd mine breve, og tænk med godhed på Deres altid hengivne Amalie Skram.

(You wrote to me once that *I* was the master of when the letters I sent you should be burned. Now I *beg* you to burn them and I *know* I will not beg in vain.... Dear, dear Hørup. Thank you for everything. Burn my letters and think with kindness of your always devoted, Amalie Skram, p. 342.)

Three years after the most intense phase of their correspondence, she writes on 22 September 1900 to make a final appeal:

Du hjalp mig, og det skal jeg aldrig glemme Dig, om end hjælpen blev en anden, end jeg havde ønsket. Du ser, jeg er ærlig og åben.
   Men nu *beder* jeg Dig kjære Hørup om at sende mig mine breve tilbage. Du *kan* ikke nægte mig denne bøn. Hvis Du gjør det, så må jeg sige, jeg forstår det ikke. Din Amalie S.

(You helped me, and for that I will never forget you, even though the help was something different than I had desired. You see, I am honest and frank.
   But now, I *beg* you, dear Hørup to send me my letters back. You *cannot* deny this request. If you do, then I must say, I do not understand. Your Amalie S., p. 363.)[15]

This letter finally brings the desired response. On 25 September 1900, Hørup finally agrees to return her letters.

Kære Fru Skram! Naturligvis skal Du have Dine Breve. Naar jeg ved, at Du ikke vil betro mig dem længer, bringer jeg dem straks, det forstaar sig. Vor Herre maa vide, hvad anden Grund jeg skulde have til at beholde dem end den ene, at jeg kan lide at have dem. Hvorfor har Du beholdt mine? Med Posten sender jeg dem imidlertid ikke, skønt de ligger i en stor Konvolut – som Du har ordineret – med Din fulde Adresse paa. Jeg bringer dem selv en af Dagene, hvis Du har Tid til at tage imod dem, ellers afleverer jeg den store Konvulut ved Døren – er det tilstrækkeligt beroligende? Din V. Hørup

(Dear Mrs. Skram! Of course you shall have your letters. Now that I know that you won't entrust them to me any longer, I'll bring them right away. Lord knows what other grounds I have for keeping them except that I like to have them. Why have you kept mine? However, I won't send them by post, although they're in a large envelope, as you ordained, with your full address on it. I'll bring them myself one of these days if you have time to receive them, otherwise I'll leave the big envelope by the door – is that reassuring enough? Your V. Hørup.)

Two weeks later on 12 October, Amalie Skram writes to tell him that she has just opened the big blue envelope of her letters and read through them:

Og jeg har den glæde at kunne sige mig selv, at der ikke findes et ord i dem, som jeg angrer på. Sandelig kunde de ikke gjerne ha ligget efter din og min død, til læsning og beskuelse af hvemsomhelst. Det var kun fordi jeg dengang, jeg skrev dem, *følte* mig som *den* mands hustru, det var kun derfor, jeg gik med dette nag, og troede jeg havde skrevet kompromiterende ting. – Aldeles ikke!!

(And I am happy to be able to say to myself that there isn't a word in them that I regret. Truthfully, they could survive after your and my death for reading and contemplation by anybody. It only was because at the time I wrote them I *felt* myself to be *that* man's wife and thought I had written compromising things, that was the reason it rankled so – Absolutely not!!, p. 365-6.)

She did notice, however, that one of the letters was missing – a letter that was '*næsten* et kjærlighedsbrev' (*almost* a love letter,

p. 365). She wonders if perhaps he burned it as she had asked him to. 'Forresten gjør det ikke noget. Nu, da jeg er så inderligt frigjort, synes det mig næsten latterligt at disse stakkels uskyldige breve har gjort mig kval. Jeg mener frigjort fra ham E.S. og fra mit forpligtelsesforhold til ham' (Anyhow it doesn't matter. Now that I am so truly liberated, it seems almost laughable that these poor innocent letters have caused me agony. I mean liberated from E.S and from the obligations of my relationship with him. pp. 365-6).[16] Looking back, she seems at peace with the physical traces of their relationship – both the feelings and words that document it.

Outcomes

How do we sum up this exchange of letters? What did each writer get from the interaction? At some level Viggo Hørup must have been flattered by Amalie Skram's admiration and attention, by her clear desire for greater intimacy with him. However problematic he found her overtures, he wrote seventeen thoughtful letters to her. Amalie Skram's thirty-six letters and cards to Hørup helped her face the situation with Erik and gain the strength to divorce him. But if she gained a degree of self-mastery, she never mastered Viggo Hørup. Like a good therapist, he refused to be drawn into an intimate relationship with his patient. Kindly, firmly, he refused to move beyond the boundaries he had established in the beginning. Although he never gave her what she most wanted from him – a face without a mask – he gave her a great deal. He listened carefully, took her seriously, and made her laugh. Using all of his literary gifts he exhorted, mocked, encouraged her. And he clothed his rejection of her overtures in the kindest of metaphorical clothes. For the next few years, until a few months before Hørup died, they continued to exchange occasional friendly letters, but Amalie Skram had turned to a new wise man, Valdemar Irminger, for the intimate and enduring friendship she wanted.[17]

Yet the letters she and Hørup exchanged were precious enough for her to preserve them. Amalie Skram's desire to possess and control her letters is on the one hand an artistic impulse – she wants control of the words and personas she has created. But her struggle to get her letters back raises uncomfortable questions for us. Did she mean for us to read them? We can sit in the Royal Library and the Danish National Archives and hold the letters in our hands. But do we betray her by taking an interest in them, by translating and speaking about them in public places? This is an issue that troubles any one who does research on correspondence. My answer is that posterity always wins these struggles. Like modern day Borchseniuses we sprawl over the letters and comfort ourselves by saying that the letters show the writers in a favourable light. They show Amalie Skram's spirit and resilience and Viggo Hørup's kindness and wit. But as we discuss their forms of self-presentation, we hide behind our own masks of disinterestedness. Epistolary relationships in their collaborative and literary aspects remain a source of endless fascination for the voyeur in all of us.

Notes

1. This was not the first crisis between them. After their marriage in 1885 she had settled in Copenhagen and dedicated herself to a literary career, with all of the financial and emotional risks that entailed. Between 1885 and 1892 she published six novels and several collections of short stories. The third volume of *Hellemyrsfolket* was published in 1890, a year after the birth of her daughter. In 1894, while working on the final volume, 'Avkom' (Offspring), she suffered a mental breakdown and was hospitalized in the Copenhagen City Hospital, under the care of Professor Knud Pontoppidan. Both her health and her marriage were damaged by this experience. *Professor Hieronimus* and *Paa St. Jørgen*, published in 1895, express her anger at both her husband and the psychiatric establishment that kept her hospitalized against her will.
2. For more about Viggo Hørup's political and personal life, see Karsten Thorborg's introduction to Chapter IX, 'Brevveksling med Amalie Skram', *Hørup i breve og digte* (København: Akademisk Forlag, 1981), p. 305.
3. Both sides of the correspondence – fifty-three letters and cards written between 1896 and 1902 – can be found in the manuscript division of the Royal Library and the Danish National Archives in Copenhagen.
4. *Hørup i breve og digte* (HBD), p. 320. All subsequent quotations from the letters of Amalie Skram and Viggo Hørup will refer to this text.
5. Translations from the Danish and Norwegian texts are my own.
6. The letter he is responding to is missing from the archives in

Copenhagen. She has apparently told him about Erik's affair.
7. In Amalie Skram's first novel *Constance Ring*, the young wife gets the same advice from all sides – Pastor Huhn, as well as her family and friends: Constance should ignore her husband's infidelity and turn the other cheek.
8. A number of her letters refer to visits with Hørup's wife and daughter, as well as to dinner invitations, and visits to the Hørup family at their country house.
9. The two previous quotes were not included in HBD. The entire text of the letter is in the Manuscript Division of the Royal Library in Copenhagen (NKS 5006).
10. In this letter Viggo Hørup refers to things she has said earlier, either in a meeting (perhaps the Saturday meeting mentioned in her letter of 31 December) or in a letter that has not been preserved. He may have burned it at her request.
11. See note 6.
12. 'Post festum' was published in the November/December 1896 issue of *Tilskueren*, pp. 823-40.
13. Borchsenius was a well-known journalist in Copenhagen. He was the editor of *Morgenbladet*, a rival paper of Hørup's *Politiken*.
14. This section of the letter was not included in HBD. The complete text can be found in the Royal Library.
15. Amalie Skram first uses the personal form of the pronoun to address him in her letter of 9 February 1899. He first addresses her as 'du' in his letter of May 19, 1899. By this time their relationship has settled into a cordial, exchange of a few letters a year. He presumably feels confident that the intimacy will not be misunderstood.
16. She was divorced from Erik Skram in January 1900.
17. Valdemar Irminger was a Danish painter with whom she corresponded from 1896 until shortly before her death in 1905.

14

Amalie Skram and her Publishers

Katherine Hanson
University of Washington

The letters Amalie Skram wrote to publishers contain the strands of multiple stories. Most prominently they document a publication history that is at times as dramatic as the fiction she wrote. They witness to the obstacles encountered by a female author who, at the end of the nineteenth century, wrote of female sexual experience, and they reveal the strategies she used to promote herself and her work. The correspondence also creates a composite picture of the personality writing the letters and, when considered chronologically, charts the emotional turmoils of her career.

Some one hundred and thirty of the letters Skram sent to publishers have been preserved and they are housed in the Manuscript Departments of two major libraries: the Royal Library in Copenhagen and the University Library in Oslo. They were written over a period of twenty years, from 1884 to her death in 1905, and the majority were addressed to five men: Frederik V. Hegel, his son Jacob Hegel, Gustav Philipsen, Paul Langhoff and Peter Nansen. Though not a publisher in the same sense as the other men (he did not own the publishing house he represented), Nansen should nonetheless be included among them because of the central role he played during his association with Gyldendal.

Frederick V. Hegel, Patriarch of Gyldendal
Amalie Skram's career as a novelist commenced with her marriage to Danish author and critic Erik Skram in the spring of 1884. She

had, of course, been writing and publishing in newspapers and journals while living in Kristiania, and indeed, her reputation as an astute and enthusiastic reviewer of contemporary literature preceded her arrival in Copenhagen. Among those who took note of Erik Skram's handsome and talented new wife was Frederik V. Hegel, legendary patriarch of Gyldendalske Boghandel.

The couple had only been married a few months when Hegel started sending books he had recently published to Amalie Skram. He probably assumed it would please her to own and read these books, but he no doubt also hoped these gifts would result in review articles sent to the Norwegian press. To a large degree it was Hegel's respect for Skram's work as a literary critic that led him, in the early spring of 1885, to accept her novel, *Constance Ring*, for publication, sight unseen.

But before she revealed her literary aspirations to Hegel, she wrote and thanked him for the books he had sent. There are two such letters, dated 22 September 1884 and 7 December 1884, full of enthusiasm and warm thanks. Skram assumes a respectful yet familiar tone, addressing Hegel by his honorary title, Justitsråd. The body of both letters is devoted to a discussion of the books she has received, and she presents herself as an observant and intelligent reader who is au courant with the contemporary literary debate. Her commentary is lively, interwoven with snatches of letters from Bjørnstjerne Bjørnson and Alexander Kielland, and while her writing seems more spontaneous than shrewd or calculating, one does sense her eagerness to establish a relationship with the old man.

It appears Skram was more interested in cultivating a friendship than establishing a strictly business relationship, for at the conclusion of the 7 December letter she confides in Hegel that he reminded her of a cherished teacher she had as a girl:

Når jeg tænker på dem er det altid som at mindes noget rigtig godt og kjært. Jeg har noget af den samme følelse for dem som ligeoverfor en gammel, elskelig lærer jeg havde i min barndom, et menneske der har sat sig fast i mit hjærte for bestandig.[1]

(When I think of you, it's always like remembering something really good and precious. I have for you some of the same feeling I have for an endearing, old teacher I had in my childhood, a person who has found a place in my heart forever.)[2]

There is a sense of confidence and ease in these words. Skram seems to be comfortable in her role as bright and diligent student and assumes Hegel will gladly accept his role as revered teacher. By sending her books and welcoming her commentary, Hegel had indeed encouraged Skram to pursue her literary interests. Wasn't it reasonable of her to interpret his expressed interest as a willingness to be her mentor?

By the following March 1885, Frederik V. Hegel had acknowledged Amalie Skram's literary aspirations and agreed to publish *Constance Ring*. Erik Skram had apparently approached Hegel about publishing his wife's manuscript, and he continued to act as go-between while the book was being typeset, until news reached the Skrams that Hegel might refuse to publish Amalie's novel. Hegel had not anticipated a book so bold in language and content, and as he read the printer's sheets, he became increasingly troubled.

When Amalie Skram realized her book was in danger, she acted with dispatch and resolve. She launched a letter campaign, in the first instance to garner support and then, when she realized Hegel's refusal was firm, to negotiate for another publisher.[3] These are among the most eloquent and persuasive of Skram's business letters, written by a woman determined to get her novel into print and thereby launch her professional career. The enthusiastic and affectionate schoolgirl is nowhere evident in the three letters Skram wrote Hegel in May 1885. The persona she projects in these letters is at once more mature and masculine as she presents her case calmly and rationally. Always courteous and respectful, she nonetheless protests his action and challenges his reasoning, claiming he has treated her book wrongly and unfairly:

den skade min bog lider ved at være bleven tilbagevist af dem efter at den sågodtsom var sat færdig er af langt større omfang i sin art og sine følger end den, det Gyldendalske forlag vilde have pådraget sig ved at stå som dens udgiver. Jeg tror at firmaet er stærkt og anset nok til at have kunnet bære den 'tort'. Hvad bogen derimod angår, så er den ved denne tilbagevisning på forhånd stemplet som en forkastelig vare.

(The damage my book suffers from being rejected by you after the typesetting was nearly completed, will be of far greater proportions in its nature and consequences than whatever Gyldendal Company would have incurred by going ahead with publication. I believe that the firm is both strong and distinguished enough to have been able to bear this 'injury'. In the book's case, this repudiation stamps it in advance as a reprehensible product. – 1 May 1885)

Although Skram was not able to persuade Hegel to retract his refusal, she did succeed in holding him to his promise to pay her honorarium and to cover printing and typesetting costs until such time as she found another publisher for *Constance Ring*. But just as she had predicted, the book's history was a deterrent to potential publishers. When Skram turned to Gustav Philipsen,[4] he said he would gladly have published *Constance Ring* had she come to him first. But for him to publish a book that Hegel had refused would be to risk accusations from the conservative press that he actively sought to promote and defend an 'immoral' book. He considered the matter for a few days, but ultimately declined.

There is no indication that Skram tried other publishing houses. In an undated letter to Georg Brandes, who had agreed to read the proof sheets and share his opinion of the book with Philipsen, Skram writes that she will not take her book to Andreas Schou, for

hvis han nu beviste mig den tjeneste at udgive bogen på sit forlag, efterat Hegel har vist den fra sig, så var det jo en selvfølgelig sag, at jeg siden gik til ham med hvad jeg fik skrevet. Og jeg vilde så langt, langt hellere ha med Philipsen at gjøre.

(if he were to show me the kindness of publishing the book, after Hegel has refused it, then it would be a matter of course that I go to him with what I subsequently write. And I would much, much rather deal with Philipsen.)

As intent as she was on finding a publisher for her first novel, she was also keeping her eye on the future. Skram was determined to bring her novel out uncensored, but she did not want to entrust her subsequent production to a publisher in whom she did not have complete confidence. Her solution was to negotiate with Olaf Huseby, a bookseller in Kristiania, to take *Constance Ring* on commission.

Reading the many letters Amalie Skram wrote on behalf and in defense of *Constance Ring* is a little like reading a novel published in instalments. The narrative is driven by suspense and intrigue, and the character of the protagonist becomes clearer with each new instalment. The fledgling novelist demonstrates that she has the poise and rhetorical skill to defend herself and her work and the courage to stand her ground. She is adamant that her novel addresses itself to the ongoing morality debate; that it is a serious and honest attempt to depict the situation as she sees it, and as such deserves a hearing. Moreover, she freely acknowledges that *Constance Ring* is just the beginning, and that she fully intends to pursue a career writing books and getting them published.

Launching a Career without a Publisher

What did it mean for Amalie Skram to lose Hegel as a publisher just as she was launching her career? The biggest publishing house in Scandinavia, Gyldendal was in a position to offer its authors unparalleled advantages: it had a market capacity that extended throughout Scandinavia; more than any other house it was the gateway to Europe; and the conditions Gyldendal offered its authors were as good as if not better than they would find elsewhere. Hegel promoted his books aggressively, made sure they were advertised in the press, even made personal visits to newspaper and journal editors to expedite review articles. But beyond his promotional activities, Frederik V. Hegel was legendary for the personal relationships he established and maintained with his authors. He was a tireless correspondent and in his letters he offered support and encouragement, gave advice on personal as well as business matters, and passed on gossip of mutual friends and acquaintances.

Amalie Skram was aware that Gyldendal's authors set great store by the letters they received from Hegel. In her letter to Hegel of 7 December 1884, she related that Alexander Kielland had complained in a letter to Erik Skram that his friends in Copenhagen wrote so seldom. "'E. Brandes er forresten ret trofast" siger han, "men" føjer han til – "den gamle herre i Klareboderne er dog den bedste"' ('E. Brandes is a faithful correspondent,' he says, 'but,' he adds, 'the old gentleman in Klareboderne is the best'). Given the auspicious beginning of Skram's relationship with Hegel, there can be little doubt that she would have been the beneficiary of his support and encouragement, had circumstances been different.

In his book *Digterne og Gyldendal* (The Authors and Gyldendal), published in 1970, Niels Wamberg chronicles the correspondence between Gyldendal's editors and authors for a little over a century. Interestingly, the first part of the book, covering Frederik V. Hegel's tenure, is dominated by Norwegian writers.

Bjørnstjerne Bjørnson was the first of the big four[5] to come to Gyldendal in the summer of 1860, and he proved to be an enthusiastic recruiter of Norwegian talent to the Danish publishing house. In a letter to Hegel he modestly claims: 'Jeg har ikke alene, kjære Hegel, skaffet Dem Ibsen og Lie, jeg har skaffet Dem hver eneste norsk på Deres lager, dels direkte (som fru Thoresen, Welhaven, fru Collett) dels indirekte' (I have not only, dear Hegel, brought you Ibsen and Lie, I have brought you every single Norwegian in your house, in part directly (as Mrs. Thoresen, Welhaven, Mrs. Collett) in part indirectly, p. 30).[6] Bjørnson was effusive in his affection for Hegel and he relied and depended on him like a father. In 1868 he wrote: 'De ejer al den sikkerhed, jeg har i verden' (You are the source of all the security I have in the world, p. 37).

Ibsen was less effusive than Bjørnson, but no less mindful of the gratitude he owed Hegel for his literary success. Ibsen came to Gyldendal in 1865 and ten years later he wrote to Hegel: 'Ingen har således som De bidraget til forskjellen mellem nu og da for mit vedkommende' (No one has contributed to the difference in my circumstances between now and then as much as you have, p. 52). And on another occasion he told Hegel: 'Det blev et vendepunkt i mit forfatterliv som i mine vilkår, da jeg kom i forbindelse med Dem som forlægger' (It marked a turning point in my life as an author as well as in my living conditions when you became my publisher, p. 52). In the early, uncertain years of their careers Hegel meant security, financial and psychological, for Bjørnson and Ibsen. And he provided this security not only with his money, but through his role as collaborator and partner. In his study *Victorian Novelists and Publishers* J. A. Sutherland argues that 'the publisher's skills were often as instrumental to success as anything the author might contribute. A good house could take material as unpromising as an unknown novelist's 'Manchester Love Story' and turn it into the bestseller we know as *Mary Barton*; a bad one could bring a novel as great as *Wuthering Heights* to still birth.'[7] Furthermore, Sutherland concurs with Wamberg that authors often valued their publisher more as friend and mentor than business partner.

In the early years of her career Amalie Skram had to manage without the encouragement and security of a publisher, though to be sure, she had her supporters. Erik Skram played an invaluable role in his wife's writing career, acting as a kind of in-house editor. And her correspondence from that period reveals that there were other mentors as well, male colleagues such as Arne Garborg, who wrote a lengthy review of *Constance Ring* in the Norwegian press, and the Danish author Sophus Schandorph. But the friend she admired more than any other, Bjørnson, is conspicuously absent from this chapter of her life. Conspicuous because of his self-appointed role as recruiter of Norwegian authors to Gyldendal, and because of the close friendship that had developed between the two since the late 1870s.

Bjørnson's failure to participate was not out of indifference, but out of a conviction that Amalie Skram did not have the makings of an author. In July 1885, after *Constance Ring* had finally come out, he wrote to her: 'At du gav dig til at skrive en bok har harmet mig; at du fik lov til at gi den ut af din man, har ærgret og skuffet mig'[8] (That you set about writing a book has angered me; that your husband allowed you to publish it has annoyed and disappointed me, p.63). This letter brought about a hiatus in their correspondence, which was not resumed until 1892. A series of letters the two exchanged in April 1893 provides a clear indication of how deeply Skram was wounded by Bjørnson's rejection. She aired her grievances and he acknowledged his mistaken judgement, albeit grudgingly. She reminded him 'Jeg skrev dengang i min vånde til Dig og klaget over at Hegel havde protesteret bogen og at Huseby gjorde vanskeligheder. Jeg tror sikkert, jeg bad Dig hjælpe mig' (At the time, I wrote to you in my distress and complained that Hegel had rejected the book and that Huseby was causing difficulties. I'm sure I asked you to help me, p. 83). And Bjørnson fired back that as long as he didn't believe she could or should become an author, 'gav jeg fæn i dine mange påfun og dit stræv for såvidt, og at Hegel ikke ville være med holdt jeg for bevis' (I didn't give a damn about all your notions or your efforts, for that matter, and the fact that Hegel wanted nothing to do with it was proof enough for me, p. 87). The gates to Gyldendal were well guarded. Bjørnson's failure to participate in 'mit livs største begivenhed' (the biggest event in my life, p. 79), as Skram puts it, was essentially a vote of no confidence. And she made clear her devastation when she wrote him 'det gav mig et knæk for livet' (it was a blow that did irreparable harm – p.79).

But Amalie Skram continued to write, even without the support of Bjørnson and Hegel, and the years between 1885 and 1893 were the most intensely creative in her life: she produced six novels, two plays and numerous stories. Two fairly long stories appeared in *Tilskueren* in 1886, and in 1887 the first two volumes of *Hellemyrsfolket* (The People of Hellemyr) were published by Salmonsen forlag, a small publishing house established in 1871. But like *Constance Ring*, *Sjur Gabriel* and *To Venner* (Two Friends) had been taken by Salmonsen on commission, an arrangement whereby Salmonsen put up the money for production, and once production costs had been covered by book sales, profits were shared by author and publisher. There remains only one letter Skram wrote to Salmonsen, from November 1887: a short, business-like letter in which she thanks him for his kind words about her book, and also for heeding her request that he not give the conservative *Morgenbladet* a review copy of her novel. She mentions an agreement that he would contact *Politiken* about a review – he still hadn't done it – and she reports that two journals, *Tilskueren* and *Nyt Tidsskrift*, would review both books together. The job of promoting the books and soliciting reviews seems to have fallen to her.

Finding a Publisher for *Lucie*

Four months later Skram was looking for a new publisher. The story of her search is revealed through her correspondence, but hardly in a straightforward manner. Unsure of herself and fearing a negative outcome, Skram withholds information and seems uncharacteristically reticent in her negotiations with a potential publisher.

On 24 March 1888 Skram wrote to Gustav Philipsen requesting a meeting with him. She states her errand at the beginning of the letter: she wants him to become her publisher. It may appear that she already has a publisher, she writes, 'men det er bare humbug, for bøgerne er forlagt af mig selv, og endskjøndt der er gode resultater, siger hr. Salmonsen dog at han ingen penger har til at udbetale honorarer' (but that's just humbug, because the books are self-published, and even though the results have been good, Mr. Salmonsen nonetheless says that he has no money to pay my honorarium). Since sales couldn't possibly have covered production costs by then, Skram hadn't earned anything from *Sjur Gabriel* and *To Venner*.[9] This must have been extremely discouraging, especially given the couple's strapped finances. Still, in this letter to Philipsen one senses that more than money even, Skram wants to have a publisher who will stand behind her and the books she writes. 'Men jeg kan ikke fordrage at *jeg* alene skal være uden forlægger; alle andre har jo en,' she exclaims, 'det er bare mig som ingen har, og det harmer mig' (But I can't bear it that I alone should be without a publisher; all the others have one, I'm the only one who doesn't, and it angers me). She has completed another novel, she goes on to tell him, not a continuation of *Hellemyrsfolket*, but something completely different 'som slår lige ned i alt sædelighedsrabalderet' (that strikes right at all the uproar over the morality debate). The book is *Lucie*, and she asks if she might come and read it to him, ostensibly because her handwriting is so bad, but she very likely thought she would be better able to influence his impression if she presented it in person. She knew her new book was as controversial in its content as *Constance Ring* had been.

Ten days later, 4 April, she sent Philipsen another letter. Contrary to what they agreed upon at their meeting, she would not be sending the manuscript. Not because of any agreement she had with Salmonsen, she assured him, because she had none. But because she was sure Philipsen wouldn't want to publish the book. 'Derfor har jeg tænkt at det er både bedre og rigtigere at spare Dem og mig for den ubehagelighet at gi og få et afslag' (I have therefore thought it was both better and more proper to save you and me from the unpleasantness of giving and receiving a refusal). Skram is very composed and business-like in this letter, but her vulnerability fairly jumps off the page. The letter gives the unmistakable impression that there is more to the story than she divulges.

A letter Skram wrote to Schandorph and his wife, Ida, reveals what she was withholding and how she finally found a publisher. The Schandorphs lived in Paris for a number of years and during that time Amalie Skram and Schandorph exchanged long letters. Toward the end of a twelve page letter dated 31 July 1888, Skram confided:

> Forresten har jeg havt en tid fuld af lejelser og modgang...Jeg havde skrevet en roman 'Lucie,' og kunde ikke få Salmonsen til at forlægge den. Han var ræd for indholdet. Så sank jeg mig ned i pessimisme, måneder igjennem og troede at min tid var forbi, tog frem gammelt linned og dækketøj og sad og stoppede og lappede og fik endda flere grå hår end jeg alt havde.

> (I've actually been through a period of unpleasantness and adversity... I had written a novel, *Lucie*, and couldn't get Salmonsen to publish it. He was afraid of the content. So I sank into despondency, for months, and thought my time was over; I took out old linen and table cloths and sat mending and darning and got more grey hairs than I already had.)

And while she was mending old linen, she relates in her letter, Herman Bang was begging her to let him take the manuscript to Schubothe. Skram, however, was sure Schubothe wouldn't take it and didn't want to go through the humiliation of refusal a second time. Then she awoke one morning and decided she should leave no stone unturned, so she sent her son to tell Herman Bang to go ahead and try Schubothe. Schubothe replied that it would be 'en ære at få mig på sit forlag' (an honor to have me in his publishing house) and asked to read the manuscript. 'Så læste han den og tog den uden at blinke, uden at ymte et muk om uanstændighed eller sligt noget. Til mig skrev han at han havde læst manuskriptet med *stor* beundring og *stor* interesse' (Then he read it and took it without blinking, without uttering a word about indecency or anything like that. To me he wrote that he'd read the manuscript with *great* admiration and *great* interest). Amalie Skram had finally found a publisher and she was overjoyed: 'Siden den dag er jeg blet som et andet menneske,' she told Schandorphs (Since that day I've become another person.)

The situation Skram found herself in with *Lucie* must have felt depressingly familiar. Once again she had written a book a publisher had refused on grounds the contents were immoral. Once again she had made an appeal to Philipsen, only this time she had not laid all her cards on the table. Presumably she kept silent about Salmonsen's unwillingness to publish *Lucie* because she feared Philipsen would respond exactly as he had when she brought him a book Hegel had refused. Perhaps she broke off negotiations with Philipsen because she felt uneasy about not having been entirely truthful with him – he might hear the whole story from Salmonsen, after all. Or perhaps she really was convinced that a woman who wrote realistic novels about relationships between contemporary women and men would be treated like a pariah by respectable publishers, and there was little use trying to interest them in her work.

In the 1990s it is hard to imagine a controversial book that would fail to bring in money hand over fist. But one hundred years ago conservative attitudes and opinions so dominated Scandinavian society that the individual who defied conventional mores risked ostracism and the economic consequences it carried. After *Ghosts* had been published, Ibsen asked Hegel if the book was not selling well because of all the controversy in the press. Hegel replied: 'De spørger: Har al denne allarm skadet bogens afsætning? Og hertil må jeg avgjort svare: ja' (You ask: has all this uproar damaged the book's sale? And to that I must decidedly answer: yes). Many preordered books were being returned. 'Også på Deres ældre arbejder har det hele udøvet tilbagevirkende kraft' (The whole affair has had a retroactive effect on your earlier works as well).[10] Hindsight tells us any damage done to Gyldendal or Ibsen was temporary and of little consequence, but the fact remains that from a publisher's point of view the economic risk involved with bringing out a controversial book was very real.

Paul Langhoff and Schubothes Boghandel
In 1888 Schubothes Boghandel was owned and directed by Paul Langhoff. The firm had been in the Langhoff family since 1828 when Paul's grandfather became owner of the house Johan Henrik

Schubothe had established in 1795. Paul's father suffered from poor health and he died before his son was able to assume ownership of the business. Family members ran the business in the interim, but it did not prosper, and when Paul Langhoff took over in 1883, he was determined to restore the publishing house to its former prominence. He actively sought to enhance his list with young writers. Twenty-one of the letters Amalie Skram wrote to Langhoff have been preserved, along with eight he wrote to her or Erik. The letters from her were written between January 1890 and November 1891, a period of almost two years. The letters from him span the years he published her books, 1888 through 1893.

The relationship between publisher and author, as seen through these letters, is strictly a business one, though on occasion Skram did write something about her personal life, usually to explain why she wasn't able to meet a deadline. Her third child, a little girl, was born in October 1889, and she is mentioned once or twice. Another time she said that she was sitting for a portrait, a project that was taking an inordinate amount of time, and in one or two letters she expresses thanks for invitations or parties. In a couple of letters she described the writing process (she was working on *Fru Inés* at the time) and these are brief, intense, hurried letters. In many more letters she complained about how hard she worked, how her writing exhausted her, and how discouraged she became because she got so little return for her efforts. The return, income earned, is a recurrent worry in most of the letters to Langhoff.

Skram wrote about money, in some form or other, in twelve of the twenty-one letters. A publisher was like a bank for an author. Once a project had been accepted, and an honorarium had been set, the author could ask for an advance, something which Skram did consistently. This meant that a good deal of the honorarium had already been spent when the author finally turned in the last chapter of the manuscript. And so the author had to come up with another project that would hopefully result in another advance.

S. G. Myhre was published in late spring 1890. *Børnefortellinger* (Childrens' Stories) came out in the fall of 1890. And on 4 January 1891 Skram wrote to Langhoff proposing another collection of stories. For the most part they were old pieces that had appeared in journals, but she also had 'en længre fortælling på stabelen, som skulle bli bogens cloû' (a longer story in the making that would be the highlight of the book) – that was *Fru Inés*. She knew that *Børnefortellinger* had not done very well, so it wouldn't surprise her if he turned her down. Still, she reasoned, he was a young man, and could figure on making money on her books after she died. She was resigned to the fact her books would not be popular during her lifetime: 'Jeg ved det nemlig så sikkert: aldrig kommer jeg at skrive min samtid tillags' (I know with certainty: never will I write what satisfies my contemporaries).

Langhoff agreed to publish the book and offered her a contract. Her immediate response was to haggle about the honorarium. An author was paid so many *kroner* per broadsheet, usually between 50 and 60, depending upon the size of the print run. The bigger the print run, the bigger the honorarium. At this point in Skram's career between 1000 and 1500 copies of her books were printed. Dickering with Langhoff for larger printings was another angle she used in an effort to increase her income.

When she had no luck convincing Langhoff to increase her honorarium or print run, she approached her publisher with another proposition. In five letters, all from January and February of 1891, she pleaded with Langhoff to buy the remaindered copies of *Sjur Gabriel* and *To Venner* from Salmonsen which, she told him, really meant buying them from her. Langhoff was already selling *Constance Ring* on commission, and she wanted to have all her books with Schubothe. Salmonsen didn't advertise the books at all, she told Langhoff, and she was sure sales would improve if he took them. Langhoff didn't reject her proposal outright – maybe, at some later date, when the fourth volume was completed, he could publish the entire cycle on subscription. Skram countered his reservations with new arguments, and finally offered him a price that seems ridiculously low. *Sjur* retailed at 2 *kroner*, *To Venner* at 3; he could have *Sjur* for 50 øre and *To Venner* for 75 øre. She didn't know how many books there were because she had not received an account sheet for several years – this was not an unusual complaint from authors whose books were taken on commission. But Langhoff presumably did his own calculations and decided it would not be a good investment.

Langhoff's letters to Skram are courteous and patient. He tried to explain the economics of his decisions, when he did not meet her demands. He did not meddle or interfere with her writing. More than once she expressed her appreciation to him on both counts. She thanked him for not being angry over her requests or outbursts, and she assured him she was glad he was her publisher: '[De] har vært så *grej* bestandig og så chemisk renset for frygt og betænkeligheder og indvendinger af nogensom helst art' ([You] have always been so *straightforward* and so chemically free of fear and misgivings and objections of any sort whatsoever, 18.11.91). But she felt discouraged and depressed that no matter how hard she worked and struggled, no matter how much she produced, she didn't advance and received no increase in her honorarium. There are veiled threats in her letters that she would stop writing and look for other work. She had no illusions she would earn significantly more, but at least the work wouldn't be so exhausting.

Langhoff did not respond to these cries of despair, at least not in writing. There are no words of encouragement or support in his letters. Paul Langhoff was Amalie Skram's much appreciated publisher with whom she 'collaborated' on the publication of six books.[11] But their business relationship does not appear to have developed into a friendship.

Jacob Hegel and the Move to Gyldendal
By the end of 1891 Skram had realized that as long as she stayed with Langhoff, she would never earn enough to meet her expenses. In November 1891 she wrote to Langhoff about the publication of a new collection of stories[12] in three letters dated the 16th, 18th and 27th. In the midst of these negotiations, marked by anger and frustration on her part and gentle but firm refusals to increase her honorarium on Langhoff's, Skram decided to make new overtures to Gyldendal, a company far exceeding Schubothes Boghandel in size and wealth.

On 20 November 1891 Amalie Skram sent a letter to Jacob Hegel, who had assumed full ownership of Gyldendalske Boghandel when his father, Frederik V. Hegel, died in 1887. The letter was written in anticipation of an annual statement from Gyldendal, a record of the debt she had incurred with Frederik V. Hegel for the printing and typesetting of *Constance Ring*. Addressing the letter to Most Honourable hr. Jacob Hegel, Skram assumes a tone that is respectful, apologetic and humble. She presents herself as the chagrined but responsible debtor who wishes to acquit herself, and she graciously acknowledges 'den mageløse tålmodighed, hvormed firmaets nuværende indehaver har optrådt imod mig' (the exceptional patience with which the firm's current owner has acted toward me). The overt purpose of her letter is to propose that she repay her debt to Gyldendal with her work, and here she is very careful not to say that she doesn't earn enough money; her failure to make payments on her debt is attributed to 'uventede udgifter' (unexpected expenses) which never cease: her sons from her first marriage continue to need her help, and now she and Erik Skram have a two-year-old daughter. But in addition to addressing this painful and embarrassing issue, Skram appears to be testing the waters. Toward the end of the letter she asks Hegel directly: 'Og nu spør jeg Dem: kunde det ikke tænkes at De tog en eller anden bog af mig i ny og næ, en som ikke var altfor gal, eller ville vække altfor stor forargelse' (And now I ask you: isn't it conceivable that you might take one or another of my books now and then, one that wasn't too bad, or wouldn't arouse too much indignation). Striking a balance between humility and confidence in her work she goes on:

Jeg har jo dog i disse 6 à 7 år, jeg har skrevet efter fattig lejlighed erhvervet mig en smule navn, og det anses ikke længer for en uoverkommelig skandale at udgi eller kjøbe en bog af mig. I altfald sælges der en god del af mine bøger oppe i Norge og hernede da også for den sags skyld.

(During the 6 to 7 years I've been writing, to the best of my abilities, I have acquired a bit of a name, and it is no longer considered to be an insurmountable scandal to publish or purchase a book by me. In any case quite a few of my books have been sold up in Norway, and down here too as far as that goes.)

  Amalie Skram apparently did not save the letters she received from Jacob Hegel, for all that remains are drafts of letters he wrote to her. One of these drafts, undated, must have been written in response to the appeal Skram made in November 1891. Hegel thanks her warmly for her letter and suggests that he pay her a visit in her home 'for at takke Dem personligt for Deres Skrivelse og for at foreslaa Dem en Maade at ordne Sagen paa' (to personally thank you for your letter and to suggest to you a way in which the matter can be taken care of). Skram sent Hegel a second letter on 26 November 1891 and the persona she projects in this letter is much less guarded; she is emotional, almost ebullient. Hegel has offered to strike her debt from the ledger and Skram is happy and relieved. Words fail her, and she instead 'rækker Dem i tankerne begge mine hænder og siger tak og atter tak!' ([I] extend both hands to you in my thoughts and say thank you, thank you!). The formality of the previous letter has been abandoned. She opens the letter 'Kjære hr. Hegel' (Dear Mr. Hegel), and the closing also indicates greater confidence and warmth on her part. She closed her first letter 'med venlig hilsen til Deres hustru er jeg Deres ærbødigst forbundne' (with friendly greetings to your wife I am most respectfully yours). Less than a week later she writes 'jeg ber Dem at hilse og takke Deres søde hustru tusen gange fra mig. Deres hengivne ...' (I beg you to greet and thank your sweet wife a thousand times from me. Sincerely yours ...).

The dynamics of the relationship that would develop between Skram and Hegel is already evident in these two letters. The persona Skram creates for Jacob Hegel is of a patient, kind and all-powerful benefactor. But the author who asserted herself so aggressively in written negotiations with Langhoff takes on a humbler persona in letters to Hegel. Skram is grateful for Hegel's generosity to the point of feeling beholden, and she seems unable to accept the fact that her account is settled. She insists there must be some way she can repay him, translation work, for example, and almost pleads with him to use her services: 'De aner vistnok neppe *hvor* glad jeg derved vilde bli. Og hvis det kun var noget ordentligt, noget rigtig slid og slæb vilde glæden bli så meget desto større' (You can scarcely know *how* glad that would make me. And if it were only something proper, some real drudgery, my happiness would be all the greater). The humiliation Skram felt over her failure to acquit herself of a debt was certainly compounded by the nature of the debt: costs covered by Gyldendal for a book Hegel's father had refused to publish.

Skram didn't write to Hegel again until May 1893, a year and a half later. She wrote three letters that month, one of them undated, and all three deal with Gyldendal's pending decision to publish the fourth volume of *Hellemyrsfolket*. The undated letter appears to be the first in the series and was clearly written by Amalie the strategist. She alludes to a meeting between Erik Skram and Hegel: 'Jeg blev *meget* glad da Skram kom hjem og sa, at De ikke i og for sig havde noget imod at forlægge mig' (I was *very* happy when Skram came home and said that you weren't opposed to publishing me per se). Once again Erik had acted as go-between for his wife and Gyldendal. Amalie's strategy at this point was to send articles, published in *Samtiden*, about the first three volumes of *Hellemyrsfolket* in the hope that they would strengthen her case with Gyldendal. She feared Hegel might not fully appreciate those books because of the Norwegian dialect her Danish readers found so difficult, and she hastened to assure him there would be much less dialect in the last volume.

But the biggest hurdle she felt she had to overcome with Hegel was her reputation as an author who wrote controversial, if not immoral, books. The spectre of *Constance Ring* must have weighed oppressively on Skram as she awaited a second verdict from Gyldendal. Exactly eight years after her unsuccessful attempt to persuade Frederik V. Hegel to publish her book, she tried to dispel any fears Jacob Hegel might have with two arguments:

For det første er nu folk vant til at det er 'fælt' hvad der kommer fra mig ... Og for det andet blir det mindre og mindre slemt det, jeg har på hjærtet. Jeg får efterhånden skrevet fra mig al min indignation og alt det pinlige jeg har set i verden og så blir det jeg har at meddele lysere og mildere, skjøndt nogen sukkergodtforfatter blir jeg aldrig.

(In the first place, people are used to the fact that anything coming from me will be 'awful' ... In the second place, what I have to say is less and less bad. Little by little I have written all my indignation and all the painful things I've seen in the world out of me. So what I have to tell is lighter and milder, though I'll never be any sugar-and-sweetness author.)

There is a disarming blend of persuasion and honesty in her argument.

Finally, she sought to assure Hegel that she was a sound financial risk. Her former publisher, Schubothe, could attest to that:

Langhoff har altid været så strålende fornøjet og har sagt at mine bøger gik udmærket, særlig var 'Lucie' og 'S.G.Myre' solgt på halvhundred eksemplarer nær (hans egne bogstavelige ord). Det var kun 'Fjældmennesker' han havde tabt på og 'Børnefortellinger' som knebent havde dækket sig.

(Langhoff has always been so wonderfully satisfied and said that my books have done well, in particular *Lucie* and *S.G.Myre* have sold to almost the last fifty copies (his very own words). *Fjældmennesker* was the only book he'd lost money on, and *Børnefortellinger* had just about covered costs.)

But, she candidly told Hegel, Langhoff had also hinted that Schubothe could no longer support her. When she had recently approached him about an advance so she could travel to Bergen and do research necessary for her book, his convoluted answer had concluded with the suggestion that she might like to try another publisher. She is careful not to speak critically of Langhoff, but to give Hegel the impression that she would be an agreeable and appreciative author.

Jacob Hegel's decision, in the spring of 1893, was to take a chance with Amalie Skram. On 12 May she wrote 'Tak for De vilde ha mig på Deres forlag' (Thank you for wanting to have me at your publishing house). And then straight to the point: 'Vilde De ha den store godhet at gi mig 600kr i forskud?' (Would you be so very kind as to give me 600 kroner in advance?). Hegel met her request willingly and promptly and took advantage of the opportunity to offer a bit of cautionary advice regarding the subject matter of future books. Her response to Hegel, in a letter dated 17 May, is remarkably acquiescent:

Deres ord til Skram om så meget som muligt at fly de 'vovede' emner, skal jeg lægge mig alvorligt og *inderligt* på sinde. Jeg har sandelig hverken glæde eller fordel af det modsatte. Tværtimod! Men det er denne forbistrede samvittighedsfuldhed og syge ærlighedstrang ligeover *mit arbejde*, som volder ulykken ... når nu manuskriptet er færdigt, skal De læse det og udpege de stygge steder, og da skal jeg rette og forandre så vidt muligt.

(Your words to Skram, about avoiding 'risqué' topics as much as possible, I shall take gravely and sincerely to heart. Indeed, it brings me neither pleasure nor profit to do the opposite. Quite the contrary! But it is this infernal scrupulousness and sick need for honesty toward *my work*, that causes all the trouble ... When the manuscript is finished, you must read it and point out the bad places, and then I'll make corrections and changes as far as possible.)

There is no evidence in the correspondence that Skram was ever censored by Jacob Hegel, but the worry that she would transgress the boundaries of propriety was never dispelled. As late as May 1900, a few months after she and Erik Skram had divorced, she expressed concern that there might be things in her new book 'som folk kalder "vovet"' (that people call 'risqué'). And she asked Hegel if he and his wife would be willing to read through her manuscript and advise her.

It is hard to detect in these words the woman who had earlier so staunchly defended *Constance Ring* to Jacob Hegel's father. Anyone familiar with the books Skram subsequently wrote knows that she did not compromise her integrity as a writer, and yet the insecurity expressed in these letters to Hegel is unmistakable. The years since her struggle to find a publisher for *Constance Ring* had taken their toll. Her books, as well as her person, were subjected to vigorous attacks by conservatives. This made it difficult to get her books published, had a negative effect on sales, and undermined her chances of receiving government stipends. Skram recognized that there was a direct relationship between her status as an author who wrote offensive and immoral books and her precarious financial situation, and understood that in order to win the backing of Gyldendalske Boghandel she would have to convince Hegel of her eagerness to avoid 'de vovede emner' (the risqué topics).

Jacob Hegel was Amalie Skram's publisher from 1893 until her death in 1905, and during this time she wrote over thirty letters to him. Money is at the heart of most of the letters, be it discussing an honorarium, asking for an advance or thanking for one, complaining about the exorbitant fee of a proof reader or the size of her debt to Gyldendal. Though these are ostensibly business letters, Skram shares much more of her personal life with Hegel than she did with Langhoff. Skram's years with Gyldendal were marked by emotional crises and failing health with resultant periods of reduced productivity. In 'begging' letters requesting additional advances, Skram was moved to explain the

Amalie Skram and her Publishers

circumstances preventing her from meeting her deadlines: domestic concerns, her own poor health, the failing health of her mother and brother.

Personal confidences culminate in a letter written 20 November 1899 in which she informed Hegel of her imminent divorce. Addressed to Hegel, Skram nonetheless intended that he share the letter with his wife. She fears that fru Hegel will somehow blame her for divorcing a second time and she asks for understanding and support: 'Jeg ber gjennem Dem Deres hustru ikke at dømme' (Through you I beg your wife not to judge). In a seven page letter she confesses her anguish over the past five years, her husband's conduct, her inability to work, her current penniless state. Finally, she makes a heartfelt appeal to the Hegels' friendship. She asks for money, 'noget forskud på fremtidigt arbejde' (some advance money for future work), but her appeal is for moral support as well: 'Bliv nu ikke kjed over dette brev, denne fornyede appel til Deres godhed. Vær snil og god. Jeg trænger hårdt til det i disse dage' (Don't be put off by this letter, this renewed appeal to your goodness. Be kind and good. I sorely need it during this time).

Throughout the years Hegel lived up to Skram's image of him and treated her with kindness, patience and support. He responded to her repeated appeals for help with money and sympathetic words. In the drafts of his letters to her are expressions of respect and admiration for her and her work. In a letter dated 2 January 1901, written to clear up a misunderstanding about payment of an honorarium, he told her she was 'en saa elskværdig Dame...for hvem jeg baade som Menneske og som Forfatterinde nærer den største Højaktelse og Beundring' (such a kind lady ... whom I hold in the highest esteem and admiration both as a human being and as an author). In November 1898 when *Afkom* (Offspring), the final volume of *Hellemyrsfolket*, was finally published, he wrote out of 'en Trang til [aa] udtale for Dem min Glæde over dette Arbejde' (a need to express to you my happiness over this work). She had, particularly in the character of Fie, 'skabt et lille Mesterværk. En saa rørende og sympatisk Skikkelse treffes sjelden i Litteraturen og hendes triste Skjæbne føles næsten som en sviende Pine' (created a little masterpiece. One seldom encounters such a touching and sympathetic character in literature and her sad fate feels almost like a searing pain). When his competitor, Ernst Bojesen, made a move to lure Skram over to Nordiske Forlag, Hegel was quick to assure her that she was 'en av vore allerkjæreste Forfattere' (one of our dearest authors) and that she could have her next advance whenever she wanted.

Skram's letters to Hegel were often written in pairs – a letter requesting money was followed a few days later by one expressing gratitude and praise. A short note sent on 20 June 1896 is a characteristic expression of her sentiments:

Kjaere hr. Hegel!
Tusen tak! De er et af verdens bedste og elskværdigste mennesker. Bare, bare god og snil har De altid vært mod mig.
    Deres altid hengivne AS

    (Dear Mr Hegel!
A thousand thanks! You are one of the world's best and kindest people. You have always been good and kind to me and only that.
    Your always devoted AS)

Her words of praise extend beyond Hegel's function as a generous banker. In a congratulatory letter written on the occasion of Hegel's fifteenth year as head of the firm she applauds Hegel for the 'enestående fordomsfrihed og humane liberalitet' (extraordinary freedom from prejudices and humane liberalism – 2.1.1902) which have guided his publishing policies. And on a more personal level the two of them clearly had occasion to discuss literature, for at the conclusion of a letter dated 4 January 1901 she exclaims: 'Jeg sætter også så stor pris på Dem, som menneske, dette at De om bøger f. eks. altid siger netop det samme jeg tænker, det blir ligesom et sjæleligt bånd mellem mennesker' (I really value you too, as a human being; take books, for example, the fact that you always say just what I'm thinking, it's like a spiritual bond between people).

But the relationship between creditor and debtor is not one of equals and is bound to sour over time. Being in debt bothered Skram deeply, and she almost never asked for a loan without referring to the means by which she would repay it, either the book she was working on or an inheritance she would one day receive. As long as she felt confident she could write books, she believed she could write herself out of debt and she was grateful to Hegel for advancing an income which she would in time earn back. 'Noblere kreditor findes vist ikke' (A more noble creditor doesn't exist), she wrote on 19 February 1897, but, she added, 'det er min natur forhadt at stå i gjæld til nogen' (but being in debt is abhorrent to my nature). When she could no longer work effectively, her outlook and her attitude toward her creditor seemed to change.

The last five years of Skram's life were not productive ones; plagued by poor health, she was often bedridden and unable to work. *Julehelg* (Christmas), published in November 1900, was the last book she completed. Issues relating to her honorarium and a second printing of *Julehelg* are discussed in a letter from Skram dated 4 January 1901, but after this her correspondence with Hegel was sporadic. She wrote to Hegel only three more times and her last letter, from 24 March 1904, was as angry and aggrieved as the earlier ones had been humble and grateful. Gyldendal had instituted a new policy whereby authors were required to pay interest on advances received, and Skram had just learned of this in a recent statement: 'Jeg har modtaget Deres opgjør, og ser deraf, at jeg er i en efter mine forhold, bundløs gjæld til Dem' (I have received your settlement and see that I am hopelessly in debt to you, given my state of affairs). She is devastated that she has been so sick for so long, humiliated that she can't pay him back immediately, and angry at being so poor. She has never received as much interest from a bank, the few times she's been able to save money, as Gyldendal is charging, she writes, but it's an old truth: 'de fattige betaler altid alting dyrere end de rige. Alt, så også penge' (the poor pay more than the rich for everything. Everything, money as well). By this time correspondence between Skram and Hegel had almost ceased – her most recent letter to him had been sent in January 1902 – and her closing salutation, while not unfriendly, underscores the estrangement in their relationship: 'Med de venligste hilsener AS' (With the kindest regards, AS).

Fortunately for Skram, the cooling of her relationship with Hegel did not result in a break with Gyldendal. In the years between 1901 and 1905, when Hegel received only four letters from Skram, another of the firm's men received over forty, and that man was Peter Nansen.

Peter Nansen, Editor and Friend

Amalie Skram's correspondence with Peter Nansen dates back to 1886, a decade before he was hired by Gyldendal. The Skrams knew Nansen socially and both had professional dealings with him as well in his capacity as journalist and editor for *Politiken*. Nansen was also a novelist and over the years Skram sent him a number of letters with enthusiastic and complimentary commentary on his books. When Nansen became managing editor at Gyldendal in January 1896, he and Amalie Skram had already established a relationship and this is very much evident in the letters she wrote to him.

Skram assumes a tone of familiarity in letters to Nansen that is seldom apparent in those to Hegel. Her prose seems freer, more conversational and is more likely to erupt in spontaneous outbursts of affection for Nansen, his wife Betty and their little baby. Toward the end of a letter from 3 January 1899 she tells Nansen: 'De har nu engang en liden krog af mit hjærte, hvor De sidder lunt og trygt...' (You do have a little corner of my heart where you are snug and safe). In a letter written 30 August 1899 she turns rhapsodic and confides: 'Jeg ved ikke hvad det er for en trolddom, der for mig er ved Dem' (I don't know what kind of sorcery you exert over me). Salutations are affectionate and warm: 'Kjære min ven!' (Dear friend!) 'Kjære, snille PN' (Dear, kind PN) 'Kjære, elskede PN' (Dear, beloved PN) 'Farvel de kjære menneske' (Farewell you dear person).

Skram sent over sixty letters to Peter Nansen after he came to Gyldendal. During her productive years all editorial matters were directed to Nansen. She would make requests to him about the size of a print run or a typesetter she emphatically wanted to avoid. In a flurry of letters in March 1899 she discusses the order of stories to be published in a new collection,[13] which should be first and which last, and asks that the book be attractively typeset and bound: 'Kan nu den bog som skal indeholde disse fortællinger ikke bli lidt pent udstyret?' (Can't the book that's going to hold these stories be nicely done?). In the spring of 1901 Skram proposed to

Nansen that Gyldendal contract with her to translate Arne Garborg's novel, *Den burtkomne Faderen* (The Lost Father), into Danish. She relied on Nansen to make all the arrangements and to be her language consultant. On 19 August 1901, when she had nearly completed the project, she sent an urgent appeal for help, sweetened with flattery: 'Og da ingen hverken kjender eller forstår at behandle det danske sprog bedre end Dem er jo De den bedste, hvis De har tid til at være så snil imod mig' (And since no one either knows or masters the Danish language better than you, you are the best one, if you have time to be so kind to me).

After she divorced Erik Skram in January 1900, her reliance on Nansen grew, not only regarding questions of language, but general management of her business affairs. Nansen began to function as a go-between to Hegel just as Erik Skram once had. Greetings to Hegel might be included in a letter to Nansen, or she might ask him to put in a good word for her, as in a letter from 20 September 1902, full of apologies and excuses for an unfinished manuscript: 'Sig til Hegel at han endelig ikke må bli vred på mig for det' (Tell Hegel that he must not be angry with me about that). Did she really fear Hegel's wrath? The correspondence surrounding the predicament she found herself in with Ernst Bojesen does give that impression.

Ernst Bojesen, the energetic and innovative head of Nordiske Forlag, represented Gyldendal's most aggressive competition. In March 1902 he proposed to Skram that she publish a 'Christmas' book with Nordiske and she agreed, seemingly unaware that this would cause Gyldendal great consternation. Both Hegel and Nansen were quick to inform her how objectionable it would be if she published with any other house, and she reluctantly agreed to break her contract with Bojesen. Though Hegel sent her two letters on this occasion, she did not write to him, preferring to communicate only with Nansen and let him play the role of mediator. At midnight, 11 April, she wrote a letter to Nansen and told him she was hard at work on her book and afraid to open a letter from Hegel that had arrived at 8 o'clock. But the next day she would write to Bojesen and tell him 'at jeg altså er en højst uvederhæftig og løgnagtig person, der går fra sit givne ord' (that I am an exceedingly untrustworthy and untruthful person who breaks her word). She protested that she did not believe she was violating her agreement with Gyldendal, but if Hegel objected, her only course of action was to comply with his wishes.

The Bojesen incident did result in another advance for Skram, but illness together with her overwrought state prevented her from sending any manuscript to Nansen. She was unsure of what she had written, afraid that it wasn't good enough. After several letters in which she offered excuses and confided her insecurity, she met with Nansen in October 1902 and he proposed she publish her novel, *Mennesker* (People), in instalments. Every month she would complete and submit four broadsheets and a booklet would be printed. Two instalments were published in the autumn of 1902, but that was all she managed to complete.

There are a half dozen letters from Skram to Nansen in 1903; she apparently wrote none to Hegel that year. Some were written from clinics where she was being treated for various ailments (phlebitis, a recurring cough), but in none did she report that she had manuscript pages to send him. Sometime in March 1904 she received the statement from Gyldendal informing her that she would henceforth be charged 5% interest on money she owed the company. She responded with a distraught letter to Hegel (see discussion above), but wrote nothing to Nansen until the following August. Evidently Nansen had written to Skram sometime that spring or summer assuring her that she had in fact been 'beskeden med at forlange forskud' (modest in asking for advances); many of Gyldendal's authors had run up much larger debts than hers.

Perhaps it was his kind, reassuring words, perhaps it was the offer of a way out she didn't want to accept, but something in Nansen's letter seems to have had a galvanizing effect on her. In the reply she was finally able to compose on 9 August 1904, she shows that her spirit was not yet defeated. After she had elaborated on her sorry state, her money worries and her ill health that now necessitated a move to an apartment without stairs, she reviewed the various possibilities she had of earning money and paying off her debt. She had inquired with Schubothe about reprinting *Constance Ring*; they had declined, but she thought she might be able to find a publisher in Norway 'da også derfra er kommen forespørgsler, sidst nu fra en norsk forlægger' (since inquiries have also come from there, most recently from a Norwegian publisher). She wouldn't dare ask Hegel to take *Constance Ring*, but what about *S.G.Myre* which had been out of print for three years: 'Vilde nu ikke Hegel, nej jeg mener Gyldendal, kjøbe forlagsretten til den bog?' (Wouldn't Hegel, no, I mean Gyldendal, buy the rights to that book?). She also mentions *Sjur Gabriel* and *To Venner* of which only a few copies remain. She is energetic and enterprising to the bitter end.

Nansen must have found her proposal reasonable and convinced Hegel of the same for on 13 January 1905, in the last letter to Nansen that has been preserved, Skram wrote:

Tusen tak kjære, mod mig uforanderlig gode og snille, PN. Tak også for 'S.G.Myrerne'. Og for alt, alt andet godt.
Deres taknemmelig hengivne AS

(A thousand thanks dear PN, always good and kind to me. Thank you also for the *S.G.Myre's*. And for everything, everything else good.
Your gratefully devoted AS)

Conclusions

Earlier I raised the question, 'What did it mean for Amalie Skram to lose Hegel as a publisher just as she was launching her career?' At this point a second question quite naturally presents itself: What did it mean for Amalie Skram to finally gain Gyldendal as her publisher?

Traces of the injury Skram suffered from Frederik V. Hegel's rejection of *Constance Ring* remained throughout her life. Her words to Bjørnstjerne Bjørnson, 'det gav mig et knæk for livet' (it was a blow that did irreparable harm), indicate just how profoundly she was affected by the difficulties she encountered in bringing out her first novel. If, as she argued to Hegel, his repudiation stamped her book as 'en forkastelig vare' (a reprehensible product), it labelled her as a controversial author who embraced 'vovede' (risqué) topics in her writing. Losing Hegel meant more than having to do without the economic and emotional rewards only Gyldendal could offer – it essentially meant having to survive without the support of any publisher during the early, uncertain years of her career. The books which most outraged conservative society and whose publication and reception caused her most trouble were her novels about marriage. All four of these, *Constance Ring, Lucie, Fru Inés, Forraadt*, had been written by 1892, a year before she became one of Gyldendal's authors.

By the time she moved to Gyldendal in the spring of 1893, Amalie Skram had been worn down by the strain of trying to make a living from her pen. Overworked and overwrought from constantly worrying about money, she was hospitalized as a result of nervous and emotional exhaustion within a year of coming to Gyldendal. Hospitalization, first in a psychiatric ward, later a mental hospital, represented a descent into hell for Amalie Skram. And while her two novels[14] based on that harrowing experience were the first books she published with Gyldendal, to great acclaim, it was a success that had cost her dearly – she was never fully to regain her health.

The benefits Skram gained from her association with Gyldendal are acknowledged in her correspondence with Jacob Hegel and Peter Nansen: an initial relief of debt, a measure of financial security, the support, encouragement and respect of the men who were her publishers. For all of this she was deeply grateful, as countless letters attest. But though the backing of Scandinavia's largest publishing house provided tangible comfort to Skram during a period in her life marked by emotional crises and failing health, it came too late to give her career a real boost.

Amalie Skram's letters to her publishers open a window onto the career of a professional writer in Scandinavia at the end of the nineteenth century. As they document her struggles to get her work into print, the letters provide evidence that Skram faced great resistance from publishers as a *female* author of controversial books. In them Skram reveals how involved she was in all aspects of bringing out her books and the degree to which she acted as her own agent. The letters also offer a glimpse of the woman who wrote them: the professional who promoted her work with determination and strategy, the writer who was wholly dedicated to her art. These letters testify to a woman who wrote in order to live, and who lived to write.

Notes

1. The teacher was O. E. Holck and he received a number of letters from Amalie during the early years of her marriage to August Müller, from ports around the world. Liv Køltzow discusses this correspondence in *Den unge Amalie Skram*.
2. All translations from the Norwegian are my own.
3. See Katherine Hanson and Judith Messick, 'Amalie Skram og forlagsverdenen – Anno 1885' in *Amalie. 'Silkestrilen sin datter'* for a discussion of the letters Skram wrote to Frederik V. Hegel, his daughter-in-law, Julie Hegel, and Olaf Huseby regarding the publication of *Constance Ring*.
4. In 1885 Gustav Philipsen, together with his brother, owned the publishing house founded by his father. The Philipsen Company was a very respected and successful house.
5. Norwegian literature during the 1870s and 1880s was dominated by four authors: Bjørnstjerne Bjørnson, Henrik Ibsen, Jonas Lie and Alexander Kielland. They came to be known as 'the big four' and were all published by Frederik V. Hegel.
6. Page references in this section are to Niels Birger Wamberg's *Digterne og Gyldendal* (Copenhagen, 1970).
7. J. A. Sutherland, *Victorian Novelists and Publishers* (Chicago, 1976), p. 1.
8. Page references in this paragraph are to Øyvind Anker and Edvard Beyer's edition, *'Og nu vil jeg tale ud' – 'Men nu vil jeg også tale ud': Brevvekslingen mellom Bjørnstjerne Bjørnson og Amalie Skram 1878-1904* (Oslo, 1982).
9. Skram complains about Salmonsen in a letter to Erik Skram written in Kongsberg, 16 May 1889: 'Jeg kan forstå at der intet har vært at få hos Salmonsen. ... Ja ja, det er nokså forgalt at jeg til dato altså har skrevet de to bøger uden at få noget honorar for dem' (I can understand that you've received nothing from Salmonsen. ... Ah yes, it really is terrible that I've written those two books and to date have received no honorarium for them). In time there were some profits to share with the author and on 10 May 1900 Skram wrote and thanked Axel Henriques for a remittance of 50 *kroner*. She was glad he and Salmonsen hadn't lost money on those two books and remarked that her earnings totalled 400 *kroner*.
10. Wamberg, p. 66.
11. Skram published *Lucie*, *S. G. Myre*, *Børnefortellinger*, *Kjærlighed i nord og syd* (which included *Fru Inés*), *Forraadt* and *Fjældmennesker* with Schubothes Boghandel.

12. The stories in this collection were, like her previous collections, a combination of old and new pieces: 'Madam Høiers leiefolk', 'Karens Jul', 'In Asiam profectus est', and 'Forraadt'.
13. The collection was *Sommer*.
14. The two novels were *Professor Hieronimus* and *Paa St. Jørgen*.

15

The Modern Breakthrough's Author and his Publisher: Mikael Lybeck and Werner Söderström

Roger Holmström
Åbo Akademi University

This essay explores an idea that originally saw the light of day some years ago when I wrote a short introduction to a new edition of Mikael Lybeck's novel *Den starkare* (The Stronger), published in 'Nya klassikerserien' (1995). My rereadings of different parts of Lybeck's literary production gave me the impression of an author extremely focused on his own image. In 1921 when his collected works were published (in ten volumes) the author sent them with his own dedication, one by one, to the Library of Åbo Akademi University. Each and every volume was specifically corrected in his own hand. When Lybeck had finished his examination of his lifelong writing he wrote the following comment on the inside of the first page of the first volume:

Många tillägg och ändringar vore ännu att göra, i synnerhet i Banden II-V, men det har sedan länge bjudit mig emot att syssla med vad som säkerligen till stor del hör glömskan till.

(Many additions and corrections could still be made, especially in Volumes II-V, but it has long since been repugnant to me to busy myself with things that will to a large extent most probably fall into oblivion.)[1]

In many respects he is completely right. On the other hand, however, some of his poetry, as well as perhaps three or four of his works in prose, belong to the classics of the Finland-Swedish literary tradition.

Aside from the literary value of Mikael Lybeck's writing, he is, from my point of view, of great interest as an artist typical of his time. Alongside Karl August Tavaststjerna he is the only relatively important and well-known Finland-Swedish writer from the period of the Modern Breakthrough. In fact, he is the only one to remain true to the ideals of the 1880s for several decades. As late as 1911 – when he published one of his literary masterpieces, the novel *Tomas Indal* – several critics drew attention to the fact that the hero of the story embodies a whole generation. One of the best-known critics of that period, Olaf Homén, makes the following statement in a two-part review article in *Hufvudstadsbladet*:

Mikael Lybecks nya bok är personskildring och tidsskildring. Huvudfiguren förkroppsligar en generation, och när natten sist faller på, som ridån för en femte akt, så är det afslutningen på en epok vi ha bevittnat. Ett märkligt skede har gått hän med sin sista representant. *Tomas Indal* är den definitiva romanen om 80-talet och det sista skådespelet om den typiska 80-talshjälten.

(Mikael Lybeck's new book is a description of character and a period. The main character is the embodiment of a whole generation, and finally when night at last falls like the curtain after a fifth act we have witnessed the end of an epoch. A remarkable period with its last representative is ended. *Tomas Indal* is the definitive novel about the eighties and the last play to describe the typical hero of the eighties.)[2]

From a retrospective point of view one can see that Tomas Indal and the hero of Mikael Lybeck's first novel *Unge Hemming* (Young Hemming, 1891) are spiritually allied to each other. There is an interval of twenty years between these two novels but as Johannes Salminen, for example, has shown in one of his essays, Lybeck is a great moralist of consistent manner in all of his works.[3] Most of the characters in Lybeck's fiction ask too much of life. The gap between their high moral ideals and gloomy, unadorned reality becomes very obvious. From a metaperspective, Lybeck himself constantly struggles with the artistic means of expression. His

Mikael Lybeck

fixation on purpose, as well as his severe self-criticism, are brought to a brilliant end in his novel *Breven till Cecilia* (Letters to Cecilia, 1920). As Karl-Erik Lundevall has shown in his exhaustive study *Från åttital till nittital*, many of the great writers of the 1880s – among them August Strindberg and Ola Hansson - are, at the end of the decade and at the beginning of the 1890s, more and more oriented towards the programme of Verner von Heidenstam which is proclaimed in his pamphlets 'Renässans' and 'Pepitas bröllop'.[4] In a similar way Lybeck's *Tomas Indal* can be seen as an epitaph of the period of the Modern Breakthrough and his last masterpiece, *Breven till Cecilia*, as an end to the aestheticism of the 1890s.

After this brief introduction, in which I have tried to pinpoint the authorship of Mikael Lybeck on the map of literary history, it is time to approach the essential question, that is to say the relationship between the young writer and his publisher. The biographical background is well-described in a comprehensive life-and-letters study published by Erik Kihlman shortly after Lybeck's death in 1925.[5] The problem is that the critic Erik Kihlman was Lybeck's son-in-law, a fact that inevitably does not lend much credence to the objectivity of Kihlman's research work. On the other hand, I want to emphasize that Kihlman, in his analysis of different parts of Lybeck's literary production, provides several examples of his good observational skills. During the last ten years Lybeck has become an almost forgotten writer and in Bonnier's *Den svenska litteraturen* he is only mentioned in a single line, in connection with some background information about Finland-Swedish modernism.[6] It is to be hoped that the authorship of Mikael Lybeck will be better favoured by fortune in the forthcoming history of Finland-Swedish literature, edited by Johan Wrede. Considering the new interest taken in literary biographies I imagine that a new comprehensive life-and-letters study is also due. In any case, there will be no lack of material in the form of manuscripts and letters for such a work.

Regarding the letters – our topic here – there is every reason to concentrate on the correspondence between Mikael Lybeck and Werner Söderström. In December 1878 the latter had, as an eighteen-year-old schoolboy, started a publishing business in co-operation with his father, the owner of a printing office. Some years later the ambitious young publisher went to Stockholm in order to develop and modernize his printing business, taking the Swedish publishing houses of P.A Norstedt & Söner and Albert Bonnier as his models. During his study visit in Stockholm in July-August 1882, Söderström met Mikael Lybeck, who as a young student had made his first trip abroad in the company of his father. By pure chance, both the publisher and Lybeck, who was to become one of his most precocious writers, acquainted themselves with the contemporary techniques of *Stockholms Dagblad*'s printing house.[7] Perhaps their common interest in different kinds of printed matter can be seen as a good omen for their collaboration almost ten years later?

Werner Söderström's entrepreneurial spirit provided his printing office with a good reputation, and at the end of the 1880s, the leading writers addressed their manuscripts to him. By that time, Söderström was publishing books in Finnish as well as in Swedish. Juhani Aho and Pietari Päivärinta are to be found among his Finnish writers, and among the Finland-Swedes, Karl August Tavaststjerna and Jac. Ahrenberg are noted. Some years later – in 1891 – the bilingual printing business had developed into so considerable an undertaking that Werner Söderström decided to split his business into two separate companies. The Swedish branch called Söderström & Co Förlags Ab was established at that time. It is still the leading publisher of Finland-Swedish fiction side by side with Schildts Förlags Ab, which was established in 1915 by Werner Söderström's nephew, Holger Schildt.

It is no exaggeration to say that in spite of his youth, Werner Söderström was a much respected publisher when Mikael Lybeck first wrote to him in January 1890. Lybeck's ambition to become a poet was not just a freak of fate. He held a Master's degree in literature and had, at the end of the 1880s, become a postgraduate student of Professor Mikael Bernays in Munich. During his study visit in Germany, Lybeck had, for instance, visited Carl Snoilsky in Dresden and Henrik Ibsen in Munich (in 1888). He had, already before his German 'Bildungsreise', published several short stories and poems in *Nya Pressen, Finsk Tidskrift* and other journals.[8] In public Lybeck was, at that time, best known for his review articles of Herman Bang's visiting lectures in the Finnish capital in the spring of 1885.

In these circumstances, it may be stated that Mikael Lybeck's first appearance on the literary stage was very well prepared. The first contact between the writer and his publisher was also promoted by the fact that they had met each other before, in Stockholm, as previously mentioned. Lybeck is thus on 'bäste bror' -level in his first letter to Werner Söderström. His acquaintance with the publisher allows him even to feel his way with Söderström prior to the completion of manuscript of his first book. On 19 January 1890, Mikael Lybeck writes to Söderström from his childhood home in Nykarleby:

Jag går rakt på sak: senast i slutet af febr. tror jag mig ha användt så pass mycket skrifpapper, att jag har något utarbetadt i skrift därhän, att det är moget för trycksvärta. När jag nämnt detta så förstår du hvarför jag nu vänder mig till dig.
    Det är en samling *dikter* – att börja med. Delvis från min sista, långa gesäll-vandring i utlandet; delvis historiska, delvis 'hvarjehanda'. Jag tänker pag:antalet i tryck (d.v.s. med de lättlästa, glesa o vackra typer, som nu äro vanliga – och måtte det förblifva!) skall blifva bortåt 200.

(I am going straight to the point: before the end of Feb(ruary) I expect to have used up so much writing-paper that I shall have something ready and worked out for printing. Having mentioned this, you will understand why I am now turning to you.
    It is a collection of poems to start with. Partly from my last long walk abroad as a journeyman; partly historic, partly 'miscellaneous'. I think the number of pages when printed will be about 200 (that is, if the very legible, sparsely printed and beautiful types which are now common are used – and may it remain so!))[9]

Each detail in the opening paragraphs of Lybeck's first letter to Söderström reveals his sense of purpose. It is significant that he speaks about a collection of poems, to start with, which implies that he has some plans concerning the field of prose as well. Lybeck's eye for typographical matters also seems to be rather unusual for a debutant. The fact is that the completed collection of poems in print consists of 184 pages. Very close to the 'about 200' which Lybeck mentions in his letter.

It must have been difficult for a publisher to respond to a book project without as much as a shred of a manuscript. Well-conscious of this, Lybeck continues his first letter to Werner Söderström:

Det är lika litet min mening, att du skall köpa grisen i säcken, som det är antagligt, att du skulle göra't. Men hvad jag önskar veta är, huruvida du öfverhufvudtaget är hågad att till våren ge ut något skönlitterärt på ditt förlag ...
　　Beroende af det svar, du som jag hoppas, *snart* ger mig, skall jag alltså i slutet af febr. (senast) sända dig ett manuskript i bästa skick, så att det underlättar sättarns arbete. Öfriga öfverenskommelser äro nu för tidiga ...

(It is no more my meaning that you should buy a pig in a poke than it could be supposed that you would do so. But what I want to know is whether you have any intentions whatever to publish any work of fiction in your publishing-house this spring....
　　Depending on the answer I hope you *soon* give me I will consequently by the end of February send you a manuscript in first-rate condition so that it makes the work of the type-setter easier. It is still too early to make any further agreements.)[10]

Lybeck's consideration for the work of the compositor must have been a publisher's dream. Again, this exemplifies the professionalism of the young debutant!

　　There is, however, another statement in Lybeck's first letter to Söderström which shows that the young poet must have been almost sure of receiving a positive answer. The fact is that Mikael Lybeck is the nephew of no less than Zacharias Topelius, and that these family ties had opened the door for the young postgraduate student to Snoilsky's home in Dresden. In his letter Lybeck refers to the close relationship with Topelius, and expresses the possibility of his sending his manuscript along with a recommendation by his famous uncle, to Albert Bonnier in Stockholm. At the same time he declares that he does not like letters of recommendation and prefers to stand on his own feet.

　　Given these facts, it is not difficult to imagine how Söderström will respond to Lybeck's inquiry. The first letter from the publisher to his new author reads as follows:

B.B. Tack för ditt bref! Jag har ingenting emot att i februari få hit ditt manuskript, sedan skall jag säga hvad jag anser mig kunna göra.

Något ovanligt vore ju visserligen att vårtiden utsända en diktsamling, men sänder du mig goda papper, skall jag icke draga mig i betänkande att utgifva dem.
På hans födelsedag uppvaktade jag jemte Borgå biskopen din morbro. Måtte du med tiden skörda rika lagrar såsom han fått göra! Tuus Werner Söderström.

(Dear Lybeck. Thank you for your letter! I have no objections to my getting your manuscript in February, then I will tell you what I think I can do.
It is true it is a little bit unusual to publish a collection of poems in the spring but if you send me good texts I will not hesitate to publish them.
Together with the bishop of Borgå I called upon your uncle on his birthday. May you in the fullness of time reap rich laurels as he has done! Tuus Werner Söderström.)[11]

This reply is dated only two days later. Söderström had acted promptly. There was a general lack of talent in the field of Finland-Swedish fiction in those days and this fact caused Söderström to place such high expectations on the young Lybeck. It is possibly the first time that Mikael Lybeck is compared to his uncle, Topelius, but certainly not the last. After Topelius's death in 1898 (which was also the same year that Karl August Tavaststjerna died) all eyes were turned to the authorship of the young Mikael Lybeck.

In the middle of February 1890 Lybeck sticks to his promise and sends the complete manuscript of his first collection of poems to Söderström. The parcel includes a long letter. Several details in the letter indicate how specifically Lybeck conceived the appearance of his first book. Moreover, as the following passages serve to illustrate, at the same time, the writer is not given to understatement. Lybeck writes:

B.b. Söderström!
Ja, här sänder jag dig nu enl. aftal manuskriptet.
Jag har ej den lyckan att tillhöra de alltför ödmjuka i denna verlden, och med den uppriktighet, som ofta nog kommit förargelse åstad, tror jag mig kunna uttrycka en förmodan, att din risk vid ett utgifvande icke borde blifva öfverhöfvan stor – du må nu själf döma. Läs då t.ex. Märchen först – innehållsförteckning finner du i slutet.
Men jag har några önskningsmål att framställa, t.o.m. *innan* ditt svar i frågan kunnat inlöpa. Jag antar att de icke kunna invärka på ditt beslut, men vill dock i tid antyda desamma. Det gäller utstyrseln – en ingalunda

obetydlig sak (särskildt i fråga om ett *diktvärk*), ehuru visserligen allt här i världen är en sammansättning af bagateller... hvar för sig.
    Du måste medge att manuskriptet är prydligt. Utom för lätt-läslighetens skull, har jag nedlagt omsorg därpå af en annan viktigare orsak. Jag vet hur störande det värkar, när, genom sidornas ombrytning, meningarne olämpligt stympas och fördelas. Må därför (allt under förutsättning att du går in på affären – naturligtvis) formatet blifva sådant, att på hvarje sida i tryck raderna så inrymmas, som manuskriptet utvisar.

(Dear Söderström!
    Well, I am now sending you my manuscript as we agreed.
    I am not so fortunate as to belong to the all-too humble in this world and with the plain speaking that has often been the cause of so much offence, I believe it is reasonable to say that your risk in the event of publication should not be too great – but you may now judge for yourself. Read for instance 'Märchen' first - you'll find the index at the end.
    But there are some things I would like to establish even *before* your response to my question can possibly come to hand. I assume they can have no effect on your decision, but I want to intimate them to you in good time. It is to do with the book's appearance – a thing that is not without importance (especially when it concerns *a collection of poems*), even if everything in this world is of course a putting together of trifles ... each in its own way.
    You must admit that the manuscript looks good. Apart from wishing it to be legible I have devoted pains to it for another and more important reason. I know how annoying it is when sentences are mutilated and broken up in an inappropriate manner through the make-up of the pages. May therefore the format be such that on every page the lines are printed in the same way as in the manuscript (always assuming you are willing to go ahead, of course).)[12]

Lybeck does not exactly speak much like a beginner. Söderström must have had the patience of Job. He seems to submit to the circumstances and comply with all the wishes of the young poet. Lybeck's advice to his publisher that he should start by reading the poem titled 'Märchen', is also an example of his self-knowledge. This poem – a love story located to Heidelberg and originally based upon Lybeck's own experiences during his stay in Germany – belongs to the best part of the book.[13] Some of the lyrical parts of 'Märchen' are among the few poems of the first collection which Lybeck accepted for his *Collected Poems* about thirty years later.

Lybeck's many demands for the typographic design of his book are manifested in his letter to Söderström by several comparisons with previous and rather recently published collections of poetry as well. Works by Karl August Tavaststjerna and Jac. Ahrenberg are mentioned as models. In particular Ahrenberg's *Hihuliter* (1889), a collection of short stories may be noted, in which type-face and the quality of paper represents a good example. Every detail is meticulously discussed in the letter. Lybeck devotes such great care to the proof-reading of his book that he is ready to make the arduous trip from Nykarleby to Helsingfors. He promptly insists on doing that, and it is worth remarking that the quality of Finland-Swedish poetry even nowadays would have a lot to benefit from better proof-reading and improved typographic design.

The debut of Mikael Lybeck is, in several respects, representative for a poet of the modern breakthrough. The collection of poems is as a whole written in an objective spirit of 'noli me tangere'. It is remarkable that the word 'I' is used only in three of the poems, in a book consisting of, in total, thirty-three poems.[14] It is an obvious fact that Lybeck wants to describe certain aspects of everyday life. A poem like 'Ångbåtsinteriör' (Steamship Interior) with its natural dialogue is an example of the poet's realistic aim. The description of life on board a steamship also belongs to the new subjects favoured by the time. Some details in a poem entitled 'Från hamnen' (From the Harbour) can be read as a poetic counterpart to the opening chapter of August Strindberg's novel *Röda rummet* (The Red Room, 1879).

About ten years ago, in August 1986, the subject of the IASS-meeting in Gothenburg was 'The Modern Breakthrough in Scandinavian Literature 1870-1905', and thus, in many ways, closely related to our present concerns. In the proceedings of that conference both Lars Nylander and Lars Peter Rømhild analysed the character of the poetry of the modern breakthrough.[15] Mikael Lybeck is not mentioned, but in my opinion Nylander and Rømhild's account of this poetry is also relevant to his work. There is, however, an important exception. Mikael Lybeck's first book contains no prose poems. On the other hand, Lybeck was very keen to emphasize the objective character of his poems. Only two weeks before the book appeared in the bookshops Lybeck sent his publisher the following message: 'Obs! Ingen lyra får finnas på titelbladet 1: emedan så föga lyrik i samlingen ingår 2: emedan det ser så rasande sockersött ut' (Please note that there must be no lyre on the title-page 1: because the collection contains so little lyric poetry 2: because it looks so awfully saccharine.)[16] Lybeck gets everything he wants. In the beginning of May 1890, the book is ready, and in an advertisement Werner Söderström launches it on the market as 'mycket talangfull' (highly talented).[17] The poet had every reason to be satisfied with the reviews of his first book,[18] but that is another story.

Regarding the relationship between a publisher and his writer as reflected in their letters the second of Mikael Lybeck's books is also of interest. It illustrates the conflict between a publisher's ideological and artistic ideals. In his study of the history of the publishing house Söderström & Co., Göran Stjernschantz reveals that Werner Söderström was at heart a religious and conservative man.[19] At the beginning of his career as a publisher Söderström tried to be open-minded to the new generation of young writers. But step by step he adopted a more negative attitude towards the so called 'smutslitteraturen' (filthy literature) of the 1880s. He rejects a co-published edition of Strindberg's *Bland franska bönder* (Among French Peasants). He rejects Minna Canth's novel *Hanna*, although he had published her first play some years before. He rejects Juhani Aho's novel *Yksin* (Alone) in 1890, well aware of the fact that Aho is one of most promising Finnish writers.

During this same period Mikael Lybeck sent Söderström the first chapters of his next work. This was *Unge Hemming*, a collection of character sketches in prose from the author's study visit in Munich. Lybeck's letter to Söderström resembles the previous ones, including as it does detailed descriptions of the typography, the quality of paper to be used, and the format of the book, etc. This time Lybeck is extremely conscious of the intrinsic value of his narrative project and allows himself such formulations as the following:

Har du det förtroendet till mitt konstnärliga omdöme, att tryckningen kan vidtaga, innan du i manuskript mottagit *fullständigt allt?* Det kan du också svara på. – Jag finge därigenom tid till att *afsluta* och slipa och putsa ännu i slutet af September.

Mikael Lybeck

Ja så vill jag tillägga, att om vi komma öfverens, så önskade jag halfva honoraret i September, andra hälften i oktober.
Hvad jag nu möjligen glömt att ange, ska jag längre fram skrifva om. Detta är skrifvet i största hast (jag arbetar ute i skären) och helt affärsmässigt. Ett vänskapligt handslag på slutet. Vi hade icke skam af hvarandra sist – böra ej få det nu häller. Men icke blir berömmet så *odeladt*, ty alla komma ej att märka den varma underströmmen på grund af en yttre brutalitet.
Mikael Lybeck

(Have you sufficient confidence in my artistic judgement that printing can start before you have received the manuscript *in its entirety*? You can give me an answer to that too. – That would give me time to *complete* and polish and put the finishing touches to it as late as the end of September.
Then I want to add, that if we do reach an agreement I wish to have half of the fee in September, the other half in October.
Later on I will write and tell you what I have perhaps now forgotten to mention. This is written in great haste (I am working out in the 'skärgård' [archipelago]) and entirely businesslike. Finally, a friendly handshake. We were no cause of disgrace to each other last time - and ought not to be so now either. But [this time] any praise will not be so *undivided*, because its outward brutality will prevent everyone from appreciating the [collection's] undercurrent of warmth.
Mikael Lybeck)[20]

Lybeck uses a peremptory tone that must have been irritating to his publisher. Nor does it make matters any better when he adds the following comment to his letter: 'Ge mig svar så snart och så fullständigt som möjligt! Eljes Bonnier' (Please, give me an answer as soon and as full as possible! Otherwise Bonnier). Maybe Lybeck's last line about 'en yttre brutalitet' (an outward brutality) encouraged Söderström to suspect mischief, too. His reply to Lybeck is lost, but it seems to have been rather negative because the next letter from Lybeck to Söderström begins with the following statement: 'B.b! Mycket möjligt att mitt bref var lustigt - vi kunna ju konstatera det att börja med' (Dear Söderström! Very probably my letter was somewhat strange - at least we can start from that).[21] As may be seen from the letter, Lybeck has in the meantime sent the second part of his manuscript to Söderström. Lybeck does not seem to worry about any possible objections from his addressee. He goes on speaking unsuspectingly about details like proof-reading and his coming fee. Obviously the publisher has not yet started his reading of the manuscript.

The situation remains unchanged, at least on the basis of the following letter from the writer in Nykarleby to his publisher in Borgå.[22] Lybeck presents some ideas about the cover of his book and promises to send the concluding part of his manuscript as ready for printing. At that point – at the end of September 1890 – Werner Söderström begins to hesitate. Again, part of Söderström's letter seems to have been lost. However, a letter from Lybeck is of such great interest that it is given here in its entirety:

B.b! Jag brukar mycket sällan och mycket ogärna försvara hvad jag gjort; det måste svara för sig själf. Men två punkter vill jag denna gång fästa din uppmärksamhet på, i största korthet.

Hela boken är så godt en förkastelsedom, men utan tendens, ty då vore den icke konstnärlig.

Rysliga personer o händelser? Nåja, om du vill. Men de äro mänskliga, och de äro behandlade så delikat som möjligt, utan grofheter. Det måste du medge. Jag intresserar mig för allt, äfven det fula, men jag söker därjemte förstå det. Jag vill icke idealisera, det strider helt och hållet mot min natur; jag söker icke upp det sinnliga, men där det uppträder som ett riktninggifvande moment, där *får* det ej förbigåas. Du är ledsen däröfver? Jag också. En annan gång blir kanske motivet soligare. Jag har velat behandla detta, emedan hvarje face af lifvet är lärorik, och medan iakttagelserna voro färska. Jag har icke varit grof, det förnekar jag. Det påstår endast skuggrädslan. – Därmed vill jag långt ifrån påstå att jag lyckats så, *som jag velat*. Vi behöfva alla tid för utveckling, och skall det ske genom ärligt, samvetsgrant arbete, så går det ej för alla med iltågsfart. Man "öder icke bläck" genom sträfsamt studium – låt vara af dystra förhållanden. – Vännen Mikael Lybeck

(*Dear Söderström*! Seldom and very unwillingly do I normally defend what I have done; it must speak for itself. But this time I want to draw your attention to two points, very briefly.

The whole book is a denunciation but without being tendentious because then it would not be artistic.

Horrible people and events? Yes, if you like. But they are human and they are dealt with in as delicate a manner as possible, without coarseness. You must admit that. I take an interest in everything, even what is unpleasant, but furthermore I try to *understand* it. I do not want to idealize, that is altogether contrary to my nature; I do not seek out the sensuous but where it appears as a directing factor it *must* not be ignored. You are sorry for this? So am I. Another time the subject will perhaps be more sunny. I have wanted to describe this because every aspect of life is instructive, and while the observations were fresh. I have *not* been coarse, I deny that. That is asserted only by timorousness. – But I am nevertheless far from pretending that I have succeeded as *I would have liked to do*. We all need time to develop and it should come to pass by honest, conscientious work so all cannot do it at express speed. One 'does not waste ink' by an industrious study – let alone of gloomy conditions. – Your friend, Mikael Lybeck)[23]

Many of the statements in this letter are well-known to a reader familiar with the 'smutslitteraturen' of the 1880s. Lybeck stands out as a lonely seeker for truth in a similar way to the more revolutionary writers such as Zola, Ibsen and Strindberg. Lybeck's arguments are similar to many of those discussed in Thure Stenström's motive study of the literature of the Modern Breakthrough, *Den ensamme*.[24] For example, Lybeck's narrative deals with a Bohemian group of Scandinavian artists and writers in Munich, a subject and location that was much in fashion during those days.

From a metaperspective Lybeck's insistence that his story is non-tendentious is of particular interest. He wishes to stress that his artistic aims are totally independent of any kind of ulterior motive. On the other hand, Werner Söderström assures Lybeck that a publisher has to avoid the possibility of his needing to censor the work of his authors. In his reply to Lybeck Söderström writes:

B.B. Tack för ditt vänliga bref. Jag skulle så oändligt gerna önska kunna vara dig till viljes, men då jag hyser så obeskrifligt litet deltagande för detta ditt barn, så vill det falla sig svårt. Ingen censur bör ju förläggaren utöfva men han bör icke heller utsända arbeten hvilka icke ega hans sympatier.
(Dear Lybeck. Thank you for your kind letter. I would so immeasurably much like to fulfil your wishes but as I have very little sympathy for this child of yours, it seems to be hard. A publisher should exert no censorship but neither should he publish works for which he feels no sympathy.)[25]

Söderström says one thing but considers another. In the following part of his letter he appeals to Lybeck by asking him to touch up the most offensive passages in the manuscript.

In this respect the threatening conflict between Mikael Lybeck and Werner Söderström is a very typical one and can be readily described in the same terms as Johan Svedjedal uses in his study of the relationship between writers and publishers.[26] Svedjedal's description verifies the fact that the impact of a publisher on the intentions of an author is a field of taboo. In order to get a more balanced view of that field of taboo – and that is my point here – it is important to investigate what the letters between a writer and his publisher have to tell us. A good example of that is to be found in the impressive collection of letters between several writers and members of the Bonnier family which was published to mark the 150th anniversary of the publishing house of Bonniers in Stockholm.[27] Many similar examples are to be found in comprehensive biographies of individual writers.

A typical difficulty connected with an analysis of the relationship between an author and his publisher is insufficient material. In the present case at least a couple of important letters from Werner Söderström to Lybeck are lacking. It is therefore necessary to reach some speculative conclusions by more or less filling the gaps in the correspondence. Söderström is not willing to publish *Unge Hemming* and urgently requests Lybeck to let his manuscript come to maturity until after Christmas. Lybeck's response, which appeared a day after Söderström's refusal, shows that the publisher was not completely sure of his own opinion and has therefore also let an anonymous reader examine the story. This makes Lybeck very indignant and in his reply to Söderström the reader's competence to judge his work is called in question. Lybeck writes:

Hvad är det för prat om Bang! Min obekante vän känner icke mycket nämnde skriftställares afstympade meningar, om han vill dra honom till jämförelse. Mina meningar äro ofta korthuggna, det är sant, men de ha i regel subjekt och predikat – och saknas någondera någon gång, t.ex. i en tanke-monolog (om jag så får säga), så är det *afsiktligt*. Jag vet själf hur jag i detalj genomarbetat hvar rad – med 3 concept. Hvar rad är afsiktlig, jag har intet att taga ifrån och intet att tillägga, utom en och annan detalj i elfte häftet. Bang! Nej, är det påvärkning i någon mån, så är det af Lie eller Garborg.

(What's all this nonsense about Bang! My unknown friend does not have much knowledge about that mentioned writer's mutilated sentences, if he's a mind to draw a parallel between us. It's true my sentences are often short but as a rule they contain a subject and a predicate – and if either of them is sometimes missing, for instance in a soliloquy of thoughts (if I may say so) it is *on purpose*. I know myself how in detail I have thoroughly dealt with every line – in 3 rough drafts. Every line is intentional, I have nothing to take away and nothing to add, except a detail or two in the eleventh section. Bang! No, if there are any slight influences they come from Lie or Garborg.)[28]

The letter is full of details, but it is not appropriate to my purpose here to bring all of them to light. Speaking about resemblances between Lybeck and his better known Danish and Norwegian forerunners, it may be of interest to mention that Åke Gulin who has studied Lybeck's relationship with Norwegian literature tends to underline the influence of Alexander Kielland in connection with *Unge Hemming*.[29] Lybeck himself calls attention to the relativity of different readers and the same can be said of a good number of literary comparisons. The main thing is that the author remains faithful to his own intentions. In that respect Mikael Lybeck remains firm. His artistic ideals are framed from the beginning and can not be remodelled. He is an uncompromising moralist and therefore he bids Werner Söderström farewell. Lybeck's second book *Unge Hemming* will consequently be published by Albert Bonnier in Stockholm in the spring of 1891, but that is an other story.

From my point of view, the correspondence between the writer and his publisher focuses on three crucial points regarding a newcomer's appearance before the public: self-criticism, self-knowledge and self-esteem. The proportions between these three characters are by no means self-evident. Every writer, sooner or later, must find his own way in relation to his publisher. By studying that relationship a good many circumstances of the background of a literary work can be clarified. As I have tried to show in this essay, the letters between a writer and his publisher can, in that perspective, be of great value.

Notes

1. This copy of Mikael Lybeck's *Samlade arbeten* now belongs to the Library of the Department of Comparative Literature at Åbo Akademi University.
2. For this quotation and further information about the reception of Lybeck's novel see my article, 'Traditionalister och modernister – linjer i finlandssvensk litteraturkritik på tio- och tjugotalet', in Sven Linnér, ed., *Från dagdrivare till feminister. Studier i finlandssvensk 1900-talslitteratur* (Helsingfors, 1986), pp. 121-4.
3. 'Mikael Lybeck moralisten' in Johannes Salminen, *Pelare av eld* (Helsingfors, 1967), pp 70-79.
4. Karl-Erik Lundevall, *Från åttital till nittital Om åttitalslitteraturen och Heidenstams debut och program* (Stockholm, 1953), pp. 293-310.
5. Erik Kihlman, *Mikael Lybeck Liv och diktning* (Helsingfors, 1932).
6. Lars Lönnroth and Sven Delblanc, eds, *Den svenska litteraturen*, Vol. 5 Modernister och arbetardiktare 1920-1950 (Stockholm, 1989), p. 149.
7. Erik Kihlman, *Mikael Lybeck*, p. 105. Mikael Lybeck's letter to Werner Söderström 19 January 1890; copy in the Library of Åbo Akademi University.
8. Erik Kihlman, *Mikael Lybeck*. pp. 154-166, 179, 197ff.
9. Mikael Lybeck to Werner Söderström, 19 January 1890; copy in the Library of Åbo Akademi University.
10. *ibid.*
11. Werner Söderström to Mikael Lybeck, 21 January 1890; copy in the Library of Åbo Akademi University.
12. Mikael Lybeck to Werner Söderström, 18 February 1890; copy in the Library of Åbo Akademi University.
13. Erik Kihlman, *Mikael Lybeck*, p. 213ff.
14. *ibid.*
15. In Bertil Nolin and Peter Forsgren, eds., *The Modern Breakthrough in Scandinavian Literature 1870-1905* (Göteborg, 1988), pp. 267-70 (Nylander) and pp. 271-4 (Rømhild).
16. Mikael Lybeck to Werner Söderström, 16 April 1890; copy in the Library of Åbo Akademi University.
17. Göran Stjernschantz, *Ett förlag och dess författare* (Helsingfors, 1991), p. 19.
18. Erik Kihlman, *Mikael Lybeck*, pp. 221-4.
19. Göran Stjernschantz, *Ett förlag och dess författare*, pp. 15-16, 20.
20. Mikael Lybeck to Werner Söderström, 24 August 1890; copy in the Library of Åbo Akademi University.
21. Mikael Lybeck to Werner Söderström, 30 August 1890; copy in the

Library of Åbo Akademi University.
22. Mikael Lybeck to Werner Söderström, 20 September 1890; copy in the Library of Åbo Akademi University.
23. Mikael Lybeck to Werner Söderström, 28 September 1890; copy in the Library of Åbo Akademi University.
24. Thure Stenström, *Den ensamme. En motivstudie i det moderna genombrottets litteratur* (Stockholm, 1961).
25. Werner Söderström to Mikael Lybeck, 21 October 1890; copy in the Library of Åbo Akademi University.
26. Johan Svedjedal, *Författare och förläggare och andra litteratursociologiska studier* (Hedemora, 1994), p. 26ff.
27. Daniel Hjorth, ed., *Excelsior! Albert Bonniers Förlag 150 år. En jubileumskavalkad i brev* (Stockholm, 1987).
28. Mikael Lybeck to Werner Söderström, 22 October 1890; copy in the Library of Åbo Akademi University.
29. Åke Gulin, 'Mikael Lybeck och den norska litteraturen', in *Historiska och litteraturhistoriska studier*, 7 (Helsingfors, 1931), p. 165ff.

16

Letters from Munich:
'En Masse Kunst og storartet Bier'

Annegret Heitmann
University of Munich

Tourists who come to Munich may take the possibility of a guided walk through one of the various quarters of the city. These walks serve to introduce a particular area, architecture or milieu, but may also take one back in time, to different periods in the nineteenth century or significant events in the first part of the twentieth. On one of his popular walks through Schwabing, the Munich Germanist Dirk Heißerer takes one back to the turn of the century, when the area was the home of many avantgarde artists. We hear the names of Thomas Mann, Franziska zu Reventlow or Joachim Ringelnatz, but also of Henrik Ibsen, Bjørnstjerne Bjørnson or Olaf Gulbransson; we can see the houses where they stayed or lived, and listen to anecdotes about Ibsen's favourite café, the 'Maximilian', and the importance of Scandinavian literature for the Munich publisher Albert Langen.[1] Such a guided tour makes vividly clear the closeness of the relationship, around a century ago, between a generation of Scandinavian writers and the south German city, and it seemed to me that a book on the correspondence by authors of the Modern Breakthrough was a good opportunity not only to document this relationship on the basis of their letters but to enquire into its status and significance.

The genre of letters has traditionally been used mainly as evidence for connections between biography and the genesis of individual works, which – after the 'death of the author' – seems a problematical approach. But as that theorem also brought about an extension of the notion of text as it was linked to a concept of intertextuality, for which 'there is nothing outside the text', the epistolary genre may well gain new interest. My aim in studying letters by a cross-section of different writers of the Modern Breakthrough about and from a single place, Munich, was – in the first instance – a cultural-historical one. Originally I intended to sketch a view of the city seen through the eyes of Scandinavian visitors, but it turned out to be impossible to construct a unified and complete picture. On the one hand, the documents offer ambivalences, contradictions or puzzling silences about the Munich experience, which are going to be part of my argument; on the other hand – and this may render my argument provisional – the relevant documents are often difficult to obtain or have even not been published. No doubt a good deal of relevant material is still to be found in the Scandinavian archives; for the present, as yet incomplete account I have relied upon the published collections of correspondence, the rather few manuscript letters preserved in the Munich archives and some samples from the manuscript collections of the Royal Library in Copenhagen.

I. Topographical survey – where, who and when?

Let me begin with some facts, dates, names and addresses that can sketch in the topography of the authors of the Modern Breakthrough in Munich. Henrik Ibsen spent the longest time there: after short stays in the 1860s (1868) he lived in the city for three longish stretches, from 1875 to 1878, 1879 to 1880 and 1885 to 1891. In these years – nine altogether – during which he wrote dramas such as *Samfundets støtter* (The Pillars of Society), *Rosmersholm* and *Hedda Gabler*, he had a whole variety of different addresses. During his first visit he rented a flat at 13 Maximiliansplatz. On his arrival in 1875 he stayed first at 17 Schönfeldstraße, then moved in 1877 to the second floor of 30 Schellingstraße. On his second stay, he moved into a house just round the corner at 50 Amalienstraße – very close to the present Institut für Nordische Philologie, which of course did not then exist. In 1885, his third stay, he moved into 32 Maximilianstraße and wrote to Hegel, his publisher: 'Vi bor nu her smukt og rummeligt i Münchens fornemste og pragtfuldeste gade og betaler dog kun det halve af hvad huslejen kostede os i Rom.' (We are now living here nice and spaciously in Munich's poshest and most splendid street, but pay only half of what the rent used to cost us in Rome).[2]

The second Norwegian to live in Munich for a considerable time was Arne Garborg. In 1889 he moved with his wife and son at first to Diessen on the Ammersee, nowadays a very desirable area with Munich house-prices but at that time an idyllic spot in the country, where they stayed at a farm 'hvor vi har det trangt, men lyst og pent' (where it is cramped, but light and pleasant).[3] It was cheap – yet at 30 marks a month for two rooms more expensive than they had expected – and they had a view of the Alps from the window which made them feel at home at once: 'Foreløbig har vi slaaet os til Ro her ved Ammensee [sic], hvor det er wunderdeiligt, og hvor vi fra vore Vinduer har stor Udsigt til Alperne. Landets Karakter er temmelig norsk, ligesaa Klimatet, dog mildere' (For the time being we have settled down at the Ammensee [sic], where it is wonderful and where from our windows we have a grand view of the Alps. The character of the country is pretty Norwegian, so is the climate, only milder).[4] But the big city called, and early in 1890 Arne and Hulda Garborg moved into a flat first in 339 Dachauer Straße in Fürstenfeldbruck, and a little later to a more central and convenient place on the third floor of 59 Heßstraße in Munich.

The second artist couple to live in Germany for a considerable period, Ola Hansson and Laura Marholm-Hansson, did something similar. Between 1894 and 1897 they lived south of Munich, off the beaten track on the Schliersee, where they were able to concentrate quietly on their work, visiting Munich only occasionally to collect materials or visit the dentist. It was at the Schliersee that Marholm wrote, among other things, her great success *Das Buch der Frauen*, which became a best-seller for Albert Langen (who had recently founded his publishing business), stirred up lively, indeed intense, debate and was translated into eight languages.[5] But they too were drawn to the big city, renting a flat in 1899 at 5 Sophienstraße and later, in 1902, moving to 61

Königinstraße. For them both, Munich was also the city of Roman Catholicism, which they came to know there, and to which they converted in 1898. Their last years in Munich, however, were overshadowed by Laura Marholm's intermittent mental illness, Hansson's moodiness and their growing isolation. The sad consequence are the most bizarre 'letters from Munich' one comes across, for example a postcard which Marholm sent to the Director of the Munich Staatsbibliothek on 3 December 1900, in which she claims that the Church has confiscated all her worldly goods.[6] As her illness developed, she saw a conspiracy between the Church and the Swedish Crown at every turn.

From 1868 onwards, Georg Brandes was a regular visitor to the south German city. At first he stayed at the Oberpollinger hotel or the Hotel Marienbad; in later years he lived with his friend and colleague Paul Heyse in his villa in Luisenstraße, which Heyse bought and converted in 1873/74 and turned into a centre of literary life as well as a Munich attraction.[7] In the summer of 1874 Brandes tells his father about Heyse's new house: 'Jeg lever i et ganske med Kunstsager udsmykt Hus. Et og andet er endog pompeiansk (!) decoreret' (I live in a house decorated all over with works of art. Some things are even decorated in the Pompeian style).[8] In a letter to his mother he mentions that he has four rooms at his disposal.[9]

Although we usually associate him with Paris, Jonas Lie was also a frequent visitor to Munich, albeit on short trips from his summer residence at Berchtesgaden. During the sixteen years that he spent away from Norway in Paris, he only lived there half the year: the rest of the time, from June to winter, he stayed with his wife in Bavaria. This was his most productive period: in sixteen summers, after his daily morning walk with Thomasine, he wrote sixteen books. They also paid and received visits to and from Ibsen in Munich. Once he came to Berchtesgaden with John Paulsen, another Norwegian visitor to Munich, who stayed in the Bamberger Hof hotel, as did Holger Drachmann, Sven Lange and Bjørnstjerne Bjørnson. In 1862 Bjørnson rented a place in 6 Theatinerstraße, in later years he often came to Munich for family reasons, since his daughter Dagny married Albert Langen: in 1895 he lived at 20b Maximilianstraße and in 1898 at 7 Leopoldstraße.

Two other addresses we may note are: 51a Kaulbachstraße, the offices of the magazine *Simplicissimus*, which Sven Lange and Knut Hamsun both give as their address in 1896; and 9 Lerchenfeldstraße, where Lange lived in 1897. We could easily extend the list of visitors: Camilla Collett came in 1877, Magdalene Thoresen and Jens Peter Jacobsen in 1879, and Verner von Heidenstam in 1886. In August Strindberg's nomadic existence, Munich was but a stop-over. But Gabriel Finne spent extensive periods in the city, his addresses being 39 Dachauer Straße in 1893 and 74 Linprun Straße in 1892, from where he wrote to his publisher: 'Vi befinder os her så godt og så frie, at vi måske bliver boende her i nogle år, ialfald så længe stipendiet bevilges' (We feel so good and so free here that we might stay for some years, at least as long as I am awarded the grant).[10]

The street-names make clear for which reasons they chose their place of living: for the sake of cheapness, convenience and proximity to each other. They may live – often, like the Garborgs and the Marholm-Hanssons, to start off with – in the country, where rooms are least costly. In Munich, they choose their living quarters mostly just north of the old city centre, near the Englischer Garten, in the Lehel or the Maxvorstadt. And although this is certainly not a complete tally of the Scandinavian writers in Munich, it is certainly a reasonable initial topography of them. We could add a large number of artists, such as – most famously – Eiliff Petersen or Markus Grønvold, who later had himself naturalized as a 'Bavarian', the Swede Julius Kronberg, the Norwegians Rusten, Ekenaes, Kittelsen, Heyerdal, Werenskiold, Lillboe, Harriet Backer, Kitty Kielland and many others. Ibsen mentions 'den herværende skandinaviske koloni' (the local Scandinavian colony) in a letter of 26 January 1876, remarking that it consisted of 'mindst 50 personer, navnlig af kunstnere og polyteknikere' (at least 50 people, mostly artists and scientists).[11]

After looking at the empirical material, we naturally turn to the issue of why the intellectual elite of Scandinavia – collectively – visited so frequently or spent such extended periods in Munich. In individual cases of course there were personal reasons of mainly biographical interest – Ibsen for example wanted his son to graduate from the famous Maximilians-Gymnasium, which Konrad

Maurer had recommended to him. But the large numbers, and the broadly representative character of the names, suggest that we should not be satisfied with individual inclination, but look rather for a more general answer.

II. Why Munich? – the antithesis of the 'hjemme' and 'ude'

Although this question has not yet been asked specifically in relation to Munich, it is, given the restless journeyings of the Scandinavians of the Modern Breakthrough, by no means new. Mainly, attention has been directed towards writers and artists who spent time in Paris and Berlin, and Gunnar Ahlström, in his *Det moderna genombrottet*, formulated the now classic thesis of 'ude og hjemme' (abroad and at home), which contrasts the writers' longing for a cosmopolitan life-style and the experience of travelling and living in big cities with the embattled lines of an uninspiring cultural milieu at home.[12] The antithesis between the freedom and modernity of There and the suffocating petty-mindedness of Here is an important motif in the literature of the Breakthrough.

On closer inspection, this obvious answer turns out to be inadequate. Ahlström himself noted that Scandinavians seem never to have forged real bonds with their host countries but preferred to remain in their own circle.[13] In their letters home they mention all the other Scandinavians who are with them abroad, recount which members of the colony they have met, conduct their social life mainly with each other. Lie visited Ibsen, Camilla Collett had a pleasant time visiting the group of Norwegian women artists and writers such as Harriet Backer and Kitty Kielland: her sixty-fourth birthday in 1877 was the occasion of a real celebration in the colony.[14] Arne Garborg, on the other hand, complained about their 'Forsvenskning' (Swedification) and felt the lack of a 'Norskhedscentrum' (centre of Norwegianness) – he did not think that Ibsen filled that role sufficiently, since he was unwilling to exercise any influence.[15] If 'ude' was then also at the same time 'hjemme', can we allow that Munich had a specific character for its visitors at all? If the Alps simply reminded Arne Garborg of Norway,[16] and Jonas Lie spent his time while he was out on his walks thinking about the Norwegian 'Fjell' and the Norwegian language question,[17] we need to think again about the significance of these writers' periods abroad. It is moreover not sufficient to ask why they left home, but we must also inquire why they came to this particular place, Munich, and what characterized the city in the second half of the nineteenth century.

Having for long been a relatively unimportant place, Munich only became a European metropolis during the nineteenth century. The city walls were razed in 1791. Bavaria became a kingdom in 1806 as a result of the Napoleonic War, and the new power concentrated its efforts on the city. By 1850 it had a hundred thousand inhabitants and was thus the fourth-largest city in Germany. The new political importance was to be symbolized architecturally by extensive new building. The Maxvorstadt (Max-suburb), the northern extension of Munich towards Schwabing (which was only incorporated into the city in 1891), with its buildings by the royal architects von Klenze and von Gärtner – including the main building of the University – was conceived and built in a single grand gesture under Ludwig the First. It was the Ludwigstraße, stretching from the Odeonsplatz with the Feldherrenhalle, to the Siegestor, and the extension of the Residenz, that gave Munich its distinction in the early nineteenth century. Under Ludwig's successor Maximilian the Second another grand quarter, the Maximilianstraße, leading up to the Maximilianeum as its climax, was planned and built in the 1850s. The area that is today the haunt of the rich and the beautiful was a brand-new quarter when Ibsen lived there, and most of the other addresses – Schellingstraße, Heßstraße, Amalienstraße, Kaulbachstraße – were part of the new and modern Munich. But it was not merely the building activity that was remarkable. Ludwig the First was greatly interested in art, and had financed the classical art collections of the Glyptothek and the Antikensammlung with the ambition of making Munich into an Athens on the River Isar. Consequently his successors also concerned themselves with the patronage of art and science. Maximilian the Second brought to Munich scholars such as Schelling and the historian von Ranke, the chemist Justus von Liebig and the cultural historian Wilhelm Heinrich von Riehl. And with the offer of a life-long pension he induced the promising young Paul Heyse to come and represent the world of letters. Heyse responded to the offer with a long list of novels and stories, and for years was at the very centre of the city's social life, embodying like no one else the taste of the 'Bürgertum' of the period.[18] The literary elite of Munich gathered round Heyse for regular meetings. He founded a group called 'die Krokodile' or 'Münchener Idealisten', to which Ibsen also belonged for a time.[19]

By the time the 80-year-old Paul Heyse received his Nobel Prize in 1910, his work and his place in Munich cultural life were already things of the past. Under the regent Luitpold (1886-1912) a new quarter north of the Maxvorstadt, Schwabing, developed into the centre of artistic life. The notorious bohemian groups around Gräfin zu Reventlow, Frank Wedekind, and the artists' pub of *Simplicissimus*, where Joachim Ringelnatz was to be seen in cabaret performances, lived quite differently, and wrote quite differently from Paul Heyse, who had not even managed to keep abreast of Naturalism. Thomas Mann wrote *Buddenbrooks* in Schwabing near the century's end, Stefan George founded his elite circle, the 'Kosmiker', and Albert Langen started his publishing house by bringing out Hamsun's *Mysterier* and, in 1896, the satirical periodical *Simplicissimus*.[20] The Jugendstil movement, the Blauer Reiter group, Paul Klee, Rainer Maria Rilke and Franz Toller are just the best known of the later names from Schwabing. Thomas Mann's famous remark that 'Die Kunst blüht, die Kunst ist an der Herrschaft, die Kunst streckt ihr rosenumwundenes Szepter über die Stadt hin und lächelt ... München leuchtet'[21] already playfully ironizes the domination of aestheticism; and we know only too well how quickly the smile froze into a grimace.

The Munich of the generation of our Scandinavian visitors was thus a city of contrasts, rapid development and immanent contradictions – growth from one hundred thousand to half a million, the grand architecture of the Bavarian Kings, three great museums and controversial literary circles, dominated respectively by the court, the bourgeoisie and the 'bohème'. If we now turn to the letters written from Munich, we first want to know which features they mention in their letters home in order to find out which of the city's aspects attracted them. Just to anticipate my answer, I can conclude that the findings are simultaneously disappointing and instructive.

III. Epistolary representations of Munich

III.1. The marginal role

On the whole, the sights and the characteristic features of the city play such a insignificant role in their correspondence that they might just as well have been writing from anywhere. Architecture, art collections, theatres, parks and the local population barely figure. Holger Drachmann had a good excuse for not going into the 'forbandet kolde Museer' (damned cold museums)[22] – he had a cold and preferred to stay by the cosy stove drinking hot chocolate, which he evidently thought a good cure. Ibsen has high praise for the healthy air, which he believes to be due to the proximity of the Alps.[23] But, by his own account, he never goes to the theatre, unless one of his own plays is being performed.[24] He had seen all the museums that everyone praised on his very first, brief, stay and to all evidence never visited them again. They are just mentioned fleetingly in a letter to Hegel of 22 September 1868, where he writes that he has 'nydt alle Münchens virkelige Kunstskatte og Befolkningens Preusserhad' (enjoyed all Munich's real art treasures and the people's hatred of Prussia).[25] The very few occasions the sights of Munich are mentioned are in family letters. Bjørnstjerne Bjørnson writes about a visit to the 'Pinakothek (Malerisamling)' in a letter to Karoline,[26] and Jens Peter Jacobsen gives a short description of the art in a letter to his mother:

Malerisamlingen her er vidunderlig, navnlig har jeg for første Gang faaet et rigtigt Begreb om Rubens, uagtet jeg i Vien, Dresden og Berlin har seet herlige Billeder af ham. Ligeledes er de gammeltydske rhinske og gammelflanderske Malerskoler mageløst repræsenterede .... men af den antike Billedhuggerkunst findes her et af de første Mesterværker: den verdensberømte 'barberiniske Faun', det er en Dejlighed man ikke aner ...

(The collection of paintings here is wonderful, I have for the first time got a real idea particularly of Rubens, although I had seen splendid pictures by him in Vienna, Dresden and Berlin. Also the old-German painting school from the Rhine and old Flemish paintings are uniquely represented .... [and] of ancient sculptures there are the first master-pieces: the world-famous 'Barberini Faun', that is a beauty one cannot imagine.)[27]

In spite of this, he does not like the city, he thinks it is 'lidt eller rettere sagt meget død og bliver det endnu mere ved den Masse af prægtige Bygninger salig Ludvig I har bygget op til Stads og meget lidt Nytte' (a bit, or rather very, dead and becomes even more so through the mass of magnificent buildings the late Ludwig I has had erected for show but very little use).[28] This is one of the rare occasions on which anyone seems to notice the then modern architecture of the city, which is in fact impressive and which continued to be added to after Ludwig the First. But although Jacobsen reports his observations, he does not do so in an objective way, his distaste overshadows the picture.

III.2. 'Irkutsk i November' – reliable testimonies?

It is only to be expected that personal impressions and subjective views of sights and experiences are reported in the letters home. But the following example shows that the same city may provoke very different reactions, even in the same person. Georg Brandes mentions visits both to the Glyptothek and to the Pinakothek in letters to his parents in 1868, where he saw works by 'Rubbens [*sic*] (90 store Malerier) og Rembrandt, ei saa mange Italienere' (Rubens (90 big paintings) and Rembrandt, not so many Italians)[29] without going into any more detail. He was evidently more taken with the statues and monuments: 'Men jeg vil tale om München. Det er uden Ende. Byen er herligt smykket med af Kong Ludvig, Monumenter overalt' (But I want to talk about Munich. It is endless. The city is beautifully adorned by King Ludwig with monuments everywhere).[30] But three years later, on returning from Italy his enthusiasm for the city has turned into contempt: although writing in the middle of July, it feels like 'Irkutsk i November' (Irkutsk in November)[31] and he thinks that 'Byen ... med al sin laante Græcitet [gjør] et eget løiet og løierligt Indtryk ... Glyptotheket er en god Samling for en By som denne af anden Rang' (The city with all its borrowed Greekness [makes] an untruthful and ridiculous impression ... The Glyptothek is a good collection for a second-rate city like this one).[32] In another letter from the same day, his negative view becomes even clearer:

Saa sidder jeg da her i dette fordømte Tyskland. Himlen er graa og tung som Bly. Det er en Kulde som er aldeles *siberisk* og Regnen har øset ned siden inat kl. 11 ... Mange andre Symptomer paa Sorg og Rædsel viste sig. Folk begyndte at kvække tydsk; ... Samtidig begyndte som ved Trylleri alle Ansigter at tabe deres Form. Kvindernes skjønne Oval blev til langagtig Magerhed, Kvindernes blide Udtryk af let jordisk Erotik tabte sig for Udtrykket af 'Øconomi', jeg veed ei bedre at betegne tydske Fruentimmers Udtryk. De see ud som forstod de at spare. Deres Jernbanehandsker er skidne og hullede; de synes at have afskaffet det kvindelige Bryst som generende ved Kjøkkenberegninger, deres Fingre er grimme, ... jeg har *aldrig* seet en distingueret Tydsker. De er fødte Plebeiere med grimt Skjæg og skidne Støvler.

(Here I am sitting again in damned Germany. The sky is as grey and heavy as lead. ... Many other symptoms of grief and terror have appeared. People have started to croak in German; ... at the same time all their faces started magically to lose their shape. Women's pretty oval turned into a longish meagreness, women's soft expression of earthly eroticism got lost in favour of an expression of 'economy', I cannot characterize the expression of German women any better. They look as though they understand how to save money. Their railway-gloves are dirty and full of holes, they seem to have abolished the female breast as being in the way with the kitchen accounts, their fingers are ugly ... I have never seen a distinguished German. They are born plebeians with ugly beards and dirty boots.)[33]

Whatever we make of such tirades, we can conclude from their generalizations and emphatic and metaphoric contempt that they probably say more about the writer than what they describe. Munich has become a metaphor for a state of mind. But if such a letter may serve as a warning not to look for a truthful, objective account of something as innocent as a city, this scepticism has to be applied to every utterance: 'letters from Munich' have to be treated – at least potentially – as no less subjective, stylized or fictitious than a novel about it. It is therefore difficult to reconstruct, at any rate from the letters of the Scandinavian authors, the aesthetic appeal of the city life of Munich, or even – reliably – their experience of it.

III.3. The clichéd picture

Instead of a reliable account of the city, we find it passed over in silence, stylized, or – most commonly – turned into a cliché. Ibsen recommends paying a visit to Munich because: 'omvejen er ikke stor og her findes mange seværdigheder' (it is not much out of your way and there are a lot of sights here).[34] Bjørnson too recommends a friend to come and visit. His praise of the city amounts to one sentence: 'Her er så morsomt og billigt og gemytligt i München, så jeg vet intet bedre sted!' (Here in Munich it is amusing and cheap and cosy, so I don't know a better place).[35] In another letter he summarizes: 'Aber hier ist es warm, billig; hier ist ausgezeichnetes essen, gutes bier, gute weine, herzliche leute, treue freundschaft von alten zeiten; hier sind Germanen!'.[36] Arne Garborg sums it all up neatly: 'Her i München er hyggeligt. En lys, vakker By med godt Theater, prægtig Opera, en Masse Kunst og storartet Bier' (Here in Munich it is pleasant. A light, beautiful city with a good theatre, magnificent opera, a lot of art and great beer).[37] The good beer, which J. P. Jacobsen also appreciated,[38] actually finds its way into a literary text, as it is mentioned in one of Garborg's *Kolbotn brev*.[39]

But this notice is unusual: the writers of the Modern, of the visual, of Realism, do not perceive Munich in such a way that it finds admittance into their work. There are texts that were written in Munich, important texts such as *Hedda Gabler*, *Das Buch der Frauen*, or *Hjaa ho mor*, but there is no Scandinavian novel or drama about Munich.[40] And the Munich of the letters is characterized by striking lacunae, stylized representation with beer as a sort of leitmotif or by projections of personal feelings, that is textual representations that hardly allow a direct equation between the reality of a city, actual experience and the literary representation of both. Was the genre itself between 1870 and 1900 capable of reflecting reality and experience directly? There is a remarkable difference between these letters and those of the Romantics from Rome, for example, who all make an effort to describe the city and their impressions of it, manifest an interest in art and knowledge of it, and are full of details of the people's lives. They also have recourse to set-piece descriptions and clichés in their accounts, but the main reason for that is that they are constantly trying to turn their experience of Rome into literature. They write poems, dramas, novels and literary travelogues that rework not only their own experience of Rome but also the images and topoi already to be found in earlier texts, and so produce a rich literature dealing with Rome, from Atterbom's travelogue to Ingemann's poems to Andersen's novels. But at the end of the nineteenth century intellectuals, artists and writers turn to Paris, London and Berlin instead of travelling to Rome: Naturalism and Realism demanded other experiences and other subjects. But Munich, with its characteristic mixture of courtly glamour and Bavarian cosiness, did – and does – not actually seem to lend itself to these experiences of modernity, speed, crowds and cosmopolitan life. The question still seems unanswered: why Munich?

Georg Brandes' experiences may take us further. We saw his violent rejection of the city when visiting in 1871, but we have also seen that three years later he feels perfectly at ease, living in Paul Heyse's Pompeian-style villa. It is not difficult to guess that it was not the wall-decorations that changed his mind about the city, but the fact that he has gained a friend and acceptance. Belonging to the literary circles of Munich and finding a share in the marketplace seems a crucial factor in the Scandinavian writers' experience of the city.

IV. Higher aims – 'Det er i udlandet vi nordboer skal vinde vore feltslag'

Paul Heyse seems to play an important role in this context. Georg Brandes' friendship with him has puzzled contemporaries and modern scholars alike. But they seem to have been close friends, the radical, liberal Brandes and Paul Heyse, the idealist and aesthete, who is nowadays thought to be so second-rate that he hardly gets a mention in the current encyclopaedias of literature, whose language is riddled with clichés, whose depictions of local life and poverty idealize, and whose plots are melodramatic. Brandes reviewed him enthusiastically early on and thereby played a crucial part in creating Heyse's reputation in Scandinavia. He also conducted a lengthy correspondence with him and exchanged ideas with him about theories of writing, of the novella, descriptions of women and erotic scenes, about the relation between art and the Zeitgeist – even though they did not always agree. They were on intimate terms – said Du to each other; Brandes especially valued the 'Strömung echter Menschlichkeit' in Heyse's novels, their edifying tone, the weight of 'allseitiger, echter Bildung'.[41] Even Heyse's uncompromising rejection of Naturalism, for example his criticism of J. P. Jacobsen and Alexander Kielland and their 'revolutionære[n] Literatur ... in welcher die Schäden und Eiterbeulen der Gesellschaft aufgedeckt werden'[42] does not seem to have bothered Brandes. Holger Drachmann reacted against this literary friendship and even linked Brandes' change of taste and attitude to what I have called the leitmotif of the 'letters from Munich', Bavarian beer:

Du har jo drukket Münchener-Bier; Dit Skarn, og er bleven som de Folk, hvorom Cæsar siger, at de ikke ere farlige. Georg B. som en godmodig, phlegmatisk, rundkindet Münchener! voila une chose très singulière. – Kan da Omgangen med den Mand, hvis Portræt du engang viste mig med de Ord: 'Han bliver for rund, det tysdke Øl gjør ham fed' ... kan Samtalerne med denne Novelleforfatter af 3die Rang, have omstemt dig saameget, Dig, den stærke, smidige Kaardeklinge ...

(You have drunk Munich-beer, you scoundrel, and have become like the people about whom Caesar says that they are not dangerous. Georg B. as a good-natured, phlegmatic Munich-person with round cheeks! Voila une chose très singulière. – Is it possible that relations with that man whose portrait you once showed me with the words: 'He is getting too round, the German beer is making him too fat', can the conversations with that third-rate novella-author have changed you so much, you, the strong, pliant sword-blade ...) [43]

Heyse's status in literary life also leads Ola Hansson to an attempt to get his attention and recognition. He writes to the 'verehrtester Meister'[44] from Schliersee, wants to introduce himself and asks his opinion of his new work: 'Ihr Urteil würde für mich ungemein viel bedeuten'.[45] But the approach fails, and Hansson recoils disappointed after hearing Heyse's negative judgements. He writes in a letter to Heyse on 8 May 1894 that:

die Kluft zwischen den Alten und den Jungen doch größer ist, als ich je gedacht. Sie waren der einzige deutsche Dichter, den ich von meiner

Kindheit an bewunderte. Ich glaubte an Kontinuität zwischen dem Früheren und dem Jetzigen, an einen Willen zum Verständnis in den älteren Dichtungen und den Jüngeren, und ich finde nur die moralische Entrüstung des Alters gegen die Jugend.[46]

The early naturalist writer Michael Georg Conrad, editor of the periodical Die Gesellschaft (Society), which soon became one of the leading organs of the 'modern' writers, might have enjoyed a mediating role between these two opposing generations. Arne Garborg, but also Henrik Ibsen and Bjørnstjerne Bjørnson, and the painter Markus Grønvold, were in contact with him. It was also Bjørnson who, surprisingly enough, had the closest contacts to the turn-of-the-century generation in Schwabing, with Frank Wedekind (to whom Georg Brandes wrote a very cool and distanced letter), with Korfiz Holm and of course the *Simplicissimus*, whose editor was his son-in-law, and of which he thought very highly. The only other of the Scandinavian writers we are discussing here to have contact with the Kaulbachstraße circle and those involved with *Simplizissimus* is Knut Hamsun, a generation younger. As his *Mysterier* and the publishing house made each other famous, he also contributed several pieces to the periodical. But his novella 'Livets Røst' (The Voice of Life), published there in 1896, did annoy Bjørnson nevertheless: he thought it was 'reine Pornographie' and demanded that Langen alter his editorial line, albeit without success.[47]

Neither the allusions to the foreign city that we can find in the letters nor the contacts between writers that we can establish through their correspondence, confirm the myth of the contrast between 'ude og hjemme', of liberation and fresh life outside the frontiers of their own stuffy country. The Scandinavian writers are actively looking for acceptance by middle-class culture, and continue the same feuds and friendships that they had initiated at home, as well as the same life-style that there they had found cramping. Their main ambition was to be recognized, find an artistic home, and so they played down the foreign. Ibsen says this once very explicitly, when in 1872 he urges Brandes too to come to Bavaria: 'Kom her ned! Det er i udlandet at vi nordboer skal vinde vore feltslag; en sejr i Tyskland, og De vil være ovenpå hjemme' (Come down here! It is abroad that we northerners have to win our battles; one victory in Germany and you will be on top at home).⁴⁸ For a young and not so famous writer like Gabriel Finne, gaining an international reputation was especially important. He is therefore pleased with the response he gets in Munich: 'thi jeg, arme Djævel, blev hilset som en ny sol af alle de elskværdige mennesker. Indbydelser til alle Kanter ... Brausewetter agter straks at skrive en artikel i Tidskriftet "Gegenwart" i Berlin om min "virksomhed" – De vil vel sige "uvirksomhed"' (as I, poor devil, was greeted like a new sun by all these lovable people. Invitations everywhere ... Brausewetter immediately intends to write an article in the Berlin journal *Gegenwart* about my 'activities' – you would probably say 'lack of activities').⁴⁹ Even if this letter may exaggerate Finne's importance, since it is directed to his publisher Hegel, whom he repeatedly has to ask for financial help and is therefore only too eager to impress, it certainly shows typical expectations and hopes.

V. The displacement of Here and There

But if internationalism was important from the point of view of reception, nationality had to become a problematic part of a writer's identity, always closely bound up with the use of language. Drachmann felt himself misrepresented as an exotic writer, and tried to get himself translated by Adolf Strodtmann: 'Man bør dog snart blive praktisk, og man føler saamegen større Opfordring dertil her i Tydskland ved stadig at præsenteres som *dansk* Forfatter: noget lignende som Chineser eller Eskimo hvis Sprog Ingen læser' (One has soon got to become practical, and one feels so much more invited to do so here in Germany where one is forever being presented as a Danish author, that is something similar to a Chinese or an Eskimo, whose language no one reads).⁵⁰ An escape-route was offered by identifying oneself as Pan-German, as for example in Bjørnson's above-quoted claim 'hier sind Germanen!'. Ibsen too adopts this course when he – repeatedly – speaks of having replaced national feeling with a sense of tribe.⁵¹ Besides, he spent his life in so many different places and lived in Munich for such a long time that the city became his second home. He expresses himself most directly in a letter to Helene Raff in which he brings his memories of Munich to an almost sentimental climax: 'Thi der hører jeg saa inderligt hjemme' (Because there I belong wholeheartedly).[52] Arne Garborg gives an ironic touch to this idea of the common Germanic roots in a letter to Sophus Schandorph, like Brandes he feels cold in Munich after he returned from a trip to Italy:

Egentlig skulle vi allesammen leve i Italien, Spanien osv. Og bruge Landet nord for Alperne bare til Sætre – Sætre og Sommersanatorier. – Jeg stemmer for, at Sahara forvandles til Hav; saa flytter Skandinavien etc. derned.... Imidlertid, med [?] alt dette, var det deiligt at komme tilbage til München og faa Øl – Øl til 22 Pfennig Literen, og Kalvekjød til 50 Pfennig! Og disse store tunge Tyskere med de grove Bevægelser og de stygge Strubelyd forekom mig at være Landsmænd. Det nytter ikke at reise til Sahara. Vi bliver Germaner alligevel.

(Really we should all live in Italy, Spain etc. And use the land north of the Alps only as summer pastures – summer pastures and summer sanatoria. – I vote in favour of the Sahara being made into sea; then we move Scandinavia etc. down there.... Meanwhile, it was nice to come back to Munich and get beer – beer for 22 Pfennig per litre and veal for 50 Pfennig! And these big, heavy Germans with their coarse movements and their ugly laryngeal sounds seemed to me to be fellow countrymen. It's no use travelling to the Sahara, we remain Germanic anyway.)[53]

In this playful geographical scenario, Garborg totally disarranges Here and There, displaces land and sea, north and south and shifts around the whole of Europe as well as the idea of belonging. The only fixed point is again the cliché of cheap Bavarian beer. The idea of a contrast between 'ude og hjemme' is beginning to look quite absurd.

As I hope to have shown there are several reasons for doubting the validity of that antithesis. Pursuit of market-share, to put it in modern terms, is one important aim in playing-down what is different and novel about the foreign city, so that, while the contrast between 'home' and 'the world' does indeed appear in the literature of the Modern Breakthrough, it is much less marked in the authors' own reported experience. They represent themselves to others not as foreigners but as cosmopolitan travellers; since hardly anyone remained at home, there was no need to extol the art-treasures of Munich. It cannot be an accident that the only letters of this kind are written to family members, not to colleagues or those who thought and lived like oneself. To that extent, the letters do indeed suggest the restlessness and rootlessness of the modern individual, including the pose of being blasé in the face of novelty.

But if the letters have hardly anything to offer as historical sources, but only as documents of subjective states of mind, and if the city of Munich appears as not much more than a cliché, should we not take their metaphoric content and their literary means seriously? Should we not look at their images, their rhetorical strategies, their lacunae? We might then finally discover, why Garborg, Ibsen, Lie or Drachmann bothered to go abroad at all if they didn't use their eyes and ears. It is in Ibsen's rather plain and boring letters that we find the answer most clearly set out, an answer which allows us to move away from cultural history to the question of writing.

VI. The poetics of the four walls

For what they did in fact was to write. All of Ibsen's letters preserved in the Monacensia manuscript library in Munich repeat the same refrain, over and over: Thank you very much for the invitation, but I am afraid I cannot come. He cannot be said to have been exactly imaginative in finding excuses: it is either too wet, or he has a cold, or he is too busy. But what he was really doing is cutting himself off, a skill he commanded to perfection. We all know how Ibsen isolated himself during his writing phases in order to concentrate; the letters make it clear that he refused any sort of distraction. A typical sentence is: 'Vi lever derfor stille indenfor vore fire vægge, og det bekommer mig bedst' (We live quietly within our four walls and that suits me best).[54] When he once went to Norway during the summer, the impressions he had of his own country affected him negatively for a considerable period and prevented him from concentrating on his writing: in a letter to Georg Brandes he says, 'Indtrykkene, erfaringerne og iattagelserne fra min rejse i Norge ifjor sommer virkede længe forstyrrende på mig' (Impressions, experiences and observations from my trip to

Norway last summer had a disturbing effect on me for a long time),[55] and he is glad now to be back in his Munich retreat. In many letters metaphors make the same point: we find images of being cut off, at rest, in peace, in a vacuum. Ibsen reports that he now has peace and quiet,[56] or that he is 'havnet'[57] – he has landed, or reached harbour. Ola Hansson describes himself, in a letter to Heyse, as a hermit.[58] Jonas Lie, whose anchoritic life in Berchtesgaden was almost overdone, writes to Brandes: 'Jeg bliver her en otte, fjorten Dage for i Ensomheden her at faa *perset* mig ind i min Bog' (my italics, A.H. – I am staying here for a week or two in order to press myself into my book in this loneliness here).[59]

Perse, havne, komme til Ro, indenfor fire vægge – this is how the writers of the Modern Breakthrough work. The significance of being abroad is once again most vividly suggested by a commentary by Arne Garborg. Writing on 22 October 1889 to Conrad he remarks, by no means for the first time, on the fact that he still cannot speak German:

Thi det gaar smaat med min Tydsk. Jeg sidder den hele Dag og skriver skandinavisk og er, saa længe jeg holder paa med det, ganske upaavirkelig. Egentlig er jeg hjemme i Kristiania. Naar jeg af og til hører, at det tales Tysk i Værelset ved Siden af, bliver jeg ganske forbavset. 'Hvad Pokker, – bor der Tyskere her?' tænker jeg. Saa kan du selv begribe. Men naar jeg bliver færdig med min Bog, flytter vi ind til München og da vil jeg forsage og afsige al skandinavisk Væsen, drikke tysk Øl og radbrække tysk Sprog indtil jeg en Dag kan sige en Sætning i Sammenhæng.

(For I am not getting on with my German. I sit the whole day and write in Scandinavian and, as long as I am doing that, am totally impervious to impressions. Really, I am at home in Kristiania. When I occasionally hear German being spoken in the room next door, I am totally surprised. 'What the hell – are there Germans living here?' I think. So you can understand. But when I finish my book, we are going to move into Munich and then I am going to abandon all Scandinavian manners, drink German beer and fumble around in German until I one day can say a complete sentence.)

Garborg too sits 'upaavirkelig' within his four walls and writes as though he were in another world. Even the bad weather seems to be arranged for the purpose of his writing process.[61] The feeling of detachment in the case of Holger Drachmann is expressed in the image of a fairy-tale-world and a time-freeze – in a letter to Cecilia Poulsen he writes: 'Jeg har med Flid levet mig ind i en saadan Ensomhedens Tilstand her i den sidste Tid, at det nu forekommer mig at Verden omkring mig maa staa ganske stille, at alle Mennesker, ligesom i Æventyret om den fortryllede Prindsesse, ere faldne isøvn paa deres Stole eller under Udøvelsen af de daglige Beskæftigelser' (I have diligently lived myself into such a state of loneliness here recently that it now seems to me that the world around me must be standing totally still, that all the people, just like in the fairy tale about the enchanted princess have fallen asleep on their chairs or while carrying out their daily business).[62]

This image carries some weight beyond being simply a matter of personal inclination; it belongs in the context of literary history, and enables us to say something about the complex relation between experience and literature, and about the ways in which authors at this period saw themselves, their writing process and their texts. Although they all observe the present and are all visual writers, the relation between life and writing is based mainly on details. These are then transmuted into fiction, by a complex process that cannot be dealt with in this context. The main inference to be drawn from looking at the letters of the writers of the Modern Breakthrough, and examining their relation to Munich, is of a writerly abstinence, an instant of isolation and emptiness, frozen time and displacement that is quite typical of Modernism. The clichéd representation of the city by means of phrases such as 'en Masse Kunst og storartet Bier' reflects precisely the real environment's insignificance in the process of writing. And it does look as if Munich had something to offer that facilitated the filtering process that made the fictionalization of experience possible, that fitted with the generally-noted de-location of the modern individual. This can perhaps best be summarized in a quotation from Theodor Fontane, who writes in a letter to Detlef von Liliencron in 1860:

> Ich höre, daß Sie an eine Übersiedelung nach München denken. Ist dem so, so gratuliere ich dazu von ganzem Herzen. Ich glaube, das ist ganz Ihr Platz. Ich gehe noch weiter: München ist die einzige Stadt in Deutschland, wo Dichter leben können! Der eigentliche Grundstock der Bevölkerung ist zwar geistig tot und verbiert wie nur möglich, aber der Kunstzuzug aus aller

Herren Länder ist so groß, daß eine Nebenbevölkerung existiert, und in dieser lebt sich's freier und frischer als irgendwo.⁶³

Frank Wedekind expresses himself in a similar way when he describes the people of Munich as 'die naivste von Deutschland'. He sees an intellectual vacuum, of the kind that the Scandinavian writers also create for themselves, which he takes to be an important pre-condition for artistic creativity. 'Das ist auch der Grund dafür, daß sich die Kunst in München so wohl fühlt und so üppig gedeiht'.⁶⁴ On the cusp between Realism and Modernism we find a poetics of the four walls. It is in that sense that the writers of the Modern Breakthrough create for themselves a 'hjemme' in the 'ude'. We need to replace a myth of opposition with the idea of an overlay, of a paradoxical revetment.

Notes

1. See also: Dirk Heißerer, *Wo die Geister wandern. Eine Topographie der Schwabinger Bohème um 1900* (München, 1993).
2. 26 October 1885 to Frederik Hegel. In Ibid., p. 77.
3. 8 August 1889 to Bolette C. Pavels Larsen. In Arne Garborg, *Mogning og Manndom. Brev*, ed. by J.A. Dale, R. Thesen, vol. 1 (Oslo, 1954), p. 229.
4. Ibid.
5. See also Susan Brantly, *The Life and Writings of Laura Marholm* (Basel & Frankfurt a.M., 1991).
6. Laubmanniana III/Marholm, Bayerische Staatsbibliothek München.
7. See also Sigrid von Moisy (Ed.), *Paul Heyse. Münchner Dichterfürst im bürgerlichen Zeitalter. Ausstellung der Bayerischen Staatsbibliothek 23 Januar bis 11. April 1981* (München, 1981), pp. 194-202.
8. 17 June 1874 to his father. In Georg Brandes, *Breve til Forældrene 1872-1904*, ed. by Torben Nielsen, vol. 1 (Copenhagen, 1994), p. 82.
9. 18 June 1874 to his mother. In ibid, p. 83.
10. 12 December 1892 to Jacob Hegel. In *NKS 3741-4°*.
11. 26 January 1876 to Alfred Sinding-Larsen. In Henrik Ibsen, *Samlede Verker*, vol. 17, p. 213.
12. Gunnar Ahlström, *Det moderna genombrottet i Nordens litteratur* (Stockholm, 1947), pp. 437-445.
13. Ibid., p. 437.

14. See: Aagot Benterud, *Camilla Collett. En skjebne og et livsverk* (Oslo, 1947), p. 292.
15. 8 August 1889 to Bolette C. Pavels Larsen. In Arne Garborg, *Mogning og Manndom*, vol. 1, p. 229.
16. Ibid.
17. 2 September 1883 to Erik Werenskjold. In *Jonas Lie og hans samtidige. Breve i udvalg*, ed. by Carl Nærup (Kristiania, 1915), pp. 173-74.
18. As a curiosity it may be mentioned that his books were among those taken along by the *Fram* on the Polar expedition over the three years 1893-96. On his return from Franz-Joseph-Land, Hjalmar Johansen thanked the author for brightening the Polar night for the explorers – he and Fridtjof Nansen had fondly remembered his books during their legendary winter on the ice. See also Sigrid von Moisy, ed., *Paul Heyse*, p. 165.
19. See also Ibid., pp. 79-86. It was through Brandes that Heyse in 1875 got to know Henrik Ibsen; and he too kept in contact with this representative of the oldest generation of Munich writers – he even became a member of 'the Crocodiles', and for a time met colleagues at their almost daily gathering at the Café Achatz to eat Bockwurst and drink beer. In his biography of Ibsen (Oslo, 1971), Michael Meyer speaks on several occasions of the two men's close and long standing friendship (pp. 414 and 459); but recent work on Heyse has made it clear, by making use of the correspondence, that there was in fact no very close relationship between them. (See: Sigrid von Moisy ed., *Paul Heyse*, p. 214.) The work of each of the two writers speaks its own different language, and makes it quite understandable that their ways did not in the end converge. This is to be seen most strikingly in Heyse's devastating criticism of Ibsen's *Gengangere* (Ghosts).
20. See also Hermann Wilhelm, *Die Münchner Bohème. Von der Jahrhundertwende bis zum Ersten Weltkrieg* (München, 1993).
21. Thomas Mann, 'Gladius Dei'. In *Die Zeit* (Wien, 1902).
22. 26 January 1876 to Edvard Brandes. In Georg og Edvard Brandes, *Brevveksling med nordiske forfattere og videnskabsmænd*, ed. by Morten Borup, vol. 2 (Copenhagen, 1940), p. 202.
23. 21 May 1875 to J.H. Thoresen. In Henrik Ibsen, *Samlede Verker*, vol. 17, p. 185.
24. 2 April 1888 to Christian Hostrup. In ibid, vol. 18, p. 162.
25. 22 September 1868 to Frederik Hegel. In ibid., vol. 16, p. 216.
26. 14 September 1862 to Karoline Bjørnson. In Bjørnstjerne Bjørnson, *Breve til Karoline 1858-1907*, ed. by Dagny Bjørnson Sautreau (Oslo, 1957), p. 92.
27. 17 August 1873 to his mother. In Jens Peter Jacobsen, *Samlede Værker*,

ed. by F. Nielsen, vol. 5 (Copenhagen, 1973), p. 98.
28. Ibid.
29. 10 August 1868 to his parents. In Georg Brandes, *Breve til Forældrene 1859-1871*, I. række, ed. by Morten Borup (Copenhagen, 1978), p. 195.
30. Ibid.
31. 12 July 1871 to his parents. In ibid., vol. II, p. 439.
32. Ibid., p. 440.
33. Ibid., p. 436.
34. 10 October 1877 to J.H. Thoresen. In Henrik Ibsen, *Samlede Verker*, vol. 17, p. 279.
35. 23 October 1895 to F.T. Borg. In *Bjørnstjerne Bjørnsons brevveksling med svenske 1858-1909*, ed. by Ø. Anker, F. Bull, Ö. Lindberger (Oslo/Stockholm, 1961), vol. 3, p. 119.
36. Between 22 and 31 December 1895 to Konrad Telman. In Aldo Keel, ed., *Bjørnstjerne Bjørnsons Briefwechsel mit Deutschen*, vol. 1 (Basel & Frankfurt a.M., 1986), p. 323.
37. 5 February 1890 to Bolette C. Pavels Larsen. In Arne Garborg, *Mogning og Manndom*, vol. 2, p. 238.
38. 17 August 1873 to his mother. In Jens Peter Jacobsen, *Samlede Værker*, vol. 5, p. 99.
39. See Arne Garborg, 'Helfesten'. In *Reiseskildringer, Kolbotnbrev, Knudaheibrev* (Oslo, 1980), pp. 40-46.
40. There are of course Munich novels by some of the Munich writers that I have already mentioned. Paul Heyse, the literary lion who managed to find time to write 150 novellas, as well as a six-decker novel in seven months, also wrote a novel about Munich artists, *Im Paradiese* (1875). Still better known was *Was die Isar rauscht* (1887), by Michael Georg Conrad, which depicts painters, patrons and girls in the milieu of Schwabing. Later still there is a whole row of Schwabing novels by the now barely remembered Oscar H. Schmidt and Franz Hessel and Franziska Gräfin zu Reventlow's autobiographical novel *Herrn Dames Aufzeichnungen oder Begebenheiten aus einem merkwürdigen Stadtteil* (1913).
41. Georg Brandes, 'Paul Heyse'. In *Deutsche Rundschau*, vol. 6, 1876, p. 403. Quoted after Sigrid von Moisy, ed., *Paul Heyse*, p. 108.
42. 7 March 1882 to Georg Brandes. In Ibid., p. 216.
43. 13 August 1873 to Georg Brandes. In *Georg og Edvard Brandes, Brevveksling med nordiske forfattere og videnskabsmænd*, vol. III (Copenhagen, 1940), p. 15-16.
44. 3 August 1893 to Paul Heyse. In Susan Brantly, *Laura Marholm*, p. 102.
45. 21 August 1893 to Paul Heyse. In Heyse-Archiv VI, Bayerische Staatsbibliothek München.

46. 8 May 1894 to Paul Heyse. In Ibid.
47. 10 May 1896 to Albert Langen. In Aldo Keel (Ed.), *Bjørnstjerne Bjørnsons Briefwechsel mit Deutschen*, vol. 1, p. 334.
48. 23 July 1872 to Georg Brandes. In Henrik Ibsen, *Samlede Verker*, vol. 17, p. 52.
49. 12 March 1893 to Jacob Hegel. In *NKS 3742-4°*.
50. 20 February 1876 to Edvard Brandes. In Georg og Edvard Brandes, *Brevveksling*, vol. II, p. 210.
51. 30 October 1888 to Georg Brandes. In Ibid., vol. IV, p. 241.
52. 30 March 1892 to Helene Raff. In Henrik Ibsen, *Samlede Verker*, vol. 18, p. 308.
53. 30 March 1890 to Sophus Schandorph. In *NKS 4640-4°*.
54. 28 January 1886 to Frederik Hegel. In Henrik Ibsen, *Samlede Verker*, vol. 18, p. 86.
55. 10 November 1886 to Georg Brandes. In Henrik Ibsen, *Samlede Verker*, vol. 18, p. 113.
56. 17 November 1887 to Frederik Hegel. In Henrik Ibsen, *Samlede Verker*, vol. 18, p. 147.
57. 23 July 1872 to Georg Brandes. In Henrik Ibsen, *Samlede Verker*, vol. 17, p. 51.
58. 5 February 1894 to Paul Heyse. In Susan Brantly, *Laura Marholm*, p. 101.
59. 15 October 1885 to Edvard Brandes. In Georg og Edvard Brandes, *Brevveksling*, vol. V, p. 256.
60. 22 October 1889 to Michael Georg Conrad. In MGC, Monacensia, Handschriftensammlung der Stadtbibliothek München.
61. 20 November 1889 to Gustav Philipsen. In *NKS 4462-4°*.
62. 6 January 1876 to Cecilia Poulsen. In *NKS 5005^5-4°*. Cecilia Poulsen was a young woman working in the 'Dybet' (probably a cellar room) in the hotel Valdemar in Copenhagen, where a circle of authors, politicians and artists generally met. Drachmann, who evidently had a relationship with her, sent her several letters from his trip to Germany and Italy. He also wrote recommendations for her to help realize her plans of becoming an actress.
63. 23 January 1890 Theodor Fontane to Detlev von Liliencron. Quoted after Werner Pleister, ed., *Fontane und München* (München, 1955), p. 142.
64. Quoted after Klaus Gallas, *München* (Köln, 1989), p. 137.

17

An English Composer at the Heart of Nordic Culture: Frederick Delius and his Friends

Lionel Carley
The Delius Trust

Delius's first journey to Scandinavia was as a nineteen-year-old agent for a Yorkshire wool concern. Since leaving school he had been apprenticed to his father's wool business in Bradford, and several months of his first year in the trade had been spent on attachments in England and in Germany. His appetite for travel by now well-developed, he next persuaded his father to send him to Sweden on business connected with the firm, duly embarking for Gothenburg some time in June 1881. In the event, his first footsteps on Scandinavian soil proved to be one of the defining moments of his life:

The affection he developed for these northern countries and their people – heightened by his subsequent friendship with some of their greatest men – has led him to spend some weeks of every year there ever since. After a few days at Gothenburg, he went to Norrköping, where business was to be transacted, and there he succeeded in getting so many orders for the firm that his father was surprised and delighted at the apparent blossoming of his commercial abilities. Owing, no doubt, to his youth and to the ingenuous charm of his personality, he was well received wherever he went, and orders poured in for the firm.

When he reached Stockholm, he quite abandoned himself to enjoyment of the lovely surroundings and the gay life of the city; and what with supper-parties, excursions by land and water, picnics, impromptu concerts in the open air, and above all the entrancingly lovely summer nights, business receded far into the background, and Stockholm seemed like Paradise after dingy Bradford, with its third-rate theatre and sordid amusements. So business was completely forgotten for a while, and an extended tour in Norway, ending up at Bergen and in no way connected with the buying and selling of wool, was the cause of considerable friction with the family, when the truant returned to England in the autumn.[1]

This particular account of Delius's first encounter with Scandinavia is echoed by another, published many years later:

After a week or so spent in Stockholm, at its very best at that time of year, he found so many opportunities of comparing life in this beautiful and civilized capital with that in his own mediocre and provincial birthplace, that he conveniently forgot all about his commercial mission, betook himself to the Swedish countryside and, later in the summer, to the Norwegian mountains and fjords ... The influence of the scenic grandeur of the Scandinavian Peninsula, particularly the western extremity of it, was profound, mystical and indelible. For the first time he realized his own secret affinity with high and lonely places.[2]

A second visit to Scandinavia, again on his father's business, was made within a year, probably, therefore, in the late spring/early summer of 1882, at the age of 20. We can only assume that Norrköping was again the principal destination, for the sources tell us no more. But the composer and writer Philip Heseltine assures us that this second business expedition 'from a commercial point of view, was a most dismal failure, though two months were spent very pleasantly in exploring the many beauties of the two countries [i.e. once again Sweden and Norway].'[3] Thomas Beecham implies, in his biography of the composer, that by now Delius 'had gained some knowledge of the Norwegian and Swedish tongues,' and that his Norwegian was even good enough for him not just to read whatever he liked of Norwegian literature, but even to understand Ibsen in the theatre. This is nonsense, as is shown in a letter Delius would write to Grieg no less that seven *years* later: 'I am just reading Peer Gynt for the 5th time, this time however in

Norwegian with the help of a dictionary, & am making good progress.'[4] Furthermore, there is no evidence that Delius made any lasting friendships during either of these first two visits to Sweden and Norway, least of all with any major figures in the world of music, art and literature, as has sometimes been suggested. What more, after all, do you do during your summer months, spent half at work and half at play, when you are aged 19 or 20 other than make no more than passing friendships with your temporary hosts and travelling companions and, hopefully (and perfectly likely in Delius's case), with a pretty girl or two?

By the time Delius next returned to Scandinavia – five years later in the summer of 1887 – he was, at the age of twenty-five, a man of the world, a traveller of some sophistication and – at long last and after tremendous battles with his father – no longer simply the prospective inheritor of a thriving wool business, but a student of music with composition very much on his mind. Much of that period of five intervening years had been spent away from home – first in France, then in America and in Germany. And it was in Germany, during the academic year of 1886-87 at the Leipzig Conservatory, that the final impulse was received that was to cause him to centre a significant part of his life and work upon Norway, Norwegians, and the music, art and literature of that country. Sweden would step into the background, later to be supplanted by Denmark as an important secondary Scandinavian source for his work.

What was it that led to this? Yes, there had been an interval of five years, but even when he was in America in the mid-1880s the Scandinavian thread had never quite been broken. From his childhood years on he had adored the music of Grieg, and despite the comparative isolation on his orange plantation on Florida's St Johns River he had to his astonishment found a friend in the Norwegian-born Jutta Bell – née Jutta Mordt – on a neighbouring plantation. She was distantly related to Grieg and had considerable musical and literary talents. Later she was to earn a living in Paris and then in New York as an admired teacher of voice-production. Fifteen items of correspondence sent to her by Delius survive in the Jacksonville University Library, Florida. Furthermore, the first two songs written by Delius that have come down to us in manuscript were written while he was in America in 1885. One is a setting of Bjørnson's 'Over the Mountains High', the other of Hans Christian Andersen's 'Two Brown Eyes'.

Delius might have expected, when he first reached Leipzig in August 1886 in order to register at the Conservatory, that he would find friends among the German and English students there. I suspect that he was both surprised and delighted to find a number of Norwegians studying music in the town too. He fell in with them as if he were one of them. He made friends very easily for this tall, handsome Englishman of German descent was blessed with an attractive and outgoing personality.

Christian Sinding was the first close friend at Leipzig. Over five years older, but a shy man whose considerable musical gifts had now begun to manifest themselves, he came, during the course of the next two or three years, very much psychologically to depend on Delius, who during his own early adult life was seen by many – not least Edvard Munch of all people – as a rock to cling to in unstable times. Next came Johan Halvorsen, later like Sinding to become a composer of repute, as well as taking his own place as one of the foremost conductors in Norway. Then there was Arve Arvesen, a talented violinist later to form a celebrated trio in Kristiania and to end his career as Principal of the Bergen Conservatory. A special bond was forged with Halfdan Jebe, a brilliant violin student who would later be Delius's chosen orchestra leader for the composer's first London concert. And finally there was Camilla Jacobsen, another young music student, whom he would visit in Kristiania in the summer of 1887.

The first significant friendships with Scandinavians, and above all with Norwegians, are now, then, established – not in Norway, but in Germany; and in consequence the first significant letters between Delius and his Scandinavian friends are penned.

I have long been involved in the task of sorting Delius's correspondence chronologically: transcribing, translating – wherever necessary – and ordering thousands of letters has taken many years, but in the process has inevitably served its purpose and has put into place the building blocks of a life. However, for present purposes, I want to some extent to compartmentalize the correspondence in order to get Delius's relationships specifically with Swedes, Norwegians and Danes into some sort of clearer perspective. One must, however, accept many points of overlap; otherwise there are risks involved. Many of us will at some stage of our lives have been cajoled into providing the late, great and omnivorous Miron Grindea with copy for his journal *Adam*. I did so on two or three occasions, once with particularly dire results. I had in 1974 published the first essay in English to survey the Scandinavian artists' colony in Grez-sur-Loing, focusing in particular on Carl Larsson's position at the heart of it. Ten years on, *Adam*'s editor asked if he might reprint it in an issue to be devoted to Sweden.[5] To my ultimate dismay I discovered that his editorial hand seemed to have been employed simply in scissoring out as many references as possible to Danes, Norwegians and Finns who had figured in my original piece – with the results that the joins are painfully evident. I hope this will not be so evident in what follows.

Delius's initial contact with Scandinavians, then, came about in Sweden – in Norrköping in the first instance and then in Stockholm. There is, however, little in the surviving correspondence to indicate any prolonged connection with Sweden or its people, and to my knowledge he never returned to that country after those first two visits in the early 1880s. Yet there continue to be various points of contact with Swedes throughout his life. After two years at the Leipzig Conservatory Delius established himself in Paris for the best part of ten years from 1888. And in Paris – no doubt through the agency of his wealthy, music-loving uncle, with whom he spent his first few weeks in the city – he got to know the then celebrated Swedish *Heldentenor* Leonard Labatt. Labatt was living at the time close to the Opéra at 41 rue Cambon, and Delius's uncle at no. 43. Labatt writes, in German, to Delius on 2 October 1888 to thank the younger man for a letter he has sent. He is off to America shortly and hopes that they can meet again before his departure:

The Swedish song that you arranged I shall take with me and sing over there – If you would have the kindness to arrange some more I should be grateful to you, it might well be useful perhaps for you too, as I would advertise 'Swedish Folksongs' arranged by Mr Delius.[6]

There is one more short note from Labatt, by now back in Paris, the following spring, but that is all. Did he keep the song – or songs? All I can say is that nothing that we, so far at least, can clearly identify as a Swedish folk-song has survived among Delius's manuscripts – something that I particularly regret. Much later, however, Delius was to make just one song-setting that derives from a Swedish original. It is of Ernst Josephson's poem, 'Svarta rosor', in a German translation, composed in 1901 and not published until 1915. Although it remains one of his least known settings, the fact that he chose a poem by Josephson does point us towards several other main lines of Swedish contact enjoyed by Delius.

A key figure during the composer's Paris years was Ida Ericson, the sculptress wife of the Franco-Norwegian amateur composer William Molard. This pair held throughout the nineties open house at their unpretentious Paris studio in Montparnasse, and Scandinavian artists, musicians and writers gravitated naturally towards their home, affording Delius the opportunity to widen still further his circle of friends and acquaintances and incidentally to introduce some of his own friends, such as Edvard Grieg, into the Molards' circle. There are no letters from Ida to Delius, although he is certainly mentioned in at least one of her own surviving letters, but we do have in the Delius Trust's archive several from her husband. At last this fascinating family and its circle, which I attempted, over twenty years ago, to document as fully as I could in my first book,[7] has received the full treatment in Thomas Millroth's *Molards salong*, published in Stockholm in 1993. Millroth tells us how Ida writes to a friend describing Delius as one of the most intelligent people she has ever met. She is very fond of him, we learn, and even goes so far as to place her bust of him prominently on the piano, simply to ensure that the young composer, although absent in person, will be pictured there too when, in March 1890, a photograph is taken of her studio.[8]

For a while in the mid-1890s Strindberg was a frequent visitor to the Molards. It was during this period that Delius would sometimes lunch with him and at other times go for walks with him, and he has left a lively memoir of their acquaintance.[9] All that, however, came virtually to an end when he and a friend ill-advisedly decided to play a practical joke on the great man – not the most of enlightened of actions in the middle of the Inferno Crisis. They were to see little of him again. I have scoured the Eklund-Meidal letter edition to see if Strindberg makes even the most oblique reference to Delius at this period, but without success. Nonetheless, we do know that Strindberg sent a telegram to Delius. It has not survived, but Delius at least recorded its content: 'I feel that the time has not yet come for me to disclose my discovery. – Strindberg.'[10] The telegram arrived after Delius and an 'eminent chemist' friend had waited for over an hour for Strindberg to come to Delius's rooms to explain how he had managed to extract gold from earth which he had collected in the Cimetière Montparnasse. We still have, in the Trust's archive, laboratory protocols – analyses confirming the presence of traces of gold in those tiny Strindbergian pebbles.

Both Strindberg and Ernst Josephson had been among that extraordinary band of Swedish artists and writers who had made of Grez-sur-Loing a temporary home in the 1880s. One hundred years on, documentation on what is now termed the Grez School has shown a dramatic increase, with scholars happy to acknowledge the area as the cradle of modern Swedish painting. In a new book,[11] the canonization – if indeed a village can be canonized – of Grez takes a further step forward, with Toru Arayashiki, a leading Japanese art historian, labelling the village for the first time as the birthplace of Japanese impressionism.

One of the Swedish artists in Grez who took the first young Japanese arrivals under her wing in the early 1890s was Caroline Benedicks Bruce, a sculptress and watercolourist married to a Canadian painter. She it was who first introduced Delius, early in 1896, to his wife-to-be Jelka Rosen. Much of her work was left on her death in 1937 to Gotlands Fornsal. Thanks to financial support from the Anglo-Swedish Literary Foundation, I was able some years ago to work through many of her letters and diaries in Visby and to discover in them a fascinating new source of Delius-related material, some of which was incorporated into a Grez-exhibition in Cheltenham in July 1994.

Emma Löwstädt Chadwick is the last of this motley collection of Swedes whom I need mention. A fine painter, married to an

American and represented in Sweden's National Gallery, she was the only one of all the Nordic painters who arrived in Grez in the 1880s to make a permanent home there and to stay on as the village gradually reverted to something approaching the somnolence that it had enjoyed for centuries. She and her husband were friends and neighbours of the Deliuses and are frequently mentioned in letters between Delius and his wife. I have a copy of Erik Bögh's book *Sanningens vallfärd*, illustrated by Carl Larsson while he was at Grez, which once belonged to the Chadwicks, and which would undoubtedly have been given to them by their friend Carl Larsson himself.

I have remained so long with the Swedes, if only because these particular relationships with Delius are relatively little documented. Leonard Labatt, a tenor of international standing in his day, Strindberg and then three gifted women artists. Hardly a letter between any of them and Delius surviving but, in many of their letters to others, fascinating glimpses of lives that have for a time been intertwined, often at crucial junctures of the artistic development of each of them.

It is in the letters between Delius and his many Norwegian friends that the greatest riches lie. The two most significant friendships formed at Leipzig have left us with 110 surviving items of correspondence between the Deliuses and the Griegs[12] and over 60 from the composer Christian Sinding to Delius.[13] Delius's letters to Sinding have gone, as Sinding was, unfortunately, one of those unhelpful people who destroy pretty well all of their incoming correspondence. The entire Grieg and Delius correspondence was published, translated into English from mainly German originals and under my own editorial hand, in 1993, as a contribution to the Grieg sesquicentennial celebrations. As for Sinding, many of his letters are reproduced in translation in my *Frederick Delius: A Life in Letters*. They are also quoted from extensively in Gunnar Rugstad's Sinding biography.[14] As with almost all the Grieg letters, the originals are written in German, inevitably the *lingua franca* of the Leipzig Conservatory students. The first essay specifically to examine the Sinding-Delius relationship – at the same time providing the most detailed English-language documentation yet of Sinding's life and career – has now been written by Gunnar

Rugstad and is published as one of a series of essays in my *Frederick Delius: Music, Art and Literature*. This collection also contains an essay by Dr John Bergsagel on Delius's Danish literary sources, as well as an examination by the late Barrie Iliffe of Delius's musical distillation of the *Folke-eventyr* collected and published by Asbjørnsen and Moe.

What of those other Leipzig friendships? A life and works of Halvorsen is under way in Norway, but neither the researches of its author, Øyvin Dybsand, nor those that I have so far undertaken have yielded up any surviving correspondence between the two. Then, from the violinist Arve Arvesen just one letter remains in the Delius Trust's archive.[15] He and Delius were often together both in Leipzig and in Paris and we might with good reason have expected there to have been a flourishing, if perhaps brief, correspondence between the two. My tentative enquiries in Norway have yielded nothing, apart from the treasured memory of a moment when some twenty years ago I interviewed, in the former Principal's room at the Bergen Conservatory, the elderly lady who had been his secretary. As our talk drew to its close, she pointed out, with a glint in her eye and an unexpected peal of laughter, that I was sitting on the sofa on which Arvesen had died, suddenly, in 1951.

Another Norwegian composer who spent a lot of time at Leipzig was Johan Selmer, generally accepted as the first Norwegian to have written programme music. Delius may not actually have first met him in Leipzig, but they *are* corresponding and meeting in Paris in the spring of 1890, with Delius expressing considerable admiration for the scores of the older man that he has studied, and hoping to get the chance actually to hear his music some time. Two letters from Delius to Selmer are conserved in the Oslo University Library and we have five from Selmer to Delius in the Delius Trust Archive.

Among the most intriguing letters in our archive are a round dozen from the brilliant violinist and composer Halfdan Jebe, the youngest of Delius's Leipzig friends. Jebe lived out the philosophy of the Kristiania Bohemia pretty well until he died, travelling the world with his violin, often in penury, and spending his latter years in Mexico rather more quietly as professor of music at a conservatory in the province of Yucatan. We find him in the early

1900s exhorting Delius to abandon his everyday life and to join him on a never-ending safari around the world, of which the main components were promised to be wine, women and song. Delius would later write of him to a mutual friend: 'Jebe is the only man I ever loved in all my life.'[16]

A sample of one of Jebe's letters written in 1903 from Ceylon – he had arrived in Colombo from Calcutta by stowing away on an Austrian ship – serves to give a flavour of the correspondence:

> You ask if people in these countries are just as moral as in Europe. My dear friend, here, or in India the women are burned alive with their dead husbands, and, I give the word to one of my acquaintances ... morals in India are therefore higher than in any other country in the world.
> It's only in Japan that you can buy young girls very cheaply. But what the devil do you want with young girls. Give me refined old whores.[17]

Not surprisingly, Jebe's lifestyle meant that little of the correspondence that he received was likely to survive, and nothing from Delius remains. In 1931, three years before his friend Delius's death, Jebe's arrival at the home of the then blind and paralysed composer is documented in two letters from Jelka Delius to Eric Fenby:

> The norwegian [sic] friend from Mexico turned up in a terrible state like the most abject dirty beggar. It affected us very much. His state was so impossible that after 2 days I had to take him to Hospital in Fontainebleau and from there we got him to Paris after the most fatiguing difficulties and we are now sending him back to Norway where he has his brother.[18]

> Our Norwegian-Mexican friend has arrived safely in Oslo – a great relief for us. It nearly killed me when they handed him back to me at the Hospital, and I knew I daren't bring him back here.[19]

So much, then, for the Leipzig Norwegians.

Soon after establishing himself in Paris, Delius met Edvard Munch. It is not known exactly where and when, but I am inclined to believe that it was in the context of those Parisian Scandinavian circles and around 1890. Munch's first portraits – pen-and-ink studies – of the young composer date from this time. One of them was reproduced in *Verdens Gang* in 1891[20] on the occasion of the first public concert anywhere of any of Delius's orchestral music. This was in Kristiania's *Tivolis Cirkuslokale* and the piece was the tone poem *Paa Vidderne* (On the Heights), inspired by Ibsen's poem of the same name. The friendship between Munch and Delius was a lifelong one and their surviving correspondence amounts to some fifty letters and postcards.[21] Translated into English, it was published in full by John Boulton Smith in 1983, together with an exemplary critical apparatus.[22] As with the Grieg and Delius letters, the availability in print of the Munch and Delius correspondence means that I propose to go no further into the subject here.

Delius spent two and a half months in Norway, largely fell-walking, in the summer of 1887. Then, bolstered by the now flourishing friendships made in Leipzig, he returned for a further stay of two months in the summer of 1889. Whereas his summer diary of 1887 has left us no names that resound to posterity, the 1899 diary does just that.[23] Arriving in Kristiania at two in the morning he is welcomed on the quayside by his violinist friend Arve Arvesen and by the latter's father, the distinguished educationist Olaus Arvesen. Jo Visdal, the sculptor, turns out to meet him too. On the next day he is lunched by Arvesen and Visdal in the company of the painter Eyolf Soot, the composer Johan Halvorsen and the conductor Iver Holter; and he spends the evening with Christian Sinding. Later in the course of the holiday comes a visit to Bergen in company with Sinding to stay with the Griegs for over a week. Then there follows some two-and-a-half weeks of touring in the Jotunheim with Grieg and Sinding, before Delius gradually makes his way back to Kristiania and from there home to Paris.

One further summer diary dating from 1891 shows Delius spending a week at Aulestad as the guest of Bjørnstjerne Bjørnson. He enjoys bathing with his host in the surely unique outdoor bathing contraption in which Bjørnson took such proprietorial pride. And Bjørnson reads aloud his 'Peace Oratorio' to Delius and the family. Other important artists we find spending time with Delius during his holiday are the soprano Gina Oselio, painters Halfdan Strøm, Harriet Backer and Hjalmar Johnsen, and once again the conductor Iver Holter, Sinding and Grieg; this year's summer tour with Grieg is in the Hardanger region. All this lively social intercourse is relatively little-documented in the correspondence, Delius's diaries providing the main source of information. Nevertheless some letters survive: one from Delius to Bjørnson, two from Holter to Delius; then Grieg writes to Bjørnson about Delius;[24] and of course the correspondence between Delius and both Grieg and Sinding continues.

Delius's extraordinary interest in and knowledge of the contemporary art scene is reflected in the many friendships he made with painters during his early adult years. Beyond Munch, three more Norwegian painters represented in the Delius Trust's archive are Gudmund Stenersen, Torstein Torsteinson and Oda Krogh, even if just one letter from each is all we have.[25] Other Norwegian artists he would get to know were Alfred Hauge, Ludvig Karsten and Christian Krohg, the latter sketching and interviewing him for the pages of *Verdens Gang*.[26]

Writers also appear on the scene. There is a single exchange of letters with Ibsen around 1890, neither surviving but both documented in a letter Delius wrote to Ibsen's German translator Emma Klingenfeld shortly afterwards.[27] Delius seems not actually to have met Ibsen until 1897, when he spent some time with him in Kristiania. No correspondence with Vilhelm Krag, if indeed there was any, has come down to us; but the young poet set out for Paris in the spring of 1893 armed by Sinding with a letter of introduction to Delius.[28] One can only surmise that it was there and then that he wrote specifically for Delius a short poem entitled 'I once had a newly-cut willow pipe', for Delius set it, in its original Norwegian, to music. The piece does not appear among any of Krag's published works, so Universal Edition's relatively recent publication of Delius's song in 1981 would seem to rank as a first edition in both a literary and a musical sense.

Then there is the novelist and critic Jappe Nilssen, whom Delius must first have got to know in the nineties. On Delius's side a postcard dating from 1900 and a letter from 1920 are all that survive in Oslo University's Library.[29] Nilssen wrote to Delius too and a couple of his communications have come down to us.[30] By the early nineties, Delius had got to know Olaf Thommessen and his wife, for he writes to Thommessen, editor of the radical *Verdens Gang*, asking him to help a young French journalist intending to travel to the North Cape and to write an account of his journey.[31] Whether or not Philippe Auquier profited by this introduction, I do not know; but Thommessen himself was to be a useful ally to Delius a few years later, when *Verdens Gang* would throw its full weight behind the composer in the extraordinary controversy surrounding the production of *Folkeraadet* at the Kristiania Theatre.

Other literary acquaintances were Sigbjørn Obstfelder, Knut Hamsun and Gunnar Heiberg. Delius did not know Obstfelder well, but liked him. As for Hamsun, we are still in the position of having to take Jelka Delius on trust, for she has left us the only brief account – a paragraph, that is all – of a 'concert tour' apparently made in the Valdres area by Delius, Jebe and Hamsun in the summer of 1896. Robert Ferguson has scoured every primary Hamsun source and I have ransacked the Delius papers and neither of us has yet managed to find any other mention of this extraordinary collaboration.[32] Delius had probably met Hamsun earlier, in Paris, but there are no letters between them, any more than with Obstfelder. Gunnar Heiberg, on the other hand, is quite a different matter, and in Kristiania in 1897 he and Delius succeeded in a collaborative endeavour that sparked off several weeks of riotous behaviour in and around the Kristiania Theatre – Norway's national theatre in all but name. Their subject? Corruption and inanity in contemporary Norwegian politics and politicians, as an overlay to the continuing quarrel with Sweden.

Delius had long been interested in the Norwegian theatre and he was at the same time reasonably well informed in respect of political developments in Norway. He knew the Blehrs, for example, quite well, both during and beyond Otto Blehr's premiership (1891-93). Nine letters that he wrote to Blehr's wife Randi have been preserved, covering a period of nearly five years up to December 1896;[33] and just one from Randi Blehr to Delius languishes in our archive, apparently dating from late 1891 and written in a dreamily affectionate style. Frankly, one does not quite know what to read into it.

On 7 August 1892 Delius writes to fru Blehr asking for news about the current political situation:

I would be very glad, for I am very interested in Norway – not just in politics, but in the development (spiritual) of a country I am so fond of and where it seems that gigantic forces in art and science are slumbering.

He continues, one might say almost ingenuously, 'Why not have a revolution right away and become a republic, quite independent of Sweden', signing off with a nonchalant 'Give my regards to Blehr'.

Delius probably met Gunnar Heiberg in Paris in the mid-1890s at a time when the writer was the Paris correspondent for *Verdens Gang*, living in the city together with Christian Krohg's wife Oda. Four letters from Heiberg – two each from 1897 and 1899 – are preserved in the Delius Trust archive, as are two postcards and a letter from Delius to Heiberg dating from the early 1900s in the Oslo University Library. Heiberg had completed his satire on Norwegian politics, *Folkeraadet*, in 1897 and asked Delius to write incidental music for it. Delius complied and was present at the première in Kristiania on 18 October that year, when his variations on 'Ja, vi elsker' for the first time affronted a Norwegian public.[34] For the next few weeks, as the play continued in repertory, the newspapers were full of reviews, critical essays, debates and readers' letters, with heavyweight musical and literary figures also having their say. Delius's letters home make for stimulating reading, telling of how, among other things, he has been thrown out of his hotel and of how

> No one speaks any more of Heiberg's piece, now it is only my music. Christiania is divided into two camps – for or against – *all* the good artists are for. All the bourgeois are against. I have been with Ibsen quite a good deal and he was delighted and congratulated me most heartily. Every night in the theatre there is a pitched battle when the music begins. Hissing and hurrahs. There was some talk about lynching me ...[35]

Erik Werenskiold and Edvard Grieg are among those who, in letters to friends, write disapprovingly of Delius's foolishness in daring to meddle with Norway's national hymn.[36] Arne Garborg vilifies him in a lead article in *Den 17de Mai* of 30 October. But Christian Krohg, Sigurd Bødtker, Johan Selmer and the actor Ludvig Bergh, leap, like Ibsen, to his defence, as, after some dithering, does the Kristiania Students Union in a debate on his music. Ibsen's words are not only congratulatory but consolatory: 'We're only barbarians up here in the north,'[37] he tells Delius as they chat together – presumably at the Grand Hotel or at Engelbrets, just across from the theatre. At all events, all the friends, wherever they are, soon get to know of events in Kristiania, and William Molard writes to Edvard Munch: '[Delius] has certainly had a real success in Norway and has kept the newspapers rather busy; this has been fortunate for him, because at any rate attention has now been drawn to Delius's name up there and this can never do any harm.'[38] The story of *Folkeraadet* is a heady one, and it is told in full for the first time in *Frederick Delius: Music, Art and Literature*.

Still elated by the fame – or perhaps notoriety – that his *Folkeraadet* music had brought him, Delius responded quickly to a request early in 1898 for more of the same. Halfdan Jebe was now conducting Centraltheatret's orchestra and, enthusiastically supported by the theatre's director, the celebrated actor-manager Johan Fahlström, he wrote (an undated letter) to ask Delius for some music for a production there of Gunnar Heiberg's *The Balcony*. Delius duly supplied a 'Serenade'. We do not, unfortunately, know what happened to the music – which was certainly given with the play – or indeed whether the manuscript may or may not have survived.

Quite apart from Heiberg's play – or plays – Norwegian literature provided Delius over a period of some thirty years with inspirational treasure trove: Ibsen, Bjørnson, Vinje, Andreas Munch, Theodor Kjerulf, Vilhelm Krag, John Paulsen, are all set by him as songs. Then Ibsen's *Paa Vidderne* is quarried twice over, once as a spoken melodrama (reciter and orchestra), and once as the source of a musically quite distinct tone poem. A later tone poem, *Eventyr*, derives from the tales of Asbjørnsen and Moe. Composed in 1917, it is, I think, the last piece that Delius wrote that specifically declares its Nordic origins.

The final section of this survey of Delius's Nordic correspondence centres upon his relations with Denmark and the Danes. The earliest of his Danish settings is very early indeed: it is a song – for voice and piano – already referred to, 'Two Brown Eyes', to words by Hans Christian Andersen, composed in 1885.

Then four years later comes a setting of Holger Drachmann's *Sakuntala*, this time for voice and orchestra. During the 1890s there follow various songs to words by J. P. Jacobsen and Drachmann, while the early 1900s continue to demonstrate a consistent interest in Danish literature, with settings of Ludvig Holstein, too, added to the canon. Another musical form is taken in the symphonic poem *Life's Dance*, which comes into being in 1899 after Delius has read *Dansen gaar*, a play by his friend Helge Rode. Ten years on, Delius's last opera *Fennimore and Gerda* is based on selected episodes from J. P. Jacobsen's novel *Niels Lyhne*. And finally comes *An Arabesque*, for baritone, chorus and orchestra – a highly original setting, albeit in German translation, of J. P. Jacobsen's poem. The work was composed in 1911.

Delius's correspondence with Danes is much more restricted than that with Norwegians, but at least it does contain more that is of interest to us than does his sparse correspondence with Swedes. Two short letters from Herman Bang survive in the Delius Trust's archive, showing that Bang was in touch with the Danish concert agent Henrik Hennings on Delius's behalf. Bang was living in Paris at the time in very straitened circumstances and had borrowed money from Delius. 'Don't be angry,' he writes, 'because I haven't sent you the fifty francs and still cannot do so. You see, I am very ill and I am not allowed to do any work.'[39] Whether Delius ever got his money back will probably never be known (he is unlikely to have pressed for it), but we do know that in the end nothing came of the modicum of interest that Hennings had shown in his work, notably in the American Indian opera *The Magic Fountain*. Even Grieg's intercession on Delius's behalf with the Danish impresario was not to succeed. The acquaintance with Herman Bang must have been short-lived, as Bang was in Paris for only a year and a half. No further correspondence between him and Delius has been found.

There remain just two really significant Danish relationships to speak of. The first is with Helge Rode, highly thought of in his day as a poet and playwright, but it seems virtually forgotten now. There are two surviving letters from him, written in a highly idiosyncratic English, in the Delius Trust's archive. They date from 14 September 1898 and 28 February 1899. Eight communications – of which two survive in part only – from Delius to Rode are today to be found among the Rode papers in Copenhagen's Royal Library. They are written over a quite lengthy period of time, from 1897 to 1922, and what clearly emerges from them is that Delius was a great admirer of Rode's work. Fired by the *succès de scandale* achieved in 1897 through his incidental music to *Folkeraadet*, Delius suggests to Rode in 1898 that he (Delius) should write incidental music for Rode's new play, *Dansen gaar*. Rode is dubious about the matter – perhaps just an overture will do, he proposes. And so Delius duly completes, in 1899, his *Life's Dance* in its first version (it was to be much revised before being premièred in London in 1912 in its present form).

From the two men's letters it is clear that we are talking about a warm and enduring friendship, even if their meetings, probably mainly in Copenhagen, only took place on an occasional basis. Rode will, I suspect, have been acquainted with little of Delius's music. But Delius kept tabs on Rode's work, much of which he greatly admired. In 1914 Rode sends him a number of books, and Delius devours them with enormous interest. The play *Morbus Tellermann* is 'very good indeed', but does not rival *Grev Bonde og hans Hus*:

I know of no modern drama which I consider so strong & so fine – Every character is so alive & worked out to its very least consequence – Since Ibsen I have read nothing that made so deep an impression on me.[40]

He even tells Rode that his wife Jelka, 'who loves the work & has translated a good deal of J. P. Jacobsen & other things *most excellently*', would like to translate *Grev Bonde* into German 'in order that it may be performed in Frankfurt', where Delius has excellent and influential connections. He also loves a number of the poems, considering them 'very original', and hopes to set several to music, above all 'Fødselen', 'Skyggekunstnerens Melodi', 'Sigbjørn Obstfelder', 'Sne', and 'Aand'. Sadly, the onset of war and, subsequently, illness, would mean that none of these wishes was to be realized.

One letter that Delius wrote to Rode, on 23 October 1915, proposing a reunion in Copenhagen at the beginning of November, serves to introduce the last of Delius's friends to be touched on here in the context of his Nordic correspondence. It is written on the headed notepaper of the old Danish *herregård* of Palsgaard, near the little ferry- and fishing-port of Juelsminde in East Jutland.

The Deliuses had first stayed at the beautiful old manor of Palsgaard in the summer of 1909, and their three-week sojourn there in the autumn of 1915 was the second and last visit they were able to make. The owner, Einar Schou, was a modest and eminently likable industrialist who had made his fortune in London in the early years of the century as the managing director of Otto Mønsted, then the largest margarine factory in the world. His wife Elisabeth was a music-lover and had already, while living in London, made the acquaintance of a number of the leading younger music-makers of the day, including Delius. There are references to the Schous in various letters in the Delius Trust's archive and it is clear that they and the Deliuses corresponded from time to time between 1908 and 1919. But, surprisingly, only three letters from Elisabeth Schou to Delius, together with just one postcard that he sent to her, have survived.[41]

With a composer like Delius, who made, over a period of forty-two years, some fifteen visits – lasting for up to two or three months at a time – to Scandinavia, one can in a survey of this brevity only skim the surface. Time and space preclude a review of the lesser-known Scandinavian names figuring in the correspondence files of the Delius Trust's archive. Delius loved the North, and he loved Norway and the Norwegians in particular. Ever-expanding testimony to this fact is supplied in the continuing publication during the 1980s and 1990s of so many of the letters that he exchanged with Scandinavian friends and acquaintances. Even today, little more than a century on from the two months or so when his name was scarcely absent from a single issue of the Norwegian national dailies, it is, I would propose, impossible to think of any leading English artist, composer, even writer, who can have been quite so intimately associated with the Nordic countries and who corresponded on equal terms with so many of the leading figures of a golden age.

Notes

1. Philip Heseltine, *Frederick Delius* (London, 1923) pp. 8-9. Heseltine's reference to Delius's spending 'some months of every year' in Scandinavia is incorrect.
2. Thomas Beecham, *Frederick Delius* (London, 1959), p. 21. Beecham would seem to be mistaken in giving the date of this first visit as 1882. Heseltine, who wrote his biography during Delius's lifetime, gives June 1881; and 1881 is also implied as the year of that first visit in a letter written by Delius's wife, Jelka, to Heseltine on 3 September 1929.
3. Heseltine, *Frederick Delius*, p. 10.
4. ALS in Bergen Offentlige Bibliotek, first published in Lionel Carley, *Grieg and Delius: A Chronicle of their Friendship in Letters* (London and New York, 1993), p. 83.
5. Lionel Carley, 'The Swedish Artists' Colony at Grez-sur-Loing in the 1880s', *Adam*, 455-67 (1985), pp. 58-67. The 'authentic' (and unadulterated) text, 'Carl Larsson and Grez-sur-Loing in the 1880s', was originally published in *The Delius Society Journal*, 45 (October 1974), pp. 8-25. I take this opportunity additionally to disavow the piece on Munch and Delius published under my name but without my permission in 1992 in *Adam*, 498-499 (1988). Taken from notes lent, at his request, to the editor, it bears as edited no relation to the illustrated lecture, originally given at the Musée d'Orsay in 1991, from which it derives.
6. ALS from Leonard Labatt to Delius, Paris, 2 October 1888. Delius Trust Archive (henceforth DTA).
7. Lionel Carley, *Delius: The Paris Years* (London, 1975).
8. In *Molards salong* (Stockholm, 1993) Thomas Millroth mistakenly takes the reference to be to a 'porträtt', rather than to Ida's (lost) bust of Delius.
9. Reprinted in full in Lionel Carley, *Delius: A Life in Letters I, 1862-1908* (London, 1983; Cambridge, Mass., 1984 – henceforth DLL 1), pp. 404-7.
10. *Ibid.*, p. 405.
11. Lionel Carley, ed., *Frederick Delius: Music, Art and Literature* (London and Brookfield, Vermont, 1998).
12. The originals of the Grieg and Delius letter are shared between the Bergen Offentlige Bibliotek and the Delius Trust Archive.
13. Originals in DTA.
14. Gunnar Rugstad, *Christian Sinding, 1856-1941: en biografisk og stilistisk studie* (Oslo, 1979).

15. ALS from Arve Arvesen to Delius, Eidsvold, 2 August 1907. DTA. Cf. DLL 1, p. 296.
16. ALS from Delius to Adey Brunel, Grez-sur-Loing, 27 April 1915. DTA. Cf. Lionel Carley, *Delius: A Life in Letters, II, 1909-1934* (London and Brookfield, Vermont, 1988 – henceforth DLL 2), p. 105.
17. ALS from Halfdan Jebe to Delius, Colombo, November 1903. DTA. Cf. DLL 1, p. 229.
18. ALS from Jelka Delius to Eric Fenby, Grez-sur-Loing, 19 February 1931. Grainger Museum, Melbourne University. Cf. DLL 2, p. 380.
19. *Ibid.*, 7 March 1931. Cf. DLL 2, p. 381.
20. The pen drawing, appearing in the issue of *Verdens Gang* of Monday, 12 October 1891, showed Delius in profile and simply bore the initials 'E.M.'. I showed it to Arne Eggum, curator of the Munch Museum, who immediately thought it likely that it was by Munch, and when together we compared notebook sketches of the period I was able to identify an until then unrecognized second, and more detailed, portrait sketch of the composer – this time full-face – which had evidently been executed at the same time.
21. The originals of the Munch and Delius letters are shared between the Munch Museum, Oslo, and the DTA.
22. John Boulton Smith, *Frederick Delius and Edvard Munch: Their Friendship and their Correspondence* (Rickmansworth, 1983).
23. The diary jottings referred to are to be found in a notebook ('The Red Notebook') in the collection of the Grainger Museum, Melbourne University. Quoted in part in DLL 1, it is planned that the notebook will be published by the Delius Trust, edited and with a critical commentary by Dr Roger Buckley.
24. ALS from Delius to Bjørnstjerne Bjørnson, Troldhaugen, 29 July 1891. Oslo University Library (henceforth UBO). Cf. DLL 1, pp. 59-60. ALSs from Iver Holter to Delius, Kristiania, 19 March 1891, and 3 May 1902. Cf. DLL 1, p. 56. ALS from Grieg to Bjørnson, Troldhaugen, 23 July 1891. Bergen Offentlige Bibliotek. Cf. DLL 1, p. 60.
25. ALSs in DTA, dated respectively Skogadalshø, 12 July 1890 (Cf. DLL 1, pp. 51-2); Paris, 11 June 1908 (Cf. DLL 1, p. 352); and Paris, 22 February 1909 (Cf. DLL 2, pp. 10-11).
26. *Verdens Gang*, 23 October 1897.
27. ALS from Delius to Emma Klingenfeld, Croissy, n.d. (c. 1890). UBO. Cf. DLL 1, p. 54.
28. Three years later, a letter from Edvard Munch to his aunt Karen Bjølstad tells of Munch, too, spending some time in Paris with Krag and Delius at this period.
29. PCS from Delius to Jappe Nilssen, Grez-sur-Loing, 15/16 October 1900;

and letter from Delius to Nilssen, in the hand of Jelka Delius, Frankfurt-am-Main, 1 December 1920. UBO. Cf. DLL 2, pp. 235-6.
30. ALS from Jappe Nilssen to Delius, n.d. DTA. The second ALS takes the form of a postscript to an unsigned letter from Edvard Munch to Delius, n.d. [February-March 1929]. The original joint letter, which was not actually sent, is in the collection of the Munch Museum. Cf. DLL 2, pp. 344-5. Munch would often draft a letter more than once – as on occasion he did to Delius – and then never send it. One letter, early in 1930, was notoriously drafted to Gustav Schiefler no less than eleven times – some 3000 words in all – and no finished letter appears to have been sent by Munch. In four of these drafts he refers to a proposed visit to Delius ('der lahme und blinde') in France – an intended last visit which, sadly, never took place. Cf. Arne Eggum, ed., *Edvard Munch / Gustav Schiefler. Briefwechsel. Band 2. 1915-1935/1943* (Hamburg, 1990), pp. 219-24.
31. ALS from Delius to Olaf Thommessen, Finisterre [Finistère], 1 July 1892. UBO. Cf. DLL 1, pp. 65-6.
32. See DLL 1, p. 412. Harald Næss, similarly, tells me that he has so far found no material to corroborate Jelka Delius's account.
33. The originals are in the State Archives, Oslo.
34. The only opportunity an English audience has so far had to see the play (as well as to hear the incidental music at the same time) was at a production at the University of Keele in March 1982, in a specially prepared translation by the present author.
35. Delius to Jelka Rosen, Holmenkollens Turisthotel, n.d. [22 October 1897]. Handwritten transcript in the Grainger Museum; whereabouts of original unknown. Cf. DLL 1, pp. 122-3.
36. Erik Werenskiold to Bernt Grønvold, 25 November 1897. Quoted in Leif Østby, *Erik Werenskiold og dikterne* (Oslo, 1985), p. 38. And Edvard Grieg to Johan Selmer, 11 November 1897; cf. Finn Benestad, ed., Edvard Grieg. *Brev i utvalg 1862-1907*. Bind I (Oslo, 1998), pp. 650-1.
37. Heseltine, *op. cit.*, p. 39.
38. ALS from William Molard to Edvard Munch, Paris, 7 March 1908. Munch Museum.
39. ALSs from Herman Bang to Delius, Paris, n.d. [?June-July 1894]; and St. Germain en Laye, 'Friday' [?July 1894]. DTA.
40. AL[S] from Delius to Helge Rode, Grez-sur-Loing, 10 March 1914 (end of letter and signature missing). Royal Library, Copenhagen.
41. ALSs from Elisabeth Schou to Delius, Ealing, 11 October 1908; Ealing, 12 October 1908; and (with Einar Schou) Palsgaard, 10 June 1909. DTA. PPCS from Delius to Elisabeth Schou, Grez-sur-Loing, n.d. [December 1908]. Palsgaard Archives. This particular Nordic

connection has at last been celebrated by a three-day festival devoted to the music of Delius and his friends, both British and Danish, in Århus and at Palsgaard in June 1988.

18

Style in the Letters of Carl Nielsen

Alan Swanson
University of Groningen

Reading other people's mail is an act of doing history. This is a fancy way of saying that, in poking through other people's letters, we are curious, prurient, treacherous, or just plain nosey about other people. I take it that this particular act of doing history has a curious temporality about it, for it is clear that the meaning of a letter changes depending upon who is reading it when. We might call these 'modes' or 'positions' which determine our understanding in this enterprise. I see three, the first of which is obvious: the writer and the intended reader, who share a world in which certain utterances in a particular context generate known and reliable responses. This cluster of responses works at its fullest only once; at the moment the intended reader first encounters the text. Every later reading is echo, and this provides the second, already historical, mode, though one coloured by personal experience with the writer. The third mode is given, then, to some other person who reads the letter, in a necessarily later time and place, and, as the original conditions no longer obtain, it operates purely historically, though overlain with intervening perceptions and experiences on the part of the new reader. None of this is news, of course, but I bring it up to remind ourselves that epistolary theory must take into central account this rhetorical aspect of doing history. As I am not Carl Nielsen, and as I am reading his letters more than sixty-five years after his death, I can only do this third mode act of history.

As an appendix to a recent compendium of articles, new and old, about Nielsen's work, I translated a selection of his letters.[1] As most of the articles are technical, it seems superficially rather odd to include a selection of private letters among them. There are, in fact, all sorts of good reasons for doing so – they illuminate Nielsen's work, expose his, often interesting, musical-philosophical ideas, grant some insight into the genesis of particular pieces, and so on. In fact, as I understand it, these worthy aims all came down in the end to high-minded commerciality: the publisher apparently thought the book would sell better this way in concert hall bookshops. So much, then, for art, scholarship, and the life of the mind. It should give one pause, however, to consider anew what it is we are doing.

Carl Nielsen (1865-1931) was certainly Denmark's leading composer around and after the turn of the century and is still so, today. An exact contemporary of Jean Sibelius, for whose work he had a guarded admiration, they both stopped composing about the same time, though Sibelius outlived Nielsen by twenty-six years. Unlike Sibelius, indeed, unlike most artists of stature, Nielsen also left a considerable body of word-work apart from his letters. If you reflect upon this fact for a moment, there will be few composers who have left an impression in another medium as well; Hector Berlioz comes first to mind, perhaps, as do Michael Tippett, Aaron Copland, and Leonard Bernstein. Similarly, we also tend to forget, say, Michelangelo's considerable reputation as a poet or Strindberg's as a painter. Around 1907, Nielsen felt he had written enough poems to make a small book he at least considered publishing, though this project seems not to have materialized.[2] In 1925, he collected his musical essays in *Levende musik* (translated as *Living Music*, 1956). These are mostly genial, occasionally somewhat philosophical, ruminations on subjects that interested him, Mozart, for instance, or the matter of program-music, or the problem of taste in music (which, incidentally, he did not feel was beyond discussion). About the same time, at the urging of his daughter, Irmelin, he also wrote a much-read autobiography, *Min fynske barndom* (1927, translated as *My Childhood on Funen*, 1953). This is a book of considerable charm and eminent readability, not least for its stylistic qualities.[3] In fact, style is its leading quality as much of its historical matter is, as with perhaps all autobiographies, more imaginative, let us say, than the general requirements of history might demand. Still, within its superficially rosy view, we can discern the larger contours and darker corners of Nielsen's early life, the relative poverty of his childhood on Fyn, his musical father, his time as a regimental bandsman, and his early musical awakening. It is difficult to know what traces all of this left on Nielsen as a person and, even more important, as an artist. Nielsen himself seems not to have known, though he was not above attributing this or that characteristic to his childhood.[4]

As a composer, Nielsen must stand in the front rank of twentieth-century symphonists. He wrote, however, in all genres: his instrumental and chamber music, for instance, is not extensive, but the large piano pieces and the wind quintet are superb works. Furthermore, his two operas are undergoing revival, and one has even had more than one commercial recording. Beyond this, his orchestral music is profound and enormously well-crafted. Until the last thirty years, however, he has been most known to Danes as a song-writer. This is because of his deep influence on the Danish hymnal and a much-used Danish school song-book.

Now, I mention this last aspect of his music because it provides us a clue to one aspect of Nielsen the epistler. I realize, of course, that it may seem odd to use the work to illuminate the letters, when we often think of the interest as going the other way around, but I am, after all, doing third mode epistolary snooping and I take clues where I can find them. What I mean by 'clue' is the following fact: Nielsen's interest in song was awakened by Thomas Laub, a musician who was to become the great renewer of Danish church music in the first half of the twentieth century. Laub had early contact with Nielsen and they discovered that they shared certain ideas about the direction song should take. They both reacted strongly, and negatively, to the direction of late-Romantic songs, whose piano parts they considered fussy, over-elaborate, and too-dominant of the words. This eventually expressed itself in two collections of Danish songs, both titled *En Snes danske Viser* (A Score of Danish Songs, 1915, 1917). Nielsen asserted that in setting the classic Danish texts they chose 'en Indlevelse i Tid og Aand uden al Stilisering har vaeret vort Maal' (an experience of [the poem's] Time and Spirit without any stylization has been our goal).[5] While it is difficult to say precisely what Nielsen meant by 'Stilisering', I use this as a sign of Nielsen's awareness of the rhetorical effect of what he and Laub wrote. Those who know Nielsen the song-writer, that is, the way most Danes think of him, will find later confirmation of that stylistic intent in his letters. Now, I do not wish to push this thesis too far, for my aim here is not to talk about all of Nielsen's correspondence, but about letters as letters. Indeed, I think too little has been said about this essential characteristic of letters. Please note that I speak here of 'personal letters' to distinguish them from letters intended to be read publicly, such as those from Voltaire to his salon correspondents or, perhaps, those in Walpole's vast correspondence with various female friends.

It seems to me that many letters we study are taken primarily as containing a code for unlocking some other information. I do not suggest that this approach is illegitimate or unuseful, but I wish to insert into the discussion an interest in letters for their own qualities, qualities which have responded to many, discernable, rhetorical and contextual gestures. An example of the difficulty to which we all fall prey is that, in searching our material for the telling citation or the quotable remark – the epistolary equivalent of the 'sound bite' – we risk losing two important contextual aspects that may impinge directly upon what it is we actually know about these letters and their correspondents, that is, their context in the historical framework outside themselves, and their context within the corpus of their writer. Do our excerpts in fact fairly represent the whole letter from which they come? Do they fairly represent the body of letters from which they come? Do they fairly take into account such central rhetorical matters as tone and level of discourse? Such an approach recognizes that (private) letters are a form of controlled conversation between the writer and the intended reader. Such an approach must recognize that each recipient is a complete and unique audience. Related to this is the understanding that letters therefore also share characteristics of the (personal) essay.

I am obviously interested in the letters themselves, as a genre, if you will. This means, then, that instead of pointing the letters outside of themselves, I wish to use the outside world to tell us something about the letters. In the present context, I cannot push this approach too far because of the limited number available. The stylistic issues I wish to address here are also admittedly difficult to focus because Nielsen's own expressed 'passion for modulation', an important aspect of musical style evident in the ingenious transitions in all his music, hardly exists in his letters.[6] Indeed, transition in the written syntactical sense is a stylistic feature prominent by its absence and its application to this body of letters is therefore potentially problematic.

 Carl Nielsen wrote many letters, though not, I think, nearly as many as such indefatigable contemporary Scandinavian epistlers as August Strindberg and Georg Brandes. Published so far are the broad, heavily edited, selection from 1954 by his daughter, Irmelin Eggert Møller, and Torben Meyer, which forms the basis for my remarks here, his letters to Emil B. Sachs, one of his earliest supporters, with whom he shared a long correspondence, and the letters to his wife, Anne Marie Carl Nielsen.[7] There are more in the Royal Library, but the available list of them does not allow a useable calculation of their number.[8]

 In reading and translating the admittedly highly selective corpus of letters with which I worked, most of which were written to good or even intimate friends, I have been struck by Nielsen's deliberate sense of rhetoric in his writing. By this I mean that his letters show a clearly defined reader and a clearly defined purpose; a letter to someone else of the same informational content will differ in ways that make it peculiar to that other reader. On the whole, this is not unexpected. After all, we each tend to have at least two styles of discourse, which we may call the Formal and the Familiar or, perhaps, Outside and Inside, and we vary them to suit the recipient. What is, I think, unusual in Nielsen's letters, and the bane of their translator, is that there is a third, fairly consistent, Middle style, for which I have yet to discover a flashy name. This Middle style is just that: to call it Semi-formal implies a direction related to formality; to call it Informal implies a direction toward Familiarity. Neither correctly calls up the position of this style, which is simply itself. I shall describe these styles and how they work, but let it be noted that I assert that a clue to understanding them lies in the music, for, loosely put, I discern three styles in Carl Nielsen's music. As all the music shares characteristics which enable us to identify it as Nielsen's as opposed, say, to Sibelius's, so do the letters also have obvious shared characteristics. But within those identities are varieties that go beyond form.

These three styles I see in Nielsen's music are not separate from one another, and my use of them here is not prescriptive. Rather, I delineate them here for their suggestive qualities. In his six symphonies, the work we non-Danes perhaps know best, there is an interesting unification of certain neo-classical rhetorical gestures of form, that is, a complex, but highly-formal, organization based largely on Mozart, with the melodic expressiveness of, say, Brahms (himself also a highly-formal composer).[9] This music is abstract and comes out of and answers to itself.

The second style, as represented for example by the overture, *Helios* (1903) is a formal piece that has yet responded to an impulse outside of itself, the movement of the sun across the sky. It does not purport to describe the emotions this raises in the observer (although, by its nature, it must contain these, because we experience this through Carl Nielsen's interpretation) but, rather, to take representative points of that movement as an organizational suggestion. In doing so, Nielsen was adamant that he had not written 'program music', something he publicly quite disliked.

The third style, as represented by the songs, is complex in the way that sophisticated complexity is often hidden by apparent simplicity. Nielsen's and Laub's song project expressly sought to let the words themselves lead the music, and Nielsen was quite proud of the result, which has an immediacy and an intimacy that propels the words rather than occludes or merely supports them. These songs are truly word-centred and their expressed aim is to draw listener and performer into a common experience. As their texts are at the heart of Danish poetry, they speak with a directness that only a Dane can fully appreciate at once and the rest of us must take on trust.

The above descriptions cannot be exclusive, for it is obvious that there are other ways of organizing our experience of music and describing it. Rather, these characterizations are intended only to help organize our survey here.

The distribution of Nielsen's letters by style is an exercise that perhaps only really concerns a translator. It was, however, through a sense of Nielsen the composer that, during the act of translation, three levels of writing became clear to me. To be sure, the discovery, if it can be called that, was eased by certain characteristics of the Danish language used in a telling way by Nielsen. You will recall that, unlike English, the Scandinavian languages have four possible forms of addressing people, of which two are largely, though by no means exclusively, restricted to Sweden. The four forms may be described as Third and Second Person Formal and Third and Second Person Familiar. Danish prefers the Second Person forms of these, as in the subject pronouns, *De* and *Du*, with their attendant oblique forms. The pronouns, then, tell us something about the relationship between writer and reader.

For instance, the Formal *De* is used consistently in Nielsen's early letters to his much-respected teacher, Orla Rosenhoff. This is only to be expected: Nielsen was, after all, still relatively young and writing to someone he greatly admired. The form also comes, again as expected, in Nielsen's letters to bureaucrats at whom he is angry. In fact, combined with the overt message, the pronouns in these latter render the complete message almost icy. In any event, for a translator, the democratic English 'you' is just not quite enough. Indeed, the very purpose of these formal pronouns is to discourage democratic communication, though, as in the case of his letters to Rosenhoff and, later, to the Swedish composer, Wilhelm Stenhammar, there were other rhetorical ways of showing that this manner contained genuine respect and an intimation of a desire for closer contact. As in Nielsen's large orchestral pieces, the content of these letters is highly organized and moves logically and smoothly from one subject to another, usually related, one. It is, however, in the letters to Stenhammar that we can see the transition to a Middle style.

From 1894, when Nielsen and Stenhammar first met, and tangled, until at least 1911, Nielsen addressed Stenhammar as *De*. From at least 1914 until Stenhammar's death in 1927, however, Nielsen used *Du*.[10] This latter use is, however, only apparently

Familiar, as there are other factors in the letters which suggest that this is the elusive Middle style. Here, we are aided by the salutations of the letters, for Nielsen has a clear hierarchy to which he holds. The Formal style always begins with something like 'Kjære Hr. Rosenhoff' or 'Kære Stenhammar'[11] and contains the expected *De*. It often ends with elaborate greetings and wishes. The Middle style usually opens 'Kære Ven' (which sounds much nicer in Danish than in English, though still suggestive of some distance). Exceptionally, a letter of 11 February 1914, addresses Stenhammar as 'Kære Sten', a salutation whose rhetorical function is difficult to ascertain. Its body uses *Du* and the letter ends with more modest wishes than in a Formal epistle. The later letters to Stenhammar seem to occupy this Middle ground. We see this style in consistent use, as well, in his long correspondence with the Dutch composer, Julius Röntgen. In the distinctions I adduce, it is obvious that Danish has a formal flexibility, denied English, which allows for considerable subtlety in controlling the distance between writer and reader. Nielsen's use of this possibility is consistent and exact, for, in the disposition of these formal elements, Nielsen shows that he has mastered his verbal as well as his musical discourse.

In the Familiar style, in addition to the expected, even necessary, Familiar *Du*, these letters almost always begin with the first name of the person addressed, as in 'Kære Johannes', and end with greetings to all and sundry or some phrase, such as 'Din gamle Ven' or 'Din hengivne'. The letters to his wife form a more intimate variation on this style. He frequently addresses her as 'Min egen Ven', or something like that. In one early case, she even becomes his 'Kjære, lille Godte!', a sticky form that only someone newly married could produce or endure.[12] Most of these letters end, simply, 'Din Carl', though there are occasions, during the period of their separation between 1915 and 1922, when he signs them, 'Din Ven, Carl'.

The selection of Carl Nielsen's letters I have used is largely centered on his musical remarks. It is, however, interesting to note that even in that selection, their contents often mirror the distinction I have here been drawing. For instance, the Formal letters talk mostly about other people's music, usually as he had heard it at a recent concert. Even in his youthful letters, he has no hesitation about assessing the musical qualities of what he had heard, and his own attitudes toward the music are always completely clear. He is rarely neutral about a piece of music. For instance, during his study in Dresden, he wrote to his early supporter, Emil B. Sachs, 'Jeg har hørt hele Nibelungen-Cyklus af Wagner i denne Uge. Han er en Karl!...en Kjæmpe i vor Tid. Og at der findes Mennesker som ikke kan lide Wagners Musik, det er ubegribeligt....Han er et vældigt Geni. Hut ab!' (I have heard the whole Nibelungen Cycle of Wagner this week. He is a real man!...a fighter in our time. And that there are people who cannot stand Wagner's music I cannot understand....He is a great Genius. Watch out!).[13] On the other hand, he could barely stand Weber's *Oberon*. 'Det er dog en græsselig Opera!' (It's a dreadful opera!)[14] In 1897, he thought the music of his Swedish friend, Bror Beckman, far better than that of Wilhelm Stenhammar, whose music and person it took a while to warm to,[15] and in 1904, he was of the opinion that Beckman's piano pieces were 'nydelige og mere indholdsrige end Grieg'ske Stykker af den Art' (useful and richer in content than Grieg-like pieces of that kind).[16] His likes and dislikes extended to the visual arts, as well. He was impressed by Ribera, Rembrandt, Carraci – and by the Danish artist, P.S. Krøyer – and was surprised to find that he did not like Corregio, Rubens, Holbein, or Dürer.[17] In the same year, in a letter to the writer Gustav Wied, he tells how he was rude when the writer and painter Holger Drachmann, called him a Symbolist. 'Jeg slog ham en Taar koldt Vand i Blodet og erklærede at De var den eneste Forfatter af danske som jeg kunde læse med Udbytte. Det Symbolistvrøvl! Ikke sandt? Drachmann er mig usympatisk; han er vist ikke noget rigtigt Mandfolk. Denne lange Spiral med en Stemme som en Kastrat. Han er ingen Mand' (I threw cold water on that and declared that you were the only writer of Danish I could get something out of. That Symbolist rubbish! Isn't that so? I am unsympathetic to Drachmann; he's not really a man. This long spiral with a voice like a castrato. He is no man).[18] It must be noted that these strong expressions come mostly early on in the letters, and that others had also commented on Drachmann's peculiarly high voice.

The Middle style letters are frequently about technical matters in music, sometimes his own, sometimes someone else's, as when, for instance, he gives Knud Harder the following advice: 'Prøv engang at komponere ganske enkelte, [sic.] tonale Melodier, uden al Harmoni (enstemmigt); forestil Dem at De ikke tør bevæge Dem udenfor Skalaens 8 Toner og at hver Tone er en Helligdom som ikke under Dødsstraf tør berøres virkningsløst' (Try once to write quite simple, tonal melodies, without any harmony (one-line); imagine that you dare not move them beyond the 8 notes of the scale and that each note is something sacred which ought not to be touched without effect, under pain of death).[19] This is an excellent exercise for learning how melody itself, something always dear to Nielsen's heart as a composer, carries its own weight and harmonic implications. He did give advice to close friends, as well, to be sure, as in this to Beckman: '...ifald Du vil modtage et Raad af mig saa siger jeg: Øv Dig meget i Kontrapunkt og Modolation, [sic.]...Skriv f. Expl. Til Studium en Kvartet ganske som Beethowens [sic.] Op. 18 Nr. 1 1'ste Allegro. Samme Antal Takter, samme Modulationer og samme Udarbejdelse helt igjennem. Du skal se, det lønner sig. Eller en Fuga af Bach!' (...in case you would take a piece of advice from me, I would say: Practice counterpoint and modulation a great deal...For example, write as an exercise a quartet just like Beethoven's Op. 18:1, the first Allegro. The same number of measures, the same modulations, and the same development from start to finish. You will see, it will repay you. Or a fugue of Bach!).[20] This splendid pedagogical counsel is, of course, derived directly from the classical practice of *imitatio* but I rather think Nielsen thought of it himself.

The Familiar letters are almost exclusively about himself and his own music. Curiously, perhaps, it is mostly in the Familiar letters that Nielsen resorts to metaphor. Metaphor is, I think, rare in any personal letter. Indeed, the writers whose use of it in letters we remember are remembered in part for that very feature. The personal letter is not a place where one needs to show off. This does not mean, of course, that one could not or did not show off in such a context.

In Nielsen's letters, as in most of his prose, the few metaphors are often quite homely. At one point, in 1905, when things are going quite well with his composition, he speaks of himself in a letter to his wife, then studying in Athens, in surprisingly Romantic terms for one who disliked many aspects of Romanticism, as having 'en Fornemmelse af at jeg slet ikke er mig selv, – Carl August Nielsen, – men kun ligesom et aabent Rør, hvorigennem der løber en Musikstrøm...' (a sense that I am not at all myself, – Carl August Nielsen, – but only like an open pipe, through which gushes a stream of music...).[21] Another time, writing to Stenhammar, he asks, 'Har De, a propos, lagt Mærke til hvormange nyere Komponister der ligesom er kommen ind paa Musiken fra den forkerte Side? De begynder med Duften, Poesien, Blomsten, Toppen af Kunsten istedetfor med Roden, Jorden, Plantningen og Formeringen' (Have you noticed, by the way, how many of our younger composers come to music from the wrong end? They begin with the smell, the poetry, the tip of the art instead of the roots, the earth, the planting, and multiplying).[22] In his 1932 essay about Nielsen's prose (not including the letters, which were unknown at the time), the great Danish novelist, Tom Kristensen, called attention to two aspects of Nielsen's use of language. First, he pointed out there are very few mentions of colour or analogies to colour in the prose, and we can now see that this is borne out in the letters. Further, Kristensen appreciated that Nielsen's rare use of metaphor often centered around farm and country-side, as in the letter just cited. Here is Nielsen again, writing to the actor and director, Johannes Nielsen: 'Du har i Dit Spil noget som altid betager mig og som jeg maa blive ved at tænke paa. Du bringer noget op i mig saa jeg føler mig som god Jord der lige er pløjet og nu skal til at tage imod Regn og Sol og Frø og Frugt...' (You have, in your acting, something that always attracts me and [gives me] something that I have to think about. You bring something out of me, so that I feel like good earth that has just been ploughed and is now ready to receive rain and sun and seed and fruit...).[23]

Most of Nielsen's letters are serious. He felt quite put upon by the administration of the Royal Theatre and he nourished a continual feud with newspaper critics. Time and again, he saw himself unfairly taken advantage of, as in a long, dark, even bitter, letter from 1914 to Johannes Nielsen, whom he saw as his only supporter in the theatre administration, which ends, 'Ak, kære Johannes, det skærer mig i Hjærtet, hvergang jeg undenfor mit Fødeland mærker at jeg er ret anset. Det som burde glæde mig, svider og stikker fordi jeg ved hvad der venter mig hjemme og kender alle de Kræfter der ønsker mig langt bort...' (Oh, dear Johannes, it cuts me to the quick every time I notice that outside the country of my birth I am well-considered. That which ought to please me sears and stabs, because I know what awaits me at home and know all those powers who wish me far away...).[24] Yet he could be humorous when he wished, as in this letter to his wife after a wildly successful performance of his opera, *Saul og David*, which the critics disliked and of whose commendation by the public his sister-in-law, Lucie Brodersen, had something to say. 'Bladene er rasende og levner mig hverken Talent, Hjerte eller Smag. Nu gaar jeg videre med mit Arbejde; jeg ved hvad jeg kan....Lucie er her. Da jeg idag fik en Lavrbærkrans sagde hun at det var nok til Grisesylte for lang Tid! Poetisk er hun ikke' (The newspapers are furious and allow me neither talent, heart, nor taste. Now I'll keep on with my work; I know what I can do....Lucie is here. When I received a laurel wreath today, she said that it would be enough for brawn for a long time. Poetic she is not).[25] He had once joked that he knew only two words of English, 'Yes', and 'Ivory'. He refers to this as his 'Ivory-period' and says that he has now learned more English. 'Jeg er helt inde i min 2'den Periode – alle store Mestre har jo som bekendt tre Perioder i deres Udvikling – og her har jeg ikke blot et enkelt Ord til Holdepunkt, som jo var saa karakterisk for Stilen fra den første Periode – men hele to korte Sætninger, hvor jeg med ikke ringe Smidighed, kan entre fra den ene til den anden uden nogensinde at støde paa Vanskeligheder eller støde an mod god Tone og selskabelig Form for gensidig Underholdning, nemlig: "I thank you" og "Werry well"' (I am well into my second period – as you know, all great masters have three periods in their development – and here I have not just one single word as my anchor, as was so characteristic of my first period – but two complete short sentences which I can use, with no small cleverness, to get from one thing to another without ever doing something odd or transgressing good tone or social form for mutual amusement, namely, 'I thank you' and 'Werry well').[26]

I have used the conceit of reading the letters through the music. But the question still nags me: why read letters, why read these letters, apart from the mere human curiosity to know more about one another, to meet an interesting person? Perhaps this is enough. To the extent that the music is important, it is instructive to know as much as possible about how that music is/was made. Though Carl Nielsen frequently discussed musical and compositional issues in letters to his friends, teachers, and colleagues, he seems usually already to have had very clear ideas about what he was doing and to have used epistolary conversation mostly to confirm those ideas. He seems seldom to have discussed his work in letter form and my sense is that, to the extent he actually discussed his music with anyone, it was done face to face. One of the rare moments in which we can see his creative process at work is in a letter written during the making of his second opera, *Maskarade*. When he had finally finished the composition and the work was in rehearsal, in November 1906, he wrote to Julius Röntgen that the orchestra liked the music, but that there were still problems: 'Desuden maatte vi [that is the librettist, Wilhelm Andersen, and himself] skrive en lille ny Scene for Pernille, som ikke var bleven helt karakteriseret i Operaen, hvad der først efterhaanden gik op for mig' (In addition, we have to write a new little scene for Pernille, who has not been completely characterised in the opera, [something] which first became clear to me afterwards).[27]

 I return, then, to my original observation, that there is a useable stylistic correspondence between Nielsen's work and his letters and that knowing Nielsen's work can suggest ways of talking about the letters as letters. What is clear is that these three styles were all used simultaneously through his life as composer and epistler. By pointing this out, I mean to suggest that Nielsen's letters, as with his music, have clear and deliberate rhetorical dimensions which are important for understanding their author. On one level, the three styles I here adduce and their variations on respect and intimacy are no more than to be expected from someone writing within a society like Nielsen's. He was always aware of the boundaries of convention, so that when he broke them, he was awake to a poetic effect. For instance, an almost telegraphic thank-you note to Vera Michaelsen begins with the near-rhyme of the salutation and gathers rhythmic speed towards its brief end, as he discovers the prosodic possibilities and even pads a bit to make it all come out:

Kære Vera! En skrækkelig Pen i en Kiosk! Meningen god nok. Dejligt Vejr! Tak for sidst! Hilsen til alle! Etty! Carl Johan! Walther Ove! Sovet skidt, spidst godt, tænkt paa Jer, gaaet en Tur. Truffet Glass, Vissevas! Kærlig Hilsen Carel Nielsen[28]

To be sure, this is intended as a light piece of thanks, of small consequence; but, on the other hand, it does demonstrate, even in his language, his rhetorical awareness, of which style is a central part. Here, he has clearly meant to delight his hostess, to tease pleasure out of words. It thus parallels the rhetorical awareness he consistently shows in his music and reminds us that the return of pleasure was also a part of his gift to us.

Alas, I cannot do more than suggest the charm of these letters, as I have here been able to do no more than suggest their craft. If I have done that, however, then, as Nielsen said, 'I thank you werry well'.

Notes

1. *The Nielsen Companion*, ed. Mina Miller (London: Faber and Faber, 1994), pp. 599-640.
2. See the letter of June 7, 1907, to the composer, Knud Harder, in Irmelin Eggert Møller and Torben Meyer, eds., *Carl Nielsens Breve* (Copenhagen: Gyldendal, 1954), pp. 85-86.
3. See Tom Kristensen, 'Carl Nielsen as a Writer', in Miller, ed., *Nielsen Companion*, pp. 151-59.
4. See, for instance the 'Introduction' to *Levende musik*, where he talks about the inheritance of the notion of 'duty' from his regimental days.
5. Letter to Gustaf Hetsch, May 8, 1915, *Breve*, pp. 148-49.
6. He refers to his *Modulationstrang* in a letter of August 19, 1913, to the pianist, Henrik Knudsen, *Breve*, p. 133.
7. See fn. 2, as well as Carl Nielsen, *Breve fra Carl Nielsen til Emil B. Sachs* (Copenhagen: Skandinavisk Grammophon A/S, 1952), and Carl Nielsen, *Dagbøger og brevveksling med Anne Marie Carl-Nielsen*, ed. by Torben Schousboe, 2 vols (Copenhagen: Gyldendal, 1983).
8. See *Det Kongelige Biblioteks Håndskriftafdeling. Erhvervelser 1924-1987*, Vol. 2 (Copenhagen: Det kongelige Bibliotek/Museum Tusculanums

Forlag, 1985), p. 470. I have not myself worked with the manuscripts.
9. See the essay by Povl Hamburger, 'The Problem of Form in the Music of Our Time with an Analysis of Nielsen's *Sinfonia espansiva*, First Movement', in Miller, ed., *Nielsen Companion*, pp. 379-95, in which he discusses the neo-Classical basis of the first movement of Nielsen's 3rd symphony, Op. 27 (1910-11). Nielsen himself had reservations about Brahms' music early on [*Breve*, p.11] but was very enthusiastic about Wagner.
10. *Breve*, pp. 111, 141.
11. *Breve*, pp. 7, 111.
12. *Breve*, p. 32.
13. *Breve*, p. 9.
14. *Breve*, p. 14.
15. *Breve*, p. 33.
16. *Breve*, p. 62.
17. *Breve*, pp. 9-10.
18. *Breve*, p. 37.
19. *Breve*, p. 84.
20. *Breve*, p. 38.
21. *Breve*, p. 68.
22. *Breve*, p. 113.
23. *Breve*, p. 110.
24. *Breve*, p. 141.
25. *Breve*, p. 65.
26. *Breve*, p. 134.
27. *Breve*, p. 81.
28. *Breve*, p. 200. The poetic qualities of this letter cannot be reproduced in English. The words mean: 'Dear Vera! A dreadful pen in a kiosk! The meaning [is] clear enough. Splendid weather! Thanks for your hospitality! Greetings to everybody! Etty! Carl Johan! Walther Ove! Slept wretchedly, ate well, thought of you, took a walk. Found ice-cream, Vissevas! Warm greetings Carel Nielsen.' Note that Nielsen even spelt his name so as to make the rhythm work.

Index

The Scandinavian letters å, ä, and æ are listed under a, and ø and ö under o.

Aalberg, Ida, 194
Adam, 380, 394
Ahlström, Gunnar, 357
Åhman, Svea, 160, 161
Aho, Juhani, 338; *Yksin*, 344
Ahrenberg, Jac, 338, 343; *Hihuliter*, 343
Albert, Karl Otto, 152
Altman, Janet, 25, 27-8, 32
Ancher, Anna, 228
Ancher, Michael, 228
Andersen, Anne Fredrikke, 43
Andersen, Hans Christian, 174, 179, 364, 379, 391
Andersen, Hildur, 26, 38, 43-6, 48, 63
Andersen, Oluf Martin, 43
Andersen, Rasmus, 249
Andersen, Vilhelm, 90, 241-2; *Bacchustoget i Norden*, 241
Andersen, Wilhelm, 410
Anker, Øyvind, 18, 36, 38, 43, 44, 63
Appia, Adolphe, 157, 169
Arayashiki, Toru, 382
Arvesen, Arve, 379, 384, 386
Arvesen, Olaus, 386
Asbjørnsen, Peter Christen, 384, 390
Atterbom, Per Daniel Amadeus, 364
Auquier, Philippe, 388

Bach, Johan Sebastian, 407
Backer, Harriet, 356, 357, 386
Baggessen, Jens, 221
Bang, Herman, 28, 207, 226-7, 240-41, 247, 315, 338, 348-9, 391

Bang, Kate, 28
Bardach, Emilie, 37-8, 42-3, 44
Bates, Henry Walter, 29
Beckman, Bror, 406
Beecham, Thomas, 377
Beethoven, Ludvig van, 407
Bell, Jutta, 378
Bellman, Carl Michael, 143
Benedictsson, Victoria, 11, 23, 28, 30, 229, 230
Bentzon, Harriet, 203-4
Bergh, Ludvig, 389
Bergman, Gösta M., 157, 169
Bergman, Hjalmar, 110
Berlioz, Hector, 399
Bernays, Mikael, 338
Berner, Hagbard, 64
Bernini, Gianlorenzo, 46
Bernstein, Leonard, 399
Bjerke, Mette, 172
Björling, Hedvig Amanda, 155, 159, 162, 163, 165
Bjørnson, Bjørnstjerne, 13, 14, 18, 21-2, 26, 28, 37, 46, 47, 50, 51, 57, 64, 80, 90, 104, 146, 152, 174, 184, 201, 211, 255, 262, 264, 265, 276, 307, 311, 312-3, 331, 352, 355, 360, 363, 366, 367, 379, 386, 387, 390; *En handske* (A Glove), 229; *Kongen* (The King), 57; *Paul Lange og Tora Parsberg*, 238; *Redaktørn* (The Editor), 57
Bjørnson, Dagny, 355
Bjørnson, Karoline, 360
Blehr, Otto, 388-9
Blehr, Randi, 388-9
Blumenthal, Oscar, 145
Bødtker, Sigurd, 389

Bögh, Erik, 383
Bojesen, Ernst, 326, 329, 330
Bonnier, Albert, 152, 340, 345, 349
Böök, Fredrik, 28
Borchsenius, Otto, 13, 207, 215, 224, 225, 237, 276, 300
Borup, Morten, 203, 206, 212, 213, 219, 223, 224
Bosse, Harriet, 12, 111-12, 152, 156, 161, 167, 170
Boswell, James, 11
Brahms, Johannes, 403
Brandes, Edith, 83, 84
Brandes, Edvard, 12, 13, 14, 23, 25, 52, 173, 180, 183, 186, 207, 209, 210, 211, 212, 213, 219, 221, 226, 229, 231, 233, 237, 248-9, 250, 252, 259, 261, 265, 276
Brandes, Ernst, 231-1
Brandes, Georg, 11, 12, 13, 14, 18, 21-2, 23, 30, 34, 35, 36, 37, 44, 50-6, 61-2, 63, 65-86, 87-107, 174, 180, 184, 194, 197, 201-2, 207, 209, 210-11, 212, 213, 214, 221, 222, 226, 229, 231, 238, 239-9, 243-4, 250-54, 261, 265, 276-7, 319, 355, 361-2, 364-5, 366, 368, 369, 402; *Hovedstrømninger i det 19de Aarhundredes Litteratur* (Main Currents in 19th Century Literature), 52, 53, 54-5, 80, 95; *Indtryck fra Polen* (Impressions from Poland), 23, 26; *Levned* (Life), 88, 89, 100, 101, 102, 105; 'Magnet for Gale' (Magnet for Madmen), 70; *Det moderne Gennembruds Mænd* (The Men of the Modern Breakthrough), 88, 202, 211, 212; 'Nadjesjda', 83
Brausewetter, Ernst, 367

Bregendahl, Marie, 247
Brøchner, Hans, 18
Brodersen, Lucie, 409
Bronte, Emily, *Wuthering Heights*, 312
Bruce, Caroline Benedicks, 382
Budkaflen, 19
Bull, Francis, 38, 90, 93, 102, 106
Byron, Lord George Gordon, 59, 247

Caesar, Julius, 70
Caillavet, Mme de, 12, 70
Calving, Henrik, 243
Canth, Minna, *Hanna*, 344
Carraci, Annibale, 406
Casanova, Mr, 71-2
Casanova, Sophia della Valle di, 71
Chadwick, Emma Löwstädt, 382-3
Christensen, Harald, 222
Clausen, Sophus, 247
Collett, Camilla, 356, 357
Collin, Christen, 252
Collin, Edvard, 50, 174
Collin, Jonas, 50, 51, 174
Conrad, Michael Georg, 366, 370, 374; *Was die Isar rauscht*, 374
Copland, Aaron, 399
Correggio, Antonio Allegri, 406
Craig, Edward Gordon, 157, 169; *On the Art of the Theatre*, 167

Dagbladet, 49, 50, 258
Dagens nyheter, 134
Dahl, Per Heggelund, 60
Dahlerup, Pil, 106
Danielsen, Dr, 104
Dante Aligheri, *Divina Commedia*, 58
Darwin, Charles, 124
Dehmel, Richard, 134
Delius, Frederick, 376-397; *An Arabesque*, 391; *Fennimore and Gerda*, 391; Incidental Music to

Folkeraadet, 392; *Life's Dance*, 391, 392; *The Magic Fountain*, 391
Derrida, Jacques, 30
Desprès, Suzanne, 155
Dickens, Charles, 110
Diderot, Denis, 25; *Le paradoxe sur le comédien*, 157
Dietrichson, Lorentz, 46, 107
Dörum, August, 155, 157-8, 159-60
Dostoyevsky, Fyodor, 110, 261, 262
Drachmann, A. G., 213
Drachmann, Emmy, 215
Drachmann, Holger, 185, 195, 196-7, 202-227, 231, 247, 276, 355, 360, 365, 367, 369, 370-1, 406; *Derovre dra Grænsen* (Across the Border), 212; *Sakuntala*, 391; *Skyggebilleder fra Rejser i Indland og Udland* (Shadows from Journeys at Home and Abroad), 212; *Til Aulestad* (To Aulestad), 211
Drewsen, Gerd, 172,174, 197
Drewsen, Jonna, 174
Drewsen, Louise, 18, 27, 177-91
Drewsen, Sten, *En kværulant ser tilbage* (A Querulous Man Looks Back), 173, 174, 175-6
Drewsen, Svend, 174, 194
Drewsen, Viggo, 18, 27, 177-91, 209; *En Livsanskuelse grundet paa Elskov* (A Philosophy Based on Love), 178, 179, 189-90, 209; *Forholdet mellem Mand og Kvinde, belyst gennem Udviklings-Hypothesen* (The Relationship Between Man and Woman, As Seen Through Evolutionary Theory), 178-9; *Grænser for Kønsfriheden. Uddrag af et ufærdigt Arbejde* (Limits for Freedom of the Sexes. Excerpts from an Unfinished Work), 179; 'Om en reaksjon mod den moderne stræben efter større sexuel sædelighed' (Concerning a Reaction against the Modern Striving for an Improvement in Sexual Morals), 179
Dreyfus, Albert, 222
Dürer, Albrecht, 406
Dybsand, Øyvin, 384

Elias, Julius, 12, 37
Elster, Kristian, Jr., 90
Erichsen, Vilhelmine, 209
Ericsen, Ida, 381
Essen, Siri von, 19, 23, 27, 31, 109-110, 112, 130, 140, 148, 152, 157, 166
Eysoldt, Gertrud, 146

Fædrelandet, 50
Fahlstedt, Eugène, 21
Fahlström, Johan, 390
Falck, August (b. 1843), 152-5, 166
Falck, August (b. 1882), 150-1, 155, 158-9, 160-1, 163, 164, 165, 166, 167, 168
Falkner, Fanny, 164
Fenby, Eric, 385
Fenger, Henning, 93
Finne, Gabriel, 356, 367
Finsk Tidskrift, 338
Flaubert, Gustave, 28
Flygare, Anna, 158-9, 165
Fontane, Theodor, 371
France, Anatole, 77
Franckenfeldt, Hilma, 154
Freud, Sigmund, 31-32
Fröding, Gustaf, 28
Fuchs, Georg, 157; *Die Schaubühne der Zukunft*, 167

Garborg, Arne, 19, 30, 257, 259, 265, 312, 348, 354, 357, 363, 366, 368, 369, 370, 389; *Bondestudentar*, 186; *Den burtkomne Faderen* (The Lost Father), 329; *Kolbotn brev*, 363
Garborg, Hulda, 354
Gardt, Fru, 154
Gaskell, Elizabeth, *Mary Barton*, 312
Gegenwart, 367
Geijerstam, Gustaf af, 135
George, Stefan, 359
Gjellerup, Karl, 216
Gjertsen, Fredrik, 58, 59
Goethe, Johan Wolfgang von, 59, 70, 140, 162, 243, 261; *Faust*, 58; *Hermann und Dorothea*, 59; *Wilhelm Meister*, 140
Gosse, Edmund, 26
Gran, Gerhard, 48
Grandinson, Emil, 156, 158
Grieg, Edvard, 377-8, 381, 383, 386, 387, 389, 391, 406
Grindea, Miron, 380
Grønvold, Markus, 356, 366
Grundtvig, Nicolaie F. S., 202
Gulbransson, Olaf, 352
Gulin, Åke, 349

Hagelstam, O. J., 143
Håkonsson, Julia, 157
Halvorsen, Johan, 379, 384, 386
Hamsun, Knut, 19, 30, 107, 246-62, 356, 388; 'Hazard', 262; *I æventyrland*, 253; 'Livets Røst' (The Voice of Life), 366; *Mysterier* (Mysteries), 249, 256, 359, 366; *Ny Jord*, 260; *Redaktør Lynge* (Editor Lynge), 258; *Sult* (Hunger), 19, 247, 248, 249, 251, 253, 262, 263; *Victoria*, 253

Hansen, Paul Botten, 46
Hansen, Peter, 58
Hansen, P. E., 247
Hansson, Alfred, 159
Hansson, Ola, 117, 134, 142, 229, 337, 354-5, 365-6, 370
Hauge, Alfred, 387
Hausemann, David, 140
Hedberg, Frans, 151, 155
Hedlund, Torsten, 27, 31, 110, 111, 151-2
Hegel, Frederik V., 37, 49-50, 208, 209, 215, 260, 306-12, 316, 319, 322, 331-2, 367
Hegel, Jacob, 13, 216, 220, 306, 319-26, 327, 329, 330, 332
Hegel, Julie, 216
Heiberg, Gunnar, 257, 388, 389; *Balkongen* (The Balcony), 390; *Folkeraadet*, 389-90
Heiberg, Johan Ludvig, 221
Heiberg, Johanne Louise, 34, 94, 110; *Peter Andreas Heiberg og Thomasine Gyllembourg. En beretning, støttet paa efterladte breve* (Peter Andreas Heiberg and Thomasine Gyllembourg. A Tale based on their Letters), 110
Heidenstam, Verner von, 14, 28, 135, 142, 152, 337, 356, 'Renässans', 337; 'Pepitas bröllop' (Pepita's Wedding), 337
Heine, Heinrich, 140; *Buch der Lieder* (Book of Songs), 140-1
Heinemann, William, 70
Heiβerer, Dirk, 352
Helland, Amund, 277
Hennings, Henrik, 391
Henningsen, Agnes, 207, 247
Herzfeld, Marie, 262
Heseltine, Philip, 377
Heyse, Paul, 355, 358-9, 364-5, 370, 373

Hilarius-Kalkau, Mrs, see Erichsen, Vilhelmine, 209
Hillberg, Gösta, 156
Hjort, Marie, 77
Høffding, Harald, 178
Hogarth, William, 406
Holberg, Ludvig, 58
Holck, O. E., 334
Holst, Johann von, 153
Holm, Korfiz, 366
Holter, Iver, 386, 387
Homer, *Iliad*, 59, *Odyssey*, 59
Horace, *Ars Poetica*, 58
Hørup, Viggo, 12, 26, 31, 209, 281-305
Høst, Else, 38-9, 43, 46
Hufvudstadsbladet, 336
Hutten, Ulrich, 141

Ibsen, Bergljot, 63
Ibsen, Henrik, 12, 14, 17, 18, 19, 25-6, 29, 33-64, 90, 125; *Brand*, 46-7, 58, 125, 153, 160, 201, 265, 311, 316, 338, 347, 352, 353-4, 355, 356, 357, 360, 363, 366, 367-8, 369-70, 373, 387, 390; *Et Dukkehjem* (A Doll's House), 17, 125; *En Folkefiende* (An Enemy of the People), 55; *Fruen fra havet* (The Lady from the Sea), 62; *Gengangere* (Ghosts), 19, 53, 124, 125, 316, 373; *Hedda Gabler*, 43, 231-2, 353, 363; *Hærmændene på Helgeland* (The Vikings at Helgeland), 48; *John Gabriel Borkman*, 157; *Kejser og Galilæer* (Emperor and Galilean), 53; *Kongsemnerne* (The Pretenders), 33; *Lille Eyolf* (Little Eyolf), 33, 252; *Når vi døde vågner* (When We Dead Awaken), 157; *Paa Vidderne* (On the Heights), 386, 390; *Peer Gynt*, 47, 50, 125; *Rosmersholm*, 33, 170, 234-5, 353; *Samfundets støtter* (The Pillars of Society), 56, 157, 353; *Vildanden* (The Wild Duck), 33, 41, 236
Ibsen, Sigurd, 37, 39, 40-1
Ibsen, Suzannah, 39-40, 41-2
Iliffe, Barry, 384
Illustreret Tidende, 88, 99, 100, 101, 102
Ingemann, B. S., 364
Ingersoll, Robert, 261
Irminger, Valdemar, 303

Jacobsen, Camilla, 379
Jacobsen, J. C., 220
Jacobsen, Jens Peter, 28, 187, 265, 356, 360-1, 363, 365, 390, 392; *Niels Lyhne*, 391
James, Henry, 21
Jansen, Kristofer, 248
Jebe, Halfdan, 379, 384-5, 388, 390
Jensen, C. E., 233
Jensen, Hans Jacob, 48-9
Jensen, Johannes V., 238, 247, 248
Jensen, Thit, 207
Johnsen, Hjalmar, 386
Johnson, Samuel, 11, 24, 31
Josephson, Ernst, 382; 'Svarta rosor' (Black Roses), 381
Josephson, Ludvig, 151, 166
Juel, Dagny, 134

Karsten, Ludvig, 387
Keats, John, 28
Key, Ellen, 77
Kielland, Alexander, 13, 14, 18, 27, 48, 72, 172-99, 225, 231, 251, 265, 274, 276, 277, 307, 310, 349, 365; *Garman & Worse*, 183; *Gift* (Married), 183, 184; *Sne* (Snow), 196; *St. Hans*

Fest (Midsummer Festival), 197;
Tre Par (Three Couples), 194, 196
Kielland, Baby, 198
Kielland, Beate, 182-3, 184, 185, 188, 192, 196, 197, 200-1
Kielland, Kitty, 356, 357
Kierkegaard, Søren, 12, 52, 58, 64, 179, 186, 197, 202
Kihlman, Erik, 337
Kinckerfuss, Margrethe, 77
Kittelsen, Theodor, 356
Kjellgren, Alrik, 164, 165
Kjerulf, Theodor, 390
Kjøbenhavns Børs Tidende, 231
Klee, Paul, 359
Kleist, Heinrich von, 112
Klingenfeld, Emma, 387
Knudtzon, Benedicte, 174
Knudtzon, Bertha, 69, 82, 83-4, 174, 194
Koch, Richert von, 153
Koht, Halvdan, 12, 36, 37, 38, 41, 42
Krag, Vilhelm, 387, 390
Kristensen, Tom, 408
Kristeva, Julia, 96-7
Krohg, Christian, 134, 228, 387-9
Krohg, Oda, 387, 389
Kronberg, Julius, 356
Krøyer, Paul Severin, 174, 228, 406
Kullenberg, Annette, 126, 128

Labatt, Leonard, 380-1, 383
Lagerlöf, Selma, 28, 254
Land, Anna, 76
Lang, Eivind, 172
Lange, Sven, 242, 247, 355, 356
Lange, Uffe, 172
Langen, Albert, 352, 354, 355, 359, 366
Langhoff, Paul, 306, 317-9, 323, 325
Larsen, Karl, 247

Larsen, Nathalie, 152, 162
Larsson, Carl, 111, 125, 127, 130-1, 152, 380, 383
Laub, Thomas, 400, 401, 403
Levertin, Oscar, 135
Lidforss, Bengt, 134-5
Lie, Jonas, 14, 18, 28, 111, 311, 348, 355, 357, 369, 370
Lie, Thomasine, 355
Liebeg, Justus von, 358
Liliencron, Detlef von, 371
Limnell, Fredrika, 34
Lindberg, August, 151, 153
Lindström, Willehad, 128-9
Littmansson, Leopold, 110, 135, 136-9, 152
Loerges, Margrethe, 205
Looström, Claes, 124, 154
Ludwig I of Bavaria, 358, 361
Lugné-Poë, Aurélian, 155
Luitpold, Regent of Bavaria, 359
Lund, Nils, 34-5
Lunde, Johs., 14, 172, 184
Lundegård, Axel, 229, 230, 238; *I Gryningen* (At Dawn), 230
Lundin, Claes, 133
Lundqvist, Ernst, 124
Lundström, Georg, 19
Luther, Martin, 140,
Lybeck, Mikael, 335-51; *Breven till Cecilia* (Letters to Ceceilia), 337; *Den starkare* (The Stronger), 335; *Tomas Indal*, 336, 337; *Unge Hemming*, 336, 344-6, 348, 349

MacArthur, Elizabeth, 23
Mann, Thomas, 352, 359; *Buddenbrooks*, 359
Marholm-Hansson, Laura, 354-5; *Das Buch der Frauen*, 354, 363
Martensen, H. L., 220
Maurer, Konrad, 356-7
Maximilian II of Bavaria, 358

Meisling, S. S., 58-9
Meyer, Torben, 402
Meyerhold, Vsevolod, 157, 163
Michaelangelo, 46, 70, 399
Michælsen, Vera, 410
Michælson, Knut, 156
Mill, John Stuart, 254
Millroth, Thomas, 381
Moe, Jörgen Engebretsen, 384, 390
Molander, Harald, 168-9
Molard, William, 381, 390
Molière, 167
Møller, Irmelin Eggert, 402
Möller, Peter von, 153
Montelius, Oscar, 131-2
Morgenbladet, 19, 313
Mozart, Wolfgang Amadeus, 403
Munch, Andreas, 390
Munch, Edvard, 134, 379, 385-6, 390, 395, 396

Nansen, Betty, 328
Nansen, Peter, 207, 240, 250, 257, 260, 306, 328-30, 332
Nansen, Fru, 146, 152
Nationaltidende, 68
Nexø, Martin Andersen, 242-3; *Pelle Erobreren*, 242
Nielsen, Anne Marie, 402
Nielsen, Carl, 398-412; *En Snes danske Viser* (A Score of Danish Songs), 400; *Helios*, 403; *Levende Musik* (Living Music), 399; *Min fynske barndom* (My Childhood on Funen), 399-400; *Saul og David*, 409
Nielsen, Johannes, 408-9
Nielsen, Rasmus, 50
Nietzsche, Friedrich, 13, 26, 254
Nilssen, Jappe, 387
Nilsson, Amanda, 205
Nilsson, Ivar, 151, 157
Nordisk tidskrift, 131
Nya Pressen, 338

Ny Jord, 248, 262
Nylander, Lars, 343
Nyt Tidsskrift, 313

Obstfelder, Sigbjørn, 388
Oehlenschläger, Adam, 221; *Haaken Jarl* (Earl Haakon), 62
Oscar II, 56
Oselio, Gina, 386

Päivärinta, Pietari, 338
Palme, August, 156
Paul, Adolf, 134, 141
Paulsen, John, 355, 390
Personne, Nils, 156
Petersen, Eiliff, 356
Petersen, Clemens, 47
Pettersen, Emil, 91, 94, 103, 104
Philipsen, Gustav, 248, 249, 258-9, 306, 319, 314-5, 316, 334
Pingel, Victorinus, 214
Pirkheimer, Willbald, 141, 144
Politiken, 219, 229, 243, 248-9, 250, 252, 253, 257, 259, 261, 296, 313, 328
Pontoppidan, Henrik, 74, 75, 146, 152, 228-44; *Det forjættede Land* (The Promised Land), 236; *Fra Hytterne*, 241; *Den gamle Adam* (The Old Adam), 236; *Lykke-Per*, 74-5, 237, 238-9; *Mimoser*, 228-9; *Skyer* (Clouds), 230
Pontoppidan, Knud, 282
Poulsen, Cecilia, 371, 375
Przybyszewski, Stanislaus, 134, 141, 144
Pushkin, Alexandr, 110

Raff, Helene, 367
Ranke, Leopold von, 358
Redford, Bruce, 24-5
Reicher, Emanuel, 146
Reimers, Sofie, 170

Reinhardt, Max, 146, 149
Rembrandt van Rijn, 361, 406
Reventlow, Franziska zu, 352, 359; *Herrn Dames Aufzeichnungen oder Begebenheiten aus einem merkwürdigen Stadtteil*, 374
Ribera, José de, 406
Richardson, Samuel, 20-1, 23-4, 30, 149, 170; *Pamela*, 182
Richardt, Christian, 97, 96
Ricoeur, Paul, 113
Riehl, Heinrich von, 358
Rilke, Rainer Maria, 359
Ring, Herman, *Teaterns historia från äldsta till nyaste tid*, 167
Ringelnatz, Joachim, 352, 359
Rode, Helge, 391-3; *Grev Bonde og hans Hus*, 392; *Morbus Tellerman*, 392
Rømhild, Lars Peter, 343
Röntgen, Julius, 410
Rosen, Jelka, 382, 385, 388, 392
Rosenhoff, Orla, 404
Rubens, Peter Paul, 361, 406
Rubow, Paul V., 204, 223, 225
Rugstad, Gunnar, 383
Rydberg, Viktor, 58, 135

Sachs, Emil B., 402, 406
Salminen, Johannes, 336
Samtiden, 322
Schandorph, Ida, 315
Schandorph, Sophus, 276, 312, 315, 368
Schering, Emil, 146-7, 148, 149, 150
Schildt, Holger, 338
Schiller, Friedrich von, 140, 'Die Götter Griechenlands' (The Gods of Greece), 140; *Maria Stuart*, 167
Schiwe, Viggo, 159
Schopenhauer, Arthur, 140, 142; *Die Welt als Wille und Vorstellung* (The World as Will and Representation), 142
Schou, Andreas, 319
Schou, Einar, 393
Schou, Elisabeth, 393
Schubothe, Johan Henrik, 317
Schulerud, Ole, 46
Schumann, Robert, 141
Seip, Didrik Arup, 38
Seligmann, Joseph, 133
Selmer, Johan, 384, 389
Shakespeare, William, 59, 69; *As You Like It*, 59; *Hamlet*, 124; *Macbeth*, 69, 124; *A Midsummer Night's Dream*, 161
Sibelius, Jean, 399
Simplicissimus, 359, 366
Sinding, Christian, 379, 383-4, 386, 387
Sjöberg, Fröken, 156
Skram, Amalie, 12, 16, 23, 26, 31, 186, 207, 230, 249, 255-6, 257, 264-79, 281-305, 306-34; *Børnefortellinger*, 318, 323; *Constance Ring*, 266, 287, 305, 307, 308-9, 312, 313, 314, 319, 322, 324, 330-1, 332; *Fru Ines*, 318, 332; *Fjældmennesker*, 323; *Forraadt* (Betrayed), 332; *Hellemyrsfolket*, 267, 281, 293, 304, 313, 314, 322, 325; *Julehelg* (Christmas), 327; *Landsforrædere* (Traitors), 270-71; *Lucie*, 313-316, 323, 332; 'Madame Høiers Leiefolk', 266; *Mennesker* (People), 330; *Paa St. Jørgen*, 304; *Professor Hieronimus*, 281, 282, 304; *S. G. Myhre*, 317-8, 323, 331; *Sjur Gabriel*, 313, 331; *To Venner* (Two Friends), 313, 318, 331
Skram, Erik, 16, 23, 209, 249, 255-6, 261, 264-79, 281, 283, 286-7, 288-9, 291, 299, 307, 308,

319, 317, 322, 324, 329, 334; *Herregårdsbilleder*, 266; Gertrude Coldbjørnsen, 266, 267
Slott-Møller, Agnes, 72-3
Smitt-Ingbretsem, Pernille, 172
Snoilsky, Carl, 135, 338, 340
Söderström, Werner, 335-51
Sømme, Andreas, 192
Sontum, Chr., 43
Soot, Eyolf, 386
Spasskaja, Vera, 77-85
Staaff, Pehr, 27, 132
Stanislavski, Konstantin, 155, 159, 164
Steffen, Gustaf, 111
Stendhal (Henri Beyle), 21; *Souvenirs d'égotisme*, 148; *La Vie de Henry Brulard*, 148
Stenersen, Gudmund, 387
Stenhammar, Wilhelm, 404-5, 406
Stenström, Thure, 347
Sternschantz, Göran, 344
Stockholms Dagblad, 338
Strindberg, August, 12, 14, 17, 18, 20, 21, 23, 26, 27, 31, 108-122, 123-145, 201, 229, 337, 347, 356, 381-2, 399, 400; *Bandet* (The Bond), 158; *En blå bok* (A Blue Book), 148; *Bland franska bönder* (Among French Peasants), 114, 344; *Blomstermålningar och djurstycken* (Flower Paintings and Animal Pieces), 114; *Brott och brott* (Crimes and Crimes), 146, 149; *Ett drömspel* (A Dream Play), 123, 150, 168; *Erik XIV*, 151; *Fadren* (The Father), 123, 124, 146, 152-5, 162, 166, 168; *Fordringsägare* (Creditors), 161, 168; *Den fredlöse* (The Outlaw), 155, 157-8; *Fröken Julie* (Miss Julie), 123, 124, 125, 128, 158, 162, 164, 168; *Gamla Stockholm* (Old Stockholm), 128, 133; *Giftas* (Getting Married), 111, 114; *Gustav Vasa*, 151; *Han och hon* (He and She), 110, 111; *Hemsöborna* (The People of Hemsö), 125; *Herr Bengts hustru* (Sir Bengts Wife), 162; 'Hjärnornas kamp' (The Battle of the Brains), 111; *I havsbandet* (By the Open Sea), 114; *Inferno*, 27, 111; *Klostret* (The Cloister), 111; *Kristina* (Queen Christina), 111, 155; *Kronbruden* (The Crown Bride), 156; *Kvarstadsresan* (The Internment Trip), 111; *Leka med elden* (Playing with Fire), 160, 161; *Mäster Olof*, 166; *Det nya riket* (The New Kingdom), 114; *Ockulta dagboken* (The Occult Diary), 111; *Öppna brev till Intima teatern* (Open Letters to the Intimate Theatre), 150; *Paria* (Pariah), 159, 161-2; *Påsk* (Easter), 156, 160; *Pelikanen* (The Pelican), 164; *Le Plaidoyer d'un fou* (A Madman's Defence), 27, 111; *Röda rummet* (The Red Room), 117, 343; *Sista riddaren* (The Last Knight), 156-7; *Skärkarlsliv* (Life in the Skerries), 114; *Spöksonaten* (The Ghost Sonata), 123, 150, 168; *Den starkare* (The Stronger), 152, 166; *Stora landsvägen* (The Great Highway), 166; *Svanevit* (Swanwhite), 163; *Svarta fanor* (Black Banners), 126; *Svenska folket* (The Swedish People), 130; *Svenska öden och äventyr* (Swedish Destinies and

Adventures), 114; *Till Damaskus*, 123, 151, 156, 158, 161; *Tjänstekvinnans son* (The Son of a Servant), 114, 120, 125; *Utopier i verkligheten* (Utopias in Reality), 114; *Vivisektioner* (Vivisections), 114
Strindberg, Axel, 20, 124
Strindberg, Elisabeth, 148
Strindberg, Greta, 152, 162, 163
Strindberg, Kerstin, 112
Strodtmann, Adolf, 367
Strøm, Hafdan, 386
Stuckenberg, Viggo, 247
Stuxberg, Anton, 126, 143
Sutherland, J. A., 311
Svedberg, The, 20
Svedjedal, Johan, 347-8
Svennberg, Tore, 151, 170

Taine, Hippolyte, 67
Tao di Bruno, Gloria, 67
Tavaststjerna, Karl August, 229, 336, 338, 341, 343
Tegner, Rudolph, 68
Tegnér, Elias, 163-4
Thadewassian, 68
Thaulow, Fritz, 13, 67
Thommessen, Olaf, 258, 387-8
Thomsen, Eli, 68
Thoresen, Cecilie, 69
Thoresen, Magdalene, 87-107, 356; *Livsbilleder* (Images of Life), 98; 'Min Bedstemoders Fortælling' (My Grandmother's Story), 98-9; *Nyere Fortællinger* (New Stories), 96, 98; *Signes Historie* (Signe's Story), 89
Thorgils, Maria Magdalena, 67
Thrale, Mrs, 24
Thyberg, Henriette O., 174
Tilskueren, 179, 248, 313
Tippett, Michael, 399
Toller, Franz, 359

Topelius, Zacharias, 340, 341
Topsøe, Vilhelm, 220
Torsteinson, Torstein, 387
Tutein, Anna, 82, 83

Uhl, Frida, 111, 112, 141
Ursin, Johannes, 202, 204

Vasenius, Valfrid, 54; *Henrik Ibsens dramatiska digtning i dess första skede*, 54; *Henrik Ibsen. Ett skaldeportrett*, 54
Vedel, Valdemar, 233, 236; *Ibsen og Danmark*, 236
Verdens Gang, 211, 386, 387-8, 389
Verdier, Anton de, 151, 165
Vergil, *Aeniad*, 59
Vinding, Andreas, 70-1
Vintergrønt, 95
Visdal, Jo, 386
Voltaire, 70
Vult von Steijern, Julius Frederik, 135

Wagner, Richard, 406
Wahl, Anders de, 156
Wahlgren, Helge, 162
Wall, Rudolf, 135
Wallace, Alfred, 29
Wamberg, Niels, 311
Weber, Carl Maria von, *Oberon*, 406
Wedekind, Frank, 359, 366, 372; *Frühlingserwachen*, 249
Wennerberg, Gunnar, 135
Werenskiold, Erik, 356, 389
Westcombe, Sophia, 24
Wied, Gustav, 406
Wilster, Christian, 59
Wirsén, Carl David af, 135
Wrangel, Carl Gustav, 23, 109

Zola, Emile, 222, 251, 267, 347